The Complete Book of
Pasta

The Complete Book of

Pasta

The definitive guide to choosing, making and cooking your own pasta,
with over 350 step-by-step recipes and over 1500 fabulous photographs

Editor **Jeni Wright**

HERMES
HOUSE

This edition is published by Hermes House, an imprint of Anness Publishing Ltd,
Hermes House, 88–89 Blackfriars Road, London SE1 8HA; tel. 020 7401 2077; fax 020 7633 9499
www.hermeshouse.com; www.annesspublishing.com

If you like the images in this book and would like to investigate using them for publishing, promotions or
advertising, please visit our website www.practicalpictures.com for more information.

ETHICAL TRADING POLICY
Because of our ongoing ecological investment programme, you, as our customer, can have the pleasure and
reassurance of knowing that a tree is being cultivated on your behalf to naturally replace the materials used
to make the book you are holding. For further information about this scheme, go to
www.annesspublishing.com/trees

A CIP catalogue record for this book is available from the British Library.

Publisher: Joanna Lorenz
Executive Editor: Linda Fraser
Senior Editor: Toria Leitch
Copy Editor: Madeline Weston
Indexer: Dawn Butcher
Production Controller: Ben Worley
Designer: Carole Perks

Additional Recipes: Catherine Atkinson, Carla Capalbo, Maxine Clark, Roz Denny, Christine France, Sarah
Gates, Shirley Gill, Norma MacMillan, Sue Maggs, Elizabeth Martin, Annie Nichols, Jenny Stacy, Liz Trigg, Laura
Washburn, Steven Wheeler

Photography: William Lingwood (recipes) and Janine Hosegood (techniques and cut-outs), also Karl
Adamson, Edward Allwright, David Armstrong, Steve Baxter, Jo Brewer, James Duncan, Michelle Garrett,
Amanda Heywood, Patrick McLeavey, Michael Michaels

Food for Photography: Lucy McKelvie and Kate Jay (recipes) and Annabel Ford (techniques), also Nichola
Fowler, Wendy Lee, Jane Stevenson, Elizabeth Wolf-Cohen

Illustrator: Anna Koska

Previously published as *Pasta Cooking*

NOTES

For all recipes, quantities are given in both metric and imperial measures and, where
appropriate, measures are also given in standard cups and spoons. Follow one set, but
not a mixture because they are not interchangeable.

Standard spoon and cup measures are level.
1 tsp = 5ml, 1 tbsp = 15ml, 1 cup = 250ml/8fl oz

Australian standard tablespoons are 20ml. Australian readers should use
3 tsp in place of 1 tbsp for measuring small quantities of salt etc.

Medium eggs are used unless otherwise stated.

CONTENTS

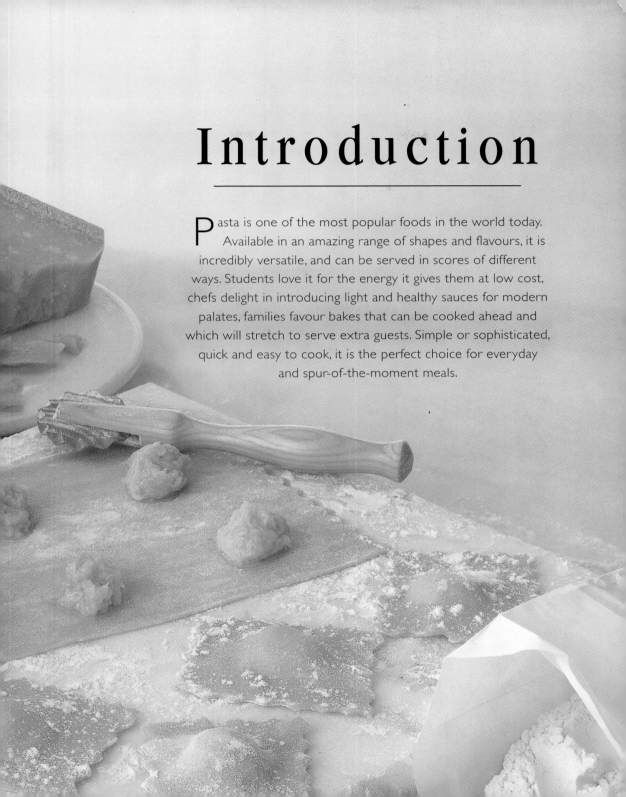

Introduction

Pasta is one of the most popular foods in the world today. Available in an amazing range of shapes and flavours, it is incredibly versatile, and can be served in scores of different ways. Students love it for the energy it gives them at low cost, chefs delight in introducing light and healthy sauces for modern palates, families favour bakes that can be cooked ahead and which will stretch to serve extra guests. Simple or sophisticated, quick and easy to cook, it is the perfect choice for everyday and spur-of-the-moment meals.

Introduction

The origin of pasta

There is a great deal of controversy surrounding the origin of pasta. Who invented it? Was it the Chinese, the Italians, or even the Arabs? There is absolutely no doubt that Marco Polo brought noodles back to Italy from China in 1295, but most food historians agree that a kind of pasta was well known in Italy long before this time. Wall paintings in an Etruscan tomb show utensils – a pastry board, rolling pin and wheel – that are remarkably similar to those used today for making pasta. There is also evidence that the Romans made an unleavened dough of flour and water which they fried, cut into pasta-like strips and ate with a sauce. Apicius, the famous Roman gastronome of the 1st century AD, described baked dishes in which a pasta-like dough was layered with other ingredients. A kind of Roman lasagne?

Wherever or whenever pasta was first "invented", it seems to have been the Sicilians who were the first to boil it in water. They learnt irrigation and cultivation from the Arabs who conquered the island in the 9th century, and by the 12th century there is evidence they were eating a long thin type of pasta like spaghetti. Meanwhile, the Calabrians had mastered the art of twisting pasta strips to make tubes that resembled modern-day macaroni.

In a 13th-century Italian cookery book published just before Marco Polo's return from China, there are recipes for making different pasta shapes, including ravioli, vermicelli and tortelli. So one way or another, pasta did exist in Italy before Marco Polo, and the pasta museum in Rome has many writings, paintings and etchings to substantiate this.

By the time of the Renaissance, pasta featured frequently on Italian menus. The rich Florentines teamed it with costly sugar and spices, but the less well-off had to content themselves with eating pasta plain or with humble ingredients, such as garlic, vegetables and cheese.

In those early days, pasta was simple, fresh and hand-made, a far cry from the many different commercially produced dried shapes

and flavours that we know today. The credit for inventing these must go to the Neapolitans.

The fertile soil in the region around Naples was found to be ideal for growing durum wheat, which makes the best flour for commercial pasta, and the unique combination of sun and wind in this part of southern Italy was just right for drying out the shapes. Once the Neapolitans discovered this, the pasta-making industry burgeoned around the city of Naples, and by the late 18th century the consumption of pasta in Italy had really taken off. Maccheroni, spaghetti and tagliatelle were among the first shapes to be produced commercially, made with flour and water only.

At this time pasta was regarded as food for the poor, and tended to be served with tomato sauces. Tomatoes loved the growing conditions in the south as much as the durum wheat, and once the Italians fell in love with the tomato there was no looking back.

The egg-enriched pasta that northern Italians favoured was not produced commercially at this time. *Pasta all'uovo* was freshly

There is no doubt that Marco Polo brought back noodles to Italy from China in the late 13th century. However, an Italian cookery book, which was published just before his return, includes recipes for making pasta. His departure from Venice is depicted in this early 14th-century painting, Romance of Alexander.

Workers in the fields at Pitti Palace, Florence, in the late 19th century tending the hard durum wheat, which Italians call grano duro. This type of wheat produces the ideal flour for pasta.

made, often with a meat filling or sauce, and was served to the rich. It was not until the 20th century that improvements in industrial equipment made the manufacture of egg pasta a viable commercial proposition.

Pasta today

Wherever Italians went, they took their pasta with them. Those that emigrated to America and Great Britain adapted pasta shapes and sauces to suit local tastes and ingredients, a tradition which happily continues to this day.

Pasta is becoming more and more popular as a healthy, quick-cooking and versatile food, and Italian manufacturers have quickly responded to the demand, constantly developing new flavours and using the latest technology to create original shapes.

Commercially produced dried pasta has always been highly regarded in Italy. It is in no way inferior to fresh home-made pasta, but is simply a different form of this fabulous food. Italian cooks always keep a few packets of dried pasta in their store cupboards and use it on a daily basis – even in the north of Italy, where the tradition of making fresh pasta at home endured for a lot longer than it did in the south of the country.

The right kind of wheat

The ideal variety of wheat for the flour used in commercial pasta making is durum (Triticum durum), which Italians call *grano duro*. This hard summer wheat produces a flour that is high in gluten. Dough made from durum wheat flour is pliable and easy to knead and shape. The majority of durum

wheat for the Italian pasta-making industry is grown in Italy or imported from North America. The flour from durum wheat, called *semola* in Italian, makes a high quality pasta that holds its shape well. Cooked properly until *al dente*, it should be just tender, with a pleasant nutty bite. When you are buying pasta in packets or boxes, always check that it is made from 100 per cent durum wheat. The Italian phrase to look out for is *pasta di semola di grano duro*. This type of pasta may be more expensive than one made with a mixture of durum wheat and soft wheat, but you will get a much better result. Inexpensive pasta made with soft wheat flour tends to stick together during cooking and its texture is often soft and flabby. Generally speaking, the Italian makes are the best. Ask the staff at your local delicatessen which brands they recommend, and spend as much as you can afford. There is a big difference in texture and taste between the higher priced Italian brands and the cheaper types of pasta, and you will quickly find that it pays to buy the best.

The northern preference for egg pasta

In southern Italy the majority of pasta is made with durum wheat and water only, and literally hundreds – if not thousands – of different shapes are manufactured. In northern Italy, the preference is for pasta with added egg, *pasta all'uovo*. The tradition for using this type of pasta began in Emilia, where filled and stuffed pasta shapes originated. Home cooks found that adding a little egg to the dough strengthened it, and helped to keep the filling in during cooking. As Italian housewives began

Above: Healthy ingredients, such as olive oil, tomatoes, garlic and peppers, combine wonderfully well with pasta and are used over and over again by Italian cooks. This may be one of the reasons that the incidence of heart disease in Italy is one of the lowest in the world.

Below: The various sizes and shapes of holes in these commercial pasta dies allow for the production of a wide range of long and short pasta shapes.

Above right: In modern pasta factories sophisticated machines are used to weigh and pack the finished product.

to make less and less fresh pasta at home and turned to buying it from the shops, small factories started making dried egg pasta to meet the demand. Now it is fast becoming a huge industry, although there are fewer fancy shapes made with egg than there are with plain pasta. This is because egg pasta is more difficult to work with. It is not used for making long thin shapes like spaghetti because they would break too easily. Commercially manufactured *pasta all'uovo* may contain as many as 7 eggs to 1kg/2¼lb flour, so it has a richer taste than plain pasta and absorbs more water.

If you buy Italian egg pasta, the packet should state that it is 100 per cent durum wheat and egg *(semola di grano duro e uova)*. *Pasta all'uovo* complements the cream and butter sauces that are popular in the north. The tomato and olive oil sauces of the south have always been traditionally served with plain pasta, although *pasta all'uovo* is now catching on in the south, too.

The nutritional value of pasta

Rich in protein, vitamins and minerals, pasta is a complex carbohydrate food. It provides as much energy as a pure protein like steak, but with little or no fat. Of the eight amino acids essential to make up a complete protein, pasta contains six, so it only needs a small quantity of cheese, meat, fish, pulses or eggs – the traditional ingredients for serving with pasta – to make it complete. If you are using *pasta all'uovo*, you need even less additional protein.

The key to healthy eating lies in eating pasta as the Italians do, with only a small amount of extra ingredients. In Italy, it is traditional for pasta to be served as a first course, before the main course of fish or meat. Eaten with a small spoonful of sauce and a light sprinkling of grated cheese, nothing could be more well-balanced and nutritionally sound.

The incidence of heart disease in Italy is one of the lowest in the civilized world, and doctors, nutritionists and scientists agree that the Italian diet plays a large and important role in this. In Italian cooking, healthy ingredients, such as extra virgin olive oil, fresh and canned tomatoes, garlic, onions, olives, red peppers and fresh parsley are used all the time, plus lots of fresh fish, vegetables and salad leaves, fruit, pulses and lemon juice. Most of these ingredients combine wonderfully well with pasta, and they are used over and over again in the recipes in this book.

Pasta is a completely natural food that contains no additives. Pasta with egg contains the most nutrients, while wholewheat pasta has the highest percentage of vitamins and fibre. Always check the label when buying coloured pasta, because some varieties include artificial colourings.

Pasta is inexpensive, quick and easy to cook, and incredibly versatile. It is the perfect convenience food: in the time it takes to boil the water and cook the pasta, most sauces are ready to serve. *Pasta all'uovo* is especially nutritious and good for children who don't like eggs in a more recognizable form. Another plus point, which athletes and other sportspeople appreciate, is that as a high-energy food, pasta is easy to digest and yet immensely satisfying.

It makes sense, therefore, to include pasta in our diets as often as possible, if not every day. Since everybody loves it, this should be very easy to do. People watching their weight may be surprised to know that a 75g/3oz portion of cooked pasta yields only about 100 calories (424kJ) and can therefore be eaten as part of a calorie-controlled diet, as long as it is only lightly sauced.

Pasta as an everyday meal

In Italy pasta is generally eaten as a first course (*primo piatto* or just *primo*) as part of the main meal of the day. This may be at lunchtime or in the evening, depending on family circumstances and whether the meal is served during the week or at the weekend. The meal usually begins with antipasto, which is followed with a *primo piatto* of either soup, pasta, rice or gnocchi. Pasta used to be served as a lunchtime first course when lunch was traditionally the main meal of the day, but now that more and more Italian women are working outside the home, these customs are changing and there are fewer hard-and-fast rules about lunch and dinner. After the *primo piatto*, the second course, *secondo piatto*, is served. This is either fish or meat followed by vegetables or salad, then cheese, fresh fruit and coffee. Desserts are normally reserved for special occasions.

When pasta is served as a first course, the usual amount is 65–90g/2¹/2–3¹/2oz uncooked weight per person. Sauce is added sparingly; this is usually tossed with the freshly drained hot pasta in the kitchen, and the mixture is then brought to the table in one large bowl.

Coloured pasta looks and tastes very good, but always check the label before buying, because some varieties include artificial colourings.

By the time the pasta reaches the dining room it has mingled with the sauce and taken on some of its flavour. In some homes the bowl is passed around the table and everyone helps themselves, while in others one person does the serving. When you are serving pasta directly from the bowl, it looks most attractive if you retain a small ladleful of the sauce to put on top of the pasta after tossing, then sprinkle this with cheese or herbs at the last moment.

If it suits your lifestyle best to serve pasta as a main course for lunch or supper, simply increase the weight of uncooked pasta to 115–175g/4–6oz per person and make more sauce. For convenience, you may prefer to serve pasta in shallow soup plates or bowls or on dinner plates. Warm these beforehand and serve and eat the pasta as soon as possible so that it can be enjoyed at its best. If you accompany your main course with a fresh leafy green salad and follow with some fresh fruit, you will have a tasty, nutritious and supremely satisfying meal. *Buon Appetito!*

Although traditionally served from one large bowl that is passed around the table, you may prefer to serve pasta in shallow soup plates or bowls.

Dried Pasta

The many hundreds of different types of dried pasta are divided into categories. Long, short and flat shapes are the most common, but there are also stuffed shapes, shapes suitable for stuffing and tiny shapes for use in soup. Among these, you will find some less well-known regional shapes and the more unusual and decorative designer shapes.

Only buy dried pasta that is made using 100 per cent durum wheat. If you decant pasta shapes into storage jars, use up any remaining pasta before adding more from a new packet. Older pasta may take longer to cook than that from a fresher packet, and different brands of the same shape may not necessarily have the same cooking time.

Long Pasta / *Pasta Lunga*

Dried long pasta in the form of spaghetti is probably the best-known pasta of all time, and was certainly one of the first types to be exported from Italy. Spaghetti is still very widely used, but nowadays there are many other varieties of long pasta that look and taste just as good. There are no hard-and-fast rules when matching pasta to sauce, so experiment with alternative varieties to add interest to your cooking, always remembering that long pasta is best served with either a thin, clinging sauce or one that is smooth and thick. If too thin and watery, the sauce will simply run off the long strands; if too chunky or heavy, the sauce will fall to the bottom of the bowl and you will be left with a bowl full of chunks and no pasta to eat it with. Clinging sauces made with olive oil, butter, cream, eggs, finely grated cheese and chopped fresh herbs are good with long pasta. When ingredients such as vegetables, fish and meat are added to a smooth thick sauce, they should be very finely chopped.

Long pasta comes in different lengths, but 30cm/12in is about the average. In specialist food shops, you may see dried pasta that is much longer than this but think twice before buying it because extra-long pasta can be tricky to cook and eat, and often not worth the bother. The width of long pasta varies too; the strands can be flat, hollow, round or square, while other types have the pasta strands coiled up into nests.

Most long shapes are available in plain durum wheat only. The shapes made with egg (*all'uovo*) are very delicate, and are either packed in nests or compressed as waves. Fine long pasta, such as spaghetti, is far too delicate to be made with egg, but a short version from Emilia-Romagna, called capricciosa all'uovo, is available.

Bavette

Bucatini

Capelli d'angelo a nidi

Capelli d'angelo

Capellini

Capellini a nidi

Bavette

This type of long pasta is known all over Italy, but is very common in the South. The noodles are narrow and flat, like tagliatelle, only slimmer. Indeed, some southern Italians use the name bavette to describe tagliatelle. Bavettine is a narrower version. Both types can be plain or all'uovo (with egg).

Bucatini

This looks like spaghetti but is slightly chunkier. The strands are hollow (*buco* means hole), like hard, inflexible drinking straws. This type of pasta is best known in the Roman dish, *Bucatini all'Amatriciana*, which has a tomato, bacon and pepper sauce, and in Sicily it is traditionally served with a sauce of fresh sardines. Bucatoni is a fatter version, while perciatelli is bucatini by another name.

Capelli d'angelo

The name means angel's hair, which is an evocative description for this extremely fine pasta. It is used in broths and soups, and is popular with children. You may find it packed in nests, labelled capelli d'angelo a nidi. These nests are easy to handle and cook – one nest per person is the usual serving, so you can use as many nests as you require. Capellini and capel Venere are similar to capelli d'angelo.

Chitarra

Also known as spaghetti alla chitarra, this type of pasta is cut on a special wooden frame strung with wires like guitar strings (*chitarra* is Italian for guitar). It is therefore square-shaped rather than round, but can be used as an alternative to spaghetti.

Fusilli

Spaghetti spirals that look like long opened-out corkscrews. You may see these labelled fusilli lunghi or fusilli col buco, to distinguish them from the more widely known short fusilli and eliche. Fusilli is often used with tomato sauces.

Lasagnette

This flat pasta resembles tagliatelle, but the noodles are slightly wider. There are several types, most of which have frilly edges. Reginette is similar. You can use lasagnette in place of any ribbon pasta.

Linguine

In Italian the name means little tongues and accurately describes a very thin spaghetti-like pasta that has flattened edges. You may also see linguinette and lingue di passera (sparrows' tongues), both of which are even narrower. Wholewheat linguine is also available. All are good with the simple olive oil-based sauces and smooth tomato sauces of southern Italy.

Maccheroni

A very familiar form of pasta. We know a short version of it as macaroni, but in Italy the long thick tubes are widely used for all kinds of sauces – in some regions the word maccheroni is even used as a generic term for pasta and maccheroncini is simply the name given to very thin, long pasta. Maccheroni comes in different lengths and thicknesses, with straight or angled ends, in plain, egg and wholewheat varieties. There is even a square-shaped chitarra version, which comes from Abruzzi. There they call it maccheroni alla chitarra, but it also goes by the name of tonnarelli. Maccheroni is useful because it goes with so many different sauces.

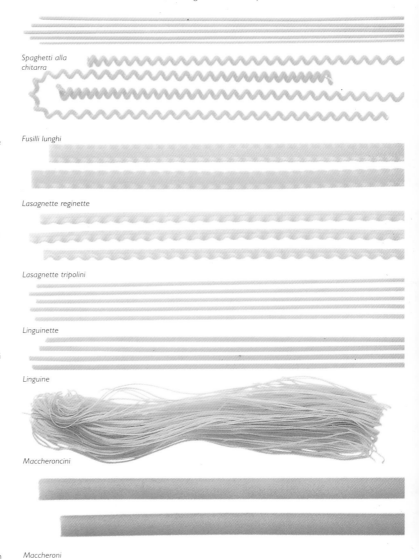

Spaghetti alla chitarra

Fusilli lunghi

Lasagnette reginette

Lasagnette tripolini

Linguinette

Linguine

Maccheroncini

Maccheroni

Spaghetti

This familiar type of pasta takes its name from the word *spago*, which means string. Spaghetti means little strings; spaghettini is a thinner variety, and spaghettoni is thicker. Spaghetti originally came from Naples, but today it is made in other parts of Italy too, and the length and width vary from one region to another.

Numerous different brands, flavours and colours are available, including whole-wheat (*integrali*), spinach (*spinaci*) and chilli (*peperoncini*) so the choice is yours, but avoid the inexpensive brands. Long Italian spaghetti tends to be very good; it is graded by number according to the thickness. Good-quality spaghetti made in Italy is still one of the best forms of pasta, despite the ever-increasing range of other shapes. It goes well with many different kinds of sauces.

Tagliatelle

The most common form of ribbon noodles, tagliatelle derives its name from the Italian verb *tagliare* meaning to cut. The noodles are usually about 8mm–1cm/ 1/3–1/2in wide, but there are fine versions called tagliatellina, tagliarini and tagliolini, and an even finer type called tagliolini fini. Traditional tagliatelle comes from Bologna. It is made both with and without egg and with spinach (*verdi*), but new flavours and colours are constantly coming on to the market.

All types of tagliatelle are sold coiled in nests, which conveniently unravel during cooking when given a good stir. Paglia e fieno, which literally means straw and hay, is a mixture consisting of half plain egg and half spinach egg pasta, packed together in separate bundles of each colour. The noodles are usually quite thin, either tagliarini or tagliolini. Both tagliatelle and paglia e fieno are very popular because they go well with most sauces, although strictly speaking, tagliatelle should not be served with a fish sauce. Meat sauce is the classic, as in *Tagliatelle alla Bolognese*.

The Roman version of tagliatelle is called fettuccine. These long, flat noodles are virtually the same as tagliatelle, but slightly thinner.

Spaghetti

Spaghetti integrali

Spaghetti con spinaci

Spaghettoni

Spaghettini

Spaghettini con peperoncini

Tagliatelle / tagliatelle verdi

Vermicelli

Ziti

Mezza zita

Vermicelli

This sounds appealing, but the name means little worms, which is rather unfortunate. It describes a very fine form of spaghetti – the original Neapolitan name for spaghetti was vermicelli, and southern Italians still sometimes refer to spaghetti as vermicelli, which can be confusing. This type of pasta comes in plain and egg (*all'uovo*) varieties and is very versatile, going well with most light sauces, but especially the light, fresh tomato and seafood sauces for which Naples is famous. There is an even finer version called vermicellini, and a similar noodle called fidelini.

Ziti

This pasta takes its name from the word *zita*, meaning fiancée. In the old days it was traditional in southern Italy to serve ziti at wedding feasts and on other special occasions. Ziti is very long, thick and hollow – like maccheroni – and the custom is to break it into the length required when you cook it. Because of their size, the tubes go well with robust and chunky sauces; they are also sometimes broken into short lengths and baked in a *timballo*, which is a cup-shaped mould. The pasta is used to line the mould, which is then filled with a savoury mixture such as mushrooms, ham or chicken livers combined with a sauce and topped with cheese. Zitoni are fatter than ziti; mezza zita are thinner.

Tagliolini all'uovo

Paglia e fieno

Tagliarini all'uovo

SOME REGIONAL TYPES OF LONG DRIED PASTA

Fettuccine comes from Lazio, and these noodles are used in classic Roman pasta dishes, such as *Fettuccine àll'Alfredo*. They are flat ribbons, like tagliatelle but narrower (about 5mm/1/4in wide), and always sold coiled into loose nests. The three most common types are plain durum wheat, with egg (*all'uovo*), and with spinach (*verdi*), and you can use them interchangeably with tagliatelle. Fettuccelle is similar, but is straight rather than coiled. Fettuccelle integrali is the wholewheat variety.

Frappe is a type of pasta from Emilia-Romagna. The 2.5–4cm/1–1¹/2in wide noodles are flat, with wavy edges, about halfway in size between tagliatelle and lasagne. Made with egg and very delicate, the noodles are packed by a special machine that presses them into waves.

Pappardelle are broad ribbon noodles (2–2.5cm/3/4–1in wide), with wavy edges. They come from Tuscany, where they are still made fresh with egg every day, but dried versions are now becoming more widely available, many of them with only one wavy edge or straight edges. They are good with heavy meat and game sauces. Nastroni are similar straight-sided noodles that are sold coiled into nests.

Trenette are noodles from Liguria, where they are traditionally served with pesto sauce. The Genoese dish, *Trenette alla Genovese*, combines trenette with pesto, potatoes and beans. The noodles are about 3mm/1/8in wide, and are made with egg. They resemble bavette and linguine, which can be substituted for them if you find trenette difficult to find.

Fettuccine al nero

Pappardelle

Trenette

Fettuccelle

Frappe

Nastroni

SHORT PASTA / PASTA CORTA

There are literally hundreds of different short pasta shapes, and new ones are constantly coming into our shops. Some people prefer short pasta simply because it is easier to cook and eat than long pasta. It also goes well with many different sauces, and in most cases you can choose any shape you fancy, regardless of whether your sauce is a smooth tomato-, cream- or olive oil-based type, or is chunky with large pieces of fish, meat or vegetables. Exceptions are regional dishes that are traditionally cooked with a specific shape, such as *Penne all'Arrabbiata* from Lazio.

Short pasta is divided into two main groups. Pasta secca is factory-made, using durum wheat flour and water. This is by far the largest group, and you will find that most packets of dried pasta list only these two ingredients on the label. *Pasta all'uovo* is made with the addition of eggs. It is naturally a brighter yellow than pasta secca and has more nutritional value. Popular in the north of Italy, especially in Emilia-Romagna, *pasta all'uovo* has different properties from plain pasta and goes especially well with the rich creamy and meaty sauces associated with that part of Italy. It has an advantage over plain durum wheat pasta in that it cooks slightly more quickly and is less likely to become overcooked and soggy. Although it is more expensive than plain pasta, egg pasta is becoming more popular and therefore more widely available, so look out for it in an increasing number of shapes.

New flavours and colours in short pasta shapes are on the increase too. For many years, tomato (**pomodoro**) and spinach (**verde**) were all that was available, but today there seems to be no end to the number of different colour and flavour combinations, ranging from garlic, chillies and herbs to beetroot, salmon, mushroom, squid ink and even chocolate. Often three colours (red, white and green) are packed together and labelled tricolore. Whole-wheat pasta, called **pasta integrale**, is made from durum wheat and other cereals. It is higher in fibre than plain durum wheat pasta and takes longer to cook. It has a chewy texture and nutty flavour.

Benfatti

Benfatti

The word *benfatti* means well made and originally described the little offcuts or scraps of pasta left over from making other shapes, such as tagliatelle. Traditionally these were used in soups so they would not be wasted, but they proved so popular that they are now made and marketed as a shape in their own right. Benfatti are available plain and with egg, and are good in salads as well as soups.

Chifferini rigatini

Chifferini

Also called chifferi, chifferoni and chifferotti, these are small curved tubes like short maccheroni that has been bent. Some versions are ridged (**rigatini**). The holes in the middle fill with sauce, making them an excellent shape for all types of pasta sauces and soups.

Conchigliette rigate

Conchiglie

As the name suggests, these shapes resemble small conch shells. Sometimes they are ridged, in which case they are called conchiglie rigate. They are one of the most useful small shapes because they are concave and trap virtually any sauce. For this reason they are extremely popular and are widely available in many different

Conchiglie rigate

Conchiglioni rigati

colours and flavours. Sizes vary too, from tiny conchigliette for soups to conchiglione, which are jumbo shells for stuffing.

Eliche

The name comes from the Italian word for screws or propellers, which is exactly what these shapes look like. They are often mis-labelled as fusilli, which are similar, but when you see the two side by side there is a marked difference. Eliche are short lengths of pasta, each twisted into a spiral, like the thread of a screw. They are available in different thicknesses, colours and flavours, including wholewheat and tricolore, and are good with most sauces, but especially those that are tomato-based. You may only be able to buy them labelled as fusilli – the two are interchangeable and their names often depend on which part of Italy they come from.

Eliche all'uovo

Eliche tricolori

Farfalle

Fusilli

Maccheroni

Farfalle verde

Fusilli con spinaci

Maccheroncelli

Farfalle salmonseppia

Fusilli all'uovo

Tubetti

Farfalle tricolore

Farfalle

The word means butterflies, but these shapes are sometimes also described as bow-ties – the Italian word for bow-tie is *cravatta a farfalla*. They are very pretty, with crinkled edges, and are sometimes ridged. Due to their popularity, farfalle are available in a wide variety of colours and flavours, including plain, with egg and tricolore (plain, tomato and spinach flavours, which are sold together in mixed packets). Farfalle can be served with any sauce, but they are particularly good with cream and tomato sauces. Children love them. In Modena, farfalle are known as strichetti.

Fusilli

These spirals of thin pasta look like tight coils or springs and are formed by winding fresh dough around a thin rod. The spiral opens out, rather than remaining solid as it does in the case of eliche, for which fusilli

are often mistaken. Check when buying, because most packets of fusilli are in fact eliche. Genuine fusilli is likely to be plain, neither made with egg nor coloured. The shapes go well with thin sauces.

Lumache rigate

Lumachoni rigati

Gomiti rigati

Lumache

Snail shells were the inspiration for this attractively shaped pasta. Unlike conchiglie, they are not shaped like conch shells, but resemble a larger version of pipe, because they are fashioned out of hollow pasta. Lumache are excellent for trapping sauces. The most common type available is lumache rigate (ridged), and there is also a large version called lumaconi. Gomiti is a similar conch shell shape.

Maccheroni

When cooks in the south of Italy speak of maccheroni, they usually mean long pasta, but in the north of the country they prefer it short. It is the short type that is generally exported as macaroni (sometimes labelled "elbow macaroni" although some brands are straighter than others). This used to be the most common short pasta shape outside Italy, but other more interesting shapes now rival its popularity. Being hollow, it is a good shape for most sauces and baked dishes, so will always remain popular. Both plain and egg maccheroni are available, and there are also many different sizes, including a thin, quick-cooking variety. Tubetti is the name given to a miniature version that is often used in soups.

Penne lisce

Penne rigate

Penne rigate con spinaci

Penne mezzanine

Mezze penne tricolori

Pennoni

Penne

Like maccheroni, penne are hollow tubes, but their ends are cut diagonally so they are pointed like quills (*penne* means feather or quill pen). In the popularity stakes, they seem to have taken over from maccheroni, possibly because of their more interesting shape. They go well with virtually every sauce and are particularly good with chunky sauces as their sturdiness means that they hold the weight well. Penne lisce are smooth; penne rigate are ridged. Other less common varieties include the small and thin pennette and even thinner pennini and penne mezzanine, the short and stubby mezze penne or "half penne", and the large pennoni. Penne made with egg and flavoured penne are very common.

Pipe rigate

Pipe

These shapes look like a cross between conchiglie and lumache. They are curved and hollow (the name means pipes) and more often than not ridged (pipe rigate). As short pasta shapes go, they are quite small. They are excellent for catching sauce and make an interesting change from other more common hollow varieties. Plain and wholewheat types are available, and there is also a smaller version called pipette.

Rigatoni

Mezzi rigatoni

Elicoidali

Elicoidali con basilico

Rigatoni

From the maccheroni family, these are ridged, hollow, chunky-looking shapes. They are very popular because they are sturdy enough to hold chunky sauces, and they come in many flavours. There is a short version called mezzi rigatoni and a straight, stubby version called millerighe. The texture of rigatoni always seems slightly chewier than that of other short pasta. Similar in shape but slightly narrower are elicoidali, which have curved ridges (their name means helixes). Elicoidali can be plain or flavoured with ingredients such as basil.

Rotelle

Rotelle tricolore

Rotelle

These are cartwheel shapes. There is a ridged variety, rotelle rigate, and sometimes this shape goes under other names such as ruote, ruote di carro and trulli. Although not a classic Italian shape, the spokes of the wheels are very good for holding chunky sauces. Children like them, and most supermarkets sell them in different colours and flavours. The plain Italian brands taste very good.

SOME REGIONAL TYPES OF SHORT DRIED PASTA

Garganelli come from Emilia-Romagna. They are tubular egg pasta shapes that resemble penne, but which look more like scrolls than quills because you can clearly see how they have been rolled. This is done on a special tool, called *il pettine*, that looks like a large comb.

Gnocchi sardi are from Sardinia. They are named after the gnocchi potato dumplings, but are smaller, like little razor shells. Gnocchetti sardi are smaller still, and are mostly used for soups. Malloreddus is another Sardinian name for gnocchi. These shapes are often flavoured with saffron, and served with traditional meat and vegetable sauces. They are quite chewy in texture.

Orecchiette, or little ears, are from Puglia in the south-east of Italy. Always made with durum wheat, they have a chewy texture and are served with the traditional sauces of the region, especially those made with broccoli.

Pizzoccheri are buckwheat noodles from Valtellina in Lombardy, not far from the border with Switzerland. They are thin and flat and usually sold in nests (*a nidi*) like fettuccine, but they are about half the length. Pizzoccheri are also sometimes cut to make short noodles. Their flavour is nutty, and they go well with the robust flavours of northern Italian cuisine, most famously with cabbage, potatoes and cheese in the baked dish of the same name.

Strozzapreti, which literally translated means priest stranglers, come from Modena. They are said to derive their name from the story of a priest who liked them so much he ate too many – and nearly choked to death. In fact, strozzapreti consist of two pieces of pasta twisted or "strangled" together. Other similar twisted shapes are caserecce, fileia and gemelli. The Genoese trofie, although not twisted, are similar, and can be substituted for strozzapreti.

Trofie are from the Ligurian port of Genoa, where it is traditional to serve them with pesto sauce. They are rolls of solid pasta with pointed ends, quite small and dainty. At one time you could only get home-made trofie, but now they are available dried in Italian deli-catessens, in which case the shapes are sometimes open along one side rather than solid. They are well worth buying if you want to make an authentic *Genoese Trofie al Pesto*.

Above from the top: Garganelli all'uovo, garganelli paglia e fieno, girondole di Puglia, gnocchi sardi integrali and gnocchetti sardi

Gnocchetti sardi

Pizzoccheri a nidi

Strozzapreti

Orecchiette

Short-cut pizzocheri

Trofie

FLAT PASTA

Although there are many kinds of long flat ribbon pasta, such as fettuccine and tagliatelle, there is really only one broad, flat pasta used for baking in the oven (*al forno*), and that is lasagne. Thin sheets of lasagne are designed to be baked between layers of sauce in the oven, or cooked in boiling water until *al dente*, rolled around a filling to make cannelloni, then baked. All types of lasagne are designed to be used in this way, and are never served with a separate sauce.

Lasagne verdi

Plain lasagne

Made from durum wheat and water, this type of lasagne comes flat-packed in boxes. There are three different colours – yellow (plain), green (*verdi*), which is made with spinach, and brown or wholewheat (*integrali*). The shape varies according to the manufacturer, from narrow or broad rectangles to squares. Most sheets are completely flat, but some are wavy all over. Others have crimped or curly edges, which help to trap the sauce and look attractive too. Get to know the different brands and their sizes and choose the ones that fit your baking dish, to avoid having to cut them to fit. This makes light work of assembling the layers before baking. Check the cooking instructions on the box because regular plain lasagne needs to be pre-cooked before being layered or rolled. The usual method is to plunge about four sheets at a time into a large pan of salted boiling water, boil for about 8 minutes until *al dente*, then carefully remove each sheet with a large slotted spoon and/or tongs and lay it flat on a damp cloth to drain. The sheets need to be drained in a single layer or they will stick to each other. This method is fairly time-consuming and messy, but once it has been completed and the lasagne has been assembled, the cooking time in the oven is usually about 30 minutes.

Lasagnette are long, narrow strips of flat pasta, which are crimped on one or two sides. They are used in the same way as lasagne, layered with sauces, then topped with grated cheese and baked in the oven. Festonelle are small squares of lasagnette,

Lasagnette

Lasagnette

Festonelle

Pantacce

Lasagne

Lasagne

Lasagne verdi

Lasagne verdi all'uovo

which are also used in baked dishes. Pantacce are tiny diagonal pieces cut from lasagnette. They are similar to the hand-cut quadrucci and can be used in baked dishes, but are more often added to soups.

Lasagne all'uovo

This type of lasagne is made with durum wheat and water like plain lasagne, but with the addition of egg. This makes it a brighter yellow than plain lasagne, and richer in

flavour and nutrients. It is available as plain egg (lasagne all'uovo) and egg and spinach (lasagne verdi all'uovo). Like the plain lasagne, it comes in different shapes and sizes with a variety of different edgings.

Lasagne

Lasagne all'uovo

Easy-cook Lasagne

Although a relatively recent innovation, easy-cook lasagne is fast becoming the number one favourite. Sometimes labelled "no pre-cooking required", it does not need to be boiled first, but is layered in the baking dish straight from the packet, so

saving lots of time and mess. As with the plain and egg lasagne, it comes in all sorts of different shapes, sizes and colours, with straight or fancy edges. It is easiest to use if it is the right shape to fit neatly into your baking dish, although it can be broken to

fit. Baking time is slightly longer than with the pre-boiled varieties, so allow at least 40 minutes. Make sure that the sauce you use is runnier than usual because this type of lasagne absorbs liquid during baking and needs extra sauce to keep it moist.

Tortellini all'uovo

Tortellini verdi

Ravioli all'uovo

Agnolotti all'uovo

DRIED STUFFED PASTA / *PASTA RIPIENA*

The most common dried stuffed pasta shapes are tortellini (little pies), a speciality of Bologna said to be modelled on the shape of Venus's navel. They are made from rounds or circles of pasta, so they look like little plump rings; another name for them is anolini. Some Italian delicatessens also sell dried cappelletti (little hats), which resemble tortellini but are made from squares of pasta so have little peaks. Cappelletti are more likely to be sold fresh than dried. The same goes for ravioli and agnolotti, although you may find them in larger supermarkets. Tortellini are popular dried because they are traditionally used *in brodo* – simmered in a clear beef or chicken stock until they swell and plump up to make a satisfying soup. Most Italian

cooks keep a packet or two of tortellini in the store cupboard for just this purpose, and *Tortellini in Brodo* is often served for an evening meal when the main meal of the day has been at lunchtime. You can also be sure that *Tortellini in Brodo* will be served as a pick-me-up if ever a member of the family is unwell. They are also traditionally served on New Year's Eve in Bologna, perhaps as an antidote to the excesses of Christmas.

Dried tortellini are generally available with a choice of fillings – with meat (*alla carne*) or cheese (*ai formaggi*). The pasta is made with egg and may be plain and yellow in colour, green if flavoured with spinach, or red if flavoured with tomato. All types of tortellini need to be cooked for at least 15 minutes to allow time for the pasta to swell and the ingredients in the filling to develop their flavour. Meat fillings are a mixture of pork sausage and beef with breadcrumbs, Parmesan cheese and spices. Cheese fillings usually consist of a minimum of 35 per cent cheese mixed with breadcrumbs and spices.

Dried tortellini are a useful store-cupboard item as they will keep for up to 12 months (but always check the use-by date on the packet). For a soup, only a handful of the filled shapes are needed and the packet can be resealed. Tortellini are also good boiled, then drained and tossed in melted butter and herbs or a cream, tomato or meat sauce, and served with grated Parmesan. Children like their shape, and they provide a good way of persuading them to eat meat and cheese. A 250g/9oz packet will serve four people.

DRIED PASTA FOR STUFFING / *PASTA DA RIPIENO*

Large pasta shapes are made commercially for stuffing and baking in the oven. Fillings vary, from meat and poultry to spinach, mushrooms and cheese, and the pasta can be baked in either a béchamel or a tomato sauce. Keep the filling moist and the sauce runny to ensure that the finished dish will not be dry. Dried shapes make an interesting change from lasagne, especially for children's meals, and they are attractive as a first course for a dinner party. They do not need to be boiled before being stuffed.

Cannelloni

Cannelloni

These large pasta tubes (their name means large reeds) are about 10cm/4in long. Plain, spinach and wholewheat versions are available. In Italy, cannelloni is traditionally made from fresh sheets of lasagne rolled around a filling, but the ready-made dried tubes are convenient and less time-consuming to use. They are easy to stuff, using either a teaspoon or a piping bag.

Conchiglie

Conchiglie

Sometimes also called conchiglioni, these jumbo conch shells are available in plain, spinach and tomato flavours, both smooth and ridged. There are often two sizes – medium and large – both of which are suitable for stuffing, although you will probably find the larger ones less fiddly.

Lumaconi

Lumaconi

These are like conchiglie, but are elbow-shaped – like large snail shells – with an opening at either end. The ones most commonly available are plain and ridged, but you may find different colours in specialist delicatessens. You may also come across similar shapes called chiocciloni, gorzettoni, manicotti and tuffolini.

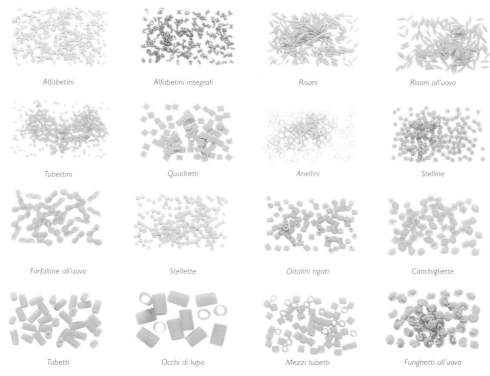

Alfabetini

Alfabetini integrali

Risoni

Risoni all'uovo

Tubettini

Quadretti

Anellini

Stelline

Farfalline all'uovo

Stellette

Ditalini rigati

Conchigliette

Tubetti

Occhi di lupo

Mezzi tubetti

Funghetti all'uovo

DRIED PASTA FOR SOUP / PASTINA

Teeny-weeny pasta shapes are called pastina in Italian, and there are literally hundreds of different ones to choose from. They are mostly made from plain durum wheat, although you may find them with egg and even flavoured with carrot or spinach. In Italy they are always served in broths and clear soups, and are regarded almost as nursery food because they are so often served for children's meals (many Italian babies are weaned on them) or as a pick-me-up for adults who are not feeling well. If you stay in an Italian hospital, you are likely to be served *Pastina in Brodo.*

Shapes of pastina vary enormously, and seem to get more and more fanciful as the market demands.

The smallest and most plain pasta per minestre (pasta for soups) are like tiny grains. Some look like rice and are in fact called risi or risoni, while others are more like barley and are called orzi. Fregola, from Sardinia, look like couscous, and have a similar nutty texture and flavour. Semi di melone are like melon seeds, as their name suggests, while acini de pepe or peperini are named after peppercorns, which they resemble in shape and size if not in colour. Coralline, grattini and occhi are three more very popular tiny shapes.

The next size up are the ones that are most popular with children. These include alfabeti and alfabetini (alphabet shapes), stelline and stellette (stars), rotellini (tiny wagon wheels) and anellini, which can be tiny rings, sometimes with ridges that make them look very pretty, or larger hoops. Ditali are similar to anellini but slightly thicker, while tubettini are thicker still.

Another category of pasta per minestre consists of slightly larger shapes, more like miniature versions of familiar types of short pasta. Their names end in "ine", "ette" or "etti", denoting that they are the diminutive forms. These include conchigliette (little shells), farfalline and farfallette (little bows), funghetti (little mushrooms), lumachine

Peperini

(little snails), quadretti and quadrettini (little squares), orecchiettini (little ears), renette (like baby penne) and tubetti (little tubes). The size of these varies: the smaller ones are for use in clear broths, while the larger ones are more often used in thicker soups, such as minestrone.

Designer Pasta

Relative newcomers to the market are the pasta shapes that bear little or no resemblance to the traditional or regional Italian varieties. Many of these are made outside Italy in any case, while the ones made in Italy are often for export only. It seems that the majority of Italians are happy enough with the pasta they know and love.

Supermarkets and food halls, gourmet food shops, specialist delicatessens and even interior design shops are the best places to find these new shapes. Quality varies enormously,

and some of them are nothing more than a gimmick, with very disappointing textures and flavours. Others are more successful, especially the ones made by long-established Italian firms. They make a change from the more usual shapes and are often an interesting talking point, especially when you are entertaining. As a general rule, flavoured pasta is best served with very simple sauces based on olive oil or butter, otherwise the flavours of the pasta and sauce tend to fight one another.

LONG SHAPES AND NOODLES

Spaghetti and tagliatelle are often flavoured and coloured. These shapes are either dramatically long or coiled in nests (*a nidi*), and you can even buy a type of pasta called spagliatelle, which is like a cross between the two. You can choose from a single flavour in one packet, or up to five different flavours mixed together, and they can be either plain durum wheat pasta or made with the addition of egg and labelled "all'uovo". Spinach, tomato, mushroom, beetroot, saffron and smoked salmon are all popular flavours, but there are also other stronger flavours, such as chilli and garlic (singly and together) and black squid ink (*nero di seppia*).

Tagliatelle flavoured with red and green chillies

Egg and smoked salmon-flavoured tagliatelle

Three-colour tagliatelle

Porcini-flavoured tagliatelle

Tagliatelle flavoured with squid ink and bottarga (mullet roe)

Garlic- and chilli-flavoured spaghetti

Porcini-flavoured tagliatelle

Poppy seed tagliatelle

Porcini-flavoured bavette

Five-colour spagliatelle

Multi-coloured arlecchino

Basil-flavoured strangozzi

One of the most fanciful combinations comes from Venice. Called arlecchino (harlequin), it is a mixture of black (squid ink), green (spinach and herbs), red (tomato and beetroot) and blue (blueberry and blue Curaçao liqueur). More common and perhaps most successful is tagliatelle speckled with herbs or seeds or, if it comes from Tuscany, flavoured with wild mushrooms (porcini). A broad variety of tagliatelle called bavette from Puglia is also flavoured with porcini. Strangozzi is an unusual thin noodle from Umbria. It comes plain and flavoured with spinach, basil or tomato. It is sometimes sold twisted into a long, thick plait, which looks pretty in the packet, but is best broken into short lengths to cook.

SHORT SHAPES

The most inventive and unusual designer shapes fall into this category. Short pasta is the easiest pasta to eat and so it's the most popular. Manufacturers, ever on the lookout to make and sell more, quickly realised that new short shapes had the most appeal and so developed this sector of the market more than any other. Ever since the 19th century competition in the pasta industry has thrived on the "design" of different short shapes, with some more successful at holding sauces than others. Among these are the frilly ballerine, fiorelli, gigli del gargano, rocchetti rigati and spaccatella, all of which trap sauces quite well but somehow give a strange sensation in the mouth. Shapes such as banane,

coralli rigati, creste di gallo, radiatori and riccioli are perhaps too gimmicky for their own good; so too are the mixed bags of highly coloured pasta shapes, such as the seven-colour orecchiette (little ears) and five-colour chioccioloni (snails), which includes chocolate-flavoured pasta along with the more run-of-the-mill plain, tomato, squid ink and wild mushroom (porcini) varieties.

These coloured designer pasta shapes are often labelled *lavorazione artigianale* or *prodotto artigianale*, to indicate that they are made by artisans or local craftsmen, but they are too often disappointing, and they rarely match up to the more traditional shapes that have been tried and tested over very many years.

Five-colour chioccioloni are made from plain pasta and pasta flavoured with squid ink, chocolate, tomato and porcini

Spinach, plain and tomato conchiglie (hand-crafted shells)

Spaccatella

Seven-colour orecchiette are made from plain pasta and pasta flavoured with spinach, tomato, saffron, squid ink, beetroot and porcini

Rocchetti rigati

Gigli del gargano

Fiorelli tricolori

Three-colour pennoti rigati

Three-colour cappelletti

Coralli rigati

Fresh Pasta

In Italy there has long been a tradition for buying fresh pasta, and now the custom has caught on in other countries too. Italians buy from their local *pastificio* or baker, where the beautiful window displays are such a tempting feast for the eye, while we have to content ourselves with delicatessens, supermarkets and food halls. Yet here too, creative talent is running wild when it comes to making fresh pasta, and the choice of different shapes, flavours and fillings is continually increasing – by popular demand. It seems that everybody loves fresh pasta, and we simply can't get enough of it. Quality is excellent, especially with the loose kinds sold in Italian delicatessens. Pre-packaged brands, although labelled fresh, are obviously not as "just-made" and silky-textured as the pasta made on a daily basis in an Italian delicatessen, but they are quite good nevertheless. Flavours vary, but the usual ingredients are spinach, tomato, chestnut, mushroom, beetroot juice, saffron, herbs, garlic, chillies and squid ink.

Buy freshly made pasta on the day you need it or you defeat the object of buying it; otherwise keep it in its wrapping and use it within 1–2 days of purchase (or according to the storage time given on the packet). If you buy fresh pasta loose from an Italian delicatessen, ask the shopkeeper for advice on storage. Fresh pasta is made with egg, which shortens its storage time, but on the plus side this increases its nutritional value and flavour, and gives the plain varieties a lovely sunshine yellow colour.

Fresh pasta takes far less time to cook than dried pasta, but the cooking technique is generally the same for each type. Most plain shapes will be *al dente* in 2–4 minutes, while stuffed shapes take 5–7 minutes, but always ask advice in the shop where it is made (or check the label).

The same rules apply for matching sauces to shapes as with dried pasta – long shapes are best with smooth sauces, while chunky sauces go better with short shapes.

LONG AND FLAT SHAPES

These were the first forms of fresh pasta to be available commercially, and were generally made in the local Italian deli- catessen by the proprietor or his wife. The choice used to be between plain egg tagliatelle and fettuccine, possibly flavoured with spinach, but now there are far more exciting varieties. Pre-packaged long fresh pasta comes in standard shapes and sizes, but Italian delicatessens sometimes have weekend specials when they offer different flavours and colours according to the seasonal availability of ingredients. This is often the case when a delicatessen supplies a local restaurant with fresh pasta. If a special order is made for a restaurant, the delicatessen may make extra to sell to customers in the shop. These occasional treats are well worth looking out for, as are regional specialities. If the owners of your local delicatessen are from Lazio you may find fresh home-made fettuccine on sale. Ligurians are more likely to make trenette, whereas pappardelle indicates that the owners of the shop probably have family ties with Tuscany or Bologna.

Fettuccine

These long, flat ribbon noodles are the narrow Roman version of tagliatelle, traditionally made about 5mm/1/4in wide.

Fettuccine are readily available, made with egg and flavoured with spinach. You may also see similar noodles called fettuccelle. The two are interchangeable, and are at their best served very simply with butter and cream.

Fettuccine all'uovo

Fettuccine al nero

Chilli-flavoured fettuccine

Fettuccine verdi

Spaghetti all'uovo

Spinach-flavoured lasagne

Tomato-flavoured lasagne

Lasagne all'uovo

Egg and spinach-flavoured capelli d'angelo

Egg and spinach-flavoured linguine

Pappardelle

Spaghetti

This pasta is widely available, in various widths. A narrow version, spaghettini, is popular, and can be found in some delicatessens. Serve fresh spaghetti or spaghettini Neapolitan style with sauces based on olive oil and tomatoes. Both spaghetti and spaghettini are also good with fish and shellfish, as long as the pieces are cut small. Capelli d'angelo, plain or flavoured with spinach, is also available.

Lasagne

Sheets of lasagne can be found plain, with egg, and flavoured with spinach or tomato. Depending on the manufacturer, they may be rectangles, squares or strips with plain or frilly edges. *Lasagne al forno* (baked lasagne) made with fresh sheets of pasta tastes much better than that made with dried pasta, so the fresh sheets are well worth buying.

Linguine

These look like strands of flattened spaghetti and are very narrow and thin. They are made with egg (*all'uovo*), and go well with a simple dressing of olive oil and flavourings such as finely chopped garlic, chillies or freshly ground black pepper. Linguine are also good with fish and shellfish sauces.

Pappardelle

Flat egg noodles, these vary in width from 2–2.5cm/³/4–1in wide. Traditional pappardelle have wavy edges, but you may see them with plain edges – the main thing is that they are wider than any of the other ribbon noodles. They originated in Tuscany, but are also popular in the city of Bologna in Emilia-Romagna. In both these regions, pasta is often served with a rich meat or game sauce, and pappardelle are the perfect choice because the noodles are wide and strong enough to support the chunkiest mixtures. Pappardelle are available plain and flavoured, sometimes with sun-dried tomatoes or porcini.

Squid ink tagliolini

Tagliolini all'uovo

Salmon-flavoured tagliolini

Spinach-flavoured tagliolini

Tagliatelle all'uovo

Spinach-flavoured tagliatelle

Tagliatelle

This is probably the best-known form of fresh pasta. The noodles are long and straight, about 1cm/½in wide. They are available everywhere, in a wide variety of flavours and colours. After plain egg tagliatelle, spinach is the most popular, but it is often flecked and flavoured with fresh herbs, garlic, porcini, sun-dried tomatoes, pepper, chillies and other spices, or beautifully coloured with saffron or tomato. When made with squid ink, it is black and dramatic. Tagliatelle comes from Bologna, where it is always served with Bolognese sauce, but it goes well with any meat sauce. Tagliarini and tagliolini are very thin versions of tagliatelle, about 3mm/⅛in wide, sold either as plain egg (all'uovo) or as paglia e fieno – half white and half green. Mixed packs are versatile and attractive because you can cook the different colours together or keep them separate, depending on the visual effect required. They go well with tomato and cream sauces.

Short Shapes

Supermarkets and other large outlets sell fresh short shapes, but the range is limited. Italian delicatessens sometimes sell a few simple home-made shapes, but because many short shapes need special machines for cutting and shaping there is seldom a wide range in small outlets, and making them by hand would be too time-consuming to be commercially viable. Short shapes tend to stick together, so in supermarkets they are kept in plastic bags in the chilled cabinets; these packs are useful in that they can be stored in the freezer. In some small shops excess moisture is removed by briefly fan-drying the shapes straight after they are made. These are then described as semi-dried and must be sold within 24–48 hours. Shapes vary widely, depending on whether they come from large manufacturers or individual shops. Conchiglie, fusilli and penne are easy to find, while other shapes, such as garganelli and ballerine, are less widely available.

Conchiglie

These shell shapes come in different sizes and colours, and conchiglie tricolore (red, white and green) are popular. They are one of the best shapes for trapping chunky sauces. If they are ridged, so much the better. Conchiglie are also good in salads because they hold dressings well.

Fusilli

Resembling the threads of screws, these should correctly be called eliche, but they are almost always labelled fusilli. Plain, spinach and tomato flavours, either sold separately or mixed together, are easy to obtain. Squid ink fusilli are made in some shops. The versatile shape of this type of pasta means that it goes well with most sauces and is also good in salads.

Garganelli

Sold in some specialist delicatessens, these are made from a very special type of egg pasta from Emilia-Romagna, and look like ridged scrolls. Garganelli need to be made

Ballerine

Penne rigate

Eliche all'uovo

Conchiglie

Semi-dried garganelli

with a special tool, called *il pettine* in Italian. Squares of fresh dough are rolled around a rod and against the *pettine*, which has teeth like a comb. The teeth produce the characteristic fine ridges on the outside of the pasta. Plain and spinach flavours are available, either sold separately or mixed together. In Emilia-Romagna, garganelli are traditionally served with a rich meat sauce, but you can use them in any recipe that calls for short maccheroni or penne. They are especially good with rich, creamy sauces.

Penne

Sometimes called quills, these come in a variety of sizes and colours, both smooth and ribbed, just like their dried counterpart. In Rome, fresh penne are served with the chilli-hot arrabbiata sauce, but they go with just about any sauce.

STUFFED SHAPES

Until recent years, the only stuffed fresh pasta shapes available were the classic ones traditionally associated with specific regions of Italy. Ravioli was the best known shape, followed by tortellini. These regional specialities are still popular, but nowadays the traditional shapes and fillings are often varied, whether they are being made by a large-scale manufacturer or a single cook working for a local delicatessen. Individual interpretations on the basic shapes, a wide variety of fresh seasonal ingredients for the fillings, plus eye-catching colour combinations for both the pasta and the fillings make variations on the theme seemingly endless. New ideas are being developed all of the time, some more successful than others, so experiment with different kinds of stuffed shapes to find the ones you like the best. Listed here are the most popular and widely available shapes, following the regional tradition.

Agnolotti

These filled pasta shapes come from northern Italy and are a speciality of Piedmont in particular. Traditionally they were shaped like plump little half moons and stuffed with meat, but this is no longer the case: nowadays you will see round and square shapes with vegetable fillings labelled as agnolotti. Square agnolotti with a pleat in the centre are called *dal plin* (with a pleat). One characteristic that all agnolotti should share is a crinkled edge, made by cutting the dough around the filling with a fluted pasta wheel.

Cappelletti

These take their name from the Italian word for little hats. In Emilia-Romagna, small squares of dough are filled and folded to make triangular shapes, then two of the ends are wrapped around

Semi-dried agnolotti all'uovo

Semi-dried cappelletti all'uovo

Cappelletti all'uovo stuffed with mushroom filling

Semi-dried tomato-flavoured cappelletti stuffed with sun-dried tomato filling

and the bottom edge turned up to make a party hat shape with a brim. In some central regions of Italy, however, cappelletti are made with either plain or fluted rounds of dough instead of squares. The dough for cappelletti can be plain or egg (*all'uovo*), or flavoured with tomato or spinach. Cappelletti are traditionally filled with minced meat and cheese and are eaten in northern and central regions of Italy at Christmas and New Year, especially in clear broth – *Cappelletti in Brodo*. You can use them in this way or serve them as a pasta course with a little melted butter and freshly grated Parmesan cheese or, alternatively, toss the cappelletti in a tomato or cream sauce.

Semi-dried raviolini all'uovo (mini egg ravioli) with a simple minced meat filling

Oval ravioli, which are sometimes called rotondi, stuffed with artichoke filling

Ravioli all'uovo with minced chicken filling

Hand-made plain and spinach-flavoured ravioli

Large rectangular ravioli stuffed with Roquefort cheese

Large ravioli stuffed with minced chicken and asparagus

Plain ravioli stuffed with asparagus filling (left), squid ink-flavoured ravioli stuffed with a herb filling and saffron-flavoured ravioli stuffed with smoked salmon and mascarpone cheese

Pansotti

Sometimes spelled pansoti, these stuffed pasta shapes are Ligurian. The word means chubby, and they are triangular in shape with little pot bellies of filling in the centre. It is traditional to fill pansotti with chopped cooked spinach, chopped hard-boiled eggs and grated Pecorino cheese, then serve them with a walnut sauce. Pansotti are made with small squares of pasta dough and may have straight or fluted edges.

Ravioli

These are usually square with fluted edges, but size and shape vary enormously. Along with tortellini, they are the most widely made of the fresh stuffed pasta shapes, and everyone seems to have their own favourite way of making them. Plain, spinach and tomato doughs are used for the pasta (although other flavours, such as squid ink and saffron, are becoming increasingly available), and the fillings can be anything from vegetables, such as spinach, artichoke and mushroom, to fish and shellfish, and minced veal and chicken. Very tiny ravioli are called raviolini, while the name for ravioli with a pumpkin filling is cappellacci. Tiny round ravioli are sometimes called medaglioni. Large round, oval and rectangular ravioli, stuffed with cheese or vegetable fillings, are occasion-ally available at Italian delicatessens. Oval ravioli are sometimes called rotondi, while the large rectangular shapes may be called cannelloni rather than ravioli.

Plain and spinach-flavoured tortellini

*Sacchetti filled with a spinach and ricotta filling
and tied with thin strips of spring onion*

Cappelli all'uovo stuffed with minced salmon

*Tomato-flavoured medaglioni all'uovo
stuffed with a prawn and trout filling*

*Tortelloni stuffed with an artichoke
and truffle oil filling*

Sacchettini

*Sweet-shaped caramelle all'uovo stuffed
with spinach and ricotta cheese*

*Spinach cannelloni stuffed with a herb
and cream cheese filling*

Tortellini

Hugely popular, these look more or less the same as cappelletti, but are made from rounds or circles of dough rather than squares so do not have peaks. They are usually slightly larger than cappelletti, while tortelloni and tortelli are larger still. Tortellini are a speciality from the city of Bologna in Emilia-Romagna, where the traditional filling is minced meats and prosciutto (Parma ham). At Christmas it is the local custom to eat *Tortellini in Brodo* as a first course soup before the main course of roast capon or turkey.

Nowadays, tortellini are available everywhere and are eaten all year round. There is a wide variety of colour combinations and fanciful fillings. Black squid ink, garlic, herbs, green olive, spinach and sun-dried tomatoes are among the many ingredients used to flavour the dough, while for the filling you can choose from such delicacies as white crabmeat, pumpkin, ricotta, asparagus, cream cheese, caramelized onions, mushrooms, marinated tuna, aubergines, sweet red peppers, artichokes and even truffles. A mixture of four cheeses is a popular filling.

Other stuffed pasta shapes

Creative cooks have started a trend for making shapes that are not based on regional traditions, so check out your local Italian delicatessen or supermarket for the latest shapes to arrive – you will find new ones appearing all the time. Two very popular pasta shapes are caramelle and sacchetti. *Caramelle* means "caramel", and this pasta shape takes its name from the familiar shape of caramels or toffees with their wrappings twisted at both ends. The filling is encased in the lozenge-shaped centre and is often ricotta-cheese based, while the pasta itself is made with egg and may be plain, spinach or tomato flavoured. Sacchetti are little purses or money bags with scrunched tops. The pasta may be plain or flavoured and the fillings based on cheese or meat. Sacchettini are a tiny version, most often served in soups but also good with smooth, creamy sauces.

Equipment

Pasta demands little in the way of specialist equipment. You are bound to have a large saucepan for cooking the pasta and a colander for draining, while for making sauces you need only a sharp knife and a chopping board for chopping ingredients, a skillet or saucepan for cooking, and a large

bowl plus spoons and forks for tossing and serving. There are a few items that will make cooking and serving easier, however, and if you eat pasta frequently you will find them a wise investment. They are all available at good kitchenware shops and department stores.

GENERAL COOKING EQUIPMENT

You may already have some of these basic items in your kitchen.

Pasta cooking pot

Made of stainless steel, this pan has straight sides with two short handles and an inner perforated draining basket, which also has two short handles. Different sizes are available, so choose the one that suits your needs best. One that will comfortably hold at least 3 litres/5 pints water is adequate if you usually cook for 2–3 people, whereas a 5 litre/8 pint pan is the one you will need if you often have to cook enough pasta for 6–8 servings. Pasta pots are quite expensive as pans go, but they are so practical that if you buy one you will wonder how you ever managed without it. The pasta is boiled in the inner basket, which is lifted out of the water once the pasta is *al dente*, making draining very easy and safe. This kind of pan is also quite versatile: you can use it with the draining basket for cooking or steaming vegetables and puddings, or use the outer pan on its own for cooking stocks, soups, stews – and even preserves. When buying a pasta cooking pot, choose one that is not too heavy or you will find it difficult to manage once it is filled with water.

Skillet

A skillet was originally a cooking pot that stood on three or four legs in the hearth. In the United States, the term came to mean a frying pan. Nowadays, it is used on both sides of the Atlantic to describe a wide, deep pan – like a cross between a wok and a frying pan – with a long handle and a lid. This is the perfect pan for making sauces. Look

for one that is at least 23cm/9in in diameter (25–30cm/10–12in is ideal) and 5–7.5cm/ 2–3in deep. If you often cook for a crowd or for varying numbers

of people, it is worth buying two of these pans, in different sizes. Choose the best quality you can afford. Some skillets have non-stick surfaces, which is fine as long as they are of good quality.

Left: This purpose-made pasta pan comes complete with an inner perforated basket for draining the pasta.

Above: A wide, deep skillet or frying pan is the ideal pan for making sauces, while a large, deep saucepan will double as a pasta pan if you don't have a purpose-made one.

Left: A large, deep-bowled ladle is extremely useful. It can be used for serving broths and soups as well as for spooning sauces over pasta.

A large perforated ladle (left) or a flatter scoop (right) are ideal for lifting short pasta shapes out of boiling water.

Right: This odd-looking tool is useful for measuring spaghetti – each hole holds a different amount of pasta.

Above: These simply designed tongs can be used for lifting long strands of pasta out of boiling water.

Left: A long-handled wooden fork is the best tool to use for stirring pasta to separate the strands during cooking.

Pasta measurer

Spaghetti is difficult to put on the scales, and measuring by the handful is not always accurate. This wooden gadget has four or five holes, each of which holds enough pasta for a given number of people.

Long-handled fork

This is useful for stirring pasta during cooking to help keep the strands or pieces from sticking together. A wooden fork is better for separating pasta than a solid wooden spoon. There are also wooden pasta rakes or hooks, which look like flat wooden spoons with prongs attached to one side. They do a good job because the pasta does not slip off when it is lifted, but sometimes the teeth come unglued in the boiling water.

Tongs

Nothing is more effective for picking strands of spaghetti and long noodles out of hot water than a good pair of tongs. Sturdy stainless steel tongs are the best, preferably with long handles for safety, but the most important thing is that they feel comfortable in your hand, so check this before buying. Some tongs have awkward mechanisms, springs and hinges – the simpler the design the better. Tongs can be used for lifting out individual strands to check for doneness and for serving.

Scoop or draining spoon

A large, deep perforated, slotted or mesh spoon is the perfect utensil for lifting short pasta shapes out of boiling water. Stainless steel is best.

Ladle

For spooning sauce over pasta and for serving soups, a deep-bowled ladle is the most effective utensil. Sizes vary from small and pointed with a lip for easy pouring, to very large, functional-looking types. Stainless steel is the best material, and it's a good idea to have several ladles in different sizes.

Parmesan knife

This is a short, quite stubby little knife with a shaped handle and a small and sturdy, double-sided blade. It is by no means an essential item, but is quite effective for scraping off shavings of Parmesan cheese from a block. It also looks good if you are serving Parmesan on a cheese board.

Below: The choice of Parmesan graters available includes a small, rotary grater with a storage space for a piece of Parmesan; a standard, stainless steel box grater; and the traditional small, hand-held Parmesan grater, which is ideal for using at the table.

EQUIPMENT FOR MAKING PASTA AT HOME

You can make pasta at home with nothing more sophisticated than a set of scales, some measuring spoons, a work surface and an ordinary rolling pin, but there are a few items of special equipment that will make the job easier. They are all available at specialist kitchenware shops and good department stores.

Tapered rolling pin

The traditional pin used in Italy for rolling out pasta dough is very long – it measures almost 80cm/32in in length. It is about 4cm/1 1/2in wide in the centre and tapers almost to a point at either end. This type of rolling pin is very easy to use and is well worth buying if you enjoy making pasta by hand and don't intend to buy a special machine. A conventional, straight rolling pin can be used instead, but try to get one that is quite slim – no more than 5cm/2in in diameter.

Mechanical pasta machine

The same type of hand-cranked pasta machine has been used in Italian kitchens for many, many years. It has stood the test of time well, because it is still manu-factured and used today, with very little modification. Made of stainless steel, it has rollers to press out the dough as thinly as possible and cutters for creating different shapes. The standard cutters usually allow you to make tagliatelle and tagliarini, but you can get attachments and accessories for other shapes

Parmesan graters

There is a huge choice of graters, ranging from the very simple hand grater to electrically operated machines. A simple stainless steel box grater will grate Parmesan and other hard cheeses, such as Pecorino, but it can be cumbersome to use with its choice of different-size teeth. It is possible to buy a small grater especially for Parmesan. This consists of a single rectangular grating plate that is designed specifically for grating hard cheese finely, and has a small handle, which can be grasped firmly. The grater is small and unobtrusive, ideal for using at the table. Mechanical Parmesan mills

are also good, as are small, hand-cranked rotary graters, and there are special Parmesan graters available with a box and a lid so that the cheese can be stored after grating. Electric Parmesan cheese graters are only worth buying if you frequently grate a lot of cheese; a less expensive alternative is to use a small electrical chopper, the kind used for chopping herbs.

including pappardelle, ravioli and cannelloni. The machine is clamped to the edge of a work surface or table and worked by turning the handle. If you make pasta frequently, it is a good buy because it is inexpensive, easy and fun to use, and makes excellent pasta in a very short time. It takes all of the hard work out of making pasta by hand, and you can even get an electric motor attachment so you don't have to turn the handle.

Above: The traditional Italian pasta rolling pin is very long, slightly wide in the centre and narrow at both ends.

Left: The traditional hand-cranked pasta machine with rollers to press out the dough and cutters for tagliatelle and tagliarini is still one of the best ways of making pasta.

Electric Pasta Machines

Tabletop electric pasta machines mix the dough, knead it and then extrude it through cutters, so all you have to do is put the ingredients in the machine and turn it on. You can make more shapes with this type of machine than the mechanical one, but you have less control over the dough because you don't actually handle it at all. Electric pasta machines are only sold in some specialist kitchenware shops. They are expensive to buy, but are a worthwhile investment if you frequently make a lot of pasta – they can make up to 1kg/2¼lb at a time – and have the space to house the machine in a convenient spot.

Left: A stainless steel pasta wheel makes light work of cutting noodles and ravioli.

Pasta wheel

This is a useful gadget for cutting lasagne and noodles such as tagliatelle when you don't have a pasta machine, and for cutting out small stuffed shapes such as ravioli. The wheel can be straight or fluted, and there are some types that will cut several lengths of noodle at a time. A sharp knife can be used instead, but a pasta wheel is easier and gives a neater finish. With a pasta wheel, the pasta edges are less likely to be dragged out of shape or torn.

Above: This special metal tray is used for making mini ravioli.

Ravioli cutter

This is virtually the same as a fluted biscuit cutter except that it has a wooden handle and can be square or round. If you want to make square ravioli and cappelletti, you can use a pasta wheel instead of this cutter, so it isn't a vital piece of equipment. For round ravioli, tortellini and anolini you can use a biscuit cutter if you have one. The most useful sizes are 5cm/2in and 7.5cm/3in.

Ravioli tray

You can buy a special metal tray for making ravioli. A sheet of rolled-out dough is laid over the tray, then pressed into the indenta-tions. The filling is then spooned into the indenta-tions and another sheet of dough placed on top. The ravioli squares are cut out by rolling a rolling pin over the serrated top. This is good for making very small ravioli, which are fiddly and time-consuming to make individually. Sometimes the tray is sold as a set with its own small rolling pin, or as an accessory for a pasta machine.

A specially designed ravioli cutter (right), which can be round or square, isn't essential, because fluted and plain biscuit cutters (left) do the same job.

How to Cook and Serve Pasta

It is very easy to cook pasta properly, but without care and attention it is equally easy to cook it badly. A few simple guidelines need to be observed if pasta is to be at its best. Once you have mastered these, you will be able to cook pasta successfully every time, no matter whether it is dried, home-made or bought fresh.

Cooking Pasta in the Microwave

Because of the large amount of water needed to boil pasta, you will not save any time by cooking it in the microwave, but for short shapes and quantities under 225g/8oz, you may find it more convenient than cooking the pasta on top of the stove. The results can be quite successful. Large and long shapes, such as lasagne sheets and spaghetti, need to be cooked in batches, so there seems hardly any point. Where the microwave comes into its own is in reheating pasta sauces, and for reheating previously baked pasta dishes, such as lasagne and cannelloni, especially individual portions of these. The microwave is also useful for thawing and reheating sauces and baked dishes that have been stored in the freezer.

How to microwave short pasta shapes

Put the pasta in a large heatproof bowl with salt to taste and pour over boiling water to cover by 2.5cm/1in. Carefully transfer the bowl to the microwave and cook on High (100 per cent power) for 3–4 minutes for fresh pasta and 8–10 minutes for dried, then leave to stand for 5 minutes before draining.

1 Synchronize sauce and pasta

Before starting to cook either sauce or pasta, read through the recipe carefully. It is important to know which needs to be cooked for the longest time – sometimes it is the pasta and sometimes the sauce, so don't always assume one or the other. The sauce can often be made ahead of time and reheated, and it is quite unusual for the timing of a sauce to be crucial, but pasta is almost like a hot soufflé – it waits for no one. This is especially true if you are cooking fresh pasta, for which timing is often only a few minutes, so the sauce needs to be ready and waiting before the pasta hits the water.

3 Use a large quantity of water

The recommended amount is 5 litres/8 pints water for every 450g/1lb pasta. If you are cooking less pasta than this, use at least 3 litres/5 pints water. If there is not enough water, the pasta shapes will stick together as they swell and the pan will become overcrowded. This will result in unpleasant, gummy-textured pasta.

WATCHPOINT

It is best not to cook more than 675g/1½lb pasta at a time, even if you have a very large saucepan, because of the danger in handling such a large amount of water. If you are using the microwave to cook pasta it is best not to cook more than 225g/8oz pasta at a time. Use a large heatproof bowl, don't overfill the bowl and transfer it carefully to and from the microwave using heatproof gloves.

2 Use a big pan

There needs to be plenty of room for the pasta to move around in the large amount of water it requires, so a big pan is essential. The best type of pan is a tall, lightweight, straight-sided, stainless steel pasta cooking pot with its own in-built draining pan. Both outer and inner pans have two handles each, which ensure easy and safe lifting and draining. If you cook pasta a lot, it is well worth investing in one of these special pans; otherwise use the largest saucepan you have for cooking the pasta and a large stainless steel colander, preferably one with feet for stability, for draining it.

4 Get the water boiling

Before adding the pasta, the water should be at a fast rolling boil. The quickest way to do this is to boil water in the kettle, then pour it into the pasta pan, which should be set over a high heat. You may need as much as 2–3 kettlefuls, so keep the water in the pan simmering, covered by the lid, while you boil the kettle again.

5 Add enough salt

Pasta cooked without salt is more or less tasteless, and with insufficient salt it is hardly any better. The recommended amount is 22.5–30ml/1 1/2–2 tbsp salt for every 450g/1lb pasta. There is no need to use sea or rock salt; cooking salt is perfectly acceptable. Add the salt when the water is boiling and just before you are ready to add the pasta. The water will bubble furiously just as the salt is added, which is your cue to shoot in the pasta.

6 Tip in the pasta all at once

Try to get all of the pasta into the boiling water at the same time so that it will cook evenly and be ready at the same time. The quickest and easiest way is literally to shake it out of the packet or the bowl of the scales, covering the surface of the water as much as possible.

7 Return the water quickly to the boil

Once the pasta is submerged in the water, give it a brisk stir with a long-handled fork or spoon and then cover the pan tightly with the lid – this will help to bring the water back to the boil as quickly as possible. Once the water is boiling, lift off the lid, turn down the heat slightly and let the water simmer over a medium to high heat for the required cooking time.

8 Stir the pasta frequently during cooking

To prevent the pasta strands or shapes from sticking together, stir them frequently during cooking so they are kept constantly on the move. Use a long-handled wooden fork or spoon so you can stir right down to the bottom of the pan.

9 Drain carefully and thoroughly

If you have a pasta pot with an inner drainer, lift the draining pan up and out of the water. Shake the draining pan vigorously and stir the pasta well so that any water trapped in pasta shapes can drain out as quickly as possible. It is a good idea to reserve a few ladlefuls of the pasta cooking water in case the pasta needs a little extra moistening when it is tossed with the sauce before serving.

Accurate Timing is Essential for Cooking Pasta

Start timing the pasta from the moment the water returns to the boil after adding the pasta. Always go by the time given on the packet or, in the case of fresh home-made pasta, by the time given in the recipe. For the greatest accuracy, use a kitchen timer with a bell or buzzer because even half a minute of overcooking can ruin pasta, especially if it is freshly made. Dried egg pasta is more difficult to spoil, so if you are new to pasta cooking and nervous about getting it right, start with this type.

For fresh pasta

As a general guide, thin fresh noodles will take only 2–3 minutes, thicker fresh noodles and pasta shapes 3–4 minutes, and stuffed fresh pasta 5–7 minutes.

For dried pasta

The cooking time for dried pasta will vary from 8–20 minutes depending on the type and the manufacturer. Always check the time on the label.

Cooking Fresh Pasta

1 For freshly made pasta that has been drying on a dish towel, gather the cloth up around the pasta in a loose cylindrical shape and hold it firmly at both ends.

2 Hold the towel over the water, then let go of the end nearest to the water so that the pasta shoots in.

Cooking Long Dried Pasta

1 For spaghetti you need to coil the pasta into the water as it softens. Take a handful at a time and dip it in the boiling water so that it touches the bottom of the pan.

2 As the spaghetti strands soften, coil them round using a wooden spoon or fork until they are all submerged.

Cooking Stuffed Pasta

1 Stuffed shapes require more gentle handling or they may break open and release their filling into the water, so stir them gently during cooking.

2 The best method of draining stuffed shapes after cooking is to lift them carefully out of the water with a large pasta scoop or slotted spoon (left).

When is it cooked?

The Italian term *al dente* is used to describe pasta that is cooked to perfection. Literally translated this means "to the tooth", meaning that it should be firm to the bite, which is how Italians like their pasta, and therefore how it should be served. Dried pasta, which is made from durum wheat, is always served *al dente*, whereas fresh pasta is made from a softer wheat and so is never as firm as dried, but it should still have some resistance to it. Overcooked pasta is limp and unpalatable and an Italian cook would not serve it.

To check that the pasta is ready, test pasta frequently towards the end of the recommended cooking time by lifting out a piece with tongs, a pasta scoop or a slotted spoon and biting into it. When you are satisfied that it is done to your liking, it is time to stop the cooking.

At-a-glance Quantities

Amounts of pasta given here are intended only as a guide to the number of people they will serve. If you are cooking fresh pasta, you may need a little more than if you are using dried, but the difference is really negligible. What is more significant is whether you are serving a light or substantial sauce with the pasta.

For an Italian-style first course (primo piatto) for 4–6 people, or a main course for 2–3 people:
3 litres/5 pints water
15ml/1 tbsp salt
250–350g/9–12oz fresh or dried pasta

For a first course for 6–8 people, or a main course for 4–6 people:
5 litres/8 pints water
22.5–30ml/1 1/2–2 tbsp salt
300–450g/11oz–1lb fresh or dried pasta

COOK'S TIP

If you are using an ordinary saucepan and a colander for cooking and draining pasta, have the colander ready in the sink. Carefully pour the contents of the pan into the colander, then shake the colander vigorously over the sink and stir the pasta to release any trapped water.

Combining the Pasta and Sauce

Recipes vary in the way they combine sauce and pasta. The majority add the sauce to the pasta, but with some it is the other way around. There are no hard-and-fast rules. If you are going to add the sauce to the drained pasta, the most important thing is to have a warmed bowl ready. The larger the bowl the better, because this will allow room for the sauce and pasta to be tossed together easily so that every piece of pasta can be thoroughly coated in sauce.

1 After draining, immediately tip the pasta into the warmed bowl, then pour the sauce over the pasta and quickly toss the two together.

2 If the pasta is not moist enough, add a little of the pasta cooking water. Some recipes call for extra butter or oil to be added at this stage, others have grated Parmesan or Pecorino cheese tossed with the pasta and sauce.

3 Use two large spoons or forks for tossing, or a large spoon and a fork. Lift the pasta and swirl it around, making sure you have scooped it up from the bottom of the bowl. The idea is to coat every piece of pasta evenly in sauce, so keep tossing until you are satisfied that this is done.

4 Occasionally, recipes call for the pasta to be returned to the cooking pan, to be combined with oil or butter and seasonings and tossed over heat until coated. A sauce may be added at this stage too, but care should be taken not to cook the pasta too much in the first place or it may overcook when it is reheated.

Serving and Presentation

Most important of all is to have your family and friends waiting at the table for the pasta, not the other way round. With the exception of baked dishes, all pasta should be eaten as soon as it is cooked and tossed with the sauce, so invite everyone to sit down just before you are ready to drain the pasta.

In most cases, pasta and sauce are tossed together in a large serving bowl in the kitchen, and the bowl is then brought straight to the table. Each person is served straight from the bowl – or the bowl is passed around the table for everyone to help themselves.

To give the pasta a finishing touch, a little Parmesan or Pecorino cheese can be grated on top, or a few chopped fresh herbs, such as parsley or basil, can be sprinkled over. The choice of garnish depends on the dish and the cook, but as a general rule, grated cheese is never served with fish and shellfish sauces. For guidance, follow the garnishing instructions in individual recipes.

Occasionally, the pasta and sauce are divided among individual plates or bowls before serving – as is the practice in restaurants. This is not the traditional custom in Italian homes, but it sometimes helps to get the pasta served quickly. It is an especially good idea when you are entertaining, because each individual serving can have its own attractive garnish.

Matching Sauces to Recipes

Some regional dishes are always made with the same pasta shape. *Bucatini all'Amatriciana*, *Penne all'Arrabbiata* and *Fettuccine all'Alfredo* are all classic Roman recipes, for example, and it is rare to see them served with anything other than the named pasta. The same applies to *Tagliatelle alla Bolognese* from Emilia-Romagna and *Trenette con Pesto* from Genoa. These classics are few and far between, however, and with the ever-increasing number of different shapes on the market it may seem difficult to know which sauces and shapes go well together. Happily, there are no rigid rules, and common sense usually prevails. Heavy sauces with large chunks of meat are unlikely to go well with thin spaghettini or tagliolini, simply because the chunks will slide off, so these sauces and others like them are always served with wide noodles, such as pappardelle, maccheroni and tagliatelle, or with short tubular shapes, such as penne, fusilli, conchiglie and rigatoni.

In the south of Italy, olive oil is used for cooking rather than butter, so sauces tend to be made with olive oil and they are usually served with the dried plain durum wheat pasta such as spaghetti and vermicelli that is also popular in the south. These long, thin shapes are traditionally served with tomato and seafood sauces, most of which are made with olive oil, and with light vegetable sauces. Spaghetti and vermicelli are also ideal vehicles for minimalist sauces like *Aglio e Olio* (garlic and olive oil) from Rome. Grated cheese is not normally used in these sauces, nor is it sprinkled over them.

Classic dishes, such as Bucatini all'Amatriciana (left), Penne all'Arrabbiata (below) and Fettuccine all'Alfredo (above), are almost always served with the named pasta.

Grated cheese is often tossed with pasta and sauce at the last moment, as well as being sprinkled over individual servings at the table.

In the North, butter and cream are used in sauces, and not surprisingly these go well with the egg pasta that is made there, especially fresh home-made egg pasta, which absorbs butter and cream and makes the sauce cling to it. Butter and cream also go well with tomato sauces when these are served with short shapes, especially penne, rigatoni, farfalle and fusilli.

Eating Pasta

Opinions vary as to whether pasta should be eaten from a plate or a bowl. There are no rules, so you can serve it on either. Large, shallow soup plates seem the ideal compromise, and setting each warmed soup plate on a large, cold underplate makes for easy carrying from kitchen to table.

If the recipe recommends extra Parmesan or Pecorino for serving, grate the cheese just before the meal and hand it round in a bowl with a small spoon so that people can help themselves. Salt and pepper mills should also be on the table for those who like to adjust the seasoning.

Pasta is traditionally eaten with a single fork. Spaghetti and other long shapes should not be difficult to manage if they have been well tossed with the sauce. The trick is to twizzle only a small amount around the fork at a time.

Wines to Serve with Pasta

It is impossible to recommend a particular wine to go with every pasta dish, but there are a few guidelines you can follow. If you know where the dish comes from, choose a wine from the same region. If a red or a white wine is used in the cooking of the sauce, select a good-quality wine for cooking and serve the rest with the meal. Otherwise, look at the main ingredient of the sauce and choose a wine that is recommended for that. Many pasta sauces are strong-tasting, garlicky or spiced with chillies, and some are served with mature Parmesan or Pecorino cheese; for these you will need to choose a robust, full-flavoured wine.

Barbaresco

A great red wine from Piedmont. Full-bodied and complex in flavour. Good with poultry and meat sauces.

Barbera

A medium-bodied red from Piedmont, which varies from young and slightly sparkling to rich and concentrated in flavour. Good with meat lasagne.

Bardolino

This fresh-tasting, light and fruity red from Veneto is very good to serve with poultry sauces.

Barolo

A full-bodied red made in Piedmont from Nebbiolo grapes. Good with red meat and game sauces.

Castel del Monte

Full-bodied smooth red and rosé wines from Puglia. Good with poultry and meat.

Chianti

Famous, uncomplicated red from Tuscany. Look for Chianti Classico to serve with red meat, poultry and game sauces.

Cirò

Fresh, zingy white and full-bodied red from Calabria. Drink the white with fish and shellfish sauces, the red with red meat and game sauces.

Est! Est!! Est!!!

A clean-tasting, dry white from the Lazio region. It is good with fish and shellfish sauces.

Frascati

A crisp and fruity dry white from the town of Frascati, which is near Rome in the Lazio region. Good with the very spicy Amatriciana sauce.

Lambrusco

This effervescent red from Emilia-Romagna is good with pork and rich meat sauces.

Orvieto Secco

Dry white, from the town of the same name in Umbria. Serve with fish, shellfish and poultry sauces.

Pinot Grigio

A fresh, fruity dry white from Friuli-Venezia. It is good with any sauce or pasta dish.

Soave

Light, dry white from Veneto made from Garganega grapes. It is good with any sauce or pasta dish, and is reasonably priced.

Valpolicella

Fruity red, sometimes with a bitter aftertaste, from Veneto. The name means valley of many cellars. It is good with red meat sauces.

Valtellina

This perfumed red from Lombardy is made from Nebbiolo grapes. Look for Grumello, Inferno, Sassella and Valgella. It is good with rich meat, poultry and game sauces.

Verdicchio

Crisp, dry white with character from Marche in central Italy. It comes in a carved bottle shaped like a Roman amphora. Good with all kinds of fish and shellfish sauces.

Vernaccia

Rich, nutty red from the island of Sardinia that goes well with fish and shellfish sauces.

How to Make Pasta

Home-made pasta has a wonderfully light, almost silky texture – quite different from the so-called fresh pasta that you buy pre-packaged in some shops. If you use egg in the mixture, which is recommended if you are making pasta at home, the dough is easy to make, either by hand or machine, and the initial process is not that different from making bread. Kneading, rolling and cutting require some patience and practice, but if you invest in an inexpensive mechanical pasta machine, this part of the process will become quick and easy – and great fun too.

Pasta all'Uovo
Pasta with Eggs

The best place to make, knead and roll out pasta dough is on a wooden kitchen table, the larger the better. The surface should be warm, so marble is not suitable.

INGREDIENTS
300g/11oz/2¾ cups flour
3 eggs
5ml/1 tsp salt

Ingredients for Pasta with Eggs

Only three inexpensive ingredients are used for making pasta with eggs: flour, eggs and salt. However, ultimate success depends as much on their quality as on the technique used for making the dough. Olive oil is added to the mixture by some cooks, especially in Tuscany, but it is by no means essential. It gives the pasta a softer texture and a slightly different flavour, and some say it helps make the dough easier to work with, especially if you don't have a pasta machine. For a 3-egg quantity of dough, use 15ml/1 tbsp olive oil and add it with the eggs.

The best flour is called Farina Bianca 00 or Tipo 00, available from Italian delicatessens. Imported from Italy, this is a very fine, soft white wheat flour. If you use ordinary plain flour, you will find the dough quite difficult to knead and roll, especially if you are doing this by hand. If you can't get 00 flour, use a strong plain white bread flour.

Very fresh eggs are essential, and the deeper the yellow of the yolks the better the colour of the pasta. Buy the eggs fresh and use them at room temperature. If they have been stored in the fridge, take them out for about 1 hour before using.

Salt is important for flavour.

1 Mound the flour on a clean work surface and make a large, deep well in the centre with your hands. Keep the sides of the well quite high so that when the eggs are added they will not run out of the well.

2 Crack the eggs into the well, then add the salt. With a table knife or fork, mix the eggs and salt together, then gradually start incorporating the flour from the sides of the well. Try not to break the sides of the well or the runny mixture will escape and quickly spread over the work surface.

3 As soon as the egg mixture is no longer liquid, dip your fingers in the flour and use them to work the ingredients together until they form a rough and sticky dough. Scrape up any dough that sticks to the work surface with a knife, then scrape this off the knife with your fingers. If the dough is too dry, add a few drops of cold water; if it is too moist, sprinkle a little flour over it.

5 Give the dough a quarter turn anti-clockwise, then continue kneading, folding and turning for 5 minutes if you intend using a pasta machine, or for 10 minutes if you will be rolling it out by hand. The dough should be very smooth and elastic. If you are going to roll it out and cut it by hand, thorough kneading is essential.

4 Press the dough into a rough ball and knead it as you would bread. Push it away from you with the heel of your hand, then fold the end of the dough back on itself so that it faces towards you and push it out again. Continue folding the dough back a little further each time and pushing it out until you have folded it back all the way towards you and all the dough has been kneaded.

6 Wrap the dough in clear film and leave to rest for 15–20 minutes at room temperature. It will then be ready to roll out.

COOK'S TIP

Don't skimp on the kneading time or the finished pasta will not be light and silky.

If you have a food processor, you can save a little time and effort by using it for making pasta dough. It will not knead the dough adequately, however, so you may find it just as quick and easy to make it by hand, especially if you take into account the washing and drying of the bowl and blade. The ingredients are the same as when making pasta by hand.

1 Put the flour and salt in the bowl of a food processor fitted with the metal blade.

2 Add 1 whole egg and then pulse-blend until the ingredients are mixed.

3 Turn the food processor on to full speed and add the remaining whole eggs through the feeder tube. Keep the machine running for just long enough to allow a dough to be formed.

4 Turn the dough out on to a clean work surface. Knead as when making pasta by hand, then wrap in clear film and leave to rest at room temperature for 15–20 minutes.

Making Pasta Shapes by Hand

Once you have made your pasta dough and let it rest, it is ready to be rolled out and cut into various shapes. If you don't have a pasta machine, the following steps show how to do it by hand. The technique is quite hard work and the pasta may not be quite as thin as that made in a machine, but it is equally good nevertheless. If you enjoy making your own pasta and think you would like to make it regularly, it is well worth buying a mechanical pasta machine to save you both time and effort.

1 Unwrap the ball of dough and cut it in half. Roll and cut one half at a time, keeping the other half wrapped in clear film as before.

2 Sprinkle a very large, clean work surface lightly with flour. Put the unwrapped dough on the surface, sprinkle it with a little flour and flatten it with the heel of your hand. Turn the dough over and repeat the process to form the dough into a 13cm/5in disc.

3 Using a lightly floured rolling pin, start to roll the dough out. Always roll the dough away from you, stretching it outwards from the centre and moving the dough round a quarter turn after each rolling. If the dough gets sticky, sprinkle the rolling pin, dough and work surface lightly with flour.

4 Continue rolling, turning and stretching the dough until it is a large oval, as thin as you can possibly get it. Ideally it should be about 3mm/$^1/8$in thick. Try to get it even all over or the shapes will not cook in the same length of time. Don't worry if the edges are not neat; this is not important.

Cutting Ribbon Noodles

1 Before you begin, have ready plenty of clean dish towels lightly dusted with flour; you will need to spread the shapes out on them after cutting. Dust the sheet of pasta (called *la sfoglia* in Italian) lightly with flour. Starting from one long edge, roll up the sheet into a loose cylinder.

2 With a large sharp knife, cut cleanly across the pasta roll. Cut at 1cm/½in intervals for tagliatelle, slightly narrower (about 5mm/¼in) for fettuccine, and as narrow as you can possibly get for tagliarini or capelli d'angelo. Take care not to drag the knife or the edges of the ribbons will be ragged.

3 With floured fingers, unravel the rolls on the work surface, then toss the noodles lightly together on the floured dish towels, sprinkling them with more flour.

4 Repeat the rolling and cutting with the remaining pasta. Leave the strips to dry on the dish towels for at least 15 minutes before cooking, tossing them from time to time and sprinkling them with a little flour if they become sticky.

Cutting Pappardelle

Cutting Lasagne and Cannelloni

1 Using a fluted pasta wheel, cut the pasta sheet into long strips about 2–2.5cm/¾–1in wide. Try to keep the strips the same width or they will not cook evenly.

2 Spread the pappardelle strips out in a single layer on floured dish towels and sprinkle them with a little more flour. Leave the pappardelle to dry on the towels for at least 15 minutes before cooking.

1 With a large sharp knife, cut the pasta sheets into 15–18 × 7.5–10cm/5–6 × 3–4in rectangles or whatever size fits your baking dish best.

2 Spread the rectangles out in a single layer on floured dish towels, sprinkle them with more flour and leave to dry for at least 15 minutes before cooking. They can be used for both lasagne and cannelloni.

COOK'S TIP

Don't throw away the trimmings when making pasta shapes, such as tagliatelle and lasagne – cut the trimmings into small pieces and pop them into soup at the last minute. You can cut leftover scraps into any rough shape you like, but there are two shapes that are made especially for soups: quadrucci and maltagliati.

Cutting Quadrucci (for Soups)

1 Stack two pasta sheets on top of each other, with a light sprinkling of flour in between. With a large sharp knife, cut the pasta diagonally into 4cm/1½in wide strips, then cut across the strips in the opposite direction to make 4cm/1½in squares.

2 Spread the squares out on floured dish towels and sprinkle with more flour. Leave to dry for at least 15 minutes before cooking.

1 Dust one pasta sheet lightly with flour. Starting from one long edge, roll the sheet up into a cylinder. Lightly flatten the cylinder, then, with a sharp knife, slice off the corners at one end, making two diagonal cuts to form two sides of a triangle. Cut straight across to complete the triangle. Repeat all the way along the cylinder, then unfold the maltagliati.

2 Spread out the maltagliati on floured dish towels. Sprinkle the shapes with a little more flour and leave them to dry for at least 15 minutes before cooking.

COOK'S TIP

Maltagliati means badly cut, so don't worry if the pasta is misshapen – it is meant to be. Quadrucci and maltagliati can also be cut from fresh lasagne rectangles, but this will take slightly longer.

Making Short Pasta Shapes

Most small pasta shapes are best left to the professionals, because they either take too long to make in any quantity or require specialist equipment. There are a couple of shapes that are an exception: garganelli and farfalle. Garganelli are traditionally made with a special tool called *il pettine*, but you can improvise with an old-fashioned butter paddle and a round pencil.

Making Garganelli

1 Cut the pasta sheets into 5cm/2in squares. Lay the butter paddle ridges horizontally on the work surface, with the ridges facing towards you. Angle the square so that it is diamond-shaped and place it over the ridges. Put a pencil diagonally across the corner of the square that is closest to you.

2 Roll the pasta square up around the pencil, pressing down hard on the ends of the pencil as you go. The ridges of the butter paddle will imprint themselves on the pasta.

3 Stand the pencil upright on the work surface and tap the end so that the tube of pasta slides off.

4 Spread the garganelli out in a single layer on floured dish towels, sprinkle them with more flour and leave them to dry for at least 15 minutes before cooking.

Making Farfalle

1 With a fluted pasta wheel, cut the pasta sheets into rectangles measuring 4 × 2.5cm/ 1¼ × 1in. Pinch the long sides of each rectangle between your index finger and thumb and squeeze hard to make a bow-tie shape. If the pasta will not hold the shape, moisten your fingers with water and squeeze again.

2 Spread the farfalle out in a single layer on floured dish towels, sprinkle them with a little more flour and leave to dry for at least 15 minutes before cooking.

Making Pasta Shapes Using a Machine

Rolling the Dough

A machine makes light work of rolling pasta dough. It makes thinner, smoother pasta than you can make by hand, and the thickness is always even. Some shapes, such as lasagne, are cut by hand, but for cutting noodles, a machine is invaluable.

1 Clamp the machine securely to your work surface and insert the handle in the roller slot. Set the rollers at their widest setting and sprinkle them lightly with flour. Unwrap the ball of pasta and cut it into quarters. Work with one quarter at a time, wrapping the other three pieces of pasta dough in clear film.

2 Flatten the quarter of dough with lightly floured hands and make it into a rough rectangle, just a little narrower in width than the rollers of the machine. Feed this through the rollers of the machine.

3 Fold the dough into thirds, then feed it lengthways through the rollers. Repeat the folding and rolling five times.

4 Turn the roller setting one notch. Sprinkle the pasta lightly with flour and feed it through the rollers again, only this time unfolded.

5 Turn the roller setting another notch and repeat the rolling, then continue in this way without folding the dough until you get to the last setting, turning the roller setting another notch after each rolling and sprinkling it lightly with flour if it becomes sticky. The dough will get longer and thinner with every rolling until it reaches 90cm–1 metre/35in–3feet in length. Once the dough has been rolled, it is ready for cutting into the required shape.

COOK'S TIPS

•About halfway through the rolling process, you may find that the pasta strip becomes too unwieldy and difficult to handle because it is so long. In this case, cut the strip in half or into thirds and work with one piece at a time. Remember to return the notch on the roller to the setting where you left off when you start with the next piece of dough.

•You may find that the dough is thin enough on the penultimate setting, in which case you can stop there. This will definitely be the case if you are going to make tonnarelli or spaghetti alla chitarra.

•Keep sprinkling the pasta dough lightly with flour if it becomes sticky, and keep the rollers lightly floured to prevent the pasta sticking to the machine.

•Any trimmings and leftover pieces of pasta dough can be re-rolled and more shapes cut from them.

•Once they are dry, noodles and pasta shapes can be stored in a paper bag for 3–4 days, or frozen in plastic bags for up to 1 month.

Cutting Lasagne and Cannelloni

COOK'S TIP

•Leave the lasagne sheets to dry on the dish towels while rolling and cutting the remaining three pieces of dough.

•Stack each successive batch of lasagne sheets on top of the previous one, with a floured dish towel in between.

1 Using a sharp knife, cut the rolled pasta strip into 15–18 x 7.5–10cm/5–6 x 3–4in rectangles, or whatever size fits your baking dish best.

2 Spread out the rectangles in a single layer on floured dish towels and sprinkle with flour.

Cutting Tagliatelle and Fettuccine

1 Insert the handle in the slot for the widest cutters and sprinkle these cutters lightly with flour. Cut the pasta strip to about 30cm/12in long if you haven't done so already, and sprinkle it lightly with flour. Feed the pasta through the widest cutters.

2 Continue turning the handle of the pasta machine slowly and steadily, guiding the strands with your other hand.

3 Toss the tagliatelle or fettuccine in flour and spread the noodles out on a floured dish towel. Leave to dry while rolling and cutting the remaining dough.

Cutting Tonnarelli and Spaghetti alla Chitarra

COOK'S TIP

When making spaghetti alla chitarra, the thickness and width of the pasta should be equal so the noodles come out square. You may need to experiment with this shape a few times until you get it just the right thickness.

VARIATIONS

To make tagliarini or spaghettini, insert the pasta machine handle in the slot for the narrowest cutters and proceed as for tonnarelli and spaghetti alla chitarra.

1 Stop rolling the pasta strip after the last but two or last but one setting, then insert the handle in the slot for the narrowest cutters and feed the pasta through the machine.

2 Proceed as for tagliatelle or fettuccine, turning the handle and guiding the long strands with your other hand. Toss the tonnarelli or spaghetti in flour and spread out on floured dish towels.

1 Using a large sharp knife, cut the rolled pasta strip into two 45–50cm/ 18–20in lengths, if this has not been done already.

2 Using a teaspoon, put 10–12 little mounds of your chosen filling along one side of one of the pasta strips, spacing them evenly.

3 Using a pastry brush, carefully brush a little water on to the pasta strip around each mound of filling.

4 Fold the plain side of the pasta strip over the filling.

5 Starting from the folded edge, press down gently with your fingertips around each mound, pushing the air out at the unfolded edge. Sprinkle lightly with flour.

6 With a fluted pasta wheel, cut along each long side, then in between each mound to make small square shapes.

7 Put the ravioli on floured dish towels, sprinkle lightly with more flour and leave to dry while repeating the process with the remaining dough. For a 3-egg dough, you should get 80–96 ravioli, more if you re-roll the trimmings.

COOK'S TIPS

• Ravioli made in this way are not perfectly square, but they look charmingly home-made. If you prefer a more precise finish, you should use a ravioli tray, which you can buy from a specialist kitchenware shop. The ravioli tray can be bought on its own or as an extra accessory to a pasta machine. Another alternative is to use a hand-held ravioli cutter or a round, plain or fluted biscuit cutter.

• Have ready 3 or 4 floured dish towels before you begin cutting the pasta shapes. Arrange the stuffed shapes on the towels, well-spaced and in one layer, because if you overlap them, they may stick together.

• Once they are dry, stuffed pasta shapes can be frozen for up to 1 month, layered between sheets of clear film in plastic bags.

Fillings for Stuffed Pasta

These vary from one or two simple ingredients to special traditional recipes. The ingredients are mixed together and often bound with beaten egg, Seasoning is added to taste.

Simple ideas

• spinach, Parmesan, ricotta and nutmeg
• crab, mascarpone, lemon, parsley and chillies
• taleggio cheese and fresh marjoram

Regional specialities

• minced pork and turkey with fresh herbs, ricotta and Parmesan
• fresh herbs, ricotta, Parmesan and garlic
• puréed cooked pumpkin, prosciutto, mozzarella and parsley

1 Using a sharp knife, cut the rolled strip of pasta dough by hand into two 45–50cm/18–20in lengths, if this has not been done already.

2 Using a teaspoon, put 8–10 little mounds of your chosen filling along one side of one of the pasta strips, spacing them evenly.

3 Using a pastry brush, carefully brush a little water on to the pasta strip around each mound of filling.

4 Fold the plain side of the pasta strip over the filling.

5 Starting from the folded edge, press down gently with your fingertips around each mound, pushing the air out at the unfolded edge. Sprinkle lightly with flour.

6 Using only half of a 5cm/2in fluted round ravioli or biscuit cutter, cut around each mound of filling to make a half-moon shape.

7 If you like, press the cut edges of the agnolotti with the tines of a fork to give a decorative effect.

8 Put the agnolotti on floured dish towels, sprinkle lightly with more flour and leave to dry while repeating the process with the remaining dough. For a 3-egg dough, you should get 64–80 agnolotti, more if you re-roll the trimmings.

COOK'S TIPS

• When cutting out the agnolotti, make sure that the folded edge is the straight edge.
• Don't re-roll the trimmings after cutting each pasta strip, but wait until you have done them all. If there is no filling left for the rolled pasta trimmings, you can use them to make noodles or small shapes for soup.

1 Using a sharp knife, cut the rolled strip of pasta dough by hand into two 45–50cm/18–20in lengths, if this has not been done already.

2 To make tortellini: with a 5cm/2in fluted ravioli or biscuit cutter, cut out 8–10 discs from one of the pasta strips. For tortelloni use a 6cm/2¹/2in cutter.

3 Using a teaspoon and a fingertip, put a little mound of your chosen filling in the centre of each disc.

4 Brush a little water around the edge of each disc.

5 Fold the disc in half over the filling so that the top and bottom edges do not quite meet. Press to seal.

6 Wrap the half-moon shape around an index finger and pinch the ends together to seal.

7 Put the tortellini or tortelloni on floured dish towels, sprinkle with flour and leave to dry while repeating the process with the remaining dough. For a 3-egg dough, you should get 64–80 tortellini, more if you re-roll the trimmings.

Making Pansotti and Cappelletti / Cappellacci

Pansotti are made from 5cm/2in squares of pasta that are folded in half over the filling to make triangles. Moisten the edges of the triangles and press to seal in the filling.

Cappelletti and cappellacci are made in the same way as tortellini, using squares of pasta rather than discs. The edges are turned up so they look like little hats.

Making Flavoured and Coloured Pasta

There are many different ingredients you can use to change the flavour and colour of pasta, whether you are making the dough by hand or machine, although you will find it easier to get a more even colour with a machine. Some flavours are more trouble than they are worth, so it is best to restrict your choice to the tried and tested ones. The following flavourings are the most successful, and the amounts of ingredients given are for a 3-egg quantity of pasta all'uovo (pasta dough with eggs).

Black pepper

Chilli

Porcini

Tomato

Black pepper

Put 30ml/2 tbsp black peppercorns or mixed peppercorns in a mortar and crush them coarsely with a pestle. Add to the eggs in the well before you start to incorporate the flour.

Chilli

Add 5–10ml/1–2 tsp crushed dried red chillies to the eggs in the well before you start to incorporate the flour.

Porcini

Soak 15g/1/2oz porcini (dried wild mushrooms) in 175ml/6fl oz/3/4 cup warm water. Drain the porcini and squeeze to remove as much water as possible. Dry the mushrooms thoroughly on kitchen paper, then chop them finely and add them to the eggs in the well before you start to incorporate the flour. The dough will be stickier than usual, so you will need to add more flour during kneading, rolling and cutting. If you like, you can add the porcini soaking water to the water for boiling the pasta. This will intensify the mushroom flavour of the pasta.

Tomato

Add 30ml/2 tbsp tomato purée to the eggs in the well before you start to incorporate the flour. The pasta dough will be stickier than usual, so you will need to add more flour during kneading, rolling and cutting.

Spinach

Wash 150g/5oz fresh spinach leaves and place them in a large saucepan with only the water that clings to the leaves. Add a pinch of salt, then cover the pan and cook over a medium heat for about 8 minutes or until the spinach is wilted and tender. Drain the spinach, leave for a few minutes until cool enough to handle, then squeeze it hard in your hands to remove as much water as possible. Dry the spinach thoroughly on several sheets of kitchen paper, then finely chop it using a large sharp knife or a food processor and add it to the eggs in the well before you start to incorporate the flour. The pasta dough will be much stickier than usual, so you will need to add a little extra flour during kneading and when rolling and cutting the dough.

Squid ink

Add two 4g sachets of squid ink to the eggs in the well before you start to incorporate the flour. The dough will be stickier than usual, so you will need to add more flour during kneading, rolling and cutting.

Herb

Wash and dry three small handfuls of fresh herbs. Basil, flat leaf parsley, sage and thyme are all good choices, either singly or together. Finely chop the herbs and add them to the eggs in the well before you start to incorporate the flour. The dough may be a little more sticky than usual, in which case you may need to add a little extra flour during kneading and when rolling and cutting it.

Saffron

Sift 3 or 4 sachets of saffron powder with the flour before starting to make the pasta dough.

Spinach

Squid ink

Herb

Saffron

Making Striped Pasta

You can use different colours to make striped dough that can be cut into rectangles for lasagne and cannelloni. It is quite fiddly, and the rolling out is best done with a pasta machine.

Plain or saffron yellow and spinach doughs look very good together, and another excellent combination is plain or saffron yellow dough contrasted with dough coloured with tomato or squid ink. To make pasta tricolore (three-coloured pasta), mix stripes of tomato dough, squid ink or spinach dough and plain dough. Some creative chefs make check and tartan patterns with coloured pasta, but this is very time-consuming for the home cook.

1 Roll out two different coloured pieces of dough on a pasta machine, keeping them separate and taking them up to and including the last setting but two.

2 With a fluted pasta wheel, cut one strip of each colour lengthways into three or four narrower strips. Select three strips of one colour and two of the other, setting the rest aside for the next batch of striped pasta.

3 The aim is to join the pasta strips together, using water as glue. Brush one long edge of one pasta strip with a little water, then join a pasta of a different colour to it, placing it over the moistened edge and pressing it firmly to seal the join. Repeat this process, alternating the pasta colours until you have a length of pasta that resembles a scarf, with three stripes of one colour and two stripes of the other.

4 Sprinkle the pasta liberally with flour, lift it very carefully and put it through the pasta machine, which should be set to the last but one setting.

5 Cut the dough into rectangles or squares for cannelloni or lasagne and spread these out in a single layer on floured dish towels. Sprinkle them with flour and leave to dry for at least 15 minutes before cooking.

COOK'S TIPS

• *When cutting flavoured tagliatelle or tagliarini on a pasta machine, sprinkle the cutters liberally with flour before putting the dough through. The noodles tend to stick together as they come through the machine, so you may need to separate them gently with floured hands before putting them on dish towels and tossing them in more flour.*

• *When cooking flavoured pasta, start testing for doneness earlier than usual. The ingredients added for some flavours make the pasta more moist and soft than usual, and this means that it cooks a little more quickly.*

• *You can use striped pasta for making ravioli: keep the strips fairly narrow and make sure that they are well sealed, otherwise the ravioli may split open during cooking.*

Making Silhouette Pasta

Fresh herbs can be rolled between sheets of pasta to give a very pretty decorative effect. The pasta needs to be very thin, so it is best to roll it out on a pasta machine. Use only soft, leafy herbs such as flat leaf parsley, chervil, green or purple basil or sage. Silhouette pasta can be boiled and served with melted butter and grated Parmesan, or cooked in a clear soup (*in brodo*).

1 Roll out a piece of dough on a pasta machine, taking it up to and including the last setting. Moisten one side of the strip of dough lightly with water. A mister or spray gun is ideal for this.

Above: Fresh herbs, such as basil (top left), flat leaf parsley (left) and sage (right), can be rolled between sheets of dough to make pretty silhouette pasta.

2 Arrange individual fresh herb leaves on the moistened half of the dough, placing them at regular intervals. Fold the dry half of the dough over the herbs and press the edges firmly to seal.

3 Sprinkle the pasta liberally with flour and put it through the machine, on the penultimate setting.

4 With a floured pasta wheel, cut around each herb leaf to make square ravioli shapes. Spread the shapes out in a single layer on floured dish towels. Sprinkle them with more flour and leave to dry for at least 15 minutes before cooking.

As an alternative to using a pasta wheel for cutting out rectangular shapes, use a small, fluted biscuit cutter and stamp out round shapes.

The Pasta Pantry

Certain ingredients crop up time and time again in sauces for pasta. Some can be kept in the pantry or storecupboard, while fresh ones must either be bought just before use, or kept in the fridge. Fresh herbs and leaves, spices, oils, vinegars and other less well-known ingredients are used to add flavour.

Canned and dried fish and shellfish are useful additions to your store cupboard, while fresh vegetables, such as aubergines, tomatoes and peppers, along with garlic and sun-dried vegetables, play an important part in many pasta dishes. Cheese and cream are used in sauces, in fillings and for baked pasta dishes.

FRESH HERBS AND LEAVES

These are used extensively for flavouring sauces for pasta, and for presentation and garnishing. Italian cooks keep pots of fresh herbs growing on the windowsill or in the garden, and think nothing of tossing in a handful of this or that herb to freshen up the flavour of their cooking. Herbs are added according to the individual cook's taste, and are seldom measured.

Marjoram

Mint

Mint
Mentuccia

Mint is not usually associated with Italian cooking, but it is frequently used in Roman dishes, in the cooking of central Italy, and even as far south as Calabria. Mentuccia is a particular kind of wild mint with small leaves grown in Rome, and there is also another variety called nepitella. You may come across the flavour of fresh mint in pasta soups, and very occasionally in sauces for pasta.

Basil

Basil
Basilico

The variety known as sweet basil is used in Italian cooking, and this is the one you are most likely to find in the shops. It is used all over Italy, but most of all in Liguria, where it grows prolifically and is used in large quantities for pesto. Basil has a special affinity with tomatoes, and is frequently used with them in sauces for pasta. It is best torn or shredded and added at the last moment. Fine chopping and long cooking spoil its pungent flavour.

Marjoram and Oregano
Maggiorana e Origano

These two herbs are closely related, but their flavours are quite different. Marjoram is sweet and delicate, while oregano, a wild variety of marjoram, is a pungent herb that should be used sparingly. They are both used in sauces for pasta, especially tomato-based ones, but marjoram is used more in Liguria and the north of Italy and oregano in the south, where it is perhaps best known for being sprinkled over pizza. Both marjoram and oregano are best chopped quite finely. They are sometimes used dried in the winter.

Parsley
Prezzemolo

Italians use the flat leaf variety of parsley, which is sometimes sold here as continental or Italian parsley. It looks very similar to coriander, and has a stronger flavour than curly parsley. It is used frequently in sauces for pasta, in fairly large quantities, and is often roughly chopped and fried in olive oil with a *battuto* of onion and garlic at the beginning of sauce making. It is popular all over Italy, and is only ever used fresh.

Bay leaves

Bay
Alloro/lauro

Both fresh and dried bay leaves are used all over Italy for flavouring soups and broths and long-cooking sauces, especially those made with meat, poultry and game. The leaves are removed before serving.

Oregano

Flat leaf parsley

Radicchio di Treviso

Rocket

Rocket
Rucola
Peppery hot *rucola* loses its pungency when cooked, so it is added to pasta sauces at the last minute, or strewn liberally over the top of pasta dishes just before serving. Bunches of large-leaved *rucola* from the greengrocer are best; the small packets sold in supermarkets are very expensive and seem to lack flavour. Use *rucola* as soon as possible after purchase because the leaves can quickly go limp and yellow, especially in warm weather.

Sage
Salvia
Along with parsley, basil and rosemary, sage is one of Italy's favourite herbs. It is frequently used by Roman cooks who sizzle fresh sage in butter to create a classic sauce to serve with ravioli. Fresh sage leaves are also used with meat, sausage, poultry and game sauces, either finely shredded or chopped or as whole leaves, which are removed before serving. Fresh sage is preferred to dried, but dried sage is occasionally used in the winter, in sauces that are cooked for a long time.

Sage

Radicchio di Verona

Radicchio
Radicchio
This ruby red and white salad leaf is a member of the chicory family. The most common variety, *radicchio di Verona*, is small and round with very tightly furled leaves, but there is another type called *radicchio di Treviso*, which is streaked creamy white and red with looser, long and tapering leaves. Both have a bitter flavour, which is much appreciated in small quantities in pasta sauces. Shredded leaves should be added at the last moment, to preserve their colour.

Rosemary

Rosemary
Rosmarino
This most fragrant and pungent herb is very popular all over Italy. Rosemary is used sparingly in meat and tomato sauces, either very finely chopped or on the sprig, which is then removed from the sauce before serving. Dried rosemary is sometimes used in the winter months.

Thyme
Timo
This aromatic and distinctively flavoured herb is used both fresh and dried. It is a Mediterranean herb that goes well with tomato-based sauces and with meat and poultry, and it is also good mixed with rosemary and bay.

Thyme

SPICES AND SALT

Spicy, highly seasoned foods are not normally associated with Italian cooking, but the use of spices in cooking dates back to Roman – and even Etruscan – times, when spices were used freely, often to excess. Nowadays, spices tend to be used more sparingly and the range tends to be limited to a few favourites.

Dried chillies

Fresh chillies

Chilli flakes

Chilli
Peperoncino

Small red chillies are immensely popular in the south of Italy and Sardinia, and they are frequently used in sauces for pasta. Sometimes the sauce is a classic that depends on chillies for its essential flavour – the hot and spicy *Penne all'Arrabbiata* from Rome being perhaps the most famous. Most often, however, chillies are added more sparingly with the aim of livening up a sauce and intensifying its flavour rather than giving it a fiery flavour.

Fresh chillies tend to be fried with a *soffritto* of olive oil, onion, garlic and parsley at the beginning of sauce making, whereas dried chillies are popped into the sauce when it is bubbling. Both fresh and dried chillies are often added whole to sauces in order to impart a subtle flavour. They are later lifted out and either discarded or chopped or crumbled, then returned to the sauce. The seeds may be included or left out, depending on the degree of heat required (the seeds contain most of the heat). Crushed dried red chillies or chilli flakes (sold in little jars) are very handy when just a pinch or two of chilli is required in a recipe.

Cinnamon
Cannella

Ground cinnamon is used in stuffings for pasta, both with meat and cheese. It gives a fragrant aroma and subtle sweetness, and is always used sparingly.

Nutmeg
Noce moscata

Whole nutmeg is grated fresh when needed. It is used for flavouring *la beschi-amella* (béchamel sauce) and is often used in combination with spinach and ricotta cheese. In Emilia-Romagna, it is traditionally used for flavouring meat sauces and stuffings for pasta.

Pepper
Pepe

Black peppercorns are ground fresh from a pepper mill as and when they are needed, both in cooking and at the table. Black pepper is used in just about every pasta sauce that is made, and it is also used to speckle and flavour home-made pasta. If coarsely crushed peppercorns are required, they are ground with a mortar and pestle.

Saffron
Zafferano

The most expensive spice in the world, saffron comes in two different forms. Threads of saffron, the actual dried stigmas of the crocus, are usually wrapped in cellophane and sold in sachets. They can be sprinkled into a sauce, but are more often soaked in warm water for 20–30 minutes, so that the water can be strained off and used for colouring and flavouring. Saffron powder is sold in sachets and can be sprinkled directly into sauces. It is less

Saffron

expensive than the threads and considered by many to be inferior, but it is more convenient to use. Saffron has a delicate but distinctive flavour, which is good with both cream and butter-based sauces as well as with fish and shellfish. The spice is also used to colour home-made pasta.

Salt
Sale

Coarse sea salt and rock salt are ground in a salt mill and used both as a seasoning in cooking and at the table. It is essential that salt is added to the water when boiling pasta to give it flavour, but for this you can use refined cooking salt rather than the more expensive sea or rock salt. Just about every pasta sauce will have salt as a seasoning, except perhaps those containing salty anchovies or bottarga (air-dried mullet or tuna roe).

Peppercorns (left) and sea salt

OILS AND VINEGARS

Oil and vinegar are essential store-cupboard items for the Italian cook. Don't buy cheap brands; it will be false economy. Good olive oil and wine or balsamic vinegar will lift the flavour of a sauce or salad and enhance the other ingredients in it.

Olive oil
Olio d'oliva

Extra virgin olive oil is the best and most expensive of the olive oils. This is literally the oil that is secreted when the olives are crushed mechanically by cold presses.

No other processing nor any heat is involved in the making of extra virgin olive oil. It should have an acidity level of one per cent or less, but as this information is seldom on the label of the bottle, this is difficult to check.

Extra virgin is the oil to use for salads, since heating may spoil its natural olive flavour. It is also the one to use for sprinkling over warm food or for tossing with pasta in dishes, such as *Spaghetti Aglio e Olio*, that rely on olive oil for their predominant flavour.

Fruity, often peppery, Tuscan oil is reputed to be among the best of the extra virgin olive oils, although some cooks prefer oil from Umbria, or from Veneto or Liguria, which are more delicate. Oils from the South are stronger and more intensely flavoured, and these may be more to your taste. Brands vary enormously, so experiment to find what suits you best.

For cooking and heating, virgin olive oil is the one to use. This is less expensive than extra virgin because it has a higher acidity

Virgin olive oil (left), extra virgin olive oil (centre) and balsamic vinegar (right)

level (up to four per cent), but it is cold pressed and not refined in any way so it still has a good, full flavour. Many pasta sauces start with the frying of flavouring ingredients, such as onion, garlic, celery, parsley, chillies and carrot. If these are fried in an oil with a good flavour, the sauce will have a strong base (*soffritto*), the flavour of which will then permeate through the other ingredients during cooking.

Vinegar
Aceto

Occasionally a splash of red or white wine vinegar may be added to a pasta sauce, but wine vinegar is more often used in salad dressings. Flavourwise, red and white vinegars are interchangeable, but the colour of the salad ingredients may dictate whether you use red or white.

Balsamic vinegar (aceto balsamico) from Modena in Emilia-Romagna is a different thing altogether. It is a dark, syrupy vinegar which is aged in wooden casks for many years. The best and most authentic *aceto balsamico* will have been aged in casks or barrels of different woods for 40–50 years. Labelled *tradizionale di Modena*, this vinegar is only used a drop at a time, usually at the moment of serving on fish or meat, salads and even fresh strawberries. For flavouring a pasta sauce or salad, use the much less expensive balsamic vinegar that has been aged between five and ten

years. Its flavour does not compare with the genuine article, but it is musky and slightly sweet, and very good.

FLAVOURINGS

Some special ingredients are used in different regions of Italy, and you may need to buy them for a particular sauce.

Salted capers

Capers bottled in brine

Capers
Capperi

Capers are the fruit of a flowering shrub that grows in the Mediterranean. They are sold in various ways. The best are the large, salted capers sold in small jars in Italian delicatessens. Check before buying that the salt is white and has not discoloured at all. Yellow salt is a sign that the capers are past their best and may have a rancid taste. Before use, salted capers need to be soaked in several changes of water for 10–15 minutes, then drained, rinsed in fresh water and dried, but after this initial preparation they taste very fresh and good. They can be chopped and used to add piquancy to sauces – you will often find them in recipes from the south of Italy and Sicily and Sardinia.

It is also possible to buy tiny capers sold in small bottles of brine or vinegar. These have a strong flavour and should be rinsed well before use. They almost always taste sharp and vinegary, so use them sparingly.

Olives
Olive

Both black and green olives are used in making sauces and salads, although black olives are more highly favoured. The best type for pasta sauces are the small, shiny, very black *gaeta* olives from Liguria. Buy the plain ones for cooking, not those with additional flavourings, such as herbs, garlic, chillies and other spices, which are intended for antipasto. Olives are best added to a sauce towards the end of cooking. They need no cooking, only heating through, and if added too early they can impart a bitter flavour. When using olives in a pasta sauce or salad, pit them first, because the stones are awkward to manage when you are eating pasta.

Olives

Pancetta
Pancetta

This is cured belly of pork, the Italian equivalent of bacon, which has a spicy, sweet flavour and aroma. Unsmoked pancetta is sold in a roll at Italian delicatessens, and is called pancetta arrotolata or pancetta coppata. A machine is used to slice it very thinly to order and it can be eaten as it is for an antipasto, or cut into strips or diced for use in cooking. Pancetta affumicata is smoked and comes in rashers, which look like streaky bacon complete

Smoked (left) and
unsmoked pancetta

with rind. There is a version called pancetta stesa, which is long and flat. Smoked pancetta is cut into strips or dice and used as the base for ragù and many other pasta sauces, the most famous of which is carbonara. Some supermarkets sell packets of ready-diced pancetta. The quality and flavour are generally good, so these are well worth buying for convenience. If you are unable to get pancetta, streaky bacon can be used instead, and you can buy smoked or unsmoked, whichever flavour you prefer.

Pine nuts
Pinoli

Best known for their inclusion in pesto, these small, creamy white nuts have an unusual waxy texture and resinous flavour. They look and taste good sprinkled over pasta salads, and they add a welcome crunchy bite. To enhance their flavour, they are often toasted before use. Only buy the quantity of pine nuts you need because they do not keep well and quickly go rancid. They are sold ready-shelled in small packets, in supermarkets and delicatessens.

Pine nuts

FISH AND SHELLFISH

Pasta sauces made with fish or shellfish are quick and delicious. Fresh seafood is often the main ingredient, but there are a few other fishy staples that are used over and over again.

Anchovies
Acciughe

The best anchovies are the salted ones that are packed in large cans. You see them on the counters of Italian delicatessens, where they are sold loose by the kilo or pound. They must be rinsed, skinned and filleted

before use, but are plumper and more flavoursome than the fillets sold in jars and cans, so repay the effort. Anchovies are used in sauces for pasta all over Italy, but particularly in the hot South and in Sicily and Sardinia where strong and salty flavours are so popular. When chopped and heated gently with a little olive oil, they melt down to a creamy paste that is packed

Anchovies in brine (left) and salt

with flavour, so you only need to use a small quantity at a time. If you can't get salted anchovies, try to locate anchovy fillets that are bottled in olive oil. These taste better than the ones canned in vegetable oil.

Bottarga
Bottarga

This is the salted and air-dried roe of mullet or tuna. The best is the mullet, bottarga di muggine. It is a great delicacy in Sardinia, Sicily and the Veneto, where they like it grated over pasta or very thinly sliced as an antipasto with lemon juice and olive oil. You can buy bottarga quite easily in Italian delicatessens, where it is kept in vacuum packs in the fridge. Mullet bottarga is delicate, moist and golden, like a pale, thin version of smoked cod's roe, and bears little resemblance to tuna bottarga, which

Tuna bottarga

Ready-grated bottarga

Mullet bottarga

comes in a thick, dark block. For grating over pasta you need only a small quantity and it can be kept in the fridge for a long time (check the use-by date). You can also buy ready-grated bottarga in small jars, but this product has a dry texture and the flavour does not compare with that of freshly grated bottarga.

Clams
Vongole

In Italy, small fresh clams are frequently used in pasta sauces on the coast and in Sicily and Sardinia, but they are not always easy to get in other parts of the country or further afield. Names vary from one region and one country to another, but the name is not important; it is the size that counts.

Fresh clams (left) and canned clams

Small *vongole* cook quickly and have a tender texture and sweet flavour, which make them ideal for pasta sauces. Don't be tempted to buy the large ones. Some fishmongers sell frozen small clams, which are a good substitute for fresh; otherwise you should buy the bottled shelled clams in natural juice that are sold at Italian delicatessens. Check labels carefully and don't buy the ones in vinegar or brine – these are intended for antipasto; their sharp flavour will spoil a pasta sauce. You can also buy bottled clams in their shells. These are packed in oil and, although intended primarily for antipasto, they also make an attractive garnish for a clam sauce.

Squid ink
Nero di seppia

If you want to colour home-made pasta black, you can buy handy little sachets of squid ink at fishmongers and Italian delicatessens. There is usually about 4g of ink in each sachet and the sachets are sold in pairs. Two sachets are enough to colour a 3-egg quantity of *pasta all'uovo*.

Tuna
Tonno

For pasta sauces, use only best-quality canned tuna in olive oil, not the kind packed in vegetable oil, water or brine. Some supermarkets sell it; otherwise you will have to go to an Italian delicatessen. The flesh of good-quality canned tuna is moist and meaty. The cost of a good can of tuna is generally less than that of fresh fish, so no matter how much you spend on it, pasta with a tuna sauce will still be an inexpensive meal.

Canned tuna

VEGETABLES

Tomatoes are not the only vegetable to be used in sauces for pasta. Many others play an important part, either as a main ingredient or in a more minor role. Dried vegetables such as porcini mushrooms, peppers and tomatoes are used almost as often as fresh; valued for the intense flavour they impart to pasta sauces and soups.

Dried chargrilled aubergines

Aubergines
Melanzane

Fresh aubergines are used as a main ingredient in many pasta sauces, especially in southern Italy, Sicily and Sardinia. Dried aubergines are not used as a substitute for fresh, but are added to fresh vegetables for their characteristic earthy flavour and meaty texture. Sold in cellophane packets, they are thin slices of aubergine that have been dried in the sun, and are a good storecupboard item in that you can use as few or as many as you like. They need to be rehydrated in boiling water with a splash of white wine vinegar for 2 minutes before use, then drained and dried. They can then be snipped into strips and either added immediately to a simmering pasta sauce or fried first in olive oil.

Garlic
Aglio

Crushed, sliced and chopped garlic is used in many pasta sauces, but especially in those from the south of Italy, and whole garlic cloves are sometimes fried in olive oil at the beginning of cooking, then removed to leave behind a subtly flavoured base for a sauce. One famous Roman pasta dish, *Spaghetti Aglio e Olio*, holds garlic in such high esteem that the sauce contains only two ingredients – garlic and olive oil – and in Rome they maintain it is the best cure for a hangover. The best Italian garlic is pink or purple tinged, with plump juicy cloves. In spring and early summer you can buy it fresh at some green-grocers, markets and Italian delicatessens.

Garlic

This is the newly picked garlic that is sweet, moist and mild. As it dries out it becomes more pungent, so you need to adjust quantities accordingly. Buy garlic little and often so it neither sprouts green shoots nor becomes papery and dry.

Porcini mushrooms
Funghi porcini

Dried porcini (*boletus edulis*) are invaluable for the intense, musky aroma and flavour they impart to pasta sauces and soups. Italians use them all year round, not as a substitute for fresh porcini, but as a valued ingredient in its own right. A few dried porcini added to ordinary fresh mushrooms, for example, will give them the flavour of wild mushrooms. Don't buy cheap porcini, but look for packets containing large pale-coloured pieces. Although they will seem expensive, a little goes a long way, and 15–25g/½–1oz is the most you will need in a recipe that serves

Dried porcini mushrooms

4–6 people. Before use, dried porcini must be reconstituted in warm water for 15–20 minutes. Drain, rinse and squeeze dry, then slice or chop as required. Don't throw the soaking liquid away. Strain it to remove any grit and use it in soups and stocks, or add it to the water when cooking pasta to impart a mushroomy flavour – this is especially effective with fresh pasta.

Peppers
Peperoni

Sun-dried red peppers are sold in cello-phane packets. They resemble sun-dried tomatoes, but their flavour is more peppery

Dried peppers

Bottled roasted peppers

and piquant. They are used in the same way as tomatoes, to add a firm meaty bite to sauces and soups, especially those made with vegetables. Before use they should be rinsed under the cold tap, then dried and cut into thin strips or chopped.

Roasted peppers can be bought loose or in jars, packed in olive oil or brine. Although you can easily roast fresh peppers yourself when you need them, it is handy to keep a jar of commercially roasted peppers in the fridge. Just one piece of roasted pepper, sliced or chopped, will add a wonderful smoky flavour to pasta sauces, salads and soups. The best ones come from Italian delicatessens, who chargrill the peppers themselves and sell them loose in extra virgin olive oil.

Tomatoes
Pomodori

In summer, when fresh Italian plum tomatoes are ripe and full of flavour, it is wonderful to use these for sauce making, but at other times of the year you will get a far better flavour and colour by using preserved tomatoes.

There are plenty of excellent tomato products to choose from, most of which come from southern Italy, where the hot sun ripens the tomatoes on the vine to an incomparable flavour.

Canned peeled plum tomatoes (*pomodori pelati*) come whole and chopped. Don't buy cheap brands; instead, opt for the top-quality Italian brands,

Chopped canned plum tomatoes

*Filetti di
pomodoro (plum
tomatoes in water and salt)*

naturale in water and salt. They are about the nearest thing you can get to bottling tomatoes yourself at home, which Italians do in summer to preserve surplus tomatoes for winter use.

Crushed tomatoes come in many guises, and are a real boon for sauce making because they take all the hard work out of peeling, seeding and chopping. They are plum tomatoes that have been mechanically peeled and crushed, then sieved to remove the seeds. You can choose from passata, which is quite smooth, to polpa and sugocasa, which are quite chunky.

Bottles and jars of these products are good in that they allow you to see what you are buying. Cartons of very smooth passata take up less room and are lighter to carry; they are very popular with Italian cooks for making almost instant sauces.

Sun-dried tomatoes (*pomodori secchi*) are sold in two different forms – as dry pieces and in oil. Both types are piquant in flavour, but the dry pieces have a chewier texture than those in oil. Dried tomatoes are sold in cellophane packets and can be snipped directly into a long-cooking pasta sauce to intensify its tomato flavour, but generally they are best if softened in hot water for 2–3 hours before use. Sun-dried tomatoes in oil are sold in jars and can also be bought loose at some delicatessens. For the best flavour, buy the ones in olive oil. They are soft and juicy and can be used as they are, either sliced or chopped, in sauces and salads.

Sun-dried tomato paste is a thick mixture of sun-dried tomatoes and olive oil. It can be used on its own as a quick sauce for pasta or added by the spoonful to tomato sauces to colour and enrich them.

Although thick in texture, the flavour of sun-dried tomato paste is sweet and mild compared with tomato purée, and the colour is paler.

*Sun-dried tomatoes bottled in oil
(top), and dry pieces*

Tomato purée or concentrate (*concentrato di pomodoro*) is a very strong, thick paste made commercially from tomatoes, salt and citric acid. You can buy it in tubes, jars or cans, and its strength varies according to the manufacturer.

*Clockwise from
left, sugocasa,
polpa and passata*

especially those that identify the tomatoes as San Marzano on the label. If you ask at your local Italian delicatessen, they will give you good advice. Plain chopped tomatoes are a good buy because they save you having to chop them yourself, but they are slightly more expensive. If they are labelled polpa di pomodoro, they are likely to be very finely chopped or even crushed. Flavourings, such as garlic and herbs, should be added fresh, so don't buy chopped canned tomatoes containing these.

Filetti di pomodoro are sold in jars at good Italian delicatessens and specialist food shops. These are plum tomatoes that have been halved or quartered and bottled *al*

*Sun-dried tomato
paste (left) and tomato purée*

Get to know the brand you like because some are quite bitter and sharp, and can overwhelm other flavours in a sauce. Only use tomato purée in small quantities or it may make a dish too acidic. A way to counteract acidity is to add a pinch or two or a lump of sugar.

Cheese and Cream

Italy's magnificent cheeses are famous all over the world, both as table cheeses and for their use in cooking. Many of them are used in sauces for pasta, in fillings for stuffed pasta and baked dishes.

Fontina

Fontina

A mountain cheese from the Val d'Aosta in the northwest of Italy, fontina is used in baked pasta dishes, such as lasagne. It has superb melting qualities and a wonderful nutty, slightly sweet flavour. Some large supermarkets sell it; otherwise you can get it at delicatessens and cheese shops.

Gorgonzola

This blue-veined cheese comes from Lombardy. Although it is a table cheese, it melts quickly and well, so it is good in sauces and stuffed pasta, and its sharp flavour tastes very good combined with cream and leafy greens, such as spinach,

Gorgonzola

sorrel and herbs. Gorgonzola piccante is the very strong version, while dolcelatte is milder and sweeter, almost buttery.

Mascarpone

This is a full-fat cream cheese with a smooth silky texture, often used in pasta

Mascarpone

sauces instead of cream. It melts without curdling and has a slightly tangy flavour. It is widely available in tubs in delicatessens and supermarkets.

Mozzarella

A soft white cheese, which is used in both salads and cooking, mozzarella melts quickly in hot sauces to serve with pasta, but must not be overcooked or it may become stringy. The whey should be drained off and discarded before the cheese is used. By

Mozzarella

tradition mozzarella should be made with buffalo's milk, but today it is often made with cow's or sheep's milk. Buy only the type that is swimming in whey in little bags – blocks of mozzarella are rubbery and tasteless. Mozzarella di bufala has the best texture and the most flavour, but it is more expensive than cow's or sheep's milk mozzarella and not so easy to find.

Parmesan

Grated Parmesan is most often used for sprinkling over pasta at the table, although it is also tossed with pasta after draining or added to sauces at the end of cooking. Genuine Parmigiano Reggiano has its name stamped on the rind and comes only from the area between Parma, Modena, Reggio-Emilia, Bologna and Mantua. It must be aged

for a minimum of 2 years, which is one of the reasons why it is so costly. Grana Padano is a similar, less expensive, cheese, which is used in the same way as Parmigiano Reggiano. Both are excellent melting cheeses, but Reggiano has a milder,

Pecorino (left) and Parmigiano Reggiano

less salty flavour and its texture is more flaky. Never buy these cheeses ready grated. Buy them in the piece and grate them as and when you need them, or shave into curls with a vegetable peeler.

Pecorino

This salty, hard sheep's milk cheese is called Pecorino Romano if it comes from Lazio and Pecorino Sardo if it is Sardinian. It is used for grating in the same way as Parmesan, but because its flavour is sharper, it is used with the strong-tasting and spicy sauces associated with southern Italian and Sardinian cooking.

Ricotta salata (right) and ricotta

Dressing up Commercial Sauces

There are lots of bottled sauces for serving with pasta, ranging from chopped tomato sugocasa to classics, such as vongole, arrabbiata and carbonara, as well as unusual combinations of ingredients created by individual manufacturers. Generally speaking it is best to stick to the Italian brands that are sold in delicatessens and supermarkets, because these are the ones that Italians keep in their own store cupboards for times when they want to serve pasta at a moment's notice. You can use these sauces just as they are, but they will taste more home-made if you liven them up by adding something fresh.

Pesto

Both classic basil pesto and red pesto – made using sun-dried tomatoes – are available in jars, and are useful store cupboard standbys. Grate a little fresh Parmesan cheese over the pasta before tossing with the pesto, and add a spoonful or two of extra virgin olive oil for a more fruity flavour. For a richer pesto sauce, add a spoonful or two of mascarpone cheese or cream (*below left*). Just before serving, sprinkle the pasta with more freshly grated Parmesan or with toasted pine nuts or shredded basil leaves.

Sugocasa/Chopped tomatoes

Add a little sun-dried tomato paste and/or a splash of red or white wine when heating up sugocasa, and season well with salt and ground black pepper. If you like a creamy tomato sauce, add up to 150ml/¼ pint/⅔ cup *panna da cucina*, double cream or crème fraîche. For a spicy kick, add a sprinkling of crushed dried red chillies. Finish the sauce off with a small handful of shredded fresh basil or rocket, or use 15–30ml/1–2 tbsp chopped fresh marjoram or oregano.

Arrabbiata

Strew a generous handful of finely shredded rocket leaves on top of the tossed pasta and sauce just before serving.

Carbonara

Stir a few spoonfuls of fresh cream into the sauce while it is heating up, then top with thin shavings of Parmesan cheese once the sauce and pasta have been tossed together.

Vongole

Add a splash of wine, some chopped fresh parsley and garlic. You can add all of these ingredients or just one or two of them. A few pitted and sliced black olives also look and taste good with a vongole sauce.

Ricotta

Fresh ricotta is a very soft white cheese, sold loose by the kilo/pound in Italian delicatessens. It has superb melting qualities and is used in fillings for stuffed and baked pasta dishes, and for tossing with fresh raw vegetables, such as tomatoes, spinach and rocket for uncooked sauces. Ricotta is low in fat and has a bland flavour, so it goes well with flavoursome ingredients, such as herbs and garlic. Fresh ricotta does not keep well, so check before buying and only buy it if it is snowy white in colour. If not, it is better to buy the ricotta sold in tubs – these are widely available at supermarkets. Ricotta salata is a hard, salted version of ricotta, cut from the block in Italian delicatessens. It too is very white and low in fat. Ricotta salata is used for grating or crumbling over soups and pasta, especially in the south of Italy. You will find it saltier than Parmesan, Grana Padano or Pecorino, so will need less.

Cream

Panna da cucina

For creamy pasta sauces, Italians use a type of cream called *panna da cucina* (cream for cooking). It is sold in little tubs, often joined together in pairs. Each tub contains 100ml/3½fl oz/scant ½ cup, which is enough to

Panna da cucina

make a pasta sauce to serve 4 people. Panna da cucina is a long-life product, so it is well worth buying to keep in the store cupboard for making impromptu sauces. It is widely available in Italian delicatessens.

Pasta Recipes

Pasta proves its enormous versatility in this section. There are complete recipes, plus many variations, and since there are very few hard-and-fast rules with sauces for pasta you can personalize them to your heart's content – and make even more. The recipes in the Broths and Soups chapter range from clear light liquids supporting delicate pieces of pasta to gutsy substantial soups that make meals in themselves. Tomato Sauces can be smooth and subtle, fiery or chunky, while Cream Sauces are deliciously rich and luxurious, and unbelievably quick to make.

The Fish and Shellfish recipes have fabulous flavours, some of which are surprisingly spicy and strong. They make good first courses and after-work suppers, as do the recipes in Meat and Poultry, many of which you will recognize as traditional and regional favourites. In Vegetables and Vegetarian, some of the recipes are classic, but most are new. They're quick and easy, colourful and light, and they look and taste absolutely stunning. There's a choice of both family favourites and dinner party dishes in Baked Pasta, while in the Stuffed Pasta chapter you can have fun making your own dough. You'll be amazed how easy it is, and delighted with the results too. The chapter devoted to Fresh and Healthy recipes proves the point that pasta not only looks and tastes good, but it's nutritionally sound too, something that can also be said of delicious Pasta Salads. And finally, there is a section on Noodles, the Chinese equivalent of pasta, to prove just how versatile this food really is.

Broths
and
Soups

Soups made with pasta range from clear broths with just a surface scattering of *pastina* to filling and substantial *minestre* or *zuppe*, which include chunkier pieces of pasta and vegetables, fish or meat. Broth, called *brodo* in Italian, is generally served as a first course or *primo piatto*, especially for evening meals. It also makes a marvellous pick-me-up if you are tired, unwell or simply under the weather. The chunkier pasta soups are more likely to make a meal in themselves, especially when served with bread.

This chapter explores the full range of pasta soups. Some, like Genoese Minestrone and Pasta, Bean and Vegetable Soup are regional classics, others are less well known yet equally delicious, but all are gloriously adaptable: use a different shape or size of pasta if you prefer, and don't worry too much about exact quantities.

Genoese Minestrone

In Genoa they often make mine-strone like this, with pesto stirred in towards the end of cooking. It is packed full of vegetables and has a good strong flavour, making it an excellent vegetarian supper dish when served with bread. There is Parmesan cheese in the pesto, so there is no need to serve extra with the soup.

INGREDIENTS

1 onion
2 celery sticks
1 large carrot
45ml/3 tbsp olive oil
150g/5oz French beans, cut into
    5cm/2in pieces
1 courgette, thinly sliced
1 potato, cut into 1cm/¹⁄₂in cubes
¹⁄₄ Savoy cabbage, shredded
1 small aubergine, cut into 1cm/¹⁄₂in cubes
200g/7oz can cannellini beans, drained
    and rinsed
2 Italian plum tomatoes, chopped
1.2 litres/2 pints/5 cups vegetable stock
90g/3¹⁄₂oz dried spaghetti or vermicelli
salt and ground black pepper

For the pesto
about 20 fresh basil leaves
1 garlic clove
10ml/2 tsp pine nuts
15ml/1 tbsp freshly grated
    Parmesan cheese
15ml/1 tbsp freshly grated
    Pecorino cheese
30ml/2 tbsp olive oil
Serves 4–6

1 Chop the onion, celery and carrot finely, either in a food processor or by hand. Heat the oil in a large saucepan, add the chopped mixture and cook over a low heat, stirring frequently, for 5–7 minutes.

2 Mix in the French beans, courgette, potato and cabbage. Stir-fry over a medium heat for about 3 minutes. Add the aubergine, cannellini beans and tomatoes, and stir-fry for 2–3 minutes more. Pour in the stock with salt and pepper to taste. Bring to the boil. Stir well, cover and lower the heat. Simmer for 40 minutes, stirring occasionally.

3 Meanwhile, process all the pesto ingredients in a food processor until the mixture forms a smooth sauce, adding 15–45ml/1–3 tbsp water through the feeder tube if necessary.

4 Break the pasta into small pieces and add it to the soup. Simmer, stirring frequently, for 5 minutes. Add the pesto sauce and stir it in well, then simmer for 2–3 minutes more, or until the pasta is *al dente*. Taste for seasoning. Serve hot, in warmed soup plates or bowls.

COOK'S TIP

If you don't want to go to the trouble of making your own pesto, use the bottled variety – the traditional green basil pesto rather than the red sun-dried tomato pesto. You will need about 45ml/3 tbsp.

Rich Minestrone

THIS IS A SPECIAL minestrone made
with chicken. Served with crusty
Italian bread, it makes a hearty meal.

INGREDIENTS

15ml/1 tbsp olive oil
2 chicken thighs
3 rindless streaky bacon rashers, chopped
1 onion, finely chopped
a few fresh basil leaves, shredded
a few fresh rosemary leaves,
    finely chopped
15ml/1 tbsp chopped fresh flat
    leaf parsley
2 potatoes, cut into 1cm/½in cubes
1 large carrot, cut into 1cm/½in cubes
2 small courgettes, cut into 1cm/½in cubes
1–2 celery sticks, cut into 1cm/½in cubes
1 litre/1¾ pints/4 cups chicken stock
200g/7oz/1¾ cups frozen peas
90g/3½oz/scant 1 cup stellette or other
    dried tiny soup pasta
salt and ground black pepper
fresh basil leaves, to garnish
coarsely shaved Parmesan cheese, to serve

Serves 4–6

1 Heat the oil in a large frying pan, add
the chicken thighs and fry for about
5 minutes on each side. Remove with a
slotted spoon and set aside.

2 Lower the heat, add the bacon,
onion and herbs to the pan and
stir well. Cook gently, stirring constantly,
for about 5 minutes. Add all the
vegetables, except the frozen peas,
and cook for 5–7 minutes more,
stirring frequently.

3 Return the chicken thighs to the
pan, add the stock and bring to
the boil. Cover and cook over a low
heat for 35–40 minutes, stirring the
soup occasionally.

4 Remove the chicken thighs with a
slotted spoon and place them on
a board. Stir the peas and pasta into the
soup and bring back to the boil. Simmer,
stirring frequently until the pasta is
al dente: 7–8 minutes or according to
the instructions on the packet.

5 Meanwhile, remove and discard
the chicken skin, then remove the
meat from the bones and cut it into
1cm/½in pieces. Return the meat to
the soup and heat through. Taste for
seasoning. Ladle into soup bowls;
scatter over Parmesan shavings and
garnish with one or two basil leaves.

COOK'S TIP

For extra flavour, add any Parmesan rind
to the simmering soup.

Red Onion and Beetroot Soup

THIS BEAUTIFUL, VIVID ruby-red soup will look stunning at any dinner-party table.

INGREDIENTS

15ml/1 tbsp olive oil
350g/12oz red onions, sliced
2 garlic cloves, crushed
50g/2oz/scant 1 cup dried small
    pasta shapes
275g/10oz cooked beetroot, cut into sticks
1.2 litres/2 pints/5 cups vegetable stock
    or water
30ml/2 tbsp raspberry vinegar
salt and ground black pepper
low-fat yogurt or fromage blanc, to garnish
snipped chives, to garnish
Serves 4–6

4 Add the beetroot, stock or water, cooked pasta and vinegar, and heat through. Season to taste with salt and pepper.

5 Ladle into warmed soup bowls. Top each one with a spoonful of low-fat yogurt or fromage blanc and sprinkle with chives.

1 Heat the olive oil in a flameproof casserole and add the red onions and garlic.

2 Cook gently for 20 minutes or until soft and tender.

3 Cook the pasta in salted boiling water according to the instructions on the packet. Drain.

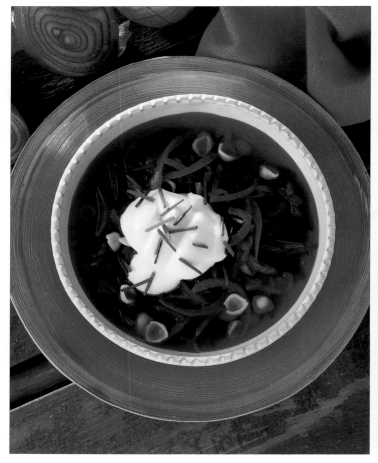

Parmesan and Cauliflower Soup

A SILKY SMOOTH, mildly cheesy soup which isn't overpowered by the cauliflower. It makes an elegant dinner-party soup served with crisp Melba toast.

INGREDIENTS

1 large cauliflower
1.2 litres/2 pints/5 cups chicken or
    vegetable stock
175g/6oz/1½ cups dried farfalle
150ml/¼ pint/⅔ cup single cream or milk
freshly grated nutmeg
pinch of cayenne pepper
60ml/4 tbsp freshly grated
    Parmesan cheese
salt and ground black pepper

For the Melba toast
3–4 slices day-old white bread
freshly grated Parmesan cheese,
    for sprinkling
1.5ml/¼ tsp paprika
Serves 6

1 Cut the leaves and central stalk away from the cauliflower and discard. Divide the cauliflower into similar-size florets.

2 Bring the stock to the boil and add the cauliflower. Simmer for about 10 minutes or until very soft. Remove the cauliflower with a slotted spoon and place in a blender or food processor.

3 Add the pasta to the stock and simmer for 10 minutes until tender. Drain, reserve the pasta, and pour the liquid over the cauliflower. Add the cream or milk, nutmeg and cayenne to the cauliflower. Blend until smooth, then press through a sieve.

4 Stir in the cooked pasta. Reheat the soup and then stir in the Parmesan. Taste and adjust the seasoning if necessary.

5 Meanwhile make the Melba toast. Preheat the oven to 180°C/350°F/Gas 4. Toast the bread lightly on both sides. Quickly cut off the crusts and split each slice in half horizontally. Scrape off any doughy bits and sprinkle with Parmesan and paprika. Place on a baking sheet and bake in the oven for about 10–15 minutes or until uniformly golden. Serve with the soup.

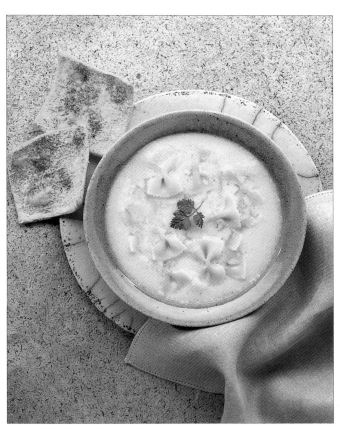

Little Stuffed Hats in Broth

THIS SOUP IS SERVED in northern Italy on Santo Stefano (St Stephen's Day – our Boxing Day) and on New Year's Day. It makes a welcome light change from all the special celebration food the day before. In Italy, the stock is traditionally made with the Christmas capon carcass.

INGREDIENTS

1.2 litres/2 pints/5 cups chicken stock
90–115g/3½–4oz/1 cup fresh or
    dried cappelletti
30ml/2 tbsp dry white wine (optional)
about 15ml/1 tbsp finely chopped fresh
    flat leaf parsley (optional)
salt and ground black pepper
about 30ml/2 tbsp freshly grated Parmesan
    cheese, to serve
shredded flat leaf parsley, to garnish
Serves 4

1 Pour the chicken stock into a large saucepan and bring to the boil. Add a little salt and pepper to taste, then drop in the pasta.

2 Stir well and bring back to the boil. Lower the heat to a simmer and cook according to the instructions on the packet, until the pasta is al dente. Stir frequently during cooking to ensure the pasta cooks evenly.

3 Swirl in the wine and parsley, if using, then taste for seasoning. Ladle into four warmed soup plates, then sprinkle with grated Parmesan and flat leaf parsley. Serve immediately.

COOK'S TIP

Cappelletti is just another name for tortellini, which come from Romagna. You can buy them or make your own.

Tiny Pasta in Broth

IN ITALY THIS SOUP is often served with bread for a light evening supper.

INGREDIENTS

1.2 litres/2 pints/5 cups beef stock
75g/3oz/¾ cup dried tiny soup pasta,
    e.g. funghetti
2 pieces bottled roasted red pepper,
    about 50g/2oz
salt and ground black pepper
coarsely shaved Parmesan cheese, to serve
Serves 4

COOK'S TIP

Stock cubes are not really suitable for a recipe like this in which the flavour of the broth is so important. If you don't have time to make your own stock, use two 300g/11oz cans of condensed beef consommé, adding water as instructed on the labels.

1 Bring the beef stock to the boil in a large saucepan. Add salt and pepper to taste, then drop in the dried soup pasta. Stir well and bring the stock back to the boil.

2 Lower the heat to a simmer and cook until the pasta is al dente: 7–8 minutes or according to the packet instructions. Stir frequently during cooking to prevent the pasta shapes from sticking together.

3 Drain the pieces of roasted pepper and dice them finely. Place them in the bottom of four warmed soup plates. Taste the soup for seasoning. Ladle into the soup plates and serve immediately, with shavings of Parmesan handed separately.

VARIATION

You can use other dried tiny soup pastas in place of the funghetti.

Pasta, Bean and Vegetable Soup

THIS IS A CALABRIAN speciality. The Italian name for it, *millecosedde*, comes from the word *millecose*, meaning "a thousand things". Literally anything edible can go in this soup. In Calabria they include a bean called *cicerchia* that is peculiar to the region.

INGREDIENTS

75g/3oz/scant ½ cup brown lentils
15g/½oz dried mushrooms
60ml/4 tbsp olive oil
1 carrot, diced
1 celery stick, diced
1 onion, finely chopped
1 garlic clove, finely chopped
a little chopped fresh flat leaf parsley
a good pinch of crushed red chillies (optional)
1.5 litres/2½ pints/6¼ cups
    vegetable stock
150g/5oz/scant 1 cup each canned red
    kidney beans, cannellini beans and
    chick-peas, rinsed and drained
115g/4oz/1 cup dried small pasta shapes,
    such as. rigatoni, penne or penne rigate
salt and ground black pepper
chopped flat leaf parsley, to garnish
freshly grated Pecorino cheese, to serve
Serves 4–6

1 Put the lentils in a medium saucepan, add 475ml/16fl oz/2 cups water and bring to the boil over a high heat. Lower the heat to a gentle simmer and cook, stirring occasionally, for 15–20 minutes or until the lentils are just tender. Meanwhile, soak the dried mushrooms in 175ml/6fl oz/¾ cup warm water for 15–20 minutes.

2 Tip the lentils into a sieve to drain, then rinse under the cold tap. Drain the soaked mushrooms and reserve the soaking liquid. Finely chop the mushrooms and set aside.

3 Heat the oil in a large saucepan and add the carrot, celery, onion, garlic, parsley and chillies, if using. Cook over a low heat, stirring constantly, for 5–7 minutes.

4 Add the stock, then the mushrooms and their soaking liquid. Bring to the boil, then add the beans, chick-peas and lentils, with salt and pepper to taste. Cover, and simmer gently for 20 minutes.

5 Add the pasta and bring the soup back to the boil, stirring. Simmer, stirring frequently, until the pasta is *al dente*: 7–8 minutes or according to the instructions on the packet. Season, then serve hot in soup bowls, with grated Pecorino and chopped parsley.

COOK'S TIP

If you like, you can freeze the soup at the end of Step 4. To serve, thaw and bring to the boil, then add the pasta and simmer until it is just tender.

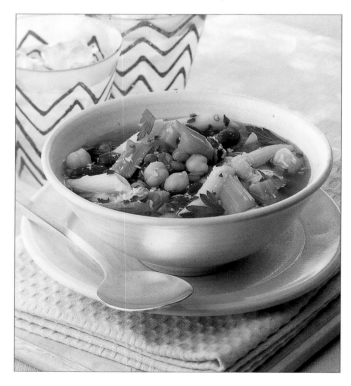

Clam and Pasta Soup

SUBTLY SWEET AND SPICY, this soup is substantial enough to be served on its own for lunch or supper. A crusty Italian loaf such as *pugliese* is the ideal accompaniment.

INGREDIENTS

30ml/2 tbsp olive oil
1 onion, finely chopped
leaves from 1 fresh or dried thyme sprig,
    chopped, plus extra to garnish
2 garlic cloves, crushed
5–6 fresh basil leaves, plus extra to garnish
1.5–2.5ml/¼–½ tsp crushed red chillies,
    to taste
1 litre/1¾ pints/4 cups fish stock
350ml/12fl oz/1½ cups passata
5ml/1 tsp granulated sugar
90g/3½oz/scant 1 cup frozen peas
65g/2½oz/⅔ cup dried small pasta
    shapes, such as chifferini
225g/8oz frozen shelled clams or bottled
    clams in their shells
salt and ground black pepper
Serves 4–6

1 Heat the oil in a large saucepan, add the onion and cook gently for about 5 minutes until softened, but not coloured. Add the thyme, then stir in the garlic, basil leaves and chillies.

2 Add the stock, passata and sugar to the saucepan, with salt and pepper to taste. Bring to the boil, then lower the heat and simmer gently, stirring occasionally, for 15 minutes. Add the frozen peas and cook for a further 5 minutes.

3 Add the pasta to the stock mixture and bring to the boil, stirring. Lower the heat and simmer, stirring frequently, until the pasta is only just *al dente*: about 5 minutes or according to the packet instructions.

4 Turn the heat down to low, add the frozen or bottled clams and heat through for 2–3 minutes. Taste for seasoning. Serve hot in warmed bowls, garnished with basil and thyme.

COOK'S TIP

Frozen shelled clams are available at good fishmongers and supermarkets; if you can't get them, use bottled or canned clams in natural juice (not vinegar). Italian delicatessens sell jars of clams in their shells. These both look and taste delicious and they are not too expensive. For a special occasion, stir some into the soup.

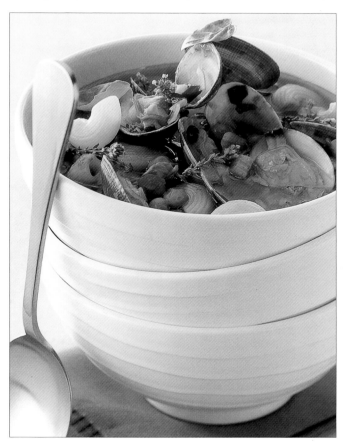

Bean and Pasta Soup

THIS HEARTY MAIN MEAL soup
sometimes goes by the name of
Pasta e Fagioli, while some Italians
refer to it as *Minestrone di Pasta e
Fagioli*. Traditional country recipes
use dried beans and a ham bone,
and require the soup to be cooked
for a long time.

INGREDIENTS

1 onion
1 carrot
1 celery stick
30ml/2 tbsp olive oil
*115g/4oz pancetta or rindless smoked
    streaky bacon, diced*
1.75 litres/3 pints/7½ cups beef stock
*1 cinnamon stick or a good pinch of
    ground cinnamon*
*90g/3½oz/scant 1 cup dried pasta shapes,
    such as conchiglie or corallini*
*400g/14oz can borlotti beans, rinsed
    and drained*
*1 thick slice cooked ham, about
    225g/8oz, diced*
salt and ground black pepper
coarsely shaved Parmesan cheese, to serve

Serves 4–6

3 Taste the soup for seasoning.
Serve hot in warmed bowls,
sprinkled with shavings of Parmesan.

VARIATIONS

• *Use spaghetti or tagliatelle instead of
the small pasta shapes, breaking it into
small pieces over the pan.*
• *Use cannellini or white haricot beans
instead of the borlotti. Alternatively, use
dried beans that have been soaked,
drained and boiled for 1 hour or until
tender. Add them to the pan after the
stock in Step 1.*
• *If you like, add 15ml/1 tbsp passata or
tomato purée, or 1 large ripe tomato,
skinned and chopped, with the beans
and diced ham.*

1 Chop the vegetables. Heat the oil in
a large saucepan, add the pancetta or
bacon and cook, stirring, until lightly
coloured. Add the chopped vegetable
mixture to the pan and cook for about
10 minutes, stirring frequently, until
lightly coloured. Pour in the stock, add
the cinnamon with salt and pepper to
taste, and bring to the boil. Cover and
simmer gently for 15–20 minutes.

2 Add the pasta. Bring back to the
boil, stirring all the time. Lower
the heat and simmer, stirring frequently,
for 5 minutes. Add the beans and diced
ham and simmer until the pasta is
al dente: 2–3 minutes or according to
the instructions on the packet.

Pasta and Chick-pea Soup

A SIMPLE, COUNTRY-STYLE soup. The shape of the pasta and the beans complement one another beautifully.

INGREDIENTS

1 onion

2 carrots

2 celery sticks

60ml/4 tbsp olive oil

400g/14oz can chick-peas, rinsed and drained

200g/7oz can cannellini beans, rinsed and drained

150ml/¹/₄ pint/²/₃ cup passata

120ml/4fl oz/¹/₂ cup water

1.5 litres/2¹/₂ pints/6¹/₄ cups vegetable or chicken stock

2 fresh or dried rosemary sprigs

200g/7oz/scant 2 cups dried conchiglie

salt and ground black pepper

freshly grated Parmesan cheese, to serve

Serves 4–6

1 Chop the onion, carrots and celery finely, either in a food processor or by hand.

2 Heat the oil in a large saucepan, add the chopped vegetable mixture and cook over a low heat, stirring frequently, for 5–7 minutes.

3 Add the chick-peas and cannellini beans, stir well to mix, then cook for 5 minutes. Stir in the passata and water. Cook, stirring, for 2–3 minutes.

4 Add 475ml/16fl oz/2 cups of the stock, one of the rosemary sprigs and salt and pepper to taste. Bring to the boil, cover, then simmer gently, stirring occasionally, for 1 hour.

5 Pour in the remaining stock, add the pasta and bring to the boil, stirring. Lower the heat and simmer, stirring frequently, until the pasta is *al dente*: 7–8 minutes or according to the instructions on the packet. Taste for seasoning. Remove the rosemary sprig and serve the soup hot, in warmed bowls, topped with grated Parmesan and a few rosemary leaves.

VARIATIONS

• *You can use other pasta shapes, but conchiglie are ideal because they scoop up the chick-peas and beans.*

• *If you like, crush 1–2 garlic cloves and fry them with the vegetables.*

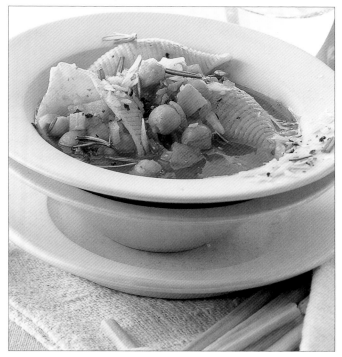

Courgette Soup with Conchigliette

A PRETTY, FRESH-TASTING soup which could be made using cucumber instead of courgettes.

INGREDIENTS

60ml/4 tbsp olive or sunflower oil
2 onions, finely chopped
1.5 litres/2¹/₂ pints/6¹/₄ cups chicken stock
900g/2lb courgettes
115g/4oz/1 cup diced conchigliette
freshly squeezed lemon juice
30ml/2 tbsp chopped fresh chervil
salt and ground black pepper
soured cream, to serve

Serves 4–6

1 Heat the oil in a large saucepan and add the finely chopped onions. Cover and cook gently for about 20 minutes until very soft but not coloured, stirring occasionally.

2 Add the chicken stock to the saucepan and bring the mixture to the boil.

3 Meanwhile grate the courgettes and stir into the boiling stock with the pasta. Reduce the heat and simmer for 15 minutes until the pasta is tender. Season to taste with lemon juice, salt and pepper.

4 Stir in the chopped fresh chervil and add a swirl of soured cream before serving.

Provençal Fish Soup with Pasta

THIS COLOURFUL SOUP has all the flavours of the Mediterranean. Serve it as a main course for a deliciously filling lunch.

INGREDIENTS

30ml/2 tbsp olive oil
1 onion, sliced
1 garlic clove, crushed
1 leek, sliced
1 litre/1¾ pints/4 cups water
225g/8oz canned chopped tomatoes
pinch of Mediterranean herbs
1.5ml/¼ tsp saffron strands (optional)
115g/4oz/1 cup dried small pasta shapes
about 8 live mussels in the shell
450g/1lb filleted and skinned white fish,
*   such as cod, plaice or monkfish*
salt and ground black pepper

For the rouille
2 garlic cloves, crushed
1 canned pimiento, drained and chopped
15ml/1 tbsp fresh white breadcrumbs
60ml/4 tbsp mayonnaise
toasted French bread, to serve

Serves 4

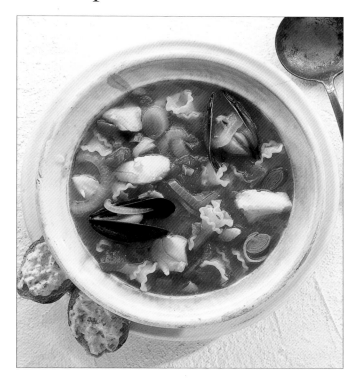

1 Heat the oil in a large saucepan and add the onion, garlic and leek. Cover and cook gently for 5 minutes, stirring until the vegetables are soft.

2 Pour in the water, the tomatoes, herbs, saffron, if using, and pasta. Season with salt and ground black pepper and cook for 15–20 minutes.

3 Scrub the mussels and pull off the "beards". Discard any that will not close when sharply tapped.

4 Cut the fish into bite-size chunks and add to the soup in the saucepan, placing the mussels on top. Then simmer with the lid on for 5-10 minutes until the mussels open and the fish is just cooked. Discard any unopened mussels.

5 To make the rouille, pound the garlic, canned pimiento and breadcrumbs together in a pestle and mortar (or in a blender or food processor). Then stir in the mayonnaise and season the mixture well.

6 Spread the toasted French bread with the rouille and serve the slices with the soup.

Farmhouse Soup

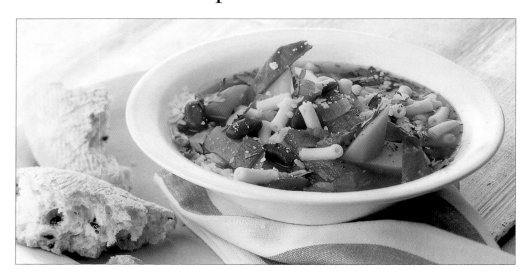

ROOT VEGETABLES FORM the base of this chunky, minestrone-style main meal soup. You can vary the vegetables according to what you have to hand.

INGREDIENTS

30ml/2 tbsp olive oil
1 onion, roughly chopped
3 carrots, cut into large chunks
175–200g/6–7oz turnips, cut into
  large chunks
about 175g/6oz swede, cut into
  large chunks
400g/14oz can chopped Italian tomatoes
15ml/1 tbsp tomato purée
5ml/1 tsp dried mixed herbs
5ml/1 tsp dried oregano
50g/2oz/½ cup dried peppers, washed and
  thinly sliced (optional)
1.5 litres/2½ pints/6¼ cups vegetable
  stock or water
50g/2oz/½ cup dried small macaroni
  or conchiglie
400g/14oz can red kidney beans, rinsed
  and drained
30ml/2 tbsp chopped fresh flat leaf parsley
salt and ground black pepper
freshly grated Parmesan cheese, to serve
Serves 4

1 Heat the oil in a large saucepan, add the onion and cook over a low heat for about 5 minutes until softened. Add the fresh vegetables, canned tomatoes, tomato purée, dried herbs and dried peppers, if using. Stir in salt and pepper to taste. Pour in the stock or water and bring to the boil. Stir well, cover, lower the heat and simmer for 30 minutes, stirring occasionally.

COOK'S TIP

Packets of dried Italian peppers are sold in many supermarkets and in delicatessens. They are piquant and firm with a "meaty" bite to them, which makes them ideal for adding substance to vegetarian soups.

2 Add the pasta and bring to the boil, stirring. Lower the heat and simmer, uncovered, until the pasta is only just *al dente*: about 5 minutes or according to the instructions on the packet. Stir frequently.

3 Stir in the beans. Heat through for 2–3 minutes, then remove from the heat and stir in the parsley. Taste the soup for seasoning. Serve hot in warmed soup bowls, with grated Parmesan handed separately.

Roasted Tomato and Pasta Soup

WHEN THE ONLY TOMATOES you can buy are not particularly flavoursome, make this soup. The roasting compensates for any lack of flavour in the tomatoes, and the soup has a wonderful smoky taste.

INGREDIENTS

450g/1lb ripe Italian plum tomatoes, halved lengthways
1 large red pepper, quartered lengthways and seeded
1 large red onion, quartered lengthways
2 garlic cloves, unpeeled
15ml/1 tbsp olive oil
1.2 litres/2 pints/5 cups vegetable stock or water
good pinch of granulated sugar
90g/3½ oz/scant 1 cup dried small pasta shapes, such as tubetti or small macaroni
salt and ground black pepper
fresh basil leaves, to garnish

Serves 4

1 Preheat the oven to 190°C /375°F/ Gas 5. Spread out the tomatoes, red pepper, onion and garlic in a roasting tin and drizzle with the olive oil. Roast for 30–40 minutes until the vegetables are soft and charred, stirring and turning them halfway.

2 Tip the vegetables into a food processor, add about 250ml/ 8fl oz/1 cup of the stock or water and process until puréed. Scrape the mixture into a sieve placed over a large saucepan and press the purée through into the pan.

3 Add the remaining stock or water to the pan, then the sugar and salt and pepper to taste. Bring to the boil, stirring.

4 Add the pasta and simmer, stirring frequently, until al dente: 7–8 minutes or according to the instructions on the packet. Taste for seasoning. Serve hot in warmed bowls, garnished with the fresh basil.

COOK'S TIPS

• You can roast the vegetables in advance, allow them to cool, then leave them in a covered bowl in the fridge overnight before puréeing.
• The soup can be frozen without the pasta. Thaw and bring to the boil before adding the pasta.

Pasta Soup with Chicken Livers

A SOUP THAT CAN BE served as either a first or main course. The fried *fegatini* are so delicious that even if you do not normally like chicken livers you will find yourself loving them in this soup.

INGREDIENTS

15ml/1 tbsp olive oil
knob of butter
4 garlic cloves, crushed
3 sprigs each fresh parsley, marjoram
    and sage, chopped
leaves from 1 fresh thyme sprig, chopped
5–6 fresh basil leaves
115g/4oz/²⁄₃ cup chicken livers, thawed
    if frozen
15–30ml/1–2 tbsp dry white wine
2 x 300g/11oz cans condensed
    chicken consommé
225g/8oz/2 cups frozen peas
50g/2oz/¹⁄₂ cup dried pasta shapes,
    such as farfalle
2–3 spring onions, diagonally sliced
salt and ground black pepper
Serves 4–6

1 Heat the oil and butter in a frying pan, add the garlic and herbs, with salt and pepper to taste, and fry gently for a few minutes. Add the livers, increase the heat to high and stir-fry for a few minutes until they change colour and become dry. Pour the wine over the livers, cook until the wine evaporates, then remove the livers from the heat and taste for seasoning.

2 Tip both cans of condensed chicken consommé into a large saucepan and add water to the condensed soup as directed on the labels. Add an extra can of water, then stir in a little salt and pepper to taste and bring to the boil.

3 Add the frozen peas to the pan and simmer for about 5 minutes, then add the small pasta shapes and bring the soup back to the boil, stirring. Allow to simmer, stirring frequently, until the pasta is only just *al dente*: about 5 minutes or according to the instructions on the packet.

4 Add the fried chicken livers and spring onions and heat through for 2–3 minutes. Taste for seasoning. Serve hot, in warmed bowls.

Meatball and Pasta Soup

EVEN THOUGH THIS SOUP comes from sunny Sicily, it is substantial enough for a hearty supper on a winter's day.

INGREDIENTS

2 x 300g/11oz cans condensed
    beef consommé
90g/3½oz/¾ cup dried very thin pasta,
    such as fidelini or spaghettini
fresh flat leaf parsley, to garnish
freshly grated Parmesan cheese, to serve

For the meatballs
1 very thick slice of white bread,
    crusts removed
30ml/2 tbsp milk
225g/8oz/1 cup minced beef
1 garlic clove, crushed
30ml/2 tbsp freshly grated
    Parmesan cheese
30–45ml/2–3 tbsp fresh flat leaf parsley
    leaves, coarsely chopped
1 egg
nutmeg
salt and ground black pepper

Serves 4

1 Make the meatballs. Break the bread into a small bowl, add the milk and set aside to soak. Meanwhile, put the minced beef, garlic, Parmesan, parsley and egg in another large bowl. Grate fresh nutmeg liberally over the top and add salt and pepper to taste.

2 Squeeze the bread with your hands to remove as much milk as possible, then add the bread to the meatball mixture and mix everything together well with your hands. Wash your hands, rinse them under the cold tap, then form the mixture into tiny balls about the size of small marbles.

3 Tip both cans of consommé into a large saucepan, add water as directed on the labels, then add an extra can of water. Stir in salt and pepper to taste and bring to the boil.

4 Drop in the meatballs, then break the pasta into small pieces and add it to the soup. Bring the soup to the boil, stirring gently. Simmer, stirring frequently, until the pasta is al dente: 7–8 minutes or according to the instructions on the packet. Taste for seasoning. Serve hot in warmed bowls, sprinkled with parsley and freshly grated Parmesan cheese.

Pea and Ham Soup

FROZEN PEAS PROVIDE flavour, freshness and colour in this delicious winter soup, which is filling enough to make a light main course.

INGREDIENTS

115g/4oz/1 cup dried small pasta shapes,
*   such as tubetti*
30ml/2 tbsp vegetable oil
1 small bunch spring onions, chopped
350g/12oz/3 cups frozen peas
1.2 litres/2 pints/5 cups chicken stock
225g/8oz raw unsmoked ham or gammon
60ml/4 tbsp double cream
salt and ground black pepper
warm crusty bread, to serve

Serves 4

1 Cook the small pasta shapes in plenty of boiling salted water according to the packet instructions. Drain through a colander, place in the pan again, cover with cold water and set aside until required.

2 Heat the vegetable oil in a large heavy saucepan and cook the spring onions gently, stirring until soft but not browned. Add the frozen peas and chicken stock to the saucepan, then simmer gently over a low heat for about 10 minutes.

3 Process the soup in a blender or food processor then return to the saucepan. Cut the ham or gammon into short fingers and add, with the pasta, to the saucepan. Simmer for 2–3 minutes and season to taste.

4 Stir in the double cream and serve the soup immediately with the warm crusty bread.

Consommé with Agnolotti

A DELICIOUS AND SATISFYING consommé with wonderful flavours.

INGREDIENTS

75g/3oz cooked peeled prawns
75g/3oz canned crab meat, drained
5ml/1 tsp fresh root ginger, peeled and finely grated
15ml/1 tbsp fresh white breadcrumbs
5ml/1 tsp light soy sauce
1 spring onion, finely chopped
1 garlic clove, crushed
1 quantity Pasta with Eggs
flour, for dusting
egg white, beaten
400g/14oz can chicken or fish consommé
30ml/2 tbsp sherry or vermouth
salt and ground black pepper
50g/2oz cooked, peeled prawns and fresh coriander leaves, to garnish

Serves 4–6

1 To make the filling, put the prawns, crab meat, ginger, breadcrumbs, soy sauce, onion, garlic and seasoning into a food processor or blender and process until smooth.

2 Roll the pasta into thin sheets and dust lightly with flour. Stamp out 32 rounds 5cm/2in in diameter, with a fluted pastry cutter.

3 Place a small teaspoon of the filling in the centre of half the pasta rounds. Brush the edges of each round with egg white and sandwich together with a second round on top. Pinch the edges together firmly to stop the filling seeping out.

4 Cook the pasta in a large pan of boiling salted water for 5 minutes (cook in batches to stop them sticking together). Remove and drop into a bowl of cold water for 5 seconds before placing on a tray. (You can make these pasta shapes a day in advance. Cover with clear film and store in the fridge until required.)

5 Heat the chicken or fish consommé in a pan with the sherry or vermouth. When piping hot, add the pasta shapes and simmer for 1–2 minutes.

6 Serve in a shallow soup bowl covered with hot consommé. Garnish with extra peeled prawns and fresh coriander leaves.

Broccoli, Anchovy and Pasta Soup

THIS SOUP IS FROM PUGLIA in the south of Italy, where anchovies and broccoli are often used together.

INGREDIENTS

30ml/2 tbsp olive oil
1 small onion, finely chopped
1 garlic clove, finely chopped
¼–⅓ fresh red chilli, seeded and
    finely chopped
2 drained canned anchovies
200ml/7fl oz/scant 1 cup passata
45ml/3 tbsp dry white wine
1.2 litres/2 pints/5 cups vegetable stock
300g/11oz/2 cups broccoli florets
200g/7oz/1¾ cups dried orecchiette
salt and ground black pepper
freshly grated Pecorino cheese,
    to serve
Serves 4

1 Heat the oil in a large saucepan. Add the onion, garlic, chilli and anchovies and cook over a low heat, stirring all the time, for 5–6 minutes.

2 Add the passata and wine, with salt and pepper to taste. Bring to the boil, cover the pan, then cook over a low heat, stirring occasionally, for 12–15 minutes.

3 Pour in the stock. Bring to the boil, then add the broccoli and simmer for about 5 minutes. Add the pasta and bring back to the boil, stirring. Simmer, stirring frequently, until the pasta is *al dente*: 7–8 minutes or according to the instructions on the packet. Taste for seasoning. Serve hot, in warmed bowls. Hand around grated Pecorino separately.

Pasta Squares and Peas in Broth

THIS THICK SOUP IS FROM LAZIO, where it is traditionally made with fresh home-made pasta and peas. In this modern version, ready-made pasta is used with frozen peas, to save time.

INGREDIENTS

25g/1oz/2 tbsp butter
50g/2oz pancetta or rindless smoked
    streaky bacon, roughly chopped
1 small onion, finely chopped
1 celery stick, finely chopped
400g/14oz/3½ cups frozen peas
5ml/1 tsp tomato purée
5–10ml/1–2 tsp finely chopped fresh flat
    leaf parsley
1 litre/1¾ pints/4 cups chicken stock
300g/11oz fresh lasagne sheets
about 50g/2oz prosciutto crudo (Parma
    ham), cut into cubes
salt and ground black pepper
freshly grated Parmesan cheese, to serve
Serves 4–6

1 Melt the butter in a large saucepan and add the pancetta or bacon, with the onion and celery. Cook over a low heat, stirring constantly, for 5 minutes.

2 Add the peas and cook, stirring, for 3–4 minutes. Stir in the tomato purée and parsley, then add the chicken stock, with salt and pepper to taste. Bring to the boil. Cover, lower the heat and simmer for 10 minutes. Meanwhile, cut the lasagne sheets into 2cm/¾in squares.

3 Taste the stock for seasoning. Drop in the pasta, stir and bring to the boil. Simmer for 2–3 minutes or until the pasta is *al dente*, then stir in the prosciutto. Serve hot in warmed bowls, with grated Parmesan handed around separately.

COOK'S TIP

Take care when adding salt, because of the saltiness of the pancetta and the prosciutto.

Italian Bean and Pasta Soup

A THICK AND HEARTY soup which,
followed by bread and cheese, makes
a substantial lunch.

INGREDIENTS

175g/6oz/1½ cups dried haricot beans,
* soaked overnight in cold water*
1.75 litres/3 pints/7½ cups chicken stock
* or water*
115g/4oz/1 cup dried conchigliette
60ml/4 tbsp olive oil, plus extra to serve
2 garlic cloves, crushed
60ml/4 tbsp chopped fresh parsley
salt and ground black pepper

Serves 6

1 Drain the beans and place in a
large saucepan with the stock or
water. Half-cover the pan, and simmer
for 2–2½ hours or until the beans
are tender.

2 In a blender or food processor,
process half the beans with a little
of their cooking liquid to form a
smooth paste. Then stir into the
unprocessed beans in the pan.

3 Add the pasta and simmer gently
for 15 minutes until tender. (Add
extra water or stock if the soup seems
too thick.)

4 Heat the oil in a small pan and fry
the garlic until golden. Stir into the
soup with the parsley and season well
with salt and pepper. Ladle into individual bowls and drizzle each with a little
extra olive oil, to serve.

Chunky Pasta Soup

SERVE THIS filling main-meal soup with tasty, pesto-topped French bread croûtons.

INGREDIENTS

115g/4oz/²/₃ cup dry beans (a mixture of
    red kidney and haricot beans), soaked in
    cold water overnight
15ml/1 tbsp oil
1 onion, chopped
2 celery sticks, thinly sliced
2–3 garlic cloves, crushed
2 leeks, thinly sliced
1 vegetable stock cube
400g/14oz can or jar of pimientos
45–60ml/3–4 tbsp tomato purée
115g/4oz/1 cup dried conchiglie
4 pieces French bread
15ml/1 tbsp pesto sauce
115g/4oz/1 cup baby sweetcorn, halved
50g/2oz each broccoli and
    cauliflower florets
few drops of Tabasco sauce, to taste
salt and ground black pepper
Serves 4

1 Drain the beans and place in a large saucepan with 1.2 litres/ 2 pints/5 cups water. Bring to the boil and simmer for about 1 hour, or until nearly tender.

2 When the beans are almost ready, heat the oil in a large pan and fry the vegetables for 2 minutes, stirring. Add the stock cube and the beans with 600ml/1 pint/ 2 cups of their liquid. Cover and simmer the mixture for 10 minutes.

3 Meanwhile, purée the pimientos with a little of their liquid and add to the pan. Stir in the tomato purée, then add the pasta and cook for 15 minutes. Preheat the oven to 200°C/400°F/Gas 6.

4 Meanwhile, make the pesto croûtons; spread the French bread with the pesto sauce and bake for 10 minutes, or until crispy.

5 When the pasta is just cooked, add the sweetcorn, broccoli and cauliflower florets, Tabasco sauce and seasoning to taste. Heat through for 2–3 minutes and serve at once with the croûtons.

Tomato Sauces

It was the Neapolitans who first discovered the delights of pasta and tomato sauce. Tomatoes originally came to Italy from the New World. They were yellow, which is why they were called golden apples (*pomodori*), and were originally used only as ornamental plants. They quickly took to the sunshine of southern Italy, however, and by the 18th century the red tomato was being enjoyed in salads. It wasn't long before they were partnered with pasta – and so began one of the most successful marriages in culinary history.

Tomato sauces, simple and uncooked or simmered for a longish while, are typically southern Italian. They go best with the dried commercially produced pasta of the south, and taste divine with those other wonderful southern ingredients – basil, garlic and olive oil. Most recipes in this chapter give advice on the best type of pasta to serve with the sauce, while some go further and include cooking the pasta as part of the recipe.

Spaghetti is the pasta most often used with tomato sauces, but all the sauces work well with a wide range of pastas, so feel free to mix and match.

Fresh Tomato Sauce

THIS IS THE FAMOUS Neapolitan sauce that is made in summer when tomatoes are very ripe and sweet. It is very simple, so that nothing detracts from the flavour of the tomatoes themselves. It is served here with spaghetti, which is the traditional choice of pasta.

INGREDIENTS

675g/1 ¹/₂lb ripe Italian plum tomatoes
60ml/4 tbsp olive oil
1 onion, finely chopped
350g/12oz fresh or dried spaghetti
1 small handful fresh basil leaves
salt and ground black pepper
coarsely shaved Parmesan cheese, to serve
Serves 4

1 With a sharp knife, cut a cross in the bottom (flower) end of each tomato. Bring a medium saucepan of water to the boil and remove from the heat. Plunge a few of the tomatoes into the water, leave for 30 seconds or so, then lift them out with a slotted spoon. Repeat with the remaining tomatoes, then peel off the skin and roughly chop the flesh.

2 Heat the oil in a large saucepan, add the onion and cook over a low heat, stirring frequently, for about 5 minutes until softened and lightly coloured. Add the tomatoes, with salt and pepper to taste, bring to a simmer, then turn the heat down to low and cover. Cook, stirring occasionally, for 30–40 minutes until thick.

3 Meanwhile, cook the pasta according to the instructions on the packet. Shred the basil leaves finely.

4 Remove the sauce from the heat, stir in the basil and taste for seasoning. Drain the pasta, tip it into a warmed bowl, pour the sauce over and toss well. Serve immediately, with shaved Parmesan handed separately.

COOK'S TIPS

• *The Italian plum tomatoes called* San Marzano *are the best variety to use. When fully ripe, they have thin skins that peel off easily.*
• *In Italy, cooks often make this sauce in bulk in the summer months and freeze it for later use. Let it cool, then freeze in usable quantities in rigid containers. Thaw before reheating.*

VARIATIONS

Some Neapolitan cooks add a little crushed garlic with the onion and some use chopped fresh oregano or flat leaf parsley with the basil; it is a matter of personal taste.

Rigatoni with Winter Tomato Sauce

IN WINTER, WHEN FRESH tomatoes are not at their best, this is the sauce the Italians make. Canned tomatoes combined with *soffritto* (the sautéed mixture of chopped onion, carrot, celery and garlic) and herbs give a better flavour than winter tomatoes.

INGREDIENTS

I onion
I carrot
I celery stick
60ml/4 tbsp olive oil
I garlic clove, thinly sliced
a few leaves each fresh basil, thyme and
*   oregano or marjoram*
2 x 400g/14oz cans chopped Italian
*   plum tomatoes*
15ml/1 tbsp sun-dried tomato paste
5ml/1 tsp granulated sugar
about 90ml/6 tbsp dry red or white
*   wine (optional)*
350g/12oz/3 cups dried rigatoni
salt and ground black pepper
coarsely shaved Parmesan cheese, to serve

Serves 6–8

1 Chop the onion, carrot and celery stick finely, either in a food processor or by hand.

2 Heat the olive oil in a medium saucepan, add the garlic slices and stir over a very low heat for 1–2 minutes.

3 Add the chopped vegetables and the fresh herbs. Cook over a low heat, stirring frequently, for 5–7 minutes until the vegetables have softened and are lightly coloured.

4 Add the canned tomatoes, tomato paste and sugar, then stir in the wine, if using. Add salt and pepper to taste. Bring to the boil, stirring, then lower the heat to a gentle simmer. Cook, uncovered, for about 45 minutes, stirring occasionally.

5 Cook the pasta according to the instructions on the packet. Drain it and tip it into a warmed bowl. Taste the sauce for seasoning, pour the sauce over the pasta and toss well. Serve immediately, with shavings of Parmesan handed separately. If you like, garnish with extra chopped herbs.

Noodles with Italian Mushrooms

PORCINI MUSHROOMS give this sauce a wonderful depth.

INGREDIENTS

25g/1oz dried Italian
  mushrooms (porcini)
175ml/6fl oz/¾ cup warm water
900g/2lb tomatoes, peeled, seeded and
  chopped or drained canned tomatoes
1.5ml/¼ tsp dried hot chilli flakes
45ml/3 tbsp olive oil
4 slices pancetta or rashers unsmoked back
  bacon, cut into thin strips
1 large garlic clove, finely chopped
350g/12oz/3 cups fresh or dried tagliatelle
  or fettuccine
salt and ground black pepper
freshly grated Parmesan cheese, to serve
Serves 2–4

1 Put the mushrooms in a bowl and cover with the warm water. Leave to soak for 20 minutes.

2 Meanwhile, put the tomatoes in a saucepan with the chilli flakes and seasoning. If using canned tomatoes, crush them coarsely with a fork or potato masher first. Bring to the boil, reduce the heat and simmer for about 30–40 minutes, until reduced to 750ml/1¼ pints/3 cups. Stir the tomatoes from time to time to prevent sticking.

3 When the mushrooms have finished soaking, lift them out and squeeze the remaining liquid into the bowl; set aside.

4 Carefully pour the soaking liquid into the tomatoes through a muslin-lined sieve. Simmer the tomatoes for a further 15 minutes.

5 Meanwhile, heat 30ml/2 tbsp of the oil in a frying pan. Add the strips of pancetta or bacon and fry until golden but not crisp. Add the garlic and mushrooms and fry for 3 minutes, stirring. Set aside.

6 Cook the pasta in a large saucepan with plenty of boiling salted water until just *al dente*.

7 Add the bacon and mushroom mixture to the tomato sauce and mix well. Season with salt and ground black pepper.

8 Drain the pasta and return to the pan. Add the remaining oil and toss to coat the strands. Divide the pasta among hot plates, spoon the sauce on top and serve with freshly grated Parmesan cheese.

Tagliatelle with Sun-dried Tomatoes

CHOOSE PLAIN sun-dried tomatoes for this sauce, instead of those preserved in oil, if you wish to reduce the fat content of the dish.

INGREDIENTS

1 garlic clove, crushed

1 celery stick, finely sliced

115g/4oz/1 cup sun-dried tomatoes, finely chopped

90ml/3 1/2fl oz/scant 1/2 cup red wine

8 plum tomatoes

350g/12oz dried tagliatelle

salt and ground black pepper

Serves 4

3 Add the plum tomatoes to the saucepan and simmer for a further 5 minutes. Season to taste.

4 Meanwhile, cook the tagliatelle in plenty of boiling salted water for 8–10 minutes, or until *al dente*. Drain well. Toss with half the sauce and serve on warmed plates, with the remaining sauce spooned over.

1 Put the garlic, celery, sun-dried tomatoes and wine into a large saucepan. Gently cook for about 15 minutes.

2 Slash the bottoms of the plum tomatoes and plunge into a saucepan of boiling water for 1 minute, then transfer them into a saucepan of cold water. Slip off their skins. Halve, remove the seeds and cores and roughly chop the flesh.

Spaghetti with Tomatoes, Anchovies, Olives and Capers

FROM CAMPANIA IN THE SOUTH, this classic sauce has a strong flavour from the anchovies and olives.

INGREDIENTS

30ml/2 tbsp olive oil
1 small onion, finely chopped
1 garlic clove, finely chopped
4 drained canned anchovies
50g/2oz/½ cup pitted black olives, sliced
15ml/1 tbsp capers
400g/14oz can chopped Italian
  plum tomatoes
45ml/3 tbsp water
15ml/1 tbsp chopped fresh flat leaf parsley
350g/12oz fresh or dried spaghetti
salt and ground black pepper
Serves 4

1 Heat the oil in a medium saucepan and add the onion, garlic and drained anchovies. Cook over a low heat, stirring constantly, for 5–7 minutes or until the anchovies break down to form a very soft pulp. Add the black olives and capers and stir-fry for a minute or so.

2 Add the tomatoes, water, half the parsley and salt and pepper to taste. Stir well and bring to the boil, then lower the heat and cover the pan. Simmer gently for 30 minutes, stirring occasionally. Meanwhile, cook the pasta according to the packet instructions.

3 Drain the pasta and tip it into a warmed bowl. Taste the sauce for seasoning, pour it over the pasta and toss well. Serve immediately, with the remaining parsley sprinkled on top.

COOK'S TIP

Use good-quality, shiny black olives – Gaeta olives from Liguria are very good.

Bucatini with Tomato and Chilli Sauce

THIS CLASSIC TOMATO sauce is called *Amatriciana* after the town of Amatrice in the Sabine hills, Lazio. If you visit Rome, you will see it on many restaurant menus served with either bucatini or spaghetti.

INGREDIENTS

15ml/1 tbsp olive oil
1 small onion, finely sliced
115g/4oz smoked pancetta or rindless
  smoked streaky bacon, diced
1 fresh red chilli, seeded and cut into
  thin strips
400g/14oz can chopped Italian
  plum tomatoes
30–45ml/2–3 tbsp dry white wine
  or water
350g/12oz dried bucatini
30–45ml/2–3 tbsp freshly grated Pecorino
  cheese, plus extra to serve (optional)
salt and ground black pepper
Serves 4

1 Heat the oil in a medium saucepan and cook the onion, pancetta and chilli over a low heat for 5–7 minutes, stirring. Add the tomatoes and wine or water, with salt and pepper to taste. Bring to the boil, stirring, then cover and simmer for 15–20 minutes, stirring occasionally. If the sauce is too dry, stir in a little of the pasta water.

2 Meanwhile, cook the pasta in a pan of salted boiling water according to the packet instructions.

3 Drain the pasta and tip it into a warmed bowl. Taste the sauce for seasoning, pour it over the pasta and add the grated Pecorino. Toss well. Serve immediately, with more grated Pecorino handed separately if liked.

COOK'S TIP

Always take care when dealing with chillies. They contain a substance called capsaicin, which will irritate delicate skin, so it's a good idea to wear rubber gloves.

Fusilli with Tomato and Balsamic Vinegar Sauce

THIS IS A MODERN CAL-ITAL recipe (Californian/Italian). The intense, sweet-sour flavour of balsamic vinegar gives a pleasant kick to a sauce made with canned tomatoes.

INGREDIENTS

2 x 400g/14oz cans chopped Italian
    plum tomatoes
2 pieces of drained sun-dried tomato in
    olive oil, thinly sliced
2 garlic cloves, crushed
45ml/3 tbsp olive oil
5ml/1 tsp granulated sugar
350g/12oz/3 cups fresh or dried fusilli
45ml/3 tbsp balsamic vinegar
salt and ground black pepper
coarsely shaved Pecorino cheese and
    rocket salad, to serve
Serves 6–8

1 Put the canned and sun-dried tomatoes in a medium saucepan with the garlic, olive oil and sugar. Add salt and pepper to taste. Bring to the boil, stirring. Lower the heat and simmer for about 30 minutes until reduced.

2 Meanwhile, cook the pasta in salted boiling water according to the instructions on the packet.

3 Add the balsamic vinegar to the sauce and stir to mix evenly. Cook for 1–2 minutes, then remove from the heat and taste for seasoning.

4 Drain the pasta and tip it into a warmed bowl. Pour the sauce over the pasta and toss well. Serve immediately, with rocket salad and the shaved Pecorino handed separately.

Linguine with Sun-dried Tomato Pesto

TOMATO PESTO WAS ONCE a rarity, but is becoming increasingly popular. To make it, sun-dried tomatoes are used instead of basil. The result is absolutely delicious.

INGREDIENTS

25g/1oz/⅓ cup pine nuts
25g/1oz/⅓ cup freshly grated
  Parmesan cheese
50g/2oz/½ cup sun-dried tomatoes
  in olive oil
1 garlic clove, roughly chopped
60ml/4 tbsp olive oil
350g/12oz fresh or dried linguine
ground black pepper
basil leaves, to garnish
coarsely shaved Parmesan cheese, to serve
Serves 4

3 Gradually add the olive oil to the mixture in the food processor through the feeder tube, with the machine running, until it has all been incorporated evenly and all the ingredients have formed a smooth-looking paste.

4 Cook the pasta according to the packet instructions. Drain well, reserving a little of the cooking water. Tip the pasta into a warmed bowl, add the pesto and a few spoonfuls of the hot water and toss well. Serve immediately garnished with basil leaves. Hand shavings of Parmesan separately.

1 Put the pine nuts in a small non-stick frying pan and toss over a low to medium heat for 1–2 minutes or until the nuts are lightly toasted and golden.

2 Tip the nuts into a food processor. Add the Parmesan, sun-dried tomatoes and garlic, with pepper to taste. Process until finely chopped.

COOK'S TIP

You can make this pesto up to 2 days in advance and keep it in a bowl in the fridge until ready to use. Pour a thin film of olive oil over the pesto in the bowl, then cover the bowl tightly with clear film to prevent the pesto from tainting other foods in the fridge.

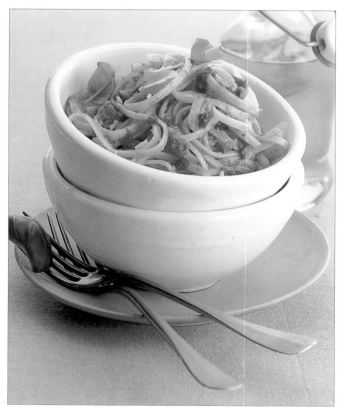

Curly Lasagne with Classic Tomato Sauce

A CLASSIC SAUCE that is simply delicious just served by itself.

INGREDIENTS

30ml/2 tbsp olive oil
1 onion, chopped
30ml/2 tbsp tomato purée
5ml/1 tsp paprika
2 x 400g/14oz cans chopped
*   tomatoes, drained*
pinch of dried oregano
300ml/¹/₂ pint/1¹/₄ cups dry red wine
large pinch of caster sugar
350g/12oz fresh or dried curly lasagne sheets
salt and ground black pepper
chopped fresh flat leaf parsley, to garnish
Parmesan cheese shavings, to serve

Serves 4

1 Heat the oil in a large frying pan and fry the onion for 10 minutes, stirring occasionally, until softened but not brown. Add the tomato purée and paprika and cook for a further 3 minutes.

2 Add the tomatoes, oregano, wine and sugar to the pan and season the mixture to taste, then bring to the boil.

3 Simmer for 20 minutes until the sauce has reduced and thickened, stirring occasionally.

4 Meanwhile, cook the pasta in plenty of boiling salted water according to the instructions on the packet. Drain thoroughly and tip into a large serving dish. Pour over the sauce and toss to coat. Serve sprinkled with Parmesan cheese shavings and the chopped fresh flat leaf parsley.

COOK'S TIP

If you cannot find curly lasagne in the supermarket use plain lasagne snipped in half lengthways.

Linguine with Clam and Tomato Sauce

THERE ARE TWO TYPES of traditional Italian clam sauce for pasta: one with tomatoes, as here, and another version without.

INGREDIENTS

900g/2lb fresh clams in the shell, or
  350g/12oz bottled clams, with
  their liquid
90ml/6 tbsp olive oil
1 garlic clove, crushed
400g/14oz tomatoes, fresh or canned,
  very finely chopped
350g/12oz linguine
60ml/4 tbsp chopped fresh parsley
salt and ground black pepper

Serves 4

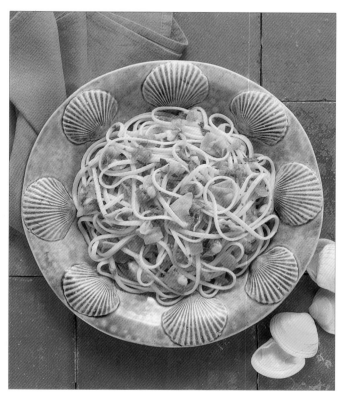

1 Scrub and rinse the clams well under cold running water discarding any that are already open. Place them in a large saucepan with a cupful of water, and heat until the clams begin to open. Lift each clam out as soon as it opens, and scoop it out of its shell using a small spoon. Place them in a separate bowl.

2 If the clams are large, you may prefer to chop them up into 2 or 3 pieces. Reserve any liquid from the shells in a separate bowl. When all the clams have opened (discard any that do not open), pour the cooking liquid into the juices from the clams, and strain them through a piece of kitchen paper to remove any sand. If using bottled clams, use the liquid from the jar.

3 Place the olive oil in a medium saucepan with the garlic. Cook, stirring, over a moderate heat until golden but not brown.

4 Remove the garlic from the pan and discard. Add the chopped tomatoes to the oil, and pour in the reserved clam liquid. Mix together well and cook over a low to moderate heat until the sauce begins to dry out and thickens slightly.

5 Cook the pasta in a large saucepan with plenty of boiling salted water until just *al dente*, following the instructions on the packet.

6 A minute or two before the pasta is cooked, stir the parsley and the clams into the tomato sauce, and increase the heat. Add pepper and taste for seasoning, adding salt if necessary. Drain the pasta and tip into a warmed serving dish. Pour on the hot sauce and mix well before serving immediately.

Cappelletti with Tomatoes and Cream

TOMATOES, CREAM AND FRESH BASIL are a winning combination. In this very quick and easy recipe, the sauce coats little pasta purses filled with soft cheeses to make a substantial supper dish for vegetarians. If you prefer a lighter dish, you can use the sauce to coat plain, unstuffed pasta. Small shapes such as penne, farfalle or conchiglie are best.

INGREDIENTS

400ml/14fl oz/1 2/3 cups passata
90ml/6 tbsp dry white wine
150ml/1/4 pint/2/3 cup double cream
225g/8oz/2 1/2 cups fresh cappelletti
1 small handful of fresh basil leaves
60ml/4 tbsp freshly grated
   Parmesan cheese
salt and ground black pepper
Serves 4–6

1 Pour the passata and wine into a medium saucepan and stir to mix. Bring to the boil over a medium heat, then add the cream and stir until evenly mixed and bubbling. Turn the heat down to low and leave to simmer.

2 Cook the cappelletti until *al dente*: 5–7 minutes or according to the instructions on the packet. Meanwhile, finely shred most of the basil leaves.

3 Drain the pasta well, return it to the pan and toss it with the grated Parmesan. Taste the sauce for seasoning, pour it over the pasta and toss well. Serve immediately, sprinkled with the shredded basil and whole basil leaves.

COOK'S TIP

• *Cappelletti with a variety of fillings are available at supermarkets and Italian delicatessens.*
• *Other stuffed pasta shapes, such as tortelloni, ravioli, or the more unusual sacchettini (little purses), can be used with this sauce.*
• *The tomato sauce can be made up to a day ahead, then chilled until ready to use. Reheat gently in a heavy-based saucepan while the pasta is cooking.*

Raw Tomato Sauce

THIS IS A WONDERFULLY simple uncooked tomato sauce that goes well with many different kinds of pasta, both long strands and short shapes. It is always made in summer when plum tomatoes have ripened on the vine in the sun and have their fullest flavour.

INGREDIENTS

500g/1 1/4lb ripe Italian plum tomatoes
1 large handful fresh basil leaves
75ml/5 tbsp extra virgin olive oil
115g/4oz ricotta salata cheese, diced
1 garlic clove, crushed
salt and ground black pepper
coarsely shaved Pecorino cheese, to serve
Serves 4

1 Roughly chop the plum tomatoes, removing the cores and as many of the seeds as you can. Tear the basil leaves into shreds with your fingers.

2 Put all the ingredients (except the cheese) in a bowl, adding salt and pepper to taste, and stir well. Cover and leave at room temperature for 1–2 hours to let the flavours mingle.

3 Taste the sauce to check the seasoning then pour it over hot, freshly cooked pasta of your choice and toss well. Serve immediately with shavings of Pecorino handed separately.

COOK'S TIPS

• *Ricotta salata is a salted and dried version of ricotta cheese. It is firmer than the traditional soft white ricotta, and can be easily diced, crumbled and even grated. It is available from some delicatessens. If you can't locate it, use feta cheese instead.*
• *Long pasta goes well with this sauce, especially bucatini or spaghetti, or you could serve it with short shapes, such as fusilli or orecchiette.*

Meaty Tomato Sauce

THIS ROMAN SAUCE came into being during the days when meat was scarce and expensive, so cooks would put a little meat fat in with the basic tomato sauce to make it taste of meat. Sometimes meat stock was used for the same purpose.

INGREDIENTS

1 small onion
1 small carrot
2 celery sticks
2 garlic cloves
1 small handful fresh flat leaf parsley
50g/2oz ham or bacon fat,
   finely chopped
60–90ml/4–6 tbsp dry white wine,
   or more to taste
500g/1¼lb ripe Italian plum
   tomatoes, chopped
salt and ground black pepper
Serves 4

1 Chop the onion, carrot and celery finely in a food processor. Add the garlic cloves and parsley and process until finely chopped. Alternatively, chop everything by hand.

2 Put the chopped vegetable mixture in a medium shallow saucepan or skillet with the ham fat and cook, stirring, over a low heat for about 5 minutes. Add the wine, with salt and pepper to taste and simmer for 5 minutes, then stir in the tomatoes. Simmer for 40 minutes, stirring occasionally and adding a little hot water if the sauce seems too dry.

3 Have ready a large sieve placed over a large bowl. Carefully pour in the sauce and press it through the sieve with the back of a metal spoon, leaving behind the tomato skins and any tough pieces of vegetable that won't go through.

4 Return the sauce to the clean pan and heat it through, adding a little more wine or hot water if it is too thick. Taste the sauce for seasoning, then toss with hot, freshly cooked pasta of your choice.

COOK'S TIPS

• Capelli d'angelo, preferably made without egg, is the traditional pasta to serve with this sauce, but you can use tagliolini or tagliarini if you prefer.
• If you like, you can add about 7g/¼oz dried porcini mushrooms, soaked, drained and squeezed dry, when first cooking the other vegetables.

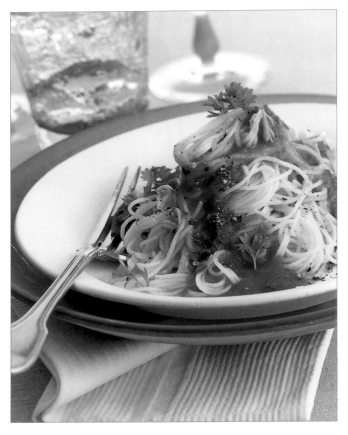

Farfalle with Tomatoes and Peas

THIS PRETTY SAUCE should be served with plain white pasta so that the red, green and white make it *tricolore*, the three colours of the Italian flag. Here farfalle (bow-tie shaped pasta) are used, but other pasta shapes will work just as well.

INGREDIENTS

15ml/1 tbsp olive oil
5–6 rindless streaky bacon rashers, cut
    into strips
400g/14oz can chopped Italian
    plum tomatoes
60ml/4 tbsp water
350g/12oz/3 cups dried farfalle
225g/8oz/2 cups frozen peas
50g/2oz/4 tbsp mascarpone cheese
a few fresh basil leaves, shredded
salt and ground black pepper
basil leaves, to garnish
freshly grated Parmesan cheese,
    to serve
Serves 4

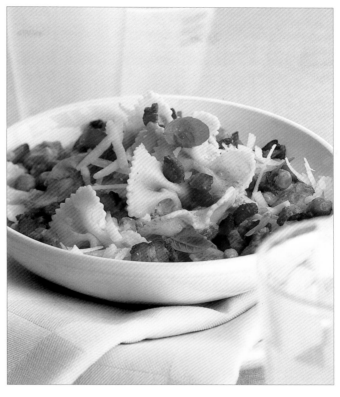

1 Heat the oil in a medium saucepan and add the bacon. Cook over a low heat, stirring frequently, for 5–7 minutes.

2 Add the tomatoes and water, with salt and pepper to taste. Bring to the boil. Lower the heat, cover and simmer gently for about 15 minutes, stirring from time to time.

3 Meanwhile, cook the pasta in salted boiling water according to the instructions on the packet.

4 Add the peas to the tomato sauce, stir well to mix and bring to the boil. Cover the pan and cook for 5–8 minutes until the peas are cooked and the sauce is quite thick. Taste the sauce for seasoning.

5 Turn off the heat under the pan and add the mascarpone and shredded basil. Mix well, cover the pan and leave to stand for 1–2 minutes. Drain the pasta and tip it into a warmed bowl. Pour the sauce over the pasta and toss well. Serve immediately, garnished with basil, and hand round some grated Parmesan separately.

Spaghetti with Tomatoes and Pancetta

THIS SAUCE comes from Spoleto in Umbria. It is a fresh, light sauce in which the tomatoes are cooked for a short time, so it should only be made in summer when tomatoes have a good flavour.

INGREDIENTS

350g/12oz ripe Italian plum tomatoes
150g/5oz pancetta or rindless streaky
*   bacon, diced*
30ml/2 tbsp olive oil
1 onion, finely chopped
350g/12oz fresh or dried spaghetti
2–3 fresh marjoram sprigs, leaves stripped
salt and ground black pepper
shredded fresh basil, to garnish
freshly grated Pecorino cheese,
*   to serve*
Serves 4

With a sharp knife, cut a cross in the bottom (flower) end of each plum tomato. Bring a medium saucepan of water to the boil and remove from the heat. Plunge a few of the tomatoes into the water, leave for 30 seconds or so, then lift them out with a slotted spoon and set aside. Repeat with the remaining tomatoes, then peel off the skin and finely chop the flesh.

COOK'S TIP

Do try to find pancetta – bacon can be substituted but the sauce will not taste precisely the same. You can buy ready diced pancetta in packets in super-markets. Alternatively, you can buy it thinly sliced, sometimes cut from a roll (arrotolata), and dice it yourself.

2 Put the pancetta or bacon in a medium saucepan with the oil. Stir over a low heat until the fat runs. Add the onion and stir to mix. Cook gently for about 10 minutes, stirring.

3 Add the tomatoes, with salt and pepper to taste. Stir well and cook, uncovered, for about 10 minutes. Meanwhile, cook the pasta according to the instructions on the packet.

4 Remove the sauce from the heat, stir in the marjoram and taste for seasoning. Drain the pasta and tip it into a warmed bowl. Pour the sauce over the pasta and toss well. Serve immediately, sprinkled with shredded basil. Hand around grated Pecorino.

Penne with Tomato and Chilli Sauce

THIS IS ONE OF ROME'S most famous pasta dishes – called *Penne all'Arrabbiata* in Italy. Literally translated, *arrabbiata* means "enraged" or "furious" but in this context it should be translated as "fiery". Make the sauce as hot as you like by adding more chillies to taste.

INGREDIENTS

25g/1oz dried porcini mushrooms
90g/3¹/₂oz/7 tbsp butter
150g/5oz pancetta or rindless smoked
   streaky bacon, diced
1–2 dried red chillies, to taste
2 garlic cloves, crushed
8 ripe Italian plum tomatoes, peeled
   and chopped
a few fresh basil leaves, torn, plus extra
   to garnish
350g/12oz/3 cups fresh or dried penne
50g/2oz/²/₃ cup freshly grated
   Parmesan cheese
25g/1oz/¹/₃ cup freshly grated
   Pecorino cheese
salt

Serves 4

1 Soak the dried mushrooms in warm water to cover for 15–20 minutes. Drain, then squeeze dry with your hands. Finely chop the mushrooms.

2 Melt 50g/2oz/4 tbsp of the butter in a medium saucepan or skillet. Add the pancetta or bacon and stir-fry over a medium heat until golden and slightly crispy. Remove the pancetta with a slotted spoon and set it aside.

3 Add the chopped mushrooms to the pan and cook in the same way. Remove and set aside with the pancetta or bacon. Crumble 1 chilli into the pan, add the garlic and cook, stirring, for a few minutes until the garlic turns golden.

4 Add the tomatoes and basil and season with salt. Cook gently, stirring occasionally, for 10–15 minutes. Meanwhile, cook the penne in a pan of salted boiling water, according to the instructions on the packet.

5 Add the pancetta or bacon and the mushrooms to the tomato sauce. Taste for seasoning, adding more chillies if you prefer a hotter flavour. If the sauce is too dry, stir in a little of the pasta water.

6 Drain the pasta and tip it into a warmed bowl. Dice the remaining butter, add it to the pasta with the cheeses, then toss until well coated. Pour the tomato sauce over the pasta, toss well and serve immediately, with a few basil leaves sprinkled on top.

Linguine with Scallops and Tomatoes

FRESH BASIL gives this sauce a distinctive flavour.

INGREDIENTS

450g/1lb fresh or dried linguine
30ml/2 tbsp olive oil
2 garlic cloves, crushed
450g/1lb sea scallops, halved horizontally
salt and ground black pepper
30ml/2 tbsp chopped fresh basil

For the sauce

30ml/2 tbsp olive oil
½ onion, finely chopped
1 garlic clove, crushed
2.5ml/½ tsp salt
2 x 400g/14oz cans plum tomatoes
Serves 4

4 Meanwhile, heat the oil in another non-stick frying pan and cook the garlic until just sizzling, for about 30 seconds.

5 Add the scallops and 2.5ml/½ tsp salt and cook over a high heat, tossing until the scallops are cooked through, about 3 minutes.

6 Add the scallops to the tomato sauce. Season with salt and pepper, stir and keep warm.

7 Drain the pasta, rinse under hot water and drain again. Place in a large serving dish. Add the sauce and the basil and toss thoroughly. Serve the pasta immediately.

1 To make the tomato sauce, heat the oil in a non-stick frying pan. Add the onion, garlic and a little salt, and cook over a medium heat for about 5 minutes until just softened, stirring occasionally.

2 Add the tomatoes to the pan, with their juice, and crush with a fork. Bring to the boil, then reduce the heat and simmer gently for 15 minutes. Remove from the heat and set aside.

3 Cook the pasta in a large saucepan with plenty of boiling salted water, according to the instructions on the packet, until the pasta is *al dente*.

Fusilli with Tomato and Smoky Bacon

PREPARE THIS SAUCE using tomatoes
that are perfectly ripe and sweet.

INGREDIENTS

900g/2lb ripe tomatoes
6 rashers smoked streaky bacon
50g/2oz/4 tbsp butter
1 onion, chopped
15ml/1 tbsp chopped fresh oregano or
*   5ml/1 tsp dried*
450g/1lb fresh or dried pasta, such as
*   fusilli col buco*
salt and ground black pepper
freshly grated Parmesan cheese, to serve
Serves 4

1 Plunge the tomatoes into boiling
water for 1 minute, then transfer
them into a bowl of cold water. Slip off
the skins. Halve the tomatoes, remove
the seeds and cores and roughly chop
the flesh.

2 Remove the rind from the streaky
bacon and roughly chop the meat.

3 Melt the butter in a saucepan and
add the chopped bacon. Fry until
lightly browned on all sides, then add
the onion and cook gently, stirring, for
5 minutes until softened.

4 Add the tomatoes, salt, pepper and
oregano to the other ingredients
in the pan. Simmer gently for 10 minutes.

5 Cook the pasta in plenty of
boiling salted water according to
the instructions on the packet. Drain
well and toss with the tomato sauce.
Serve with plenty of freshly grated
Parmesan cheese.

Cream Sauces

The northern Italians love cream sauce with pasta. Its unctuous texture goes well with *pasta all'uovo* – pasta made with egg. The pasta in the north is often fresh rather than dried, and cream sauces complement it perfectly. The cream used in Italy is different from our fresh cream. Called *panna da cucina* (cream for cooking), it has a thin, almost runny, consistency and a slight tang. You can buy it fresh in Italy, but beyond its borders you are more likely to see long-life *panna da cucina* in delicatessens and specialist stores.

Oddly enough, the most famous cream sauce of all does not come from northern Italy, but from Rome. *Fettuccine all'Alfredo* – a simple dish of fresh fettuccine tossed in nothing more than cream, butter and grated Parmesan – is one of the best pasta dishes of all time, and very hard to beat. You will find the recipe in this chapter, plus many other simple sauces based on cream to rival Alfredo's creation. From classic favourites, such as Spaghetti Carbonara and Vermicelli with Lemon to recipes using seasonal vegetables, such as asparagus and wild mushrooms, or more unusual ingredients, such as radicchio, there is plenty of choice.

Pasta with a cream sauce is always special and makes a good dinner party first course, but keep portions small, because flavours are rich.

Spaghetti Carbonara

AN ALL-TIME FAVOURITE that needs no introducing. This version has plenty of pancetta or bacon and is not too creamy, but you can vary the amounts as you please.

INGREDIENTS

30ml/2 tbsp olive oil
1 small onion, finely chopped
8 pancetta or rindless smoked streaky bacon rashers, cut into 1cm/1/2in strips
350g/12oz fresh or dried spaghetti
4 eggs
60ml/4 tbsp crème fraîche
60ml/4 tbsp freshly grated Parmesan cheese, plus extra to serve
salt and ground black pepper
Serves 4

1 Heat the oil in a large saucepan or skillet, add the finely chopped onion and cook over a low heat, stirring frequently, for about 5 minutes until softened but not coloured.

2 Add the strips of pancetta or bacon to the onion in the pan and cook for about 10 minutes, stirring almost all of the time. Meanwhile, cook the pasta in a pan of salted boiling water according to the instructions on the packet until *al dente*.

3 Put the eggs, crème fraîche and grated Parmesan in a bowl. Grind in plenty of pepper, then beat everything together well.

4 Drain the pasta, tip it into the pan with the pancetta or bacon and toss well to mix. Turn the heat off under the pan. Immediately add the egg mixture and toss vigorously so that it cooks lightly and coats the pasta.

5 Quickly taste for seasoning, then divide among four warmed bowls and sprinkle with black pepper. Serve immediately, with extra grated Parmesan handed separately.

Fusilli with Wild Mushrooms

A VERY RICH DISH WITH AN earthy flavour and lots of garlic, this makes an ideal main course for vegetarians, especially if it is followed by a crisp green salad.

INGREDIENTS

1/2 x 275g/10oz jar wild mushrooms in olive oil
25g/1oz/2 tbsp butter
225g/8oz/2 cups fresh wild mushrooms, thinly sliced
5ml/1 tsp finely chopped fresh thyme
5ml/1 tsp finely chopped fresh marjoram or oregano, plus extra to serve
4 garlic cloves, crushed
350g/12oz/3 cups fresh or dried fusilli
200ml/7fl oz/scant 1 cup panna da cucina or double cream
salt and ground black pepper
Serves 4

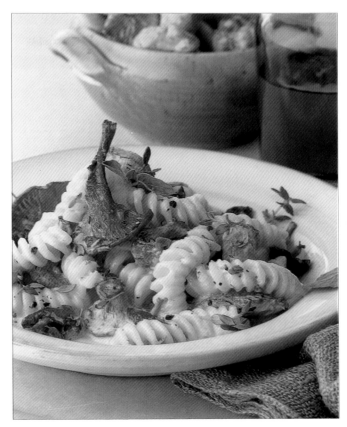

1 Drain about 15ml/1 tbsp of the oil from the mushrooms into a medium saucepan. Slice or chop the bottled mushrooms into bite-size pieces, if they are large.

2 Add the butter to the oil in the pan and place over a low heat until sizzling. Add the bottled and the fresh mushrooms, the chopped herbs and the garlic, with salt and pepper to taste. Simmer over a medium heat, stirring frequently, for about 10 minutes or until the fresh mushrooms are soft and tender. Meanwhile, cook the pasta in salted boiling water according to the instructions on the packet.

3 As soon as the mushrooms are cooked, increase the heat to high and toss the mixture with a wooden spoon to drive off any excess liquid. Pour in the cream and bring to the boil, stirring, then taste and add more salt and pepper if needed.

4 Drain the pasta and tip it into a warmed bowl. Pour the sauce over the pasta and toss well. Serve immediately, sprinkled with finely chopped fresh herbs.

Fusilli with Walnuts

A CLASSIC ITALIAN DISH with a strong, nutty flavour, this should be served with a delicately flavoured salad.

INGREDIENTS

350g/12oz/3 cups dried fusilli col buco
50g/2oz/½ cup walnut pieces
25g/1oz/2 tbsp butter
300ml/½ pint/1¼ cups milk
50g/2oz/1 cup fresh breadcrumbs
25g/1oz/2 tbsp freshly grated
   Parmesan cheese
pinch of freshly grated nutmeg
salt and ground black pepper
fresh rosemary sprigs, to garnish
Serves 4

1   Cook the pasta in plenty of boiling salted water according to the instructions on the packet. Meanwhile, preheat the grill.

2   Spread the walnuts evenly over the grill pan. Grill for about 5 minutes, turning occasionally until evenly toasted.

3   Remove the walnuts from the heat, place in a clean dish towel and rub away the skins. Roughly chop the nuts.

4   Heat the butter and milk in a saucepan until the butter is completely melted.

5   Stir in the breadcrumbs and nuts and heat gently for 2 minutes, stirring constantly until the mixture has thickened.

6   Add the Parmesan cheese, nutmeg and seasoning to taste.

7   Drain the pasta thoroughly through a colander then pour over the sauce and combine thoroughly. Serve immediately, garnished with fresh sprigs of rosemary.

Farfalle with Mushrooms and Cheese

FRESH WILD MUSHROOMS are very good in this sauce, but they are expensive. To cut the cost, use half wild and half cultivated, or as many wild as you can afford — even a small handful will intensify the mushroom flavour of the sauce.

INGREDIENTS

15g/^{1}/$_2$ oz/^{1}/$_4$ cup dried porcini mushrooms
250ml/8fl oz/1 cup warm water
25g/1 oz/2 tbsp butter
1 small onion, finely chopped
1 garlic clove, crushed
225g/8oz/3 cups fresh mushrooms,
    thinly sliced
a few fresh sage leaves, very finely chopped,
    plus a few whole leaves, to garnish
150ml/^{1}/$_4$ pint/ ^{2}/$_3$ cup dry white wine
225g/8oz/2 cups dried farfalle
115g/4oz/^{1}/$_2$ cup mascarpone cheese
115g/4oz/1 cup Gorgonzola or torta di
    Gorgonzola cheese, crumbled
salt and ground black pepper
Serves 4

1 Put the dried porcini in a small bowl with the warm water and leave to soak for 20–30 minutes. Remove the porcini from the liquid with a slotted spoon and squeeze over the bowl to extract as much liquid as possible. Strain the liquid and set it aside. Finely chop the porcini.

2 Melt the butter in a large saucepan, add the onion and chopped porcini and cook gently, stirring for about 3 minutes until the onion is soft. Add the garlic and fresh mushrooms, chopped sage, salt and plenty of black pepper. Cook over a medium heat, stirring frequently, for about 5 minutes or until the mushrooms are soft and juicy. Stir in the soaking liquid and the wine and simmer gently.

3 Cook the farfalle in a large saucepan of rapidly boiling salted water, for about 10 minutes or until it is al dente.

4 Meanwhile, stir the mascarpone and Gorgonzola into the mushroom sauce. Heat through, stirring, until melted. Taste for seasoning and adjust if necessary. Drain the pasta thoroughly, add to the sauce and toss to mix. Serve at once, with black pepper ground liberally on top. Garnish with sage leaves.

VARIATION

For a lighter sauce, use crème fraîche instead of mascarpone.

Pink and Green Farfalle

IN THIS MODERN RECIPE, pink prawns and green courgettes combine prettily with cream and pasta bows to make a substantial main course. Serve with crusty Italian rolls or chunks of warm ciabatta bread.

INGREDIENTS

50g/2oz/¼ cup butter

2–3 spring onions, very thinly sliced on
   the diagonal

350g/12oz courgettes, thinly sliced on
   the diagonal

60ml/4 tbsp dry white wine

300g/11oz/2⅔ cups dried farfalle

75ml/5 tbsp crème fraîche

225g/8oz/1⅓ cups peeled cooked
   prawns, thawed and thoroughly dried
   if frozen

15ml/1 tbsp finely chopped fresh marjoram
   or flat leaf parsley, or a mixture

salt and ground black pepper

Serves 4

1 Melt the butter in a large saucepan, add the spring onions and cook over a low heat, stirring frequently, for about 5 minutes until softened. Add the courgettes, with salt and pepper to taste, and stir-fry for 5 minutes. Pour over the wine and let it bubble, then cover and simmer for 10 minutes.

VARIATION

Use penne instead of the farfalle, and asparagus tips instead of the courgettes.

2 Cook the pasta in a saucepan of salted boiling water according to the instructions on the packet. Meanwhile, add the crème fraîche to the courgette mixture and simmer for about 10 minutes until well reduced.

3 Add the prawns to the courgette mixture, heat through gently and taste for seasoning. Drain the pasta and tip it into a warmed bowl. Add the sauce and chopped herbs and toss well. Serve immediately.

Penne with Prawns and Pernod

THIS IS A MODERN RECIPE, typical of those found on menus in the most innovative Italian restaurants. The Pernod and dill go well together, but you could use white wine and basil.

INGREDIENTS

200ml/7fl oz/scant 1 cup panna da cucina
   or double cream

250ml/8fl oz/1 cup fish stock

350g/12oz/3 cups dried penne

30–45ml/2–3 tbsp Pernod

225g/8oz/1⅓ cups peeled cooked prawns,
   thawed and thoroughly dried if frozen

30ml/2 tbsp chopped fresh dill, plus extra
   to garnish

salt and ground black pepper

Serves 4

1 Put the cream and the fish stock in a medium saucepan and bring to the boil. Lower the heat and simmer, stirring occasionally, for 10–15 minutes until reduced by about half. Meanwhile, cook the dried pasta in a saucepan of salted boiling water according to the instructions on the packet.

2 Add the Pernod and prawns to the cream sauce, with salt and pepper to taste, if necessary. Heat the prawns through very gently. Drain the pasta and tip it into a warmed bowl. Pour the sauce over the pasta, add the dill and toss well. Serve immediately, sprinkled with chopped dill.

Pipe Rigate with Peas and Ham

3 Add about half the cream, increase the heat to high and let the cream bubble, stirring constantly, until it thickens and coats the peas. Remove from the heat, stir in the prosciutto and taste for seasoning.

4 Cook the pasta according to the instructions on the packet. Tip into a colander and drain well.

5 Immediately melt the remaining butter with the cream in the pan in which the pasta was cooked. Add the pasta and toss over a medium heat until it is evenly coated. Pour in the sauce, toss lightly to mix with the pasta and heat through. Serve immediately, sprinkled with fresh herbs.

PRETTILY FLECKED WITH PINK and green, this is a lovely dish for a spring or summer supper party.

INGREDIENTS

25g/1oz/2 tbsp butter
15ml/1 tbsp olive oil
150–175g/5–6oz/1¼–1½ cups frozen
    peas, thawed
1 garlic clove, crushed
150ml/¼ pint/⅔ cup chicken stock, dry
    white wine or water
30ml/2 tbsp chopped fresh flat leaf parsley
175ml/6fl oz/¾ cup panna da cucina or
    double cream
115g/4oz prosciutto crudo (Parma
    ham), shredded
350g/12oz/3 cups dried pipe rigate
salt and ground black pepper
chopped fresh herbs, to garnish
Serves 4

1 Melt half the butter with the olive oil in a medium saucepan until foaming. Add the thawed frozen peas and the crushed garlic to the pan, followed by the chicken stock, wine or water.

2 Sprinkle in the chopped parsley and add salt and pepper to taste. Cook over a medium heat, stirring frequently, for 5–8 minutes or until most of the liquid has been absorbed.

COOK'S TIPS

• Prosciutto is quite expensive, but it tastes very good in this dish. To cut the cost you could use ordinary cooked ham or pancetta.
• If you can't get pipe rigate, use conchiglie or orecchiette instead, all of which trap the peas.

Alfredo's Fettuccine

THIS SIMPLE RECIPE WAS invented by a Roman restaurateur called Alfredo, who became famous for serving it with a gold fork and spoon.

INGREDIENTS

50g/2oz/¼ cup butter
200ml/7fl oz/scant 1 cup panna da cucina
    or double cream
50g/2oz/⅔ cup freshly grated Parmesan
    cheese, plus extra to serve
350g/12oz fresh fettuccine
salt and ground black pepper
Serves 4

1 Melt the butter in a large saucepan or skillet. Add the cream and bring it to the boil. Simmer for 5 minutes, stirring, then add the Parmesan, with salt and pepper to taste, and turn off the heat under the pan.

2 Bring a large saucepan of salted water to the boil. Drop in the pasta all at once and quickly bring back to the boil, stirring occasionally. Cook until *al dente*: 2–3 minutes, or according to the instructions on the packet. Drain well.

3 Turn on the heat under the pan of cream to low, add the pasta all at once and toss until it is coated in the sauce. Taste for seasoning. Serve immediately, with extra grated Parmesan handed around separately.

COOK'S TIPS

• *With so few ingredients, it is particularly important to use only the best-quality ones for this dish to be a success. Use good unsalted butter and top-quality Parmesan cheese. The best is Parmigiano-Reggiano – available from Italian delicatessens – which has its name stamped on the rind. Grate it only just before using.*
• *Fresh fettuccine is traditional, so either make it yourself or buy it from an Italian delicatessen. If you cannot get fettuccine, you can use tagliatelle instead.*

Vermicelli with Lemon

FRESH AND TANGY, this makes an excellent first course for a dinner party. It doesn't rely on fresh seasonal ingredients, so it is good at any time of year. It is also a recipe to remember when you're pushed for time, because the sauce can easily be made in the time it takes to cook the pasta.

INGREDIENTS

350g/12oz dried vermicelli
juice of 2 large lemons
50g/2oz/¼ cup butter
200ml/7fl oz/scant 1 cup panna da cucina
 or double cream
115g/4oz/1⅓ cups freshly grated
 Parmesan cheese
salt and ground black pepper
Serves 4

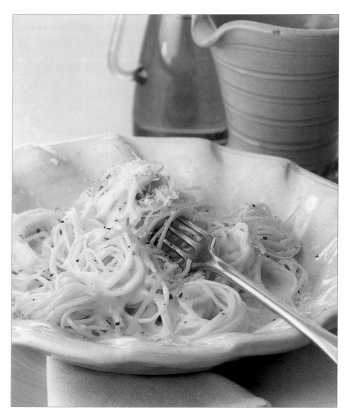

1 Cook the pasta in salted boiling water according to the instructions on the packet.

2 Meanwhile, pour the lemon juice into a medium saucepan. Add the butter and cream, then salt and pepper to taste.

3 Bring to the boil, then lower the heat and simmer for about 5 minutes, stirring occasionally, until the cream reduces slightly.

4 Drain the pasta and return it to the pan. Add the grated Parmesan, then taste the sauce for seasoning and pour it over the pasta. Toss quickly over a medium heat until the pasta is evenly coated with the sauce, then divide among four warmed bowls and serve immediately.

COOK'S TIP

Lemons vary in the amount of juice they yield. On average, a large fresh lemon will yield 60–90ml/4–6 tbsp. The lemony flavour of this dish is supposed to be quite sharp – you can use less juice if you prefer.

VARIATIONS

• *Use spaghettini or spaghetti, or even small pasta shapes, such as fusilli, farfalle or orecchiette.*
• *For an even tangier taste, add a little grated lemon rind to the sauce when you add the butter and the cream to the pan in Step 2.*

Spaghetti with Saffron

A QUICK AND EASY DISH THAT makes a delicious midweek supper. The ingredients are all staples that you are likely to have in the fridge, so this recipe is perfect for impromptu meals.

INGREDIENTS

350g/12oz dried spaghetti
a few saffron strands
30ml/2 tbsp water
150g/5oz cooked ham, cut into matchsticks
200ml/7fl oz/scant 1 cup panna da cucina or double cream
50g/2oz/²⁄₃ cup freshly grated Parmesan cheese, plus extra to serve
2 egg yolks
salt and ground black pepper
Serves 4

3 Add the strips of ham to the pan containing the saffron. Stir in the cream and Parmesan, with a little salt and pepper to taste. Heat gently, stirring all the time. When the cream starts to bubble around the edges, remove the sauce from the heat and add the egg yolks. Beat well to mix, then taste for seasoning.

4 Drain the pasta and tip it into a warmed bowl. Immediately pour the sauce over the pasta and toss well. Serve immediately, with extra grated Parmesan handed separately.

COOK'S TIPS

• Individual sachets of saffron powder, enough for four servings, are sold at Italian delicatessens and some supermarkets, and one sachet can be used for this sauce instead of the saffron strands. Simply sprinkle in the powder in Step 3, when adding salt and pepper.
• Use a heavy-based pan for heating the cream so that it does not catch on the bottom. Make sure you beat the sauce immediately the eggs are added.

1 Cook the pasta in a saucepan of salted boiling water according to the instructions on the packet.

2 Meanwhile, put the saffron strands in a saucepan, add the water and bring to the boil immediately. Remove the pan from the heat and leave to stand for a while.

Fettuccine with Ham and Cream

PROSCIUTTO IS PERFECT for this rich and delicious dish, which makes a very elegant starter.

INGREDIENTS

115g/4oz prosciutto crudo or other
*   unsmoked ham (raw or cooked)*
50g/2oz/¼ cup butter
2 shallots, very finely chopped
150ml/¼ pint/⅔ cup double cream
350g/12oz fresh or dried fettucine
50g/2oz/½ cup grated Parmesan cheese
salt and ground black pepper
fresh parsley sprig, to garnish

Serves 4

1 Cut the fat from the ham and chop both lean and fat parts separately into small squares.

2 Melt the butter in a medium frying pan and add the shallots and the squares of ham fat. Cook, stirring, until golden. Add the lean ham, and cook for a further 2 minutes. Season with black pepper. Stir the cream into the cooked ham, and keep the sauce warm over a low heat while the pasta is cooking.

3 Cook the pasta in plenty of boiling salted water until *al dente*. Drain, tip into a warmed serving dish and toss with the sauce. Stir in the cheese and serve immediately, garnished with a sprig of parsley.

Tagliatelle with Smoked Salmon

IN ITALY SMOKED SALMON is imported and quite expensive. This elegant creamy sauce makes a little go a long way. Use a mixture of green and white pasta if you wish.

INGREDIENTS

175g/6oz smoked salmon slices or ends,
*   fresh or frozen*
300ml/½ pint/1¼ cups single cream
pinch of ground mace or grated nutmeg
350g/12oz fresh or dried green and
*   white tagliatelle*
salt and ground black pepper
45ml/3 tbsp snipped fresh chives,
*   to garnish*

Serves 4–5

1 Cut the salmon into thin strips, each about 5cm/2in long. Place the strips in a bowl and add the cream and the mace or nutmeg. Stir to combine, cover and allow to stand for at least 2 hours in a cool place (not the fridge).

2 Cook the pasta in a large saucepan with plenty of boiling salted water according to the instructions on the packet, or until it is just *al dente*.

3 Meanwhile, gently warm the cream and salmon mixture in a small saucepan, without boiling.

4 Drain the pasta, pour the sauce over and mix well. Season to taste and garnish with the chives.

Fusilli with Mascarpone and Spinach

THIS CREAMY, GREEN SAUCE tossed in lightly cooked pasta is best served with plenty of sun-dried tomato ciabatta bread.

INGREDIENTS

350g/12oz/3 cups fresh or dried fusilli
50g/2oz/¼ cup butter
1 onion, chopped
1 garlic clove, chopped
30ml/2 tbsp fresh thyme leaves
225g/8oz frozen spinach leaves, thawed
225g/8oz/1 cup mascarpone cheese
salt and ground black pepper
fresh thyme sprigs, to garnish

Serves 4

1 Cook the pasta in plenty of boiling salted water according to the instructions on the packet.

2 Melt the butter in a large saucepan and fry the onion for 10 minutes until softened.

3 Stir in the garlic, fresh thyme, spinach and seasoning and heat gently for about 5 minutes, stirring occasionally, until heated through.

4 Stir in the mascarpone cheese and cook gently until heated through. Do not boil.

5 Drain the pasta thoroughly and stir into the sauce. Toss until well coated. Serve immediately, garnished with fresh thyme.

COOK'S TIP

Mascarpone is a rich Italian cream cheese. If you cannot find any, use ordinary full-fat cream cheese instead.

Ravioli with Four-cheese Sauce

THIS IS A SMOOTH, cheesy sauce that
coats the pasta very evenly.

INGREDIENTS

350g/12oz fresh or dried ravioli
50g/2oz/¼ cup butter
50g/2oz/¼ cup plain flour
450ml/¾ pint/1¾ cups milk
50g/2oz freshly grated Parmesan cheese
50g/2oz freshly grated Edam cheese
50g/2oz freshly grated Gruyère cheese
50g/2oz freshly grated fontina cheese
salt and ground black pepper
chopped fresh flat leaf parsley, to garnish
Serves 4

1 Cook the pasta in plenty of boiling
salted water according to the
instructions on the packet.

2 Melt the butter in a saucepan,
stir in the flour and cook for
2 minutes, stirring occasionally.

3 Gradually stir in the milk until
completely blended.

4 Bring the milk slowly to the boil,
stirring constantly until the sauce
is thickened.

5 Stir the grated cheeses into the
sauce. Mix together until they are
just beginning to melt. Remove from
the heat and season.

6 Drain the pasta thoroughly and
turn into a large serving dish. Pour
over the sauce and toss to coat. Serve
immediately, garnished with the
chopped fresh parsley.

Linguine with Ham and Mascarpone

MASCARPONE CHEESE masquerades as cream in this recipe. Its thick, unctuous consistency makes it perfect for sauces. Have the water boiling, ready for the pasta, before you start making the sauce, because everything cooks so quickly.

INGREDIENTS

25g/1oz/2 tbsp butter
150g/5oz/³⁄₄ cup mascarpone cheese
90g/3¹⁄₂oz cooked ham, cut into thin strips
30ml/2 tbsp milk
45ml/3 tbsp freshly grated Parmesan
cheese, plus extra to serve
500g/1¹⁄₄lb fresh linguine
salt and ground black pepper
Serves 6

1 Melt the butter in a medium saucepan, add the ham, mascarpone and milk and stir well over a low heat until the mascarpone has melted. Add 15ml/1 tbsp of the grated Parmesan and plenty of pepper and stir well.

2 Cook the pasta in a large saucepan of salted boiling water for 2–3 minutes until al dente.

3 Drain the cooked pasta well and tip it into a warmed bowl. Pour the sauce over the pasta, add the remaining Parmesan and toss well until thoroughly combined.

4 Taste for seasoning and serve the pasta immediately, with more ground black pepper and extra grated Parmesan handed separately.

Farfalle with Gorgonzola Cream

SWEET AND SIMPLE, this sauce has a nutty tang from the blue cheese. It is also good with long pasta, such as spaghetti or trenette.

INGREDIENTS

350g/12oz/3 cups dried farfalle
175g/6oz Gorgonzola cheese, any rind
removed, diced
150ml/¹⁄₄ pint/²⁄₃ cup panna da cucina or
double cream
pinch of granulated sugar
10ml/2 tsp finely chopped fresh sage, plus
fresh sage leaves (some whole, some
shredded) to garnish
salt and ground black pepper
Serves 4

1 Cook the pasta until al dente: 8–10 minutes or according to the instructions on the packet.

2 Meanwhile, put the Gorgonzola and cream in a medium saucepan. Add the sugar and plenty of ground black pepper and heat gently, stirring frequently, until the cheese has melted. Remove the pan from the heat.

3 Drain the cooked pasta well and return it to the pan in which it was cooked. Pour the sauce into the pan with the pasta.

4 Add the chopped sage to the pasta and toss over a medium heat until the pasta is evenly coated. Taste for seasoning, adding salt if necessary, then divide among four warmed bowls. Garnish each portion with sage and serve immediately.

Garganelli with Asparagus and Cream

A LOVELY RECIPE FOR LATE SPRING when bunches of fresh young asparagus are found on sale in shops and markets everywhere.

INGREDIENTS

1 bunch fresh young asparagus,
    250–300g/9–11oz
350g/12oz/3 cups dried garganelli
25g/1oz/2 tbsp butter
200ml/7fl oz/scant 1 cup panna da cucina
    or double cream
30ml/2 tbsp dry white wine
90–115g/3½–4oz/1–1⅓ cups freshly
    grated Parmesan cheese
30ml/2 tbsp chopped fresh mixed herbs,
    such as basil, flat leaf parsley, chervil,
    marjoram and oregano
salt and ground black pepper

Serves 4

3 Cook the pasta according to the instructions on the packet. Meanwhile, put the butter and cream in a medium saucepan, add salt and pepper to taste and bring to the boil. Simmer for a few minutes until the cream reduces and thickens, then add the asparagus, wine and about half the grated Parmesan. Taste for seasoning and keep on a low heat.

4 Drain the pasta when cooked and tip it into a warmed bowl. Pour the sauce over the pasta, sprinkle with the fresh herbs and toss well. Serve immediately, topped with the remaining grated Parmesan.

COOK'S TIPS

• When buying asparagus look for thin stalks, which will be sweet and tender. Don't buy asparagus with thick or woody stalks, which will be tough.

• Garganelli all'uovo (with egg) are just perfect for this dish. You can buy packets of this pasta in Italian delicatessens.

• Penne (quills) or penne rigate (ridged quills) are an alternative pasta for this recipe. They are similar in shape and size to garganelli.

1 Trim off and throw away the woody ends of the asparagus – after trimming, you should have about 200g/7oz asparagus spears. Cut the spears diagonally into pieces that are roughly the same length and shape as the garganelli.

2 Blanch the asparagus spears in salted boiling water for 2 minutes, the tips for 1 minute. Immediately after blanching drain the asparagus spears and tips, rinse in cold water and set aside.

Tagliatelle with Radicchio and Cream

3 Add the butter, onion and garlic to the pan and stir-fry for 5 minutes more. Add the radicchio and toss for 1–2 minutes until wilted.

4 Pour in the cream and add the grated Parmesan, with salt and pepper to taste. Stir for 1–2 minutes until the cream is bubbling and the ingredients are evenly mixed. Taste for seasoning.

THIS IS A MODERN RECIPE that is very quick and easy to make. It is deliciously rich, and makes a good dinner party first course.

INGREDIENTS

225g/8oz dried tagliatelle
75–90g/3–3½oz pancetta or rindless
  streaky bacon, diced
25g/1oz/2 tbsp butter
1 onion, finely chopped
1 garlic clove, crushed
1 head of radicchio, about
  115–175g/4–6oz, finely shredded
150ml/¼ pint/⅔ cup panna da cucina or
  double cream
50g/2oz/⅔ cup freshly grated
  Parmesan cheese
salt and ground black pepper
Serves 4

1 Cook the pasta according to the instructions on the packet.

2 Meanwhile, put the pancetta or bacon in a medium saucepan and heat gently until the fat begins to run. Increase the heat slightly and stir-fry the pancetta or bacon for a further 5 minutes until crisp and golden.

5 Drain the pasta and tip it into a warmed bowl. Pour the sauce over and toss well. Serve immediately.

COOK'S TIP

In Italy, cooks use a type of radicchio called radicchio di Treviso. It is very striking to look at, having long leaves that are dramatically striped in dark red and white. Radicchio di Treviso is available in some supermarkets and specialist green-grocers, but if you cannot get it you can use the round radicchio instead, which is very easy to obtain.

Fish
and
Shellfish

It is not surprising that seafood sauces are often served with pasta along the Italian coastline, and on the islands of Sicily and Sardinia, but they're very popular inland, too. Clams, mussels, tuna, prawns, anchovies, salmon, scallops and squid are the most common fish and shellfish used, but cooks in coastal areas also create unique pasta dishes using the local catch. These are hard to replicate elsewhere.

Sometimes seafood is cooked with tomatoes, sometimes with a cream-based sauce, so the look and taste of seafood pasta can vary considerably from one dish to another. Intense flavours are found in Sicilian recipes, such as Spaghetti with Anchovies and Olives and Spaghetti with Bottarga, while the popular modern classic Penne with Cream and Smoked Salmon is mild and creamy. Linguine with Clams, Leeks and Tomatoes offers a fresh and light alternative. When partnered with seafood, pasta really proves its versatility. Spaghetti is the traditional pasta to serve with seafood sauces, since so many of them are based on olive oil and tomatoes, and it remains the all-time favourite, but other shapes work equally well.

Vermicelli with Clam Sauce

THIS RECIPE COMES from the city of Naples, where both fresh tomato sauce and seafood are traditionally served with vermicelli. Here the two are combined to make a very tasty dish.

INGREDIENTS

1kg/2¼lb fresh clams
250ml/8fl oz/1 cup dry white wine
2 garlic cloves, bruised
1 large handful fresh flat leaf parsley
30ml/2 tbsp olive oil
1 small onion, finely chopped
8 ripe Italian plum tomatoes, peeled, seeded and finely chopped
½–1 fresh red chilli, seeded and finely chopped
350g/12oz dried vermicelli
salt and ground black pepper
Serves 4

1 Scrub the clams thoroughly under cold running water and discard any that are open or that do not close when sharply tapped against the work surface.

2 Pour the wine into a large saucepan, add the garlic cloves and half the parsley, then the clams. Cover tightly with the lid and bring to the boil over a high heat. Cook for about 5 minutes, shaking the pan frequently, until the clams have opened.

3 Tip the clams into a large colander set over a bowl and let the liquid drain through. Leave the clams until cool enough to handle, then remove about two-thirds of them from their shells, tipping the clam liquor into the bowl of cooking liquid. Discard any clams that have failed to open. Set both shelled and unshelled clams aside, keeping the unshelled clams warm in a bowl covered with a lid.

4 Heat the oil in a saucepan, add the onion and cook gently, stirring frequently, for about 5 minutes until softened and lightly coloured. Add the tomatoes, then strain in the clam cooking liquid. Add the chilli and salt and pepper to taste.

5 Bring to the boil, half cover and simmer gently for 15–20 minutes. Meanwhile, cook the pasta according to the instructions on the packet. Chop the remaining parsley finely.

6 Add the shelled clams to the tomato sauce, stir well and heat through very gently for 2–3 minutes.

7 Drain the cooked pasta well and tip it into a warmed bowl. Taste the sauce for seasoning, then pour the sauce over the pasta and toss everything together well. Garnish with the reserved clams, sprinkle the parsley over the pasta and serve immediately.

Seafood Conchiglie

THIS IS A VERY SPECIAL MODERN dish, a warm salad composed of scallops, pasta and fresh rocket flavoured with roasted pepper, chilli and balsamic vinegar. It makes a substantial and impressive dinner party starter, or a main course for a light lunch.

INGREDIENTS

8 large fresh scallops
300g/11oz/2³/₄ cups dried conchiglie
15ml/1 tbsp olive oil
15g/1¹/₂oz/1 tbsp butter
120ml/4fl oz/¹/₂ cup dry white wine
90g/3¹/₂oz rocket leaves, stalks trimmed
salt and ground black pepper

For the vinaigrette

60ml/4 tbsp extra virgin olive oil
15ml/1 tbsp balsamic vinegar
1 piece bottled roasted pepper, drained and
   finely chopped
1–2 fresh red chillies, seeded and chopped
1 garlic clove, crushed
5–10ml/1–2 tsp clear honey, to taste
Serves 4

1 Cut each scallop into 2–3 pieces. If the corals are attached, pull them off and cut each piece in half. Season the scallops and corals with salt and pepper.

2 To make the vinaigrette, put the oil, vinegar, chopped pepper and chillies in a jug with the garlic and honey and whisk well.

3 Cook the pasta according to the instructions on the packet.

4 Meanwhile, heat the oil and butter in a non-stick frying pan until sizzling. Add half the scallops and toss over a high heat for 2 minutes. Remove with a slotted spoon and keep warm. Cook the remaining scallops in the same way.

5 Add the wine to the liquid remaining in the pan and stir over a high heat until the mixture has reduced to a few tablespoons. Remove from the heat and keep warm.

6 Drain the pasta and tip it into a warmed bowl. Add the rocket, scallops, the reduced cooking juices and the vinaigrette and toss well to combine. Serve immediately.

COOK'S TIPS

• Use only fresh scallops for this dish – they are available all year round in most fishmongers and from fish counters in supermarkets. Frozen scallops tend to be watery and tasteless, and often prove to be rubbery when cooked.
• For a more formal presentation, arrange the rocket leaves in a circle on each of four individual serving plates. Toss the pasta, scallops, reduced cooking juices and vinaigrette together and spoon into the centre of the rocket leaves.

Salmon Rigatoni with Parsley Sauce

THIS DISH IS SO QUICK and easy to
make – and delicious.

INGREDIENTS

450g/1lb salmon fillet, skinned
225g/8oz/2 cups dried rigatoni
175g/6oz cherry tomatoes, halved
150ml/¼ pint/⅔ cup low-fat
   crème fraîche
45ml/3 tbsp finely chopped parsley
finely grated rind of ½ orange
salt and ground black pepper
Serves 4

1 Cut the salmon into bite-size
pieces, arrange on a heatproof
plate and cover with foil.

2 Bring a large pan of salted water
to the boil, add the pasta and
return to the boil. Place the plate of
salmon on top of the pan and simmer
for 10–12 minutes, until the pasta and
salmon are cooked.

3 Drain the pasta and toss with the
tomatoes and salmon. In a
separate bowl mix together the crème
fraîche, parsley, orange rind and pepper
to taste. Spoon this mixture over the
salmon and pasta, toss well and serve
hot or cold.

Tagliatelle with Saffron Mussels

MUSSELS IN A SAFFRON and cream sauce are served with tagliatelle in this recipe, but you can use any other pasta if you prefer.

INGREDIENTS
1.75kg/4–4½lb live mussels in the shell
150ml/¼ pint/⅔ cup dry white wine
2 shallots, chopped
350g/12oz dried tagliatelle
25g/1oz/2 tbsp butter
2 garlic cloves, crushed
250ml/8fl oz/1 cup double cream
generous pinch of saffron strands
1 egg yolk
salt and ground black pepper
30ml/2 tbsp chopped fresh parsley,
    to garnish
Serves 4

1 Scrub the mussels well under cold running water. Remove the "beards" and discard any mussels that are open.

2 Place the mussels in a large pan with the shallots and pour over the wine. Cover and cook over a high heat, shaking the pan occasionally, for 5–8 minutes until the mussels have opened. Drain the mussels, reserving the liquid. Discard any that remain closed. Shell all but a few of the mussels and keep warm.

3 Bring the reserved cooking liquid to the boil in the pan, then reduce by half. Strain the liquid into a jug to remove any grit.

4 Cook the tagliatelle in plenty of boiling salted water for about 10 minutes, until al dente.

5 Meanwhile, melt the butter and fry the garlic for 1 minute. Pour in the mussel liquid, cream and saffron strands. Heat gently until the sauce thickens slightly. Off the heat, stir in the egg yolk and shelled mussels and season the sauce to taste.

6 Drain the tagliatelle and transfer to warmed serving dishes. Spoon the sauce over and sprinkle with chopped parsley. Garnish with the mussels in shells and serve at once.

Orecchiette with Anchovies and Broccoli

WITH ITS ROBUST FLAVOURS, this pasta dish is typical of southern Italian and Sicilian cooking. Anchovies, pine nuts, garlic and Pecorino cheese are all very popular ingredients. Serve with crusty Italian bread for a light lunch or supper.

INGREDIENTS
300g/11oz/2 cups broccoli florets
40g/1¹/₂oz/¹/₂ cup pine nuts
350g/12oz/3 cups dried orecchiette
60ml/4 tbsp olive oil
1 small red onion, thinly sliced
50g/2oz jar anchovies in olive oil
1 garlic clove, crushed
*50g/2oz/²/₃ cup freshly grated
   Pecorino cheese*
salt and ground black pepper
Serves 4

COOK'S TIP

Orecchiette (little ears) from Puglia are a special type of pasta with a chewy texture. You can get them in Italian delicatessens, or use conchiglie instead.

1 Break the broccoli florets into small sprigs and cut off the stalks. If the stalks are large, chop or slice them. Cook the broccoli florets and stalks in a saucepan of boiling salted water for 2 minutes, then drain and refresh under cold running water. Leave to drain on kitchen paper.

2 Put the pine nuts in a dry non-stick frying pan and toss over a low to medium heat for 1–2 minutes or until the nuts are lightly toasted and golden. Remove and set aside.

3 Cook the pasta according to the instructions on the packet.

4 Meanwhile, heat the oil in a skillet, add the red onion and fry gently, stirring frequently, for about 5 minutes until softened. Add the anchovies with their oil, then add the garlic and fry over a medium heat, stirring frequently, for 1–2 minutes until the anchovies break down to form a paste. Add the broccoli and plenty of pepper and toss over the heat for a minute or two until the broccoli is hot. Taste for seasoning.

5 Drain the pasta and tip it into a warmed bowl. Add the broccoli mixture and grated Pecorino and toss well to combine. Sprinkle the pine nuts over the top and serve immediately.

Trenette with Shellfish

COLOURFUL AND DELICIOUS, this typical Genoese dish is ideal for a dinner party. The sauce is quite runny, so serve it with crusty bread and spoons as well as forks.

INGREDIENTS

45ml/3 tbsp olive oil
1 small onion, finely chopped
1 garlic clove, crushed
$^1/_2$ fresh red chilli, seeded and chopped
200g/7oz can chopped Italian
   plum tomatoes
30ml/2 tbsp chopped fresh flat leaf parsley
400g/14oz fresh clams
400g/14oz fresh mussels
60ml/4 tbsp dry white wine
400g/14oz/3$^1/_2$ cups dried trenette
a few fresh basil leaves
90g/3$^1/_2$oz/$^2/_3$ cup peeled cooked prawns,
   thawed and thoroughly dried if frozen
salt and ground black pepper
chopped fresh herbs, to garnish

Serves 4

1 Heat 30ml/2 tbsp of the oil in a skillet or medium saucepan. Add the onion, garlic and chilli and cook over a medium heat for 1–2 minutes, stirring constantly. Stir in the tomatoes, half the parsley and pepper to taste. Bring to the boil, lower the heat, cover and simmer for 15 minutes.

2 Meanwhile, scrub the clams and mussels under cold running water. Discard any that are open or that do not close when sharply tapped against the work surface.

3 In a large saucepan, heat the remaining oil. Add the clams and mussels, with the rest of the parsley and toss over a high heat for a few seconds. Pour in the wine, then cover tightly. Cook for about 5 minutes, shaking the pan frequently, until the clams and mussels have opened.

4 Remove the pan from the heat and transfer the clams and mussels to a bowl with a slotted spoon, discarding any shellfish that have failed to open.

5 Strain the cooking liquid into a measuring jug and set aside. Reserve eight clams and four mussels in their shells for the garnish, then remove the rest from their shells.

6 Cook the pasta according to the instructions on the packet. Meanwhile, add 120ml/4fl oz/$^1/_2$ cup of the reserved seafood liquid to the tomato sauce. Bring to the boil over a high heat, stirring. Lower the heat, tear in the basil leaves and add the prawns with the shelled clams and mussels. Stir well, then taste for seasoning.

7 Drain the pasta and tip it into a warmed bowl. Add the seafood sauce and toss well to combine. Serve in individual bowls, sprinkle with herbs and garnish each portion with two reserved clams and one mussel in their shells.

Seafood Conchiglie with Spinach Sauce

YOU'LL NEED VERY LARGE pasta shells, measuring about 4cm/1¹/2in long for this dish; don't try stuffing smaller shells – they will be much too fiddly!

INGREDIENTS

15g/¹/2oz/1 tbsp margarine
8 spring onions, finely sliced
6 tomatoes
32 large dried conchiglie
225g/8oz/1 cup low-fat soft cheese
90ml/6 tbsp skimmed milk
pinch of freshly grated nutmeg
225g/8oz/2 cups prawns
175g/6oz can white crab meat, drained
    and flaked
115g/4oz frozen chopped spinach, thawed
    and drained
salt and ground black pepper
Serves 4

1 Preheat the oven to 150°C/300°F/ Gas 2. Melt the margarine in a small saucepan and gently cook the spring onions for 3–4 minutes, or until softened but not brown.

2 With a sharp knife, slash the bottoms of the tomatoes, plunge into a saucepan of boiling water for 45 seconds, then into a bowl of cold water. Slip off the skins. Halve the tomatoes, remove and discard the seeds and cores and roughly chop the flesh.

3 Cook the conchiglie in plenty of boiling salted water for about 10 minutes, or until al dente. Drain well and set aside.

4 Heat the soft cheese and milk in a saucepan, stirring until blended. Season with salt, pepper and nutmeg. Measure 30ml/2 tbsp of the sauce into a large bowl.

5 Add the spring onions, chopped tomatoes, prawns, and crab meat to the bowl. Mix well. When the shells are cool enough to handle, spoon the filling into them and place in a single layer in a shallow ovenproof dish. Cover with foil and cook in the preheated oven for 10 minutes.

6 Stir the spinach into the remaining sauce in the pan. Bring to the boil and simmer gently for 1 minute, stirring all the time.

7 Transfer the pasta onto plates and drizzle the spinach sauce over. Serve hot.

Spaghetti with Tomato and Clam Sauce

SMALL SWEET CLAMS make this a delicately succulent sauce. Cockles would make a good substitute, but don't be tempted to use seafood pickled in vinegar.

INGREDIENTS

900g/2lb live small clams in the shell,
  or 2 x 400g/14oz cans clams in
  brine, drained
90ml/6 tbsp olive oil
2 garlic cloves, crushed
500g/1¼lb canned chopped tomatoes
45ml/3 tbsp chopped fresh parsley
450g/1lb dried spaghetti
salt and ground black pepper
Serves 4

1 If using live clams, place them in a bowl of cold water and rinse several times to remove any grit or sand, then drain well.

2 Heat the oil in a saucepan and add the clams. Stir over a high heat until the clams open. Discard any that do not open. Transfer the clams to a bowl with a slotted spoon and set the bowl aside.

3 Reduce the clam juice left in the pan to almost nothing by boiling fast. Add the garlic and fry until golden. Pour in the tomatoes, bring to the boil and cook for 3–4 minutes until reduced. Stir in the clam mixture or canned clams and half the parsley and heat through. Season to taste.

4 Cook the pasta in plenty of boiling salted water according to the instructions on the packet. Drain well and tip into a warm serving dish. Pour the sauce over and sprinkle with the remaining chopped parsley.

Rigatoni with Tuna and Anchovies

THIS PIQUANT SAUCE could be made without the addition of tomatoes — just heat the oil, add the other ingredients and heat through gently before tossing with the pasta.

INGREDIENTS

400g/14oz can tuna fish in oil
30ml/2 tbsp olive oil
2 garlic cloves, crushed
800g/1¾lb canned chopped tomatoes
6 canned anchovy fillets, drained
30ml/2 tbsp capers in vinegar, drained
30ml/2 tbsp chopped fresh basil
400g/14oz/3½ cups dried rigatoni
salt and ground black pepper
fresh basil sprigs, to garnish
Serves 4

1 Drain the oil from the can of tuna fish into a large saucepan, add the olive oil and heat gently until the oil mixture stops spitting.

2 Add the garlic and fry until golden. Stir in the tomatoes and simmer for about 25 minutes until the sauce has thickened.

3 Flake the tuna and cut the anchovies in half. Stir into the sauce with the capers and chopped basil. Season well.

4 Cook the pasta in plenty of boiling salted water according to the instructions on the packet. Drain well and toss with the sauce. Garnish with fresh basil sprigs and serve.

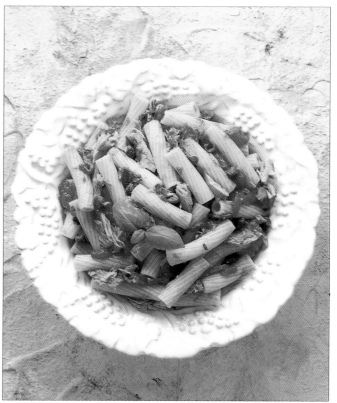

Fish with Fregola

THIS SARDINIAN SPECIALITY is a cross between a soup and a stew. Serve it with crusty Italian country bread to mop up the juices.

INGREDIENTS

75ml/5 tbsp olive oil
4 garlic cloves, finely chopped
½ small fresh red chilli, seeded and
finely chopped
1 large handful fresh flat leaf parsley,
roughly chopped
1 red snapper, about 450g/1lb, cleaned,
with head and tail removed
1 red or grey mullet, about 500g/1¼lb,
cleaned, with head and tail removed
350–450g/12oz–1lb thick cod fillet
400g/14oz can chopped Italian
plum tomatoes
175g/6oz/1½ cups dried fregola
salt and ground black pepper
Serves 4–6

1 Heat 30ml/2 tbsp of the olive oil in a large flameproof casserole. Add the chopped garlic and chilli, with about half the chopped parsley. Fry over a medium heat, stirring occasionally, for about 5 minutes.

2 Cut all of the fish into large chunks – including the skin and the bones in the case of the snapper and mullet – and add the pieces to the casserole as you cut them. Sprinkle the pieces with a further 30ml/2 tbsp of the olive oil and fry for a few minutes more.

3 Add the tomatoes, then fill the empty can with water and pour this into the pan. Bring to the boil. Stir in salt and pepper to taste, lower the heat and cook for 10 minutes, stirring occasionally.

4 Add the fregola and simmer for 5 minutes, then add 250ml/8fl oz/ 1 cup water and the remaining oil. Simmer for 15 minutes until the fregola is *al dente*.

5 If the sauce becomes too thick, add more water, then taste for seasoning. Serve hot, in warmed bowls, sprinkled with the remaining parsley.

COOK'S TIPS

• *You can make the basic fish sauce several hours in advance or even the day before, bringing it to the boil and adding the fregola just before serving.*
• *Fregola is a tiny pasta shape from Sardinia. If you can't get it, use a tiny soup pasta (pastina), such as corallini or semi de melone.*

Farfalle with Tuna

A QUICK AND SIMPLE DISH that makes a good weekday supper if you have canned tomatoes and tuna in the storecupboard.

INGREDIENTS

30ml/2 tbsp olive oil
I small onion, finely chopped
I garlic clove, finely chopped
400g/14oz can chopped Italian
  plum tomatoes
45ml/3 tbsp dry white wine
8–10 pitted black olives, cut into rings
10ml/2 tsp chopped fresh oregano or
  5ml/1 tsp dried oregano, plus extra fresh
  oregano to garnish
400g/14oz/3½ cups dried farfalle
175g/6oz can tuna in olive oil
salt and ground black pepper
Serves 4

1 Heat the olive oil in a medium skillet or saucepan, add the onion and garlic and fry gently for 2–3 minutes until the onion is soft and golden.

2 Add the plum tomatoes to the pan and bring to the boil, then pour over the white wine and simmer the mixture for a minute or so. Stir in the olives and oregano, with salt and pepper to taste, then cover and cook for 20–25 minutes, stirring from time to time.

3 Meanwhile, cook the pasta in a large saucepan of salted boiling water according to the instructions on the packet.

4 Drain the canned tuna and flake it with a fork. Add the tuna to the sauce with about 60ml/4 tbsp of the water used for cooking the pasta. Taste and adjust the seasoning.

5 Drain the cooked pasta well and tip it into a warmed large serving bowl. Pour the tuna sauce over the top and toss to mix. Serve immediately, garnished with sprigs of oregano.

Capelli d'Angelo with Spinach Sauce

DELICIOUSLY EARTHY, this would make a good starter or light supper dish. Add some sultanas to the sauce to ring the changes.

INGREDIENTS

900g/2lb fresh spinach or 500g/1¼lb
    frozen leaf spinach, thawed
450g/1lb fresh capelli d'angelo
salt, to taste
60ml/4 tbsp olive oil
45ml/3 tbsp pine nuts
2 garlic cloves
6 canned anchovy fillets, drained and
    chopped, or whole salted anchovies,
    rinsed, boned and chopped
butter, for tossing the pasta
salt

Serves 4

1 If using fresh spinach, wash it well and remove any tough stalks before cooking. Drain thoroughly. Place in a large saucepan with only the water that clings to the leaves. Cover with a lid and cook over a high heat, shaking the pan occasionally, until the spinach is just wilted and still bright green. Drain well.

2 Cook the pasta in plenty of boiling salted water according to the instructions on the packet.

3 Heat the oil in a saucepan and fry the pine nuts until golden. Remove with a slotted spoon and set aside. Add the garlic to the oil in the pan and fry until golden. Add the chopped anchovies to the pan.

4 Stir in the spinach and cook for 2–3 minutes or until heated through. Stir in the reserved pine nuts.

5 Drain the pasta, toss in a little butter and tip into a warmed serving dish. Top with the hot sauce and toss roughly before serving.

Tagliatelle with Haddock and Avocado

YOU WILL NEED to start this recipe the day before because the haddock should be left to marinate overnight.

INGREDIENTS

350g/12oz fresh haddock fillets, skinned
2.5ml/½ tsp each ground cumin, ground
  coriander and turmeric
150ml/¼ pint/⅔ cup fromage frais
150ml/¼ pint/⅔ cup double cream
15ml/1 tbsp lemon juice
25g/1oz/2 tbsp butter
1 onion, chopped
15ml/1 tbsp plain flour
150ml/¼ pint/⅔ cup fish stock
350g/12oz fresh or dried tagliatelle
1 avocado, peeled, stoned and sliced
2 tomatoes, seeded and chopped
salt and ground black pepper
fresh rosemary sprigs, to garnish
Serves 4

1 Carefully cut the haddock into bite-size pieces.

2 Mix together all the spices, seasoning, fromage frais, cream and lemon juice.

3 Stir in the haddock to coat. Cover the dish and leave to marinate overnight in the fridge.

4 Heat the butter in a frying pan and fry the onion for about 10 minutes until softened but not brown. Stir in the flour, cook for a minute, then blend in the stock until the sauce is smooth.

5 Carefully stir in the haddock mixture until well blended. Bring to the boil, stirring, cover and simmer for about 30 seconds. Remove from the heat.

6 Meanwhile, cook the pasta in plenty of boiling salted water according to the instructions on the packet until al dente.

7 Stir the avocado and tomatoes into the haddock mixture.

8 Drain the pasta thoroughly and divide among four serving plates. Spoon the sauce over and serve immediately, garnished with fresh rosemary sprigs.

Tagliatelle with Scallops

SCALLOPS AND BRANDY make this a relatively expensive dish, but it is so delicious that you will find it well worth the cost. Serve it for a dinner party first course.

INGREDIENTS

200g/7oz scallops, sliced
30ml/2 tbsp plain flour
40g/1½oz/3 tbsp butter
2 spring onions, cut into thin rings
½–1 small fresh red chilli, seeded and
    very finely chopped
30ml/2 tbsp finely chopped fresh flat
    leaf parsley
60ml/4 tbsp brandy
105ml/7 tbsp fish stock
275g/10oz fresh spinach-flavoured
    tagliatelle
salt and ground black pepper

Serves 4

1 Toss the scallops in the flour, then shake off the excess. Bring a saucepan of salted water to the boil, ready for cooking the pasta.

2 Meanwhile, melt the butter in a skillet or large saucepan. Add the spring onions, finely chopped chilli and half the parsley and fry, stirring frequently, for 1–2 minutes over a medium heat. Add the scallops and toss over the heat for 1–2 minutes.

3 Pour the brandy over the scallops, then set it alight with a match. As soon as the flames have died down, stir in the fish stock and salt and pepper to taste. Mix well. Simmer for 2–3 minutes, then cover the pan and remove it from the heat.

4 Add the pasta to the boiling water and cook it according to the instructions on the packet. Drain, add to the sauce and toss over a medium heat until mixed. Serve at once, in warmed bowls sprinkled with the remaining parsley.

COOK'S TIP

Buy fresh scallops, with their corals if possible. Fresh scallops always have a better texture and flavour than frozen scallops, which tend to be watery.

Spaghetti with Squid and Peas

IN TUSCANY, SQUID IS OFTEN cooked with peas in a tomato sauce. This recipe is a variation on the theme, and it works very well.

INGREDIENTS

450g/1lb prepared squid
30ml/2 tbsp olive oil
1 small onion, finely chopped
400g/14oz can chopped Italian
    plum tomatoes
1 garlic clove, finely chopped
15ml/1 tbsp red wine vinegar
5ml/1 tsp granulated sugar
10ml/2 tsp finely chopped fresh rosemary
115g/4oz/1 cup frozen peas
350g/12oz fresh or dried spaghetti
15ml/1 tbsp chopped fresh flat leaf parsley
salt and ground black pepper

Serves 4

1 Cut the prepared squid into strips about 5mm/¼in wide. Finely chop any tentacles.

2 Heat the oil in a skillet or medium saucepan, add the finely chopped onion and cook gently, stirring, for about 5 minutes until softened. Add the squid, tomatoes, garlic, red wine vinegar and sugar.

3 Add the rosemary, with salt and pepper to taste. Bring to the boil, stirring, then cover and simmer gently for 20 minutes. Uncover the pan, add the peas and cook for 10 minutes. Meanwhile, cook the pasta according to the instructions on the packet, then drain and tip it into a warmed bowl. Pour the sauce over the pasta, add the parsley, then toss well and serve.

Capelli d'Angelo with Lobster

THIS IS A SOPHISTICATED, stylish dish for a special occasion. Some cooks make the sauce with champagne rather than sparkling white wine, especially when they are planning to serve champagne with the meal.

INGREDIENTS

meat from the body, tail and claws of
*   1 cooked lobster*
juice of ¹/₂ lemon
40g/1¹/₂oz/3 tbsp butter
4 fresh tarragon sprigs, leaves stripped
*   and chopped*
60ml/4 tbsp double cream
90ml/6 tbsp sparkling dry white wine
60ml/4 tbsp fish stock
300g/11oz fresh capelli d'angelo
salt and ground black pepper
about 10ml/2 tsp lumpfish roe, to garnish
*   (optional)*
Serves 4

1 Cut the lobster meat into small pieces and put it in a bowl. Sprinkle with the lemon juice. Melt the butter in a skillet or large saucepan, add the lobster meat and tarragon and stir over the heat for a few seconds. Add the cream and stir for a few seconds more, then pour in the wine and stock, with salt and pepper to taste. Simmer for 2 minutes, then remove from the heat and cover.

2 Cook the pasta according to the instructions on the packet. Drain well, reserving a few spoonfuls of the cooking water.

3 Place the pan of lobster sauce over a medium to high heat, add the pasta and toss for just long enough to combine and heat through; moisten with a little of the reserved water from the pasta. Serve immediately in warmed bowls, sprinkled with lumpfish roe if you like.

COOK'S TIP

To remove the meat from a lobster, place the lobster on a board with its underbelly facing uppermost. With a large sharp knife, cut the lobster in half lengthways. Spoon out the green liver and any pink roe (coral) and reserve these, then remove and discard the gravel sac (stomach). Pull the white tail meat out from either side of the shell and discard the black intestinal vein. Crack the claws with a nutcracker just below the pincers and remove the meat from the base. Pull away the small pincer, taking the white membrane with it, then remove the meat from this part of the shell. Pull the meat from the large pincer shell.

Linguine with Crab

THIS RECIPE COMES FROM Rome. It makes a very rich and tasty first course on its own, or can be served for a lunch or supper with crusty Italian bread. Some cooks like a finer sauce, and work the crabmeat through a sieve after pounding. If you fancy following their example, be warned – it's hard work.

INGREDIENTS

about 250g/9oz shelled crabmeat
45ml/3 tbsp olive oil
1 small handful fresh flat leaf parsley,
* roughly chopped, plus extra to garnish*
1 garlic clove, crushed
350g/12oz ripe Italian plum tomatoes,
* skinned and chopped*
60–90ml/4–6 tbsp dry white wine
350g/12oz fresh or dried linguine
salt and ground black pepper
Serves 4

1 Put the crabmeat in a mortar and pound to a rough pulp with a pestle. If you do not have a pestle and mortar, use a sturdy bowl and the end of a rolling pin. Set aside.

2 Heat 30ml/2 tbsp of the oil in a large saucepan. Add the parsley and garlic, with salt and pepper to taste, and fry for a few minutes until the garlic begins to brown.

3 Add the tomatoes, pounded crabmeat and wine, cover the pan and simmer gently for 15 minutes, stirring occasionally.

4 Meanwhile, cook the pasta according to the instructions on the packet, draining it the moment it is *al dente*, and reserving a little of the cooking water.

5 Return the pasta to the clean pan, add the remaining oil and toss quickly over a medium heat until the oil coats the strands.

6 Add the tomato and crab mixture to the pasta and toss again, adding a little of the reserved cooking water if you think it necessary. Adjust the seasoning to taste. Serve hot, in warmed bowls, sprinkled with parsley.

COOK'S TIP

The best way to obtain crabmeat is to ask a fishmonger to remove it from the shell for you, or buy dressed crab from the supermarket. For this recipe you will need one large crab, and you should use both the white and dark meat.

Spaghetti with Salmon and Prawns

THIS IS A LOVELY FRESH-TASTING pasta dish, perfect for an *al fresco* meal in summer. Serve it as a main course lunch with warm ciabatta or focaccia and a dry white wine.

INGREDIENTS

300g/11oz salmon fillet
200ml/7fl oz/scant 1 cup dry white wine
a few fresh basil sprigs, plus extra basil
*   leaves, to garnish*
6 ripe Italian plum tomatoes, peeled and
*   finely chopped*
150ml/¼ pint/⅔ cup double cream
350g/12oz/3 cups fresh or dried spaghetti
115g/4oz/⅔ cup peeled cooked prawns,
*   thawed and thoroughly dried if frozen*
salt and ground black pepper

Serves 4

1 Put the salmon skin-side up in a wide shallow pan. Pour the wine over, then add the basil sprigs to the pan and sprinkle the fish with salt and pepper. Bring the wine to the boil, cover the pan and simmer gently for no more than 5 minutes. Using a fish slice, lift the fish out of the pan and set aside to cool a little.

2 Add the tomatoes and cream to the liquid remaining in the pan and bring to the boil. Stir well, then lower the heat and simmer, uncovered, for 10–15 minutes. Meanwhile, cook the pasta according to the instructions on the packet.

3 When cool enough to handle, flake the fish into large chunks, discarding the skin and any bones. Add the fish to the sauce with the prawns, shaking the pan until the fish and shellfish are well coated. Taste for seasoning.

4 Drain the pasta and tip it into a warmed bowl. Pour the sauce over the pasta and toss to combine. Serve immediately, garnished with fresh basil leaves.

COOK'S TIP

Check the salmon fillet carefully for small bones when you are flaking the flesh. Although the salmon is already filleted, you will always find a few stray "pin" bones. Pick them out carefully using tweezers or your fingertips.

Tagliolini with Clams and Mussels

SERVED ON WHITE CHINA, this makes a stunning looking dish for a dinner party first course. The sauce can be prepared a few hours ahead of time, then the pasta cooked and the dish assembled at the last minute.

INGREDIENTS

450g/1lb fresh mussels
450g/1lb fresh clams
60ml/4 tbsp olive oil
1 small onion, finely chopped
2 garlic cloves, finely chopped
1 large handful fresh flat leaf parsley, plus
  extra chopped parsley to garnish
175ml/6fl oz/³/₄ cup dry white wine
250ml/8fl oz/1 cup fish stock
1 small fresh red chilli, seeded and chopped
350g/12oz squid ink tagliolini or tagliatelle
salt and ground black pepper
Serves 4

1 Scrub the mussels and clams under cold running water and discard any that are open or damaged, or that do not close when sharply tapped against the work surface.

2 Heat half the oil in a large saucepan, add the onion and cook gently for about 5 minutes until softened. Sprinkle in the garlic, then add about half the parsley sprigs, with salt and pepper to taste. Add the mussels and clams and pour in the wine. Cover with the lid and bring to the boil over a high heat. Cook for about 5 minutes, shaking the pan frequently, until the shellfish have opened.

3 Tip the mussels and clams into a fine sieve set over a bowl and let the liquid drain through. Discard the aromatics in the sieve, together with any mussels or clams that have failed to open. Return the liquid to the clean pan and add the fish stock. Chop the remaining parsley finely and add it to the liquid with the chopped chilli. Bring to the boil, then lower the heat and simmer, stirring, for a few minutes until slightly reduced. Turn off the heat.

4 Remove and discard the top shells from about half the mussels and clams. Put all the mussels and clams in the pan of liquid and seasonings, then cover the pan tightly and set aside.

5 Cook the pasta according to the instructions on the packet.

6 Drain well, then return to the clean pan; toss with the remaining olive oil. Put the pan of shellfish over a high heat and toss to heat the shellfish through quickly and combine with the liquid and seasonings.

7 Divide the pasta among four warmed plates, spoon the shellfish mixture over and around, then serve immediately, sprinkled with parsley.

Spaghetti with Anchovies and Olives

THE STRONG FLAVOURS of this dish are typical of Sicilian cuisine.

INGREDIENTS

45ml/3 tbsp olive oil
1 large red pepper, seeded and chopped
1 small aubergine, finely chopped
1 onion, finely chopped
8 ripe Italian plum tomatoes, peeled, seeded
*   and finely chopped*
2 garlic cloves, finely chopped
120ml/4fl oz/¹/₂ cup dry red or white wine
120ml/4fl oz/¹/₂ cup water
1 handful fresh herbs, such as basil, flat leaf
*   parsley and rosemary*
300g/11oz dried spaghetti
50g/2oz canned anchovies, roughly chopped,
*   plus extra whole anchovies to garnish*
12 pitted black olives
15–30ml/1–2 tbsp capers, to taste
salt and ground black pepper
Serves 4

1 Heat the oil in a saucepan and add all the finely chopped vegetables and garlic. Cook gently, stirring frequently, for 10–15 minutes until the vegetables are soft. Pour in the wine and water, add the fresh herbs and pepper to taste and bring to the boil. Lower the heat and simmer, stirring occasionally, for 10–15 minutes. Meanwhile, cook the pasta in a large saucepan of salted boiling water according to the instructions on the packet.

2 Add the chopped anchovies, olives and capers to the sauce, heat through for a few minutes and taste for seasoning. Drain the pasta and tip it into a warmed bowl. Pour the sauce over the pasta, toss well and serve immediately.

COOK'S TIP

If the anchovies are omitted, this makes a good sauce for vegetarians.

Spaghetti with Tuna, Anchovies, Olives and Mozzarella

THIS RECIPE FROM CAPRI is fresh, light and full of flavour, so serve it as soon as it is cooked to enjoy it at its best.

INGREDIENTS

300g/11oz dried spaghetti
30ml/2 tbsp olive oil
6 ripe Italian plum tomatoes, chopped
5ml/1 tsp granulated sugar
50g/2oz jar anchovies in olive oil, drained
about 60 ml/4 tbsp dry white wine
50g/2oz/¹/₂ cup pitted black olives,
*   quartered lengthways*
200g/7oz can tuna in olive oil, drained
125g/4¹/₂oz packet mozzarella cheese,
*   drained and diced*
salt and ground black pepper
fresh basil leaves, to garnish
Serves 4

1 Cook the pasta according to the instructions on the packet. Meanwhile, heat the oil in a medium saucepan. Add the tomatoes, sugar and pepper to taste, and toss over a medium heat for a few minutes until the tomatoes soften and the juices run. Snip a few anchovies at a time into the pan of tomatoes with kitchen scissors.

2 Add the wine, tuna and olives and stir once or twice until they are just evenly mixed into the sauce. Add the mozzarella and heat through without stirring. Taste and add salt if necessary. Drain the pasta and tip it into a warmed bowl. Pour the sauce over, toss gently and sprinkle with basil leaves. Serve immediately.

Mixed Summer Pasta

A PRETTY AND COLOURFUL sauce with bags of flavour makes this a popular dish for the summer.

INGREDIENTS

115g/4oz French beans, cut into
   2.5cm/1in pieces
350g/12oz fresh or dried fusilli col buco
30ml/2 tbsp olive oil
½ fennel bulb, sliced
1 bunch spring onions, sliced diagonally
115g/4oz yellow cherry tomatoes
115g/4oz red cherry tomatoes
30ml/2 tbsp chopped fresh dill
225g/8oz/2 cups peeled prawns
15ml/1 tbsp lemon juice
15ml/1 tbsp wholegrain mustard
60ml/4 tbsp soured cream
salt and ground black pepper
fresh dill sprigs, to garnish
Serves 4

1 Cook the beans in a saucepan of boiling salted water for about 5 minutes until tender. Drain through a colander.

2 Cook the pasta in plenty of boiling salted water, according to the instructions on the packet, until *al dente*.

3 Heat the oil in a frying pan and fry the sliced fennel and spring onions for about 5 minutes.

4 Stir in all the cherry tomatoes and fry for a further 5 minutes, stirring the pan occasionally.

5 Add the dill and prawns and cook for a further minute.

6 Stir in the lemon juice, wholegrain mustard, soured cream, seasoning and beans and simmer for 1 minute.

7 Drain the pasta and toss with the sauce. Serve immediately, garnished with fresh dill.

Spaghetti with Seafood Sauce

THE ITALIAN NAME for this popular tomato-based seafood sauce is *marinara*.

INGREDIENTS

45ml/3 tbsp olive oil
1 onion, chopped
1 garlic clove, finely chopped
225g/8oz fresh or dried spaghetti
600ml/1 pint/2½ cups passata
15ml/1 tbsp tomato purée
5ml/1 tsp dried oregano
1 bay leaf
5ml/1 tsp sugar
115g/4oz/1 cup cooked peeled shrimps, rinsed well if canned
115g/4oz/1 cup cooked peeled prawns

175g/6oz/1½ cups cooked clam or cockle meat, rinsed well if canned or bottled
15ml/1 tbsp lemon juice
45ml/3 tbsp chopped fresh parsley
25g/1oz/2 tbsp butter
salt and ground black pepper
4 whole cooked prawns, to garnish
Serves 4

1 Heat the oil in a pan and add the onion and garlic. Fry over a moderate heat for 6–7 minutes, until the onions have softened.

2 Meanwhile, cook the spaghetti in a large saucepan of boiling salted water for 10–12 minutes until *al dente*.

3 Stir the passata, tomato purée, oregano, bay leaf and sugar into the cooked onions and season well. Bring to the boil, then simmer for 2–3 minutes.

4 Add all the shellfish, lemon juice and 30ml/2 tbsp of the parsley. Stir well, then cover and cook for 6–7 minutes.

5 Meanwhile, drain the spaghetti when it is ready and add the butter to the pan. Return the drained spaghetti to the pan and toss in the butter. Season well.

6 Divide the spaghetti among four warmed plates and top with the seafood sauce. Sprinkle with the remaining chopped parsley, garnish each plate with whole prawns and serve immediately.

Farfalle with Smoked Salmon and Dill

IN ITALY, pasta cooked with smoked salmon is very fashionable. This is a quick and luxurious sauce.

INGREDIENTS

6 spring onions
50g/2oz/4 tbsp butter
90ml/6 tbsp dry white wine or vermouth
450ml/¾ pint/1¾ cups double cream
freshly grated nutmeg
225g/8oz smoked salmon
30ml/2 tbsp chopped fresh dill or
    15ml/1 tbsp dried
freshly squeezed lemon juice
450g/1lb/4 cups dried farfalle
salt and ground black pepper
Serves 4

1 Slice the spring onions finely making diagonal cuts along the length. Melt the butter in a saucepan and gently fry the spring onions for 1 minute until softened.

2 Add the wine or vermouth and boil hard to reduce to about 30ml/2 tbsp. Stir in the cream and add salt, pepper and nutmeg to taste. Bring to the boil and simmer for 2–3 minutes until the sauce is slightly thickened.

3 On a board, cut the smoked salmon into 2.5cm/1 in squares. Transfer into the prepared sauce with the dill and stir to combine thoroughly. Taste and add a little lemon juice. Keep the sauce warm while you cook the pasta.

4 Cook the pasta in plenty of boiling salted water according to the instructions on the packet. Drain well. Then add the pasta to the sauce in the pan and toss thoroughly. Transfer the pasta to warmed plates and serve immediately.

Spaghetti with Mixed Shellfish Sauce

A SPECIAL OCCASION sauce for an evening of entertaining is just what this is, so serve it in bountiful portions to your guests.

INGREDIENTS

50g/2oz/4 tbsp butter
2 shallots, chopped
2 garlic cloves, chopped
350g/12oz fresh or dried spaghetti
2 tbsp finely chopped fresh basil
300ml/¹/₂ pint/1¹/₄ cups dry white wine
450g/1lb mussels, scrubbed
115g/4oz squid, washed
5ml/1 tsp chilli powder
350g/12oz raw peeled prawns
300ml/¹/₂ pint/1¹/₄ cups soured cream
50g/2oz/¹/₃ cup freshly grated
    Parmesan cheese
salt and ground black pepper
chopped fresh flat leaf parsley, to garnish
Serves 4

4 Discard any mussels that are open and do not shut when tapped on the work surface. Quickly add the remaining mussels to the pan, cover and simmer for about 5 minutes until all the shells have opened. Discard any mussels that do not open. Using a slotted spoon, transfer the mussels to a plate, remove them from their shells and return to the pan. Reserve a few mussels in the shells for garnishing.

5 Meanwhile, slice the squid into thin circles. Melt the remaining butter in a frying pan and fry the remaining shallot and garlic for about 5 minutes until softened.

6 Add the remaining basil, the squid, chilli powder and prawns to the pan and stir-fry for 5 minutes until the prawns have turned pink and tender.

7 Turn the mussel mixture into the prawn mixture and bring to the boil. Stir in the soured cream and season to taste. Bring almost to the boil and simmer for 1 minute.

8 Drain the pasta thoroughly and stir it into the sauce with the Parmesan cheese until well coated. Serve immediately, garnished with chopped flat leaf parsley and the reserved mussels in their shells.

1 Melt half the butter in a frying pan and fry 1 shallot and 1 garlic clove for about 5 minutes until softened.

2 Cook the pasta in plenty of boiling salted water according to the instructions on the packet.

3 Add half the basil and pour over the wine. Stir the ingredients together and bring to the boil.

Zite with Fresh Sardine Sauce

IN THIS CLASSIC Sicilian dish, fresh sardines are combined with raisins and pine nuts.

INGREDIENTS

30g/1¼oz/3 tbsp sultanas
450g/1lb fresh sardines
90ml/6 tbsp breadcrumbs
1 small fennel bulb
90ml/6 tbsp olive oil
1 onion, very thinly sliced
30g/1¼oz/3 tbsp pine nuts
2.5ml/½ tsp fennel seeds
400g/14oz fresh or dried zite
salt and ground black pepper
Serves 4

1 Soak the sultanas in warm water for 15 minutes. Drain and pat dry.

2 Clean the sardines. Open each one out flat and remove the central bones and head. Wash well and shake dry. Sprinkle evenly with the breadcrumbs.

3 Coarsely chop the top fronds of fennel and reserve. Pull off a few outer leaves and wash. Fill a large saucepan with enough water to cook the pasta. Add the fennel leaves and bring to the boil.

4 Heat the oil in a large frying pan and sauté the onion lightly until soft but not brown. Remove to a side dish. Add the sardines, a few at a time, and cook over a moderate heat until golden on both sides, turning once. When all the sardines have been cooked, gently return them to the pan. Add the onion, and the sultanas, pine nuts and fennel seeds. Season with salt and pepper.

5 Take about 60ml/4 tbsp of the boiling water for the pasta, and add it to the sauce. Add salt to the boiling water, and cook the pasta until *al dente*. Drain, and remove the fennel leaves. Toss the pasta with the sauce to combine. Divide among four individual serving plates, arranging several sardines on each. Sprinkle with the reserved chopped fennel tops and serve at once.

Spaghetti with Olives and Capers

THIS SPICY SAUCE originated in the Naples area. It can be quickly assembled using a few store-cupboard ingredients.

INGREDIENTS

60ml/4 tbsp olive oil
2 garlic cloves, finely chopped
small piece of dried red chilli, crumbled
50g/2oz can anchovy fillets, chopped
350g/12oz tomatoes, fresh or
    canned, chopped
115g/4oz/1 cup pitted black olives
30ml/2 tbsp capers, rinsed
15ml/1 tbsp tomato purée
400g/14oz fresh or dried spaghetti
30ml/2 tbsp chopped fresh parsley
Serves 4

1 Heat the oil in a large frying pan. Add the garlic and the dried red chilli, and cook for 2–3 minutes over a moderate heat until the garlic has just turned golden.

2 Add the chopped anchovies to the pan, and mash them into the garlic with the back of a fork so that they form a paste-like consistency.

3 Add the fresh or canned tomatoes, olives, capers and tomato purée to the ingredients in the pan. Stir well and continue to cook over a moderate heat.

4 Cook the spaghetti in a large saucepan with plenty of boiling salted water until al dente. Drain well.

5 Tip the spaghetti into the sauce. Increase the heat and cook for 3–4 minutes, turning the pasta constantly. Divide between four plates, sprinkle with parsley and serve at once.

Paglia e Fieno with Prawns and Vodka

THE COMBINATION OF PRAWNS, vodka and pasta may seem unusual, but it has become something of a modern classic in Italy. Here it is stylishly presented with two-coloured pasta, but the sauce goes equally well with short shapes such as penne, rigatoni and farfalle.

INGREDIENTS

30ml/2 tbsp olive oil
¼ large onion, finely chopped
I garlic clove, crushed
15–30ml/1–2 tbsp sun-dried tomato paste
200ml/7fl oz/scant I cup panna da cucina
    or double cream
350g/12oz fresh or dried paglia e fieno
12 raw tiger prawns, peeled and chopped
30ml/2 tbsp vodka
salt and ground black pepper
Serves 4

1 Heat the oil in a medium saucepan, add the onion and garlic and cook gently, stirring frequently, for about 5 minutes until softened.

2 Add the tomato paste and stir for 1–2 minutes, then add the cream and bring to the boil, stirring. Season with salt and pepper to taste and let the sauce bubble until it starts to thicken slightly. Remove from the heat.

3 Cook the pasta according to the instructions on the packet. When it is almost ready, add the prawns and vodka to the sauce; toss quickly over a medium heat for 2–3 minutes until the prawns turn pink.

4 Drain the pasta well and tip it into a warmed bowl. Pour the sauce over and toss well. Divide among warmed bowls and serve immediately.

COOK'S TIP

The sauce is best served as soon as it is ready, otherwise the prawns will overcook and become tough. Make sure that the pasta has only a minute or two of cooking time left before adding the prawns to the sauce.

Penne with Cream and Smoked Salmon

THIS MODERN WAY OF serving pasta is popular all over Italy. The three essential ingredients combine together beautifully, and the dish is very quick and easy to make.

INGREDIENTS

350g/12oz/3 cups dried penne
115g/4oz thinly sliced smoked salmon
2–3 fresh thyme sprigs
25g/1oz/2 tbsp butter
150ml/¼ pint/⅔ cup single cream
salt and ground black pepper
Serves 4

1 Cook the pasta in a saucepan of salted boiling water according to the instructions on the packet.

2 Meanwhile, using kitchen scissors, cut the smoked salmon into thin strips, about 5mm/¼in wide. Strip the leaves from the thyme sprigs.

3 Melt the butter in a large saucepan. Stir in the cream with about a quarter of the salmon and thyme leaves, then season with pepper. Heat gently for 3–4 minutes, stirring all the time. Do not allow the sauce to boil. Taste for seasoning.

4 Drain the pasta, return to the pan, and toss in the cream and salmon sauce. Divide among four warmed bowls and top with the remaining salmon and thyme leaves. Serve hot.

VARIATION

Although penne is traditional with this sauce, it also goes very well with fresh ravioli stuffed with spinach and ricotta.

Fusilli with Vegetable and Prawn Sauce

YOU WILL NEED to start this recipe the day before because the prawns should be left to marinate overnight.

INGREDIENTS

450g/1lb/4 cups peeled prawns
60ml/4 tbsp soy sauce
45ml/3 tbsp olive oil
350g/12oz fusilli col buco
1 yellow pepper, cored, seeded and cut
    into strips
225g/8oz broccoli florets
1 bunch spring onions, shredded
2.5cm/1in piece fresh ginger root, peeled
    and shredded
15ml/1 tbsp chopped fresh oregano
30ml/2 tbsp dry sherry
15ml/1 tbsp cornflour
300ml/$\frac{1}{2}$ pint/1$\frac{1}{4}$ cups fish stock
salt and ground black pepper

Serves 4

1   Place the prawns in a mixing bowl. Stir in half the soy sauce and 30ml/2 tbsp of the olive oil. Cover and marinate overnight in the fridge.

2   Cook the pasta in plenty of boiling salted water according to the instructions on the packet.

3   Meanwhile, heat the remaining oil in a wok or frying pan and fry the prawns for 1 minute.

4   Add the pepper, broccoli, spring onions, ginger and oregano and stir-fry for about 1–2 minutes.

5   Drain the pasta thoroughly, set aside and keep warm. Meanwhile, in a bowl, blend together the sherry and cornflour until smooth. Stir in the stock and remaining soy sauce until well blended.

6   Pour the stock mixture into the wok or pan, bring to the boil and stir-fry for 2 minutes until thickened. Pour over the pasta and serve.

Rigatoni with Tuna and Olive Sauce

THIS COLOURFUL SAUCE combines well
with a thicker and shorter pasta.

INGREDIENTS

350g/12oz/3 cups dried rigatoni
30ml/2 tbsp olive oil
1 onion, chopped
2 garlic cloves, chopped
400g/14oz can chopped tomatoes
50g/2oz/4 tbsp tomato purée
50g/2oz/1/2 cup pitted black
  olives, quartered
15ml/1 tbsp chopped fresh oregano
225g/8oz can tuna in oil, drained
  and flaked
2.5ml/1/2 tsp anchovy purée
15ml/1 tbsp capers, rinsed
115g/4oz/1 cup grated Cheddar cheese
45ml/3 tbsp fresh white breadcrumbs
salt and ground black pepper
flat leaf parsley sprigs, to garnish
Serves 4

1 Cook the pasta in plenty of boiling
salted water according to the
instructions on the packet.

2 Meanwhile, heat the oil in a frying
pan and fry the onion and garlic
for about 10 minutes until softened.

3 Add the tomatoes, tomato purée,
and salt and pepper, and bring to
the boil. Simmer gently for 5 minutes,
stirring occasionally.

4 Stir the olives, oregano, tuna,
anchovy purée and capers into
the pan. Spoon the mixture into a
separate mixing bowl.

5 Drain the pasta, toss well in the
sauce and spoon into flameproof
serving dishes.

6 Preheat the grill and sprinkle the
cheese and breadcrumbs evenly
over the pasta. Place under the grill for
about 10 minutes until the pasta is
heated through and the cheese
topping has melted. Serve at once,
garnished with flat leaf parsley.

Spaghetti with Bottarga

ALTHOUGH THIS MAY SEEM an unusual recipe, with bottarga (salted and air-dried mullet or tuna roe) as the principal ingredient, it is very well known in Sardinia – and also in Sicily and parts of southern Italy. It is simplicity itself to make and tastes very, very good.

INGREDIENTS

350g/12oz fresh or dried spaghetti
about 60ml/4 tbsp olive oil
2–3 garlic cloves, peeled
ground black pepper
60–90ml/4–6 tbsp grated bottarga, to taste
Serves 4

1 Cook the pasta according to the instructions on the packet.

2 Meanwhile, heat half the olive oil in a large saucepan. Add the garlic and cook gently, stirring, for a few minutes. Remove the pan from the heat, scoop out the garlic with a slotted spoon and discard, leaving the garlic-flavoured oil in the bottom.

3 Drain the pasta very well. Return the pan of oil to the heat and add the pasta. Toss well, season with pepper and moisten with the remaining oil, or more to taste. Divide the pasta among four warmed bowls, sprinkle the grated bottarga over the top and serve immediately.

COOK'S TIP

You can buy bottarga in Italian delicatessens. Small jars of ready-grated bottarga are convenient, but the best flavour comes from vacuum-packed slices of mullet bottarga. This is very easy to grate on a box grater. Keep any leftover bottarga in the fridge, tightly wrapped so that it does not taint other foods.

Spaghetti with Tuna, Mushrooms and Bacon

THE ITALIAN TERM for this dish, *alla carrettiera*, means "cart-driver's style". The Romans lay claim to the recipe, as do the Neapolitans and Sicilians, so there are lots of versions.

INGREDIENTS

15g/¹/₂oz dried porcini mushrooms
175ml/6fl oz/³/₄ cup warm water
30ml/2 tbsp olive oil
1 garlic clove
75g/3oz pancetta or rindless streaky bacon,
*   cut into 5mm/¹/₄in strips*
225g/8oz/3 cups button
*   mushrooms, chopped*
400g/14oz fresh or dried spaghetti
200g/7oz can tuna in olive oil, drained
salt and ground black pepper
freshly grated Parmesan cheese, to serve
Serves 4

1 Put the porcini in a small bowl. Pour the warm water over and leave to soak for 15–20 minutes.

2 Heat the oil in a large saucepan, add the garlic clove and cook gently for about 2 minutes, crushing it with a wooden spoon to release the flavour. Remove the garlic and discard. Add the pancetta or bacon to the oil remaining in the pan and cook for 3–4 minutes, stirring occasionally.

3 Meanwhile, drain the dried mushrooms, reserving the soaking liquid, and chop them finely.

4 Add both types of mushroom to the pan and cook, stirring, for 1–2 minutes, then add 90ml/6 tbsp of the reserved liquid from soaking the dried mushrooms, with salt and pepper to taste. Simmer for 10 minutes, stirring occasionally. Meanwhile, cook the pasta according to the instructions on the packet, adding the remaining soaking liquid from the mushrooms to the pasta cooking water.

5 Add the drained canned tuna to the mushroom sauce and fold it in gently. Taste for seasoning.

6 Drain the cooked pasta well and tip it into a warmed serving bowl. Pour the sauce over the top, toss well and sprinkle liberally with some freshly grated Parmesan. Serve immediately, with more Parmesan handed around separately.

Penne with Prawns and Feta Cheese

THIS DISH COMBINES the richness of fresh prawns with the tartness of feta cheese. If you find feta cheese a little too salty, soak it in fresh, cold water or milk for a few minutes, to make it less salty.

INGREDIENTS

450g/1lb raw prawns in the shell
6 spring onions
225g/8oz feta cheese
50g/2oz/4 tbsp butter
small bunch fresh chives
450g/1lb penne, garganelle or rigatoni
salt and ground black pepper
Serves 4

COOK'S TIP

If fresh prawns are not available, use well-thawed frozen, and add to the sauce at the last minute together with the spring onions.

VARIATION

Another cheese that works well with this dish is goat's cheese.

1 Remove the heads from the prawns by twisting gently and pulling off. Peel the body of the prawns and discard the shells.

2 On a nylon chopping board, chop the spring onions and the feta cheese using a sharp knife. Put them to one side.

3 Melt the butter in a large saucepan and stir in the peeled prawns. When they turn pink, add the chopped spring onions and cook gently over a low heat for about 1 minute, stirring.

4 Stir the chopped feta cheese into the prawn mixture in the saucepan and season with ground black pepper.

5 Snip the chives into 2.5cm/1in lengths on a plate. Tip half of them into the prawn mixture and toss well to combine.

6 Cook the pasta in plenty of boiling salted water according to the instructions on the packet.

7 Drain well and spoon into warmed serving dishes. Top with the sauce. Scatter with the remaining chives and serve immediately.

Black Tagliatelle with Scallops

A STUNNING PASTA DISH using black tagliatelle with a contrasting white fish sauce.

INGREDIENTS

120ml/4fl oz/ 1/2 cup low-fat crème fraîche

10ml/2 tsp wholegrain mustard

2 garlic cloves, crushed

30–45ml/2–3 tbsp fresh lime juice

60ml/4 tbsp chopped fresh parsley

30ml/2 tbsp snipped chives

350g/12oz fresh or dried black tagliatelle

12 large scallops

60ml/4 tbsp white wine

150ml/ 1/4 pint/ 2/3 cup fish stock

salt and ground black pepper

lime wedges and parsley sprigs, to garnish

Serves 4

1 To make the tartare sauce, mix the crème fraîche, mustard, garlic, lime juice, herbs and seasoning together in a bowl.

2 Cook the pasta in a large pan of boiling, salted water until *al dente*: 8–10 minutes, or according to the instructions on the packet. Drain the pasta thoroughly.

3 Slice each of the scallops in half horizontally. Keep any coral whole. Put the white wine and fish stock into a medium saucepan and heat until the mixture reaches simmering point. Add the scallops to the pan and cook very gently for 3–4 minutes (do not be tempted to cook them for any longer or they will become tough).

4 Remove the scallops from the pan with a slotted spoon. Boil the wine and stock to reduce by half and add the tartare sauce to the pan.

5 Heat the combined mixture gently to warm, replace the scallops and cook gently for 1 minute. Spoon over the pasta and garnish with lime wedges and sprigs of parsley.

Tagliatelle with Smoked Salmon

THIS IS A PRETTY PASTA DISH with the light texture of the cucumber complementing the fish perfectly.

INGREDIENTS

350g/12oz fresh or dried tagliatelle
1/2 cucumber
75g/3oz/6 tbsp butter
grated rind of 1 orange
30ml/2 tbsp chopped fresh dill
300ml/1/2 pint/1 1/4 cups single cream
15ml/1 tbsp orange juice
115g/4oz smoked salmon, skinned
salt and ground black pepper
Serves 4

1 Cook the pasta in plenty of boiling salted water according to the instructions on the packet.

4 Melt the butter in a large saucepan, add the orange rind and dill and stir well. Add the sliced cucumber and cook gently for 2 minutes, stirring occasionally.

6 Meanwhile, cut the salmon into thin strips. Stir into the sauce and heat through.

5 Add the cream and orange juice, and season to taste. Then simmer for 1 minute.

7 Drain the pasta thoroughly and toss in the sauce until well coated. Serve immediately.

2 Using a sharp knife, cut the cucumber in half lengthways then, using a small spoon, scoop out the seeds and discard.

3 Turn the cucumber over onto the flat side and slice thinly along the length.

Spaghetti with Clam Sauce

THIS IS ONE OF ITALY'S most famous pasta dishes, sometimes known as "white clam sauce" to distinguish it from that other classic, clams in tomato sauce. It is how they serve clams with pasta in Venice.

INGREDIENTS

1kg/2¼lb fresh clams
60ml/4 tbsp olive oil
45ml/3 tbsp chopped fresh flat leaf parsley
120ml/4fl oz/½ cup dry white wine
350g/12oz dried spaghetti
2 garlic cloves
salt and ground black pepper
Serves 4

1 Scrub the clams under cold running water, discarding any that are open or that do not close when sharply tapped against the work surface.

2 Heat half the oil in a large saucepan, add the clams and 15ml/1 tbsp of the parsley and cook over a high heat for a few seconds. Pour in the wine, then cover tightly. Cook for about 5 minutes, shaking the pan frequently, until the clams have opened. Meanwhile, cook the pasta in salted boiling water according to the instructions on the packet.

3 Using a slotted spoon, transfer the clams to a bowl, discarding any that have failed to open. Strain the liquid and set it aside. Put eight clams in their shells to one side for the garnish, then remove the rest from their shells.

4 Heat the remaining oil in the clean pan. Fry the whole garlic cloves over a medium heat until golden, crushing them with the back of a spoon. Remove the garlic with a slotted spoon and discard.

5 Add the shelled clams to the oil remaining in the pan, gradually add some of the strained liquid from the clams, then add plenty of pepper. Cook for 1–2 minutes, gradually adding more liquid as the sauce reduces. Add the remaining parsley and cook for 1–2 minutes.

6 Drain the pasta, add it to the pan and toss well. Serve in individual dishes, scooping the shelled clams from the bottom of the pan and placing some of them on top of each serving. Garnish with the reserved clams in their shells and serve immediately.

Penne with Prawns and Artichokes

THIS IS A GOOD DISH TO MAKE in late spring or early summer, when greeny-purple baby artichokes appear in shops and on market stalls.

INGREDIENTS

juice of ¹/₂ lemon
4 baby globe artichokes
90ml/6 tbsp olive oil
2 garlic cloves, crushed
30ml/2 tbsp chopped fresh mint
30ml/2 tbsp chopped fresh flat leaf parsley
350g/12oz/3 cups dried penne
8–12 peeled cooked king or tiger prawns,
   each cut into 2–3 pieces
25g/1oz/2 tbsp butter
salt and ground black pepper

Serves 4

1 Have ready a bowl of cold water to which you have added the lemon juice. To prepare the artichokes, cut off the artichoke stalks, if any, and cut across the tops of the leaves. Peel off and discard any tough or discoloured outer leaves.

2 Cut the artichokes lengthways into quarters and remove any hairy chokes from their centres. Finally, cut the pieces of artichoke lengthways into 5mm/¹/₄in slices and put these in the bowl of acidulated water.

3 Drain the slices of artichoke and pat them dry. Heat the olive oil in a non-stick frying pan and add the artichokes, the crushed garlic and half the mint and parsley to the pan.

4 Season with plenty of salt and pepper. Cook over a low heat, stirring frequently, for about 10 minutes or until the artichokes feel tender when pierced with a sharp knife.

5 Meanwhile, cook the pasta in a large saucepan of salted boiling water according to the instructions on the packet.

6 Add the prawns to the artichokes, stir well to mix, then heat through gently for 1–2 minutes.

7 Drain the pasta and tip it into a warmed bowl. Add the butter and toss until it has melted. Spoon the artichoke mixture over the pasta and toss to combine. Serve immediately, sprinkled with the remaining herbs.

Spaghetti with Mussels

MUSSELS ARE POPULAR in all the coastal regions of Italy, and are delicious with pasta. This simple dish is greatly improved by using the freshest mussels available.

INGREDIENTS

900g/2lb fresh mussels, in the shell
75ml/5 tbsp olive oil
3 garlic cloves, finely chopped
60ml/4 tbsp chopped fresh parsley
60ml/4 tbsp white wine
400g/14oz fresh or dried spaghetti
salt and ground black pepper
Serves 4

1 Scrub the mussels well under cold running water, carefully cutting off the "beards" with a small sharp knife. Discard any that do not close when tapped sharply on the work surface.

COOK'S TIP

Mussels should be firmly closed when fresh. If a mussel is slightly open, pinch it closed. If it remains closed on its own, it is alive. If it remains open, discard it. Fresh mussels should be consumed as soon as possible after being purchased. They may be kept in a bowl of cold, salted water in the fridge.

2 Place the mussels with a cupful of water in a large saucepan over a moderate heat. As soon as they open, lift them out one by one with a slotted spoon and set aside.

3 When all the mussels have opened (discard any that do not), strain the cooking liquid in the saucepan through a layer of kitchen paper to remove any grit, and reserve until needed.

4 Heat the oil in a large frying pan. Add the garlic and parsley, and cook for 2–3 minutes. Add the mussels, their cooking liquid and the wine. Cook the sauce over a moderate heat until heated through.

5 Add a generous amount of pepper to the sauce. Taste for seasoning; add salt if necessary.

6 Cook the pasta in plenty of boiling salted water until *al dente*. Drain, then tip it into the frying pan with the sauce, and stir well over a moderate heat for 3–4 minutes. Serve immediately on individual plates.

Spaghetti with Hot-and-Sour Fish

A TRULY CHINESE spicy taste is what makes this sauce so different.

INGREDIENTS

350g/12oz fresh or dried spaghetti
450g/1lb monkfish, skinned
225g/8oz courgettes
1 green chilli, cored and seeded (optional)
15ml/1 tbsp olive oil
1 large onion, chopped
5ml/1 tsp turmeric
115g/4oz/1 cup shelled peas, thawed
  if frozen
10ml/2 tsp lemon juice
75ml/5 tbsp hoisin sauce
150ml/¹/₄ pint/²/₃ cup water
salt and ground black pepper
fresh dill sprig, to garnish

Serves 4

1   Cook the pasta in plenty of boiling salted water according to the instructions on the packet.

2   Cut the monkfish into bite-size pieces. Thinly slice the courgettes, then finely chop the chilli, if using.

3   Heat the oil in a large frying pan and fry the onion for 5 minutes until softened. Add the turmeric.

4   Add the chilli, if using, courgettes and peas, and fry over a medium heat for 5 minutes until the vegetables have softened.

5   Stir in the fish, lemon juice, hoisin sauce and water. Bring the mixture to the boil, then simmer, uncovered, for about 5 minutes or until the fish is tender. Season.

6   Drain the pasta thoroughly and tip into a serving dish. Toss in the sauce to coat. Serve at once, garnished with fresh dill.

Saffron Pappardelle

A WONDERFUL DISH with a delicious shellfish sauce.

INGREDIENTS

large pinch of saffron strands
4 sun-dried tomatoes, chopped
5ml/1 tsp fresh thyme
60ml/4 tbsp hot water
12 large prawns in their shells
225g/8oz baby squid
225g/8oz monkfish fillet
2–3 garlic cloves
2 small onions, quartered
1 small bulb fennel, trimmed and sliced
150ml/¼ pint/⅔ cup white wine
225g/8oz fresh or dried pappardelle
salt and ground black pepper
chopped fresh parsley, to garnish
Serves 4

1 Put the saffron strands, sun-dried tomatoes and thyme into a bowl and pour over the hot water. Mix together and then leave to soak for at least 30 minutes.

2 Wash the prawns and carefully remove the shells, leaving the heads and tails intact.

3 Pull the body from the squid, remove the quill and cut off the tentacles, then rinse. Pull off the outer skin and cut into 5mm/¼in rings. Cut the monkfish into 2.5cm/1in cubes.

4 Put the garlic, onions and fennel into a pan and pour over the wine. Cover and simmer for 5 minutes until tender.

5 Add the monkfish, saffron, tomatoes and thyme in their liquid. Cover and cook for 3 minutes. Then add the prawns and squid. Cover and cook gently for a further 1–2 minutes (do not overcook or the squid will become tough).

6 Meanwhile, cook the pasta in a large pan of boiling, salted water until *al dente*. Drain the pasta thoroughly in the colander.

7 Divide the pasta among four serving dishes and top each one with the fish and shellfish sauce. Sprinkle with chopped fresh parsley and serve at once.

Linguine with Clams, Leeks and Tomatoes

CANNED CLAMS make this a speedy dish for those in a real hurry.

INGREDIENTS

350g/12oz fresh or dried linguine
25g/1oz/2 tbsp butter
2 leeks, thinly sliced
150ml/¼ pint/⅔ cup dry white wine
4 tomatoes, skinned, seeded and chopped
pinch of turmeric (optional)
250g/9oz can clams, drained
30ml/2 tbsp chopped fresh basil
60ml/4 tbsp crème fraîche
salt and ground black pepper
Serves 4

1 Cook the pasta in plenty of boiling salted water according to the instructions on the packet.

2 Meanwhile, melt the butter in a small saucepan and fry the sliced leeks for about 5 minutes until softened but not coloured.

3 Add the wine, tomatoes and turmeric, bring to the boil and boil until reduced by half.

4 Stir in the clams, basil, crème fraîche and seasoning and heat through gently without boiling the sauce.

5 Drain the pasta thoroughly and toss in the clam and leek sauce. Serve immediately.

Macaroni with King Prawns and Ham

COOKED RADICCHIO makes a novel addition to this sauce. The bitter flavour of this salad vegetable mellows on cooking and perfectly complements the rich prawns.

INGREDIENTS

350g/12oz dried short macaroni
45ml/3 tbsp olive oil
12 shelled raw king prawns
1 garlic clove, chopped
175g/6oz/generous 1 cup diced
  smoked ham
150ml/¼ pint/⅔ cup red wine
½ small radicchio lettuce, shredded
2 egg yolks, beaten
30ml/2 tbsp chopped fresh flat leaf parsley
150ml/¼ pint/⅔ cup double cream
salt and ground black pepper
shredded fresh basil, to garnish
Serves 4

1 Cook the pasta in plenty of boiling salted water, according to the instructions on the packet.

2 Meanwhile, heat the oil in a frying pan and cook the prawns, garlic and ham for about 5 minutes, stirring occasionally until the prawns are just opaque and tender. Be careful not to overcook.

3 Add the wine and radicchio, bring to the boil and boil rapidly until the juices are reduced by about half.

4 Tip the egg yolks into the sauce and stir.

5 Now add the parsley and cream and bring almost to the boil, stirring constantly, then simmer until the sauce thickens slightly. Check the seasoning and adjust if necessary.

6 Drain the pasta thoroughly once it is cooked and toss in the sauce to coat. Serve immediately, garnished with some shredded fresh basil.

Rigatoni with Scallop Sauce

A JEWEL FROM THE SEA, the scallop is what makes this sauce so special. Serve with a green salad, if liked.

INGREDIENTS

350g/12oz fresh or dried rigatoni
350g/12oz queen scallops
45ml/3 tbsp olive oil
1 garlic clove, chopped
1 onion, chopped
2 carrots, cut into matchsticks
30 ml/2 tbsp chopped fresh parsley
30ml/2 tbsp dry white wine
30ml/2 tbsp Pernod
150ml/ 1/4 pint/ 2/3 cup double cream
salt and ground black pepper
Serves 4

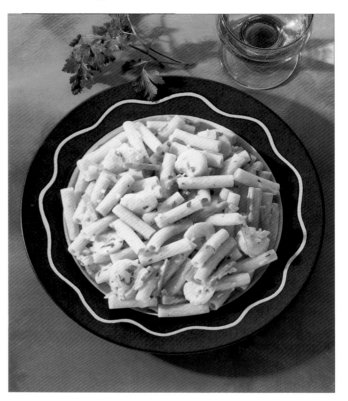

1 Cook the pasta in plenty of boiling salted water according to the instructions on the packet.

2 Trim the scallops, separating the corals from the white eye part of the meat.

3 Using a sharp knife on a board, cut the white eye sections in half lengthways.

4 Heat the oil in a frying pan and fry the garlic, onion and carrots for 5–10 minutes, stirring occasionally, until the carrots are softened.

5 Stir in the scallops, parsley, wine and Pernod and bring to the boil. Cover and simmer for about 1 minute. Using a slotted spoon, transfer the scallops and vegetables to a plate and keep them warm until required.

6 Bring the pan juices back to the boil and boil rapidly until reduced by half. Stir in the cream and heat the sauce through.

7 Return the scallops and cooked vegetables to the sauce in the pan and heat them through. Season the mixture to taste.

8 Drain the pasta thoroughly and toss with the sauce until thoroughly combined. Serve the rigatoni immediately.

Spaghetti with Mussels and Saffron

IN THIS RECIPE the pasta is tossed with a delicious pale yellow mussel sauce, streaked with yellow strands of saffron. Powdered saffron will do just as well, but don't use turmeric – the flavour will be too strong.

INGREDIENTS

900g/2lb live mussels, in the shell
150ml/ $^1/_4$ pint/ $^2/_3$ cup dry white wine
2 shallots, finely chopped
25g/1oz/2 tbsp butter
2 garlic cloves, crushed
10ml/2 tsp cornflour
300ml/ $^1/_2$ pint/1 $^1/_4$ cups double cream
pinch of saffron strands
juice of $^1/_2$ lemon
1 egg yolk
450g/1lb fresh or dried spaghetti
salt and ground black pepper
chopped fresh parsley, to garnish
Serves 4

1 Scrub the mussels and rinse well. Pull off any "beards" and leave the mussels to soak in cold water for 30 minutes. Tap each mussel sharply after this time. Discard any that do not close straightaway.

2 Drain the mussels and place them in a large saucepan. Pour over the wine and add the finely chopped shallots.

3 Cover and cook the mussels, shaking frequently, over a high heat for 5–10 minutes until they are all open. Discard any that do not open.

4 Drain the mussels through a sieve, reserving the liquid. Remove most of the mussels from their shells, reserving some in the shell to use as a garnish. Boil the reserved liquid rapidly until reduced by half.

5 Melt the butter in another saucepan, add the garlic and cook until golden. Stir in the cornflour and gradually stir in the cooking liquid and the cream. Add the saffron and seasoning and simmer until slightly thickened.

6 Stir in lemon juice to taste, then the egg yolk and mussels. Keep warm, but do not boil.

7 Cook the pasta according to the instructions on the packet. Drain well. Toss the mussels with the spaghetti, spoon into individual bowls, top with the reserved mussels and sprinkle with the parsley. Serve with crusty bread, if you like.

Meat
and
Poultry

When we think of a meat sauce to serve with pasta, our minds automatically turn to Bolognese sauce, or *ragù alla Bolognese*, as it is correctly called in Italian. Thanks to Italian emigrés, Bolognese sauce has become one of the most famous pasta sauces outside Italy, especially in Great Britain and the United States. Beef, pork and pancetta simmered with wine and tomatoes until rich, intensely meaty and satisfying, is very hard to beat. Unfortunately, this superb sauce is almost always served with spaghetti outside Italy, which is incorrect. It should be teamed with tagliatelle.

Many meat sauces hail from the north of Italy, especially from the region of Emilia-Romagna, where both fresh meat and the famous hams, salami and sausages are enjoyed in abundance. The actual quantity of meat in the sauce is never very large, however, and the size of the pieces must be small or the sauce will simply slide off the pasta. The egg-enriched pasta of the northern regions is good with meat sauces because it holds the sauce well, but it is by no means the only possibility. Long, thin types of pasta like spaghetti and vermicelli, find favour precisely because they do not hold a great deal of sauce with each forkful, a point worth considering when a meat sauce is very rich.

Tagliatelle with Bolognese Sauce

THIS RECIPE IS an authentic meat sauce – ragù – from the city of Bologna in Emilia-Romagna. It is very rich, and is always served with tagliatelle, never with spaghetti.

INGREDIENTS

450g/1lb fresh or dried tagliatelle
salt and ground black pepper
freshly grated Parmesan cheese, to serve

For the Bolognese meat sauce

25g/1oz/2 tbsp butter
15ml/1 tbsp olive oil
1 onion, finely chopped
2 carrots, finely chopped
2 celery sticks, finely chopped
2 garlic cloves, finely chopped
130g/4½oz pancetta or rindless streaky bacon, diced
250g/9oz lean minced beef
250g/9oz lean minced pork
120ml/4fl oz/½ cup dry white wine
2 x 400g/14oz cans crushed Italian plum tomatoes
475–750ml/16fl oz–1¼ pints/2–3 cups beef stock
100ml/3½fl oz/scant ½ cup panna da cucina or double cream

Serves 6–8

| Make the meat sauce first. Heat the butter and oil in a large skillet or saucepan until sizzling. Add the garlic, vegetables and the pancetta or bacon and cook over a medium heat, stirring frequently, for 10 minutes or until the vegetables have softened.

2 Add the minced beef and pork, lower the heat and cook gently for 10 minutes, stirring frequently and breaking up any lumps in the meat with a wooden spoon. Stir in salt and pepper to taste, then add the wine and stir again. Simmer for about 5 minutes, or until reduced.

3 Add the canned tomatoes and 250ml/8fl oz/1 cup of the beef stock and bring to the boil. Stir the sauce well, then lower the heat. Half cover the pan with a lid and leave to simmer very gently for 2 hours. Stir occasionally during this time and add more stock as it becomes absorbed.

4 Pour the cream into the sauce, stir well to mix, then simmer, without a lid, for another 30 minutes, stirring frequently. Meanwhile, cook the pasta according to the packet instructions. Taste the sauce to check the seasoning. Drain the cooked pasta and tip it into a warmed bowl. Pour the sauce over the pasta and toss well. Serve immediately, sprinkled with grated Parmesan.

VARIATION

Some cooks add a few chopped chicken livers when frying the meat at the beginning of Step 2. This gives the sauce a stronger, almost gamey, flavour.

Spaghetti with Meatballs

TINY MEATBALLS SIMMERED in a sweet and spicy tomato sauce are truly delicious with spaghetti. Children love them and you can easily leave out the chillies.

INGREDIENTS

350g/12oz minced beef
1 egg
60ml/4 tbsp roughly chopped fresh flat
*   leaf parsley*
2.5ml/½ tsp crushed dried red chillies
1 thick slice white bread, crusts removed
30ml/2 tbsp milk
about 30ml/2 tbsp olive oil
300ml/½ pint/1¼ cups passata
400ml/14fl oz/1¾ cups vegetable stock
5ml/1 tsp granulated sugar
350–450g/12oz–1lb fresh or
*   dried spaghetti*
salt and ground black pepper
freshly grated Parmesan cheese, to serve
Serves 6–8

1 Put the minced beef in a large bowl. Add the egg, and half the parsley and crushed chillies. Season with plenty of salt and pepper.

2 Tear the bread into small pieces and place in a small bowl. Moisten with the milk. Leave to soak for a few minutes, then squeeze out the excess milk and crumble the bread over the meat mixture. Mix everything together with a wooden spoon, then use your hands to squeeze and knead the mixture so that it becomes smooth and quite sticky.

3 Wash your hands, rinse them under the cold tap, then pick up small pieces of the mixture and roll them between your palms to make about 60 very small balls. Place the meatballs on a tray and chill in the fridge for about 30 minutes.

4 Heat the oil in a large, deep non-stick frying pan. Cook the meatballs in batches until browned on all sides. Pour the passata and stock into the pan. Heat gently, then add the remaining chillies and the sugar, with salt and pepper to taste. Return all the meatballs to the pan. Bring to the boil, lower the heat and cover. Simmer for 20 minutes.

5 Cook the pasta according to the packet instructions. When it is *al dente*, drain and tip it into a warmed large bowl. Pour the sauce over the pasta and toss gently. Sprinkle with the remaining parsley and serve with grated Parmesan handed separately.

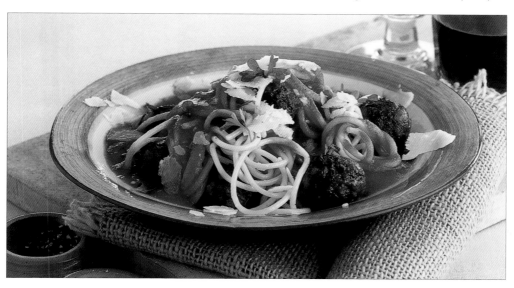

Lamb and Sweet Pepper Sauce

THIS SIMPLE SAUCE is a speciality of
the Abruzzo-Molise region, east of
Rome, where it is traditionally
served with *maccheroni alla chitarra*
– square-shaped long macaroni.

INGREDIENTS

60ml/4 tbsp olive oil
250g/9oz boneless lamb neck fillet, diced
    quite small
2 garlic cloves, finely chopped
2 bay leaves, torn
250ml/8fl oz/1 cup dry white wine
4 ripe Italian plum tomatoes, peeled
    and chopped
2 large red peppers, seeded and diced
salt and ground black pepper
Serves 4–6

1 Heat half the olive oil in a medium
skillet or saucepan, add the small
pieces of lamb and sprinkle with a
little salt and pepper. Cook the meat
over a medium to high heat for about
10 minutes, stirring often, until it is
browned on all sides.

2 Sprinkle in the garlic and add the
bay leaves, then pour in the wine
and let it bubble until reduced.

3 Add the remaining oil, the
tomatoes and the peppers; stir to
mix with the lamb. Season again. Cover
with the lid and simmer over a low
heat for 45–55 minutes or until the
lamb is very tender. Stir occasionally
during cooking and moisten with water
if the sauce becomes too dry. Remove
the bay leaves from the sauce before
serving it with pasta.

COOK'S TIPS

• *The peppers don't have to be red. Use
yellow, orange or green if you prefer;
either one colour or a mixture.*
• *If you need to add water to the sauce
towards the end of cooking, take it from
the pan used for cooking the pasta.*
• *You can make your own fresh*
maccheroni alla chitarra *or buy the
dried pasta from an Italian delicatessen.
Alternatively, this sauce is just as good
with ordinary long or short macaroni. You
will need 350–425g/12–15oz.*

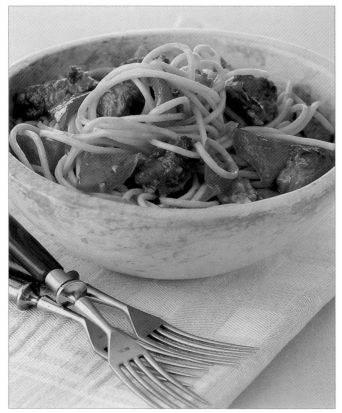

Fusilli with Sausage

SPICY HOT SAUSAGE and tomato sauce combine with spirals of pasta to make this really tasty dish from southern Italy. Pecorino cheese, with its strong and salty flavour, is the perfect accompaniment. Serve for an informal supper party with a full-bodied red wine and crusty country bread.

INGREDIENTS

400g/14oz spicy pork sausages
30ml/2 tbsp olive oil
1 small onion, finely chopped
2 garlic cloves, crushed
1 large yellow pepper, seeded and cut
   into strips
5ml/1 tsp paprika
5ml/1 tsp dried mixed herbs
5–10ml/1–2 tsp chilli sauce
400g/14oz can Italian plum tomatoes
250–300ml/8–10fl oz/1–1¼ cups
   vegetable stock
300g/11oz/2¾ cups fresh or dried fusilli
salt and ground black pepper
freshly grated Pecorino cheese, to serve
Serves 4

1 Grill the sausages for 10–12 minutes until they are browned on all sides, then drain them on kitchen paper.

2 Heat the oil in a large skillet or saucepan, add the onion and garlic and cook over a low heat, stirring frequently, for 5–7 minutes until soft. Add the yellow pepper, paprika, herbs and chilli sauce to taste. Cook gently for 5–7 minutes, stirring occasionally.

3 Tip in the canned tomatoes, breaking them up with a wooden spoon, then add salt and pepper to taste and stir well. Cook over a medium heat for 10–12 minutes, adding the vegetable stock gradually as the sauce reduces.

4 While the tomato sauce is cooking, cut the grilled sausages diagonally into 1cm/½in pieces.

5 Add the sausage pieces to the sauce, reduce the heat to low and cook for 10 minutes. Meanwhile, cook the pasta according to the instructions on the packet.

6 Taste the sauce for seasoning. Drain the pasta and add it to the pan of sauce. Toss well, then divide among four warmed bowls. Sprinkle each serving with a little grated Pecorino and serve immediately, with more Pecorino handed separately.

Rigatoni with Garlic Crumbs

A HOT AND SPICY DISH — halve the quantity of chilli if you like a milder flavour. The bacon is an optional addition; you can leave it out if you are cooking for vegetarians.

INGREDIENTS

45ml/3 tbsp olive oil

2 shallots, chopped

8 rashers streaky bacon, chopped (optional)

10ml/2 tsp crushed dried red chillies

400g/14oz can chopped tomatoes with
garlic and herbs

6 slices white bread

115g/4oz/½ cup butter

2 garlic cloves, chopped

450g/1lb/4 cups fresh or dried rigatoni

salt and ground black pepper

Serves 4–6

COOK'S TIP

To keep the breadcrumbs crisp and dry after frying, drain them on kitchen paper and place in a low oven until ready to use.

1 Heat the oil in a medium saucepan and fry the shallots and bacon, if using, gently for about 6–8 minutes, stirring continuously until golden. Add the dried chillies and chopped tomatoes, half-cover the pan and simmer for 20 minutes.

2 Meanwhile, cut the crusts off the bread and discard them. Reduce the bread to crumbs in a blender or food processor.

3 Heat the butter in a frying pan, add the garlic and breadcrumbs and stir-fry until golden and crisp. (Keep stirring and don't let the crumbs catch and burn or the final result will be ruined.)

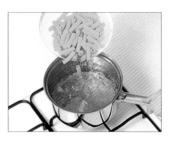

4 Cook the pasta in plenty of boiling salted water according to the instructions on the packet, until *al dente*. Drain well.

5 Toss the pasta with the tomato sauce and divide among four or six warmed serving plates.

6 Sprinkle the pasta with the golden breadcrumbs and serve immediately.

Spaghetti with Eggs and Bacon

ONE OF THE CLASSIC pasta sauces, about which a debate still remains: whether or not it should contain cream. Pasta purists believe that it should not.

INGREDIENTS

30ml/2 tbsp olive oil

150g/5oz bacon, cut into matchsticks

1 garlic clove, crushed

400g/14oz fresh or dried spaghetti

3 eggs, at room temperature

75g/3oz/¾ cup freshly grated
  Parmesan cheese

salt and ground black pepper

Serves 4

1 In a medium frying pan, heat the oil and sauté the bacon and the garlic until the bacon renders its fat and starts to brown. Remove and discard the garlic. Keep the bacon and its fat hot, until needed.

2 Cook the spaghetti in a large saucepan in plenty of rapidly boiling salted water according to the instructions on the packet or until *al dente*.

3 Meanwhile, warm a large serving bowl and break the eggs into it. Beat in the Parmesan cheese with a fork, and season with salt and pepper.

4 As soon as the pasta is done, drain it quickly, and mix it into the egg mixture. Pour on the hot bacon and its fat. Stir well. The heat from the pasta and bacon fat will lightly cook the beaten eggs. Serve immediately.

Piquant Chicken with Spaghetti

THE ADDITION of cucumber and tomatoes adds a deliciously fresh flavour to this unusual dish.

INGREDIENTS

1 onion, finely chopped
1 carrot, diced
1 garlic clove, crushed
300ml/¹/₂ pint/1¹/₄ cups vegetable stock
4 chicken breasts, boned and skinned
1 bouquet garni
115g/4oz button mushrooms, thinly sliced
5ml/1 tsp wine vinegar or lemon juice
350g/12oz fresh or dried spaghetti
¹/₂ cucumber, peeled and cut into fingers
2 tomatoes, skinned, seeded and chopped
30ml/2 tbsp crème fraîche
15ml/1 tbsp chopped fresh parsley
15ml/1 tbsp snipped chives
salt and ground black pepper
Serves 4

1 Put the onion, carrot, garlic, vegetable stock, chicken and bouquet garni into a saucepan.

2 Bring to the boil, cover and simmer for 15–20 minutes or until the chicken is tender. Transfer the chicken to a plate with a slotted spoon and cover with foil.

3 Strain the remaining cooking liquid in the pan. Discard the vegetables and return the liquid to the pan. Add the sliced mushrooms, wine vinegar or lemon juice, then stir and simmer for 2–3 minutes.

4 Cook the spaghetti in plenty of boiling salted water according to the instructions on the packet or until *al dente*. Drain thoroughly.

5 Blanch the cucumber in boiling water for 10 seconds. Drain and rinse under cold water.

6 Cut the chicken breasts into bite-size pieces. Boil the stock to reduce by half, then add the chicken, tomatoes, crème fraîche, cucumber and herbs. Season with salt and pepper to taste.

7 Transfer the spaghetti to a warmed serving dish and spoon over the piquant chicken and tomato sauce. Serve at once.

Eliche with Sausage and Radicchio

SAUSAGE AND RADICCHIO may seem odd companions, but the combined flavour of these ingredients is really delicious. This robust and hearty dish makes a good main course.

INGREDIENTS

30ml/2 tbsp olive oil
1 onion, finely chopped
200g/7oz Italian pure pork sausage
175ml/6fl oz/¾ cup passata
90ml/6 tbsp dry white wine
300g/11oz/2¾ cups dried eliche
50g/2oz radicchio leaves
salt and ground black pepper
Serves 4

1 Heat the olive oil in a large, deep skillet or saucepan. Add the finely chopped onion and cook over a low heat, stirring frequently, for about 5 minutes until softened.

2 Snip the end off the sausage skin and squeeze the sausagemeat into the pan. With a wooden spoon, stir the sausagemeat to mix it with the oil and onion and break it up into small pieces.

3 Continue to fry the mixture, increasing the heat if necessary, until the sausagemeat is brown all over and looks crumbly. Stir in the passata, then sprinkle in the wine, with salt and pepper to taste. Simmer over a low heat, stirring occasionally, for 10–12 minutes.

4 Meanwhile, cook the pasta according to the instructions on the packet. Just before draining the pasta, add a ladleful or two of the cooking water to the sausage sauce and stir it in well. Taste the sauce to check the seasoning.

5 Finely shred the radicchio leaves. Drain the cooked pasta and tip it into the pan of sausage sauce. Add the shredded radicchio and toss well to combine. Serve immediately.

COOK'S TIPS

• *The best sausage to use is the one you buy from the Italian delicatessen called salsiccia puro suino. It is made from 100 per cent pure pork plus flavourings and seasonings.*

• *If you can get it, use the long, tapering radicchio di Treviso for this dish; otherwise the tightly furled, round radicchio can be used.*

Spaghetti with Minced Beef Sauce

SPAGHETTI BOLOGNESE is not an authentic Italian dish. It was "invented" by Italian emigrés in America in the sixties in response to popular demand for a spaghetti dish with meat sauce. This is a rich, spicy version.

INGREDIENTS

30ml/2 tbsp olive oil
1 onion, finely chopped
1 garlic clove, crushed
5ml/1 tsp dried mixed herbs
1.25ml/¼ tsp cayenne pepper
350–450g/12oz–1lb minced beef
400g/14oz can chopped Italian
  plum tomatoes
45ml/3 tbsp tomato ketchup
15ml/1 tbsp sun-dried tomato paste
5ml/1 tsp Worcestershire sauce
5ml/1 tsp dried oregano
450ml/¾ pint/1¾ cups beef or
  vegetable stock
45ml/3 tbsp red wine
400–450g/14oz–1lb dried spaghetti
salt and ground black pepper
freshly grated Parmesan cheese, to serve
Serves 4–6

2 Stir in the canned tomatoes, ketchup, sun-dried tomato paste, Worcestershire sauce, oregano and plenty of black pepper. Pour in the stock and red wine and bring to the boil, stirring. Cover the pan, lower the heat and leave the sauce to simmer for 30 minutes, stirring occasionally.

3 Cook the pasta according to the instructions on the packet. Drain well and divide among warmed bowls. Taste the sauce and add a little salt if necessary, then spoon it on top of the pasta and sprinkle with a little grated Parmesan. Serve immediately, with grated Parmesan handed separately.

1 Heat the oil in a medium saucepan, add the onion and garlic and cook over a low heat, stirring frequently, for about 5 minutes until softened. Stir in the mixed herbs and cayenne and cook for 2–3 minutes more. Add the minced beef and cook gently for about 5 minutes, stirring frequently and breaking up any lumps in the meat with a wooden spoon.

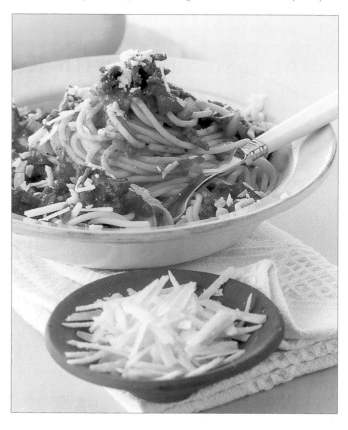

Tortellini with Ham

THIS IS A VERY EASY RECIPE that can be made quickly from storecupboard ingredients. It is therefore ideal for an after-work supper.

INGREDIENTS

250g/9oz packet tortellini alla carne
    (meat-filled tortellini)
30ml/2 tbsp olive oil
1/4 large onion, finely chopped
115g/4oz cooked ham, diced
150ml/1/4 pint/2/3 cup strained crushed
    Italian plum tomatoes
100ml/31/2fl oz/scant 1/2 cup panna da
    cucina or double cream
about 90g/31/2oz/generous 1 cup freshly
    grated Parmesan cheese
salt and ground black pepper
Serves 4

1 Cook the pasta according to the instructions on the packet.

2 Meanwhile, heat the oil in a large skillet or saucepan, add the onion and cook over a low heat, stirring frequently, for about 5 minutes until softened. Add the ham and cook, stirring occasionally, until it darkens.

3 Add the strained crushed tomatoes. Fill the empty carton with water and pour it into the pan. Stir well, then add salt and pepper to taste. Bring to the boil, lower the heat and simmer the sauce for a few minutes, stirring occasionally, until it has reduced slightly. Stir in the cream. Drain the pasta well and add it to the sauce.

4 Add a handful of grated Parmesan to the pan. Stir, toss well and taste for seasoning. Serve in warmed bowls, topped with the remaining Parmesan.

COOK'S TIP

Cartons of strained crushed tomatoes are handy for making quick sauces.

Bolognese Sauce with Red Wine

THIS IS A VERSATILE meat sauce. You can toss it with freshly cooked pasta – the quantity here is enough for 450g/1lb tagliatelle, spaghetti or a short pasta shape such as penne or fusilli – or alternatively you can layer it in a baked dish like lasagne.

INGREDIENTS

1 medium onion
1 small carrot
1 celery stick
2 garlic cloves
45ml/3 tbsp olive oil
400g/14oz minced beef
120ml/4fl oz/1/2 cup red wine
200ml/7fl oz/scant 1 cup passata
15ml/1 tbsp tomato purée
5ml/1 tsp dried oregano
15ml/1 tbsp chopped fresh flat leaf parsley
about 350ml/12fl oz/11/2 cups beef stock
8 baby Italian tomatoes (optional)
salt and ground black pepper
Serves 4–6

1 Chop all the vegetables finely, either in a food processor or by hand. Heat the oil in a large saucepan, add the chopped vegetable mixture and cook over a low heat, stirring frequently, for 5–7 minutes.

2 Add the minced beef and cook for 5 minutes, stirring frequently and breaking up any lumps in the meat with a wooden spoon. Stir in the wine and mix well.

3 Cook for 1–2 minutes, then add the passata, tomato purée, herbs and 60ml/4 tbsp of the stock. Season with salt and pepper to taste. Stir well and bring to the boil.

4 Cover the pan and cook over a gentle heat for 30 minutes, stirring from time to time and adding more stock as necessary. Add the tomatoes, if using, and simmer for 5–10 minutes more. Taste for seasoning and toss with hot, freshly cooked pasta, or use in baked pasta dishes.

Tagliatelle with Parma Ham and Asparagus

A STUNNING SAUCE, this is worth every effort to serve at a dinner party or as a special treat.

INGREDIENTS

350g/12oz fresh or dried tagliatelle
25g/1oz/2 tbsp butter
15ml/1 tbsp olive oil
225g/8oz asparagus tips
1 garlic clove, chopped
115g/4oz Parma ham, sliced into strips
30ml/2 tbsp chopped fresh sage
150ml/¼ pint/⅔ cup single cream
115g/4oz/1 cup grated chive-and-onion
   double Gloucester cheese
115g/4oz/1 cup grated Gruyère cheese
salt and ground black pepper
fresh sage sprigs, to garnish
Serves 4

4 Stir in the chopped sage and fry for a further 1 minute.

5 Pour in the cream and bring the mixture to the boil.

6 Add the cheeses and simmer gently, stirring occasionally, until thoroughly melted. Season.

7 Drain the pasta thoroughly and toss with the sauce to coat. Serve immediately in four warmed plates, garnished with fresh sage sprigs.

1 Cook the pasta in plenty of boiling salted water according to the instructions on the packet.

2 Melt the butter and oil in a frying pan and gently fry the asparagus tips for about 5 minutes, stirring occasionally, until they are almost tender.

3 Stir the garlic and Parma ham into the pan with the asparagus and fry everything for 1 minute.

Tagliatelle with Chicken and Herb Sauce

SERVE THIS DELICIOUS dish with its wine-flavoured sauce and a fresh green salad.

INGREDIENTS

30ml/2 tbsp olive oil
1 red onion, cut into wedges
350g/12oz fresh or dried tagliatelle
1 garlic clove, chopped
350g/12oz chicken, diced
300ml/ ½ pint/1 ¼ cups dry vermouth
45ml/3 tbsp chopped fresh mixed herbs
150ml/ ¼ pint/ ⅔ cup fromage frais
salt and ground black pepper
shredded fresh mint, to garnish

Serves 4

1 Heat the oil in a large frying pan and fry the red onion for 10 minutes until softened but not coloured and the layers have separated.

2 Cook the pasta in plenty of boiling salted water according to the instructions on the packet.

3 Add the garlic and chicken to the frying pan and fry for 10 minutes, stirring occasionally, until the chicken is browned all over and cooked through.

4 Pour in the vermouth, bring to boiling point and boil rapidly until reduced by about half.

5 Stir in the herbs, fromage frais and seasoning and heat through gently, but do not boil.

6 Drain the pasta thoroughly and spoon the sauce over. Toss the mixture to coat the pasta. Serve immediately, garnished with shredded fresh mint.

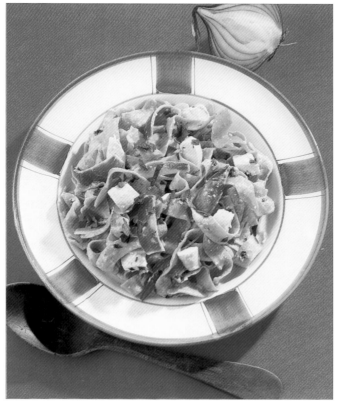

Farfalle with Chicken and Cherry Tomatoes

QUICK TO PREPARE and easy to cook, this colourful dish is full of flavour. Serve it for a midweek supper, with a green salad to follow.

INGREDIENTS

350g/12oz skinless chicken breast fillets, cut into bite-size pieces
60ml/4 tbsp Italian dry vermouth
10ml/2 tsp chopped fresh rosemary, plus 4 fresh rosemary sprigs, to garnish
15ml/1 tbsp olive oil
1 onion, finely chopped
90g/3½oz piece Italian salami, diced
275g/10oz/2½ cups dried farfalle
15ml/1 tbsp balsamic vinegar
400g/14oz can Italian cherry tomatoes
good pinch of crushed dried red chillies
salt and ground black pepper

Serves 4

1 Put the pieces of chicken in a large bowl, pour in the dry vermouth and sprinkle with half the chopped rosemary and salt and pepper to taste. Stir well and set aside.

2 Heat the oil in a large skillet or saucepan, add the onion and salami and fry over a medium heat for about 5 minutes, stirring frequently.

3 Cook the pasta according to the instructions on the packet.

4 Add the chicken and vermouth to the onion and salami, increase the heat to high and fry for 3 minutes or until the chicken is white on all sides. Sprinkle the vinegar over the chicken.

5 Add the cherry tomatoes and dried chillies. Stir well and simmer for a few minutes more. Taste the sauce for seasoning.

6 Drain the pasta and tip it into the skillet or saucepan. Add the remaining chopped rosemary and toss to mix the pasta and sauce together. Serve immediately in warmed bowls, garnished with the rosemary sprigs.

COOK'S TIP

The tomatoes look good left whole, but if you prefer you can crush them with the back of a wooden spoon while they are simmering in the pan.

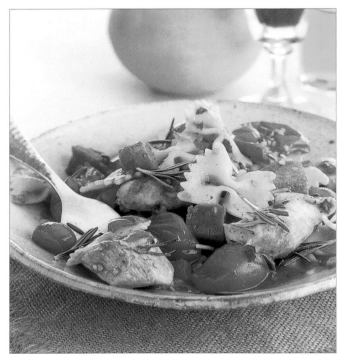

Penne with Chicken, Broccoli and Cheese

THE COMBINATION OF BROCCOLI, garlic and Gorgonzola is very good, and goes especially well with chicken.

INGREDIENTS

115g/4oz/scant 1 cup broccoli florets, divided into tiny sprigs
50g/2oz/¼ cup butter
2 skinless chicken breast fillets, cut into thin strips
2 garlic cloves, crushed
400g/14oz/3½ cups dried penne
120ml/4fl oz/½ cup dry white wine
200ml/7fl oz/scant 1 cup panna da cucina or double cream
90g/3½oz Gorgonzola cheese, rind removed and diced small
salt and ground black pepper
freshly grated Parmesan cheese, to serve

Serves 4

1 Plunge the broccoli into a saucepan of boiling salted water. Bring back to the boil and boil for 2 minutes, then drain in a colander and refresh under cold running water. Shake well to remove the surplus water and set aside to drain completely.

2 Melt the butter in a large skillet or saucepan, add the chicken and garlic, with salt and pepper to taste, and stir well. Fry over a medium heat for 3 minutes or until the chicken becomes white. Meanwhile, start cooking the pasta according to the instructions on the packet.

3 Pour the wine and cream over the chicken mixture in the pan, stir to mix, then simmer, stirring occasionally, for about 5 minutes until the sauce has reduced and thickened. Add the broccoli, increase the heat and toss to heat it through and mix it with the chicken. Taste for seasoning.

4 Drain the pasta and tip it into the sauce. Add the Gorgonzola and toss well. Serve with grated Parmesan.

VARIATION

Use leeks instead of broccoli if you prefer. Fry them with the chicken.

Penne with Sausage and Parmesan Sauce

SPICY SAUSAGE tossed in a cheesy tomato sauce is delicious served on a bed of cooked pasta.

INGREDIENTS

350g/12oz/3 cups dried penne
450g/1lb ripe tomatoes
30ml/2 tbsp olive oil
225g/8oz chorizo sausage,
*   diagonally sliced*
1 garlic clove, chopped
30ml/2 tbsp chopped fresh flat leaf parsley
grated rind of 1 lemon
50g/2oz/½ cup freshly grated
*   Parmesan cheese*
salt and ground black pepper
finely chopped fresh flat leaf parsley,
*   to garnish*

Serves 4

1 Cook the pasta in plenty of boiling salted water according to the instructions on the packet.

2 Slash the bottoms of the tomatoes with a knife, making a cross. Place in a large bowl, cover with boiling water and leave to stand for 45 seconds. Plunge into cold water for 30 seconds, then peel off the skins and roughly chop the flesh.

3 Heat the oil in a frying pan and fry the sliced chorizo sausage for 5 minutes, stirring from time to time, until browned.

4 Add the chopped tomatoes, garlic, parsley and grated lemon rind. Heat through gently, stirring, for 1 minute.

5 Finally, add the grated Parmesan cheese to the sauce, stir to combine and season to taste.

6 Drain the pasta well through a colander and toss it with the sauce to coat. Serve immediately, garnished with finely chopped fresh flat leaf parsley.

Fusilli with Chicken and Tomato

A RECIPE FOR a speedy supper –
serve this dish with a mixed
bean salad.

INGREDIENTS

15ml/1 tbsp olive oil
1 onion, chopped
1 carrot, chopped
50g/2oz sun-dried tomatoes in olive oil,
   drained weight
1 garlic clove, chopped
400g/14oz can chopped tomatoes, drained
15ml/1 tbsp tomato purée
150ml/¼ pint/⅔ cup chicken stock
350g/12oz/3 cups dried fusilli
225g/8oz chicken, diagonally sliced
salt and ground black pepper
fresh mint sprigs, to garnish
Serves 4

3 Stir the garlic, tomatoes, tomato
purée and stock into the onions
and carrots in the frying pan and bring
to the boil. Simmer for 10 minutes,
stirring occasionally.

4 Cook the pasta in plenty of
boiling salted water according to
the instructions on the packet.

5 Pour the sauce into a blender or
food processor and process until
smooth and well blended.

6 Return the sauce to the pan and
stir in the sun-dried tomatoes and
chicken. Bring back to the boil and then
simmer for 10 minutes until the
chicken is cooked. Adjust the
seasoning, if necessary.

7 Drain the pasta thoroughly and
toss in the sauce. Serve at once,
garnished with sprigs of fresh mint.

1 Heat the oil in a large frying pan
and fry the chopped onion and
carrot for 5 minutes, stirring the
vegetables occasionally.

2 Chop the sun-dried tomatoes and
set aside until needed.

Sardinian Sausage and Pasta

IN SARDINIA THEY CALL this dish simply "malloreddus", which is the local name for the type of pasta traditionally used to make it.

INGREDIENTS

30ml/2 tbsp olive oil

6 garlic cloves

200g/7oz Italian pure pork sausage, diced small

2 small handfuls fresh basil leaves

400g/14oz can chopped Italian plum tomatoes

a good pinch of saffron threads

15ml/1 tbsp granulated sugar

350g/12oz/3 cups dried malloreddus (gnocchi sardi)

75g/3oz/1 cup freshly grated Pecorino sardo cheese

salt and ground black pepper

Serves 4–6

1 Heat the oil in a medium skillet or saucepan. Add the garlic, sausage and half the basil leaves. Fry, stirring frequently, until the sausage is browned all over. Remove and discard the garlic. Add the tomatoes. Fill the empty can with water, pour it into the pan, then stir in the saffron, sugar, 5ml/1 tsp salt and pepper to taste. Bring to the boil, lower the heat and simmer for 20–30 minutes, stirring occasionally.

2 Meanwhile, cook the pasta in a pan of salted boiling water according to the packet instructions.

3 Drain the pasta and tip it into a warmed bowl. Taste the sauce for seasoning, pour it over the pasta and toss well. Add about one-third of the grated Pecorino and the remaining basil and toss well to mix again. Serve immediately, with the remaining Pecorino sprinkled on top.

COOKS TIP

In Sardinia, a special type of sausage is used for malloreddus. It is flavoured with aniseed and black pepper and is called sartizzu sardo. A good alternative to sartizzu sardo would be the piquant salsiccia piccante. If, however, you prefer a slightly milder flavour, try luganega, which is much more widely available. Some butchers make their own Italian-style sausage on the premises, in which case you can always ask the butcher if he will season it for you with aniseed and black pepper if you want to try and create the authentic taste for yourself.

Rigatoni with Bresaola and Peppers

BRESAOLA – CURED RAW BEEF – is usually served thinly sliced as an antipasto. Here its strong, almost gamey, flavour is used to good effect.

INGREDIENTS

30ml/2 tbsp olive oil

1 small onion, finely chopped

150g/5oz bresaola, cut into thin strips

4 peppers (red and orange or yellow), diced

120ml/4fl oz/½ cup dry white wine

400g/14oz can chopped plum tomatoes

450g/1lb/4 cups dried rigatoni

50g/2oz/⅔ cup freshly shaved Parmesan cheese

1 small handful fresh basil leaves

salt and ground black pepper

Serves 6

1 Heat the oil in a medium saucepan, add the onion and bresaola. Cover the pan and cook over a low heat for 5–8 minutes until the onion has softened. Stir in the basil leaves, then add the peppers, wine, 5ml/1 tsp salt and plenty of pepper. Stir well, then simmer for 10–15 minutes.

2 Add the canned tomatoes to the pan and increase the heat to high. Bring to the boil, stirring, then lower the heat and replace the lid again. Simmer gently, stirring occasionally, for 20 minutes or until the peppers are very soft and quite creamy. Meanwhile, cook the pasta in a pan of salted boiling water according to the instructions on the packet.

3 Drain the cooked pasta and tip it into a warmed bowl. Taste the sauce for seasoning, then pour it over the pasta and add half the Parmesan. Toss well and serve immediately, with the basil leaves and the remaining Parmesan sprinkled on top.

Pappardelle with Chicken and Mushrooms

RICH AND CREAMY, this is a good supper party dish.

INGREDIENTS

15g/½oz dried porcini mushrooms
175ml/6fl oz/¾ cup warm water
25g/1oz/2 tbsp butter
1 small leek or 4 spring onions, chopped
1 garlic clove, crushed
1 small handful fresh flat leaf parsley,
    roughly chopped
120ml/4fl oz/½ cup dry white wine
250ml/8fl oz/1 cup chicken stock
400g/14oz fresh or dried pappardelle
2 skinless chicken breast fillets, cut into
    thin strips
105ml/7 tbsp mascarpone cheese
salt and ground black pepper
fresh basil leaves, shredded, to garnish

Serves 4

1 Put the dried mushrooms in a bowl. Pour in the warm water and leave to soak for 15–20 minutes. Tip into a fine sieve set over a bowl and squeeze the mushrooms with your hands to release as much liquid as possible.

2 Chop the mushrooms finely and set aside the strained soaking liquid until required.

3 Melt the butter in a medium skillet or saucepan, add the chopped mushrooms, leek or spring onions, garlic and parsley, with salt and pepper to taste. Cook over a low heat, stirring frequently, for about 5 minutes, then pour in the wine and stock and bring to the boil. Lower the heat and simmer for about 5 minutes or until the liquid has reduced and is thickened.

4 Meanwhile, start cooking the pasta in salted boiling water according to the packet instructions, adding the reserved soaking liquid from the mushrooms to the water.

5 Add the chicken strips to the sauce and simmer for 5 minutes or until just tender. Add the mascarpone a spoonful at a time, stirring well after each addition, then add one or two spoonfuls of the water used for cooking the pasta. Taste for seasoning.

6 Drain the pasta and tip it into a warmed large bowl. Add the chicken and sauce and toss well. Serve immediately, topped with the shredded basil leaves.

VARIATIONS

• Add 115g/4oz/1 cup sliced button or chestnut mushrooms with the chicken.
• Add blanched sprigs of broccoli before the mascarpone in Step 5.

Conchiglie with Chicken Livers and Herbs

FRESH HERBS AND CHICKEN livers are a good combination, often used together on crostini in Tuscany. Here they are tossed with pasta shells to make a very tasty supper dish.

INGREDIENTS

50g/2oz/¼ cup butter

115g/4oz pancetta or rindless streaky
    bacon, diced

250g/9oz frozen chicken livers, thawed,
    drained and diced

2 garlic cloves, crushed

10ml/2 tsp chopped fresh sage

300g/11oz/2¾ cups dried conchiglie

150ml/¼ pint/⅔ cup dry white wine

4 ripe Italian plum tomatoes, peeled
    and diced

15ml/1 tbsp chopped fresh flat
    leaf parsley

salt and ground black pepper

Serves 4

1 Melt half the butter in a medium skillet or saucepan, add the pancetta or bacon and fry over a medium heat for a few minutes until it is lightly coloured but not crisp.

2 Add the chicken livers, garlic, half the sage and plenty of pepper. Increase the heat and toss the livers for about 5 minutes, until they change colour all over. Meanwhile, start cooking the pasta according to the instructions on the packet.

3 Pour the wine over the chicken livers in the pan and let it sizzle, then lower the heat and simmer gently for 5 minutes. Add the remaining butter to the pan. As soon as it has melted, add the diced tomatoes, toss to mix, then add the remaining sage and the parsley. Stir well. Taste and add salt if needed.

4 Drain the pasta and tip it into a warmed bowl. Pour the sauce over and toss well. Serve immediately.

Twin Cities Meatballs

SERVE THESE meatballs without gravy
as drinks party nibbles.

INGREDIENTS

30ml/2 tbsp butter or margarine
½ small onion, minced
350g/12oz/2¼ cups minced beef
115g/4oz/1 cup minced veal
225g/8oz/2 cups minced pork
1 egg
40g/1½oz/½ cup mashed potatoes
30ml/2 tbsp finely chopped fresh dill
  or parsley
1 garlic clove, crushed
5ml/1 tsp salt
2.5ml/½ tsp black pepper
2.5ml/½ tsp ground allspice
1.5ml/¼ tsp grated nutmeg
40g/1½oz/¾ cup fresh breadcrumbs
175ml/6fl oz/¾ cup milk
25g/1oz/¼ cup plain flour plus
  15ml/1 tbsp extra
30ml/2 tbsp olive oil
350g/12oz fresh or dried fettucini
175ml/6fl oz/¾ cup evaporated milk
Serves 6

1 Melt the butter or margarine in a
large frying pan. Add the onion and
cook, stirring, over a low heat until
softened but not brown, about
8–10 minutes. Remove the pan from
the heat. Using a slotted spoon,
transfer the cooked onion to a large
mixing bowl.

2 Add the beef, veal and pork, the
egg, mashed potatoes, dill or
parsley, garlic, salt, pepper, allspice and
nutmeg to the bowl.

3 Put the breadcrumbs in a
separate small bowl and add the
milk. Stir until well moistened, then add
to the other ingredients in the large
mixing bowl. Mix well.

4 Shape the mixture into balls
about 2.5cm/1in in diameter.

5 Place 25g/1oz/¼ cup of the flour
on a plate and roll the meatballs
in the flour until coated all over. Shake
off the excess flour.

6 Add the olive oil to the frying pan
and heat over a medium heat.
Add the meatballs to the pan and
brown on all sides for 8–10 minutes.
Shake the pan occasionally to roll the
balls so that they colour and cook
evenly. With a slotted spoon, remove
the meatballs to a serving dish. Cover
with foil and keep warm.

7 Cook the pasta in salted boiling
water until al dente.

8 Meanwhile, stir the 15ml/1 tbsp of
flour into the fat in the frying pan.
Add the evaporated milk and mix in
thoroughly with a small whisk. Simmer
for 3–4 minutes.

9 Drain the pasta and serve hot with
the meatballs and gravy poured over.

Peasant Bolognese

A SPICY VERSION of a popular dish.
Worcestershire sauce and chorizo
sausages add an extra element to
this perfect family standby.

INGREDIENTS

15ml/1 tbsp oil
225g/8oz/2 cups minced beef
1 onion, chopped
5ml/1 tsp chilli powder
15ml/1 tbsp Worcestershire sauce
25g/1oz/2 tbsp plain flour
150ml/¼ pint/⅔ cup beef stock
4 chorizo sausages
50g/2oz baby sweetcorn
200g/7oz can chopped tomatoes
15ml/1 tbsp chopped fresh basil
salt and ground black pepper
fresh basil, to garnish
450g/1lb cooked spaghetti, to serve

Serves 4

1 Heat the oil in a large pan and fry
the minced beef for
5 minutes. Add the onion and chilli
powder to the pan and cook for a
further 3 minutes.

COOK'S TIP

*Make the Bolognese sauce and freeze
in conveniently sized portions for up to
two months.*

2 Stir the Worcestershire sauce and
flour into the pan, making sure it is
well combined.

3 Continue to cook for 1 minute
then pour in the stock.

4 Slice the chirozo sausages and
halve the corn lengthways.

5 Stir the sliced sausages, tomatoes,
sweetcorn and chopped basil into
the pan. Season and bring the sauce to
the boil. Reduce the heat and simmer
for 30 minutes.

6 Serve hot, with spaghetti,
garnished with fresh basil leaves.

Fettuccine with Ham and Peas

THIS SIMPLE DISH MAKES a very good first course for six people, or a main course for three to four. The ingredients are all easily available from the supermarket, so the recipe makes an ideal impromptu supper.

INGREDIENTS

50g/2oz/¼ cup butter
1 small onion, finely chopped
200g/7oz/1¾ cups fresh or frozen peas
100ml/3½fl oz/scant ½ cup
  chicken stock
2.5ml/½ tsp granulated sugar
175ml/6fl oz/⅔ cup dry white wine
350g/12oz fresh fettuccine
75g/3oz piece cooked ham, cut into
  bite-size chunks
115g/4oz/1⅓ cups freshly grated
  Parmesan cheese
salt and ground black pepper
Serves 3–6

1 Melt the butter in a medium skillet or saucepan, add the onion and cook over a low heat for about 5 minutes until softened but not coloured. Add the peas, stock and sugar, with salt and pepper to taste.

2 Bring to the boil, then lower the heat and simmer for 3–5 minutes or until the peas are tender. Add the wine, increase the heat and boil until the wine has reduced.

3 Cook the pasta according to the instructions on the packet. When it is almost ready, add the ham to the sauce, with about a third of the grated Parmesan. Heat through, stirring, then taste for seasoning.

4 Drain the pasta and tip it into a warmed large bowl. Pour the sauce over the pasta and toss well. Serve immediately, sprinkled with the remaining grated Parmesan.

Pappardelle with Rabbit Sauce

THIS RICH-TASTING DISH comes from the north of Italy, where rabbit sauces for pasta are very popular.

INGREDIENTS

15g/½oz dried porcini mushrooms
175ml/6fl oz/¾ cup warm water
1 small onion
½ carrot
½ celery stick
2 bay leaves
25g/1oz/2 tbsp butter
15ml/1 tbsp olive oil
40g/1½oz pancetta or rindless streaky
   bacon, chopped
15ml/1 tbsp roughly chopped fresh flat
   leaf parsley, plus extra to garnish
250g/9oz boneless rabbit meat
90ml/6 tbsp dry white wine
200g/7oz can chopped Italian plum
   tomatoes or 200ml/7fl oz/scant
   1 cup passata
300g/11oz fresh or dried pappardelle
salt and ground black pepper
Serves 4

1 Put the dried mushrooms in a bowl, pour over the warm water and leave to soak for 15–20 minutes. Finely chop the vegetables, either in a food processor or by hand. Make a tear in each bay leaf, so that they will release their flavour when added to the sauce.

2 Heat the butter and oil in a skillet or medium saucepan until just sizzling. Add the chopped vegetables, pancetta or bacon and the parsley and cook for about 5 minutes.

3 Add the pieces of rabbit and fry on both sides for 3–4 minutes. Pour the wine over and let it reduce for a few minutes, then add the tomatoes or passata. Drain the mushrooms and pour the soaking liquid into the pan. Chop the mushrooms and add them to the mixture, with the bay leaves and salt and pepper to taste. Stir well, cover and simmer for 35–40 minutes until the rabbit is tender, stirring occasionally.

4 Remove the pan from the heat and lift out the pieces of rabbit with a slotted spoon. Cut them into bite-size chunks and stir them into the sauce. Remove and discard the bay leaves. Taste the sauce and add more salt and pepper, if needed. Cook the pasta according to the instructions on the packet. Meanwhile, reheat the sauce. Drain the pasta and toss with the sauce in a warmed bowl. Serve immediately, sprinkled with parsley.

Tagliatelle with Devilled Kidneys

ASK YOUR BUTCHER to prepare the kidneys for you if you prefer.

INGREDIENTS
8–10 lambs' kidneys
15ml/1 tbsp sunflower oil
25g/1oz/2 tbsp butter
10ml/2 tsp paprika
5–10ml/1–2 tsp mild grainy mustard
salt
225g/8oz fresh tagliatelle
chopped fresh parsley, to garnish
Serves 4

1 Cut the kidneys in half and neatly cut out the white cores with scissors. Cut the kidneys in half again if very large.

2 Heat the oil and butter together. Add the kidneys and cook, turning frequently, for about 2 minutes. Blend the paprika and mustard together with a little salt and stir into the pan.

3 Continue cooking the kidneys, basting frequently, for a further 3–4 minutes.

4 Cook the pasta for about 10–12 minutes, or according to the instructions on the packet. Serve the kidneys and their sauce, topped with the chopped fresh parsley, and accompanied by the pasta.

Golden-topped Eliche

WHEN IT COMES TO the children helping you to plan the menus, this is the sort of dish that always wins hands down. It is also perfect for "padding out" if you have to feed eight instead of four people.

INGREDIENTS
225g/8oz/2 cups dried eliche
115g/4oz/²⁄₃ cup chopped cooked ham, beef or turkey
350g/12oz par-cooked mixed vegetables, such as carrots, cauliflower, beans, etc
5–10ml/1–2 tsp oil

For the cheese sauce
25g/1oz/2 tbsp butter
25g/1oz/2 tbsp plain flour
300ml/½ pint/1¼ cups milk
175g/6oz/1½ cups grated Cheddar cheese
5–10ml/1–2 tsp mustard
salt and ground black pepper
Serves 4–6

1 Cook the pasta according to the instructions on the packet. Drain and place in a flameproof dish with the chopped meat, the mixed vegetables and oil.

2 Melt the butter in a saucepan, stir in the flour and cook for 1 minute, stirring. Remove from the heat and gradually stir in the milk. Return to the heat, bring to the boil, stirring and cook for 2 minutes. Add half the cheese, the mustard and seasoning to taste.

3 Spoon the sauce over the meat and vegetables. Sprinkle with the rest of the cheese and grill quickly until golden and bubbling. Allow to stand for a few minutes before serving.

VARIATION

Any mature hard cheese is suitable for the topping. Red Leicester will give the sauce a deep golden colour and is always a favourite with hungry children.

Fusilli Col Buco with Pepperoni

A WARMING SUPPER DISH, perfect for a cold winter's night. All types of sausage are suitable, but if using raw sausages, add them with the onion to cook thoroughly.

INGREDIENTS

1 onion
1 red pepper
1 green pepper
30ml/2 tbsp olive oil, plus extra for tossing the pasta
800g/1¾ lb canned chopped tomatoes
30ml/2 tbsp tomato purée
10ml/2 tsp paprika
175g/6oz pepperoni or chorizo sausage
45ml/3 tbsp chopped fresh parsley
450g/1lb dried fusilli col buco
salt and ground black pepper
Serves 4

1 Chop the onion. Halve, core and seed the peppers. Cut the flesh into dice.

2 Heat the oil in a medium saucepan, add the onion and cook for 2–3 minutes until beginning to colour and soften, but before they go brown.

3 Add the peppers, tomatoes, tomato purée and paprika to the pan and bring to the boil. Simmer uncovered for about 15–20 minutes until reduced and thickened.

4 Slice the pepperoni or chorizo and stir into the sauce with 30ml/2 tbsp of the chopped parsley. Season to taste with salt and pepper.

5 While the sauce is simmering, cook the pasta in plenty of boiling salted water according to the instructions on the packet. Drain well. Toss the pasta with the remaining parsley in a little extra olive oil. Divide among four warmed bowls and top with the prepared sauce.

Tagliatelle with Prosciutto and Parmesan

THIS IS A REALLY SIMPLE DISH, prepared in minutes from the best ingredients.

INGREDIENTS

115g/4oz prosciutto
450g/1lb fresh or dried tagliatelle
75g/3oz/6 tbsp butter
50g/2oz/½ cup freshly grated
  Parmesan cheese
salt and ground black pepper
a few fresh sage leaves, to garnish
Serves 4

1 Cut the prosciutto into strips the same width as the tagliatelle. Cook the pasta in plenty of boiling salted water according to the instructions on the packet.

2 Meanwhile, melt the butter gently in a saucepan, stir in the prosciutto strips and heat through over a very gentle heat, being careful not to let them colour.

3 Drain the tagliatelle through a colander and pile into a warmed serving dish.

4 Sprinkle the Parmesan cheese over and pour the buttery prosciutto on the top. Season well with black pepper and garnish with the sage leaves.

Bucatini with Sausage and Pancetta

THIS IS A VERY RICH and satisfying main course dish. It hardly needs grated Parmesan cheese as an accompaniment, but you can hand some round in a separate bowl if you wish.

INGREDIENTS

115g/4oz pork sausagemeat
400g/14oz can Italian plum tomatoes
15ml/1 tbsp olive oil
1 garlic clove, crushed
115g/4oz pancetta or rindless streaky bacon, roughly chopped
30ml/2 tbsp chopped fresh flat leaf parsley
400g/14oz dried bucatini
60–75ml/4–5 tbsp panna da cucina or double cream
2 egg yolks
salt and ground black pepper
Serves 4

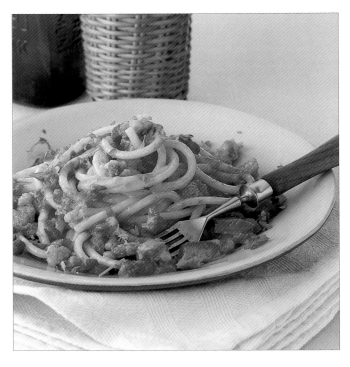

1 Remove any skin from the sausage-meat and break the meat up roughly with a knife. Purée the tomatoes in a food processor or blender.

2 Heat the oil in a medium skillet or saucepan, add the garlic and fry over a low heat for 1–2 minutes. Remove the garlic with a slotted spoon and discard it.

3 Add the pancetta or bacon and the pork sausagemeat and cook over a medium heat for 3–4 minutes. Stir constantly with a wooden spoon to break up the sausagemeat – it will become brown and look crumbly.

4 Add the puréed tomatoes to the pan with half the parsley and salt and pepper to taste. Stir well and bring to the boil, scraping up any sediment from the sausagemeat that has stuck to the bottom of the pan.

5 Lower the heat, cover and simmer for 30 minutes, stirring from time to time. Taste the sausagemeat sauce for seasoning.

6 Meanwhile, cook the pasta according to the instructions on the packet. Put the cream and egg yolks in a warmed large bowl and mix with a fork. As soon as the pasta is *al dente*, drain it well and add it to the bowl of cream mixture. Toss until the pasta is coated, then pour the sausage-meat sauce over the pasta and toss again. Serve immediately, sprinkled with the remaining parsley.

COOK'S TIPS

• *To save time puréeing the tomatoes, use passata.*
• *For authenticity, buy salsiccia a metro, a pure pork sausage sold in lengths at Italian delicatessens.*
• *Bucatini is a long hollow pasta that looks like hard drinking straws; spaghetti works equally well.*

Rigatoni with Pork

THIS IS AN EXCELLENT meat sauce using minced pork rather than the more usual minced beef. Here it is served with rigatoni, a short tubular pasta shape, but you could serve it with tagliatelle or spaghetti to make a pork version of Bolognese.

INGREDIENTS

1 small onion
1/2 carrot
1/2 celery stick
2 garlic cloves
25g/1oz/2 tbsp butter
30ml/2 tbsp olive oil
150g/5oz minced pork
60ml/4 tbsp dry white wine
400g/14oz can chopped Italian
   plum tomatoes
a few fresh basil leaves, plus extra basil
   leaves, to garnish
400g/14oz/3 1/2 cups dried rigatoni
salt and ground black pepper
freshly shaved Parmesan cheese,
   to serve

Serves 4

1 Chop all the fresh vegetables finely, either in a food processor or by hand. Heat the butter and oil in a large skillet or saucepan until just sizzling, add the chopped vegetables and cook over a medium heat, stirring frequently, for 3–4 minutes.

2 Add the minced pork and cook gently for 2–3 minutes, breaking up any lumps in the meat with a wooden spoon.

3 Lower the heat and fry for a further 2–3 minutes, stirring frequently, then stir in the wine. Mix in the tomatoes, whole basil leaves, salt to taste and plenty of pepper. Bring to the boil, then lower the heat, cover and simmer for 40 minutes, stirring from time to time.

4 Cook the pasta according to the instructions on the packet. Just before draining it, add a ladleful or two of the cooking water to the sauce. Stir well, then taste the sauce for seasoning.

5 Drain the pasta, add it to the pan of sauce and toss well. Serve immediately, sprinkled with the shredded basil and shaved Parmesan.

VARIATION

To give the sauce a more intense flavour, soak 15g/1/2oz dried porcini mushrooms in 175ml/6fl oz/3/4 cup warm water for 15–20 minutes, then drain, chop and add with the meat.

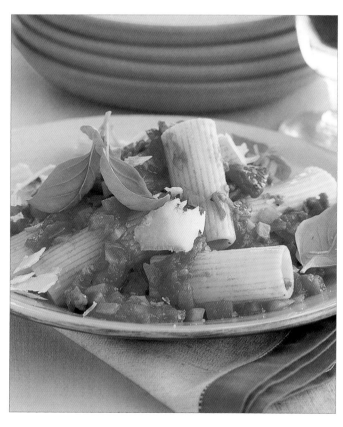

Cavatappi with Mushroom and Chorizo

THE DELICIOUS COMBINATION of wild mushrooms and spicy sausage make this a tempting supper dish.

INGREDIENTS

350g/12oz dried cavatappi
60ml/4 tbsp olive oil
1 garlic clove, chopped
1 celery stick, chopped
225g/8oz chorizo sausage, sliced
225g/8oz mixed mushrooms, such as
*   oyster, brown cap and shiitake*
15ml/1 tbsp lemon juice
30ml/2 tbsp chopped fresh oregano
salt and ground black pepper
finely chopped fresh parsley, to garnish
Serves 4

1 Cook the pasta in plenty of boiling salted water according to the instructions on the packet.

2 Heat the oil in a frying pan and cook the garlic and celery for 5 minutes until the celery is softened but not browned.

COOK'S TIP

Use any combination of mushrooms for this full-bodied sauce, but take care not to overcook them or they will lose their robust, earthy flavour.

3 Add the chorizo and cook for 5 minutes, stirring from time to time, until browned.

4 Next add the mushrooms, either chopped or whole, depending on their size, and cook for a further 4 minutes, stirring from time to time, until they are slightly softened.

5 Stir in the remaining ingredients, and heat through.

6 Drain the pasta well through a colander and tip into a large serving dish. Add the sauce to the pasta and toss to coat. Serve immediately, garnished with finely chopped fresh parsley.

Penne with Chicken and Ham Sauce

A MEAL IN ITSELF, this colourful pasta sauce is perfect for lunch or supper.

INGREDIENTS

350g/12oz/3 cups dried penne
25g/1oz/2 tbsp butter
1 onion, chopped
1 garlic clove, chopped
1 bay leaf
450ml/³⁄4 pint/1³⁄4 cups dry white wine
150ml/¹⁄4 pint/²⁄3 cup crème fraîche
225g/8oz cooked chicken, skinned, boned and diced
115g/4oz cooked lean ham, diced
115g/4oz Gouda cheese, grated
15ml/1 tbsp chopped fresh mint
salt and ground black pepper
finely shredded fresh mint, to garnish
Serves 4

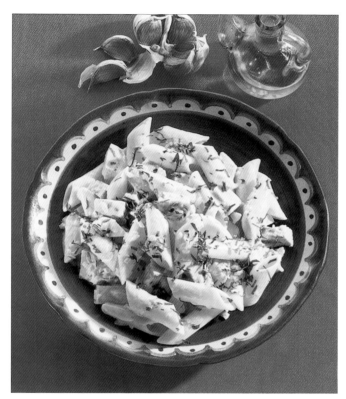

1 Cook the pasta in plenty of boiling salted water according to the instructions on the packet.

2 Heat the butter in a large frying pan and fry the onion for about 10 minutes, or until softened.

3 Add the garlic, bay leaf and wine and bring to the boil. Boil rapidly until reduced by about half. Remove the bay leaf, then stir in the crème fraîche and return to the boil.

4 Add the chicken, ham and grated Gouda cheese and simmer for 5 minutes, stirring occasionally until heated through.

5 Add the chopped fresh mint and season to taste.

6 Drain the pasta thoroughly and tip it into a large serving dish. Toss the pasta with the sauce, garnish with finely shredded fresh mint and serve immediately.

Spaghetti with Bacon and Tomato Sauce

THIS SUBSTANTIAL SAUCE is a meal in itself, so serve it up as a warming winter supper.

INGREDIENTS

15ml/1 tbsp olive oil
225g/8oz smoked streaky bacon, rinded and roughly chopped
250g/9oz fresh or dried spaghetti
5ml/1 tsp chilli powder
1 quantity Classic Tomato Sauce (see Curly Lasagne with Classic Tomato Sauce)
salt and ground black pepper
roughly chopped fresh flat leaf parsley, to garnish
Serves 4

1 Heat the oil in large frying pan and fry the bacon for about 10 minutes, stirring occasionally until crisp and golden.

2 Cook the pasta following the instructions on the packet, until *al dente*.

3 Add the chilli powder to the bacon and cook for 2 minutes. Stir in the tomato sauce and bring to the boil. Cover and simmer for 10 minutes. Season with salt and pepper to taste.

4 Drain the pasta thoroughly and toss it together with the sauce. Serve garnished with the roughly chopped fresh parsley.

Tagliatelle with Pea and Ham Sauce

A COLOURFUL SAUCE, this is ideal served with crusty Italian or French bread.

INGREDIENTS

350g/12oz fresh or dried tagliatelle
225g/8oz/1 1/2 cups shelled peas
300ml/1/2 pint/1 1/4 cups single cream
50g/2oz/1/3 cup freshly grated fontina cheese
75g/3oz prosciutto (Parma ham), sliced into strips
salt and ground black pepper
Serves 4

1 Cook the pasta following the instructions on the packet until *al dente*.

2 Plunge the peas into a pan of boiling salted water and cook for about 7 minutes or until tender. Drain.

3 Place the cream and half the fontina cheese in a small saucepan and heat gently, stirring constantly until heated through.

4 Drain the pasta thoroughly and tip it into a large serving bowl. Toss together the pasta, ham and peas and pour on the sauce. Add the remaining cheese and season with salt and pepper to taste.

Two-way Chicken and Vegetables

THIS TENDER slow-cooked chicken makes a tasty lunch or supper, with the stock and remaining vegetables providing a nourishing soup as a second meal.

INGREDIENTS

1.5 kg/3¹/₂ lb chicken

2 onions, quartered

3 carrots, thickly sliced

2 celery sticks, chopped

1 parsnip or turnip, thickly sliced

50 g/2 oz/¹/₂ cup button mushrooms, with
    stalks, roughly chopped

1–2 fresh thyme sprigs or 5 ml/1 tsp
    dried thyme

4 bay leaves

large bunch of fresh parsley

pasta, mangetouts or French beans, to serve
    with the chicken

115 g/4 oz/1 cup dried wholemeal
    pasta shapes, for the soup

sea salt and ground black pepper

Serves 6

1   Trim the chicken of any extra fat. Put it in a flameproof casserole and add the vegetables and herbs. Pour in water to cover. Bring to the boil over a medium heat, skimming off any scum. When the water boils, lower the heat and simmer for 2–3 hours.

2   Carve the meat neatly, discarding the skin and bones, but returning any small pieces of chicken to the pan. Serve the chicken with some of the vegetables from the pan, plus the pasta of your choice and mangetouts or French beans, if you like.

3   Remove any large pieces of parsley and thyme from the pan, let the remaining mixture cool, then chill it overnight. Next day, lift off the fat that has solidified on the surface. Reheat the soup gently.

4   When the soup comes to the boil, add the pasta shapes, with salt, if required, and cook for 10–12 minutes or until the pasta is tender. Season the soup with salt and plenty of ground black pepper and garnish with sprigs of fresh parsley.

Pork Meatballs with Spaghetti

SERVE THESE TASTY MEATBALLS on a bed
of freshly cooked corn spaghetti,
which is gluten-free.

INGREDIENTS

450g/1lb lean minced pork
1 leek, finely chopped
115g/4oz/1½ cups mushrooms, finely
   chopped
15ml/1 tbsp chopped fresh thyme
15ml/1 tbsp tomato purée
1 egg, beaten
30ml/2 tbsp potato flour
15ml/1 tbsp sunflower oil
350–500g/12oz–1¼lb fresh or dried
   corn spaghetti
fresh thyme sprigs, to garnish

For the tomato sauce

1 onion, finely chopped
1 carrot, finely chopped
1 celery stick, finely chopped
1 garlic clove, crushed
675g/1½lb ripe tomatoes, skinned, seeded
   and chopped
150ml/¼ pint/⅔ cup dry white wine
150ml/¼ pint/⅔ cup well-flavoured
   vegetable stock
15ml/1 tbsp tomato purée
15ml/1 tbsp chopped fresh basil
salt and ground black pepper

Serves 6

1 Preheat the oven to 180°C/350°F/
Gas 4. Put the pork, leek,
mushrooms, chopped thyme, tomato
purée, egg and potato flour in a bowl
and mix together. Shape into small
balls, place on a plate, cover and chill.

2 Place all the sauce ingredients in a
small saucepan, season to taste,
then bring to the boil. Boil, uncovered,
for 10 minutes until thickened.

3 Heat the oil in a frying pan, add
the meatballs and cook in batches
until lightly browned.

4 Place the meatballs in a shallow,
ovenproof dish and pour the
sauce over. Cover and bake for 1 hour.

5 Meanwhile, cook the pasta in a
pan of lightly salted, boiling water
for 8–12 minutes, or according to the
packet instructions, until al dente. Rinse
under boiling water and drain. Divide
the pasta into warmed bowls, spoon
the meatballs and sauce over the top
and serve garnished with fresh thyme.

Rigatoni with Meat and Cheese Sauce

THE TWO SAUCES complement each other perfectly in this wonderfully flavoursome dish.

INGREDIENTS

350g/12oz/3 cups dried rigatoni
salt and ground black pepper
fresh basil sprigs, to garnish

For the meat sauce
15ml/1 tbsp olive oil
350g/12oz/3 cups minced beef
1 onion, chopped
1 garlic clove, chopped
400g/14oz can chopped tomatoes
15ml/1 tbsp dried mixed herbs
30ml/2 tbsp tomato purée

For the cheese sauce
50g/2oz/¼ cup butter
50g/2oz/½ cup plain flour
450ml/¾ pint/1¾ cups milk
2 egg yolks
50g/2oz/½ cup freshly grated
  Parmesan cheese
Serves 4

1 To make the meat sauce, heat the oil in a large frying pan and fry the beef for 10 minutes, stirring occasionally until browned all over. Add the onion to the pan and cook for 5 minutes, stirring occasionally.

2 Stir in the garlic, tomatoes, herbs and tomato purée. Bring to the boil, cover, and simmer for about 30 minutes.

3 Meanwhile, to make the cheese sauce, melt the butter in a small saucepan, then add in the flour and cook for 2 minutes, stirring constantly.

4 Remove the pan from the heat and gradually pour in the milk, stirring constantly. Return the pan to the heat and bring to the boil, stirring the mixture occasionally, until creamy and thickened.

5 Add the egg yolks, cheese and seasoning and stir until the sauce is well blended.

6 Preheat the grill. Meanwhile, cook the pasta in plenty of salted boiling water according to the instructions on the packet. Drain thoroughly and tip into a large mixing bowl. Pour the meat sauce over and toss to coat.

7 Divide the pasta among four flameproof dishes. Spoon over the cheese sauce and place under the grill until brown. Serve immediately, garnished with fresh basil.

Spaghetti in a Cream and Bacon Sauce

THIS IS A LIGHT and creamy sauce flavoured with bacon and lightly cooked eggs.

INGREDIENTS

350g/12oz fresh or dried spaghetti
15ml/1 tbsp olive oil
1 onion, chopped
115g/4oz rindless streaky bacon or
  pancetta, diced
1 garlic clove, chopped
3 eggs
300ml/½ pint/1¼ cups double cream
50g/2oz freshly grated Parmesan cheese
chopped fresh basil, to garnish
Serves 4

1 Cook the pasta in plenty of boiling salted water according to the instructions on the packet.

2 Heat the oil in a frying pan and fry the onion and bacon or pancetta for 10 minutes, until softened. Stir in the garlic and fry for a further 2 minutes, stirring occasionally.

3 Meanwhile, beat the eggs in a bowl, then stir in the cream and seasoning. Add the Parmesan cheese and stir into the egg and cream mixture.

4 Stir the cream mixture into the onion and bacon or pancetta and cook over a low heat for a few minutes, stirring constantly, until heated through. Season to taste.

5 Drain the pasta thoroughly and tip into a large serving dish. Pour the sauce over and toss to coat. Serve immediately, garnished with chopped fresh basil.

Classic Meat Sauce

THIS IS A RICH meat sauce which is ideal to serve with all types of pasta. The sauce definitely improves if kept overnight in the fridge. This allows the flavours time to mature.

INGREDIENTS

450g/1lb/4 cups minced beef
115g/4oz smoked streaky beacon, rinded
    and chopped
1 onion, chopped
2 celery sticks, chopped
15ml/1 tbsp plain flour
150ml/¼ pint/⅔ cup chicken stock
    or water
45ml/3 tbsp tomato purée
1 garlic clove, chopped
45ml/3 tbsp chopped fresh mixed herbs,
    such as oregano, parsley, marjoram
    and chives or 15ml/1 tbsp dried
    mixed herbs
15ml/1 tbsp redcurrant jelly
350g/12oz dried pasta shapes, such
    as fusilli
salt and ground black pepper
chopped oregano, to garnish
Serves 4

1 Heat a large saucepan and fry the beef and bacon for about 10 minutes, stirring occasionally until lightly browned.

2 Add the chopped onion and celery and cook for 2 minutes, stirring occasionally.

COOK'S TIP

The redcurrant jelly helps to draw out the flavour of the tomato purée. You can use a sweet mint jelly or chutney instead, if you like.

3 Stir in the flour and cook for 2 minutes, stirring constantly.

4 Pour in the stock or water and bring to the boil.

5 Stir in the tomato purée, garlic, herbs, redcurrant jelly and seasoning. Bring to the boil, cover and simmer for about 30 minutes.

6 Cook the pasta in plenty of boiling salted water according to the instructions on the packet until *al dente*. Drain thoroughly and turn into a large serving dish. Pour the sauce over and toss to coat. Serve the pasta immediately, garnished with chopped fresh oregano.

Penne with Pancetta and Cream

THIS MAKES a gloriously rich supper dish. Follow it with a simple salad.

INGREDIENTS

300g/11oz/2¾ cups dried penne
30ml/2 tbsp olive oil
1 small onion, finely chopped
175g/6oz pancetta rashers, any rinds
   removed, cut into bite-size strips
1–2 garlic cloves, crushed
5 egg yolks
175ml/6fl oz/¾ cup double cream
115g/4oz/1⅓ cups grated Parmesan
   cheese, plus extra to serve
salt and freshly ground black pepper
Serves 3–4

COOK'S TIP

Serve this dish the moment it is ready or it will not be hot enough. Having added the egg yolks, don't return the pan to the heat or attempt to reheat the pasta and cream sauce together or the egg yolks will scramble and give the pasta a curdled appearance.

1 Cook the penne in a large pan of rapidly boiling salted water for about 10 minutes or until *al dente*.

2 Meanwhile, heat the oil in a large flameproof casserole. Add the onion and cook gently for about 5 minutes, stirring, until softened. Add the pancetta and garlic. Cook over a medium heat until the pancetta is cooked but not crisp. Remove the pan from the heat and set aside.

3 Put the egg yolks in a jug and add the cream and Parmesan cheese. Grind in plenty of black pepper. Beat well to mix.

4 Drain the penne thoroughly, tip into the casserole and toss over a medium to high heat until the pancetta mixture is evenly mixed with the pasta.

5 Remove from the heat, pour in the egg yolk mixture and toss well to combine. Spoon into a large shallow serving dish, grind a little black pepper over and sprinkle with some of the extra Parmesan. Serve the rest of the Parmesan separately.

Cannelloni Stuffed with Meat

CANNELLONI ARE RECTANGLES of home-made egg pasta which are spread with a filling, rolled up and baked in a sauce. In this recipe, they are baked in a béchamel sauce.

INGREDIENTS

30ml/2 tbsp olive oil
1 onion, very finely chopped
225g/8oz/1½ cups very lean minced beef
75g/3oz/½ cup finely chopped
  cooked ham
15ml/1 tbsp chopped fresh parsley
30ml/2 tbsp tomato purée, softened in
  15ml/1 tbsp warm water
1 egg
1 quantity Pasta with Eggs
750ml/1¼ pints/3 cups béchamel sauce
50g/2oz/½ cup freshly grated
  Parmesan cheese
40g/1½oz/3 tbsp butter
salt and ground black pepper
Serves 6–8

1 Prepare the meat filling by heating the oil in a medium saucepan. Add the onion and sauté gently until translucent. Stir in the beef, crumbling it with a fork, and stirring constantly until it has lost its raw red colour. Cook for about 3–4 minutes.

2 Remove from the heat and turn the beef mixture into a large bowl with the ham and parsley. Add the tomato purée mixture and the egg, and mix well to combine. Season with salt and pepper. Set aside.

3 If you are making the pasta yourself, do not let it dry before cutting it into rectangles, about 13–15cm/5–6in long and as wide as they come from the machine (7.5cm/3in if you are not using a pasta machine).

4 Bring a very large pan of water to the boil. Place a large bowl of cold water near the cooker. Cover a large work surface with a tablecloth. Add salt to the rapidly boiling water. Drop in three or four of the egg pasta rectangles. Cook very briefly, for about 30 seconds. Remove them from the pan and plunge them into the cold water, shake off the excess and lay them out flat on the tablecloth. Continue until all the pasta has been cooked in this way.

5 Preheat the oven to 220°C/425°F/Gas 7. Select a shallow baking dish large enough to take all the cannelloni in one layer. Butter the base and sides of the dish and smear about 30–45ml/ 2–3 tbsp of béchamel sauce over the base.

6 Stir about one-third of the remaining sauce into the meat filling. Spread a thin layer of filling on each pasta rectangle. Roll the rectangles up loosely starting from a long side, Swiss-roll style. Place the filled cannelloni in the baking dish with their open edges underneath.

7 Spoon the rest of the sauce over the cannelloni, pushing a little down between each pasta roll. Sprinkle the top with the grated Parmesan and dot with butter. Bake in the oven for about 20 minutes. Allow to rest for 5–8 minutes before serving on warmed plates.

Vegetables
and
Vegetarian

Pasta really comes into its own when it is served
with a vegetable sauce. After all, when pasta was first
"invented" it was a food for the poor, and vegetables were
often all they could afford.

Vegetable sauces are invariably simple, in fact the simpler
the better. Modern recipes often consist of nothing more
elaborate than chopped or sliced raw vegetables "cooked" by
the heat of freshly drained pasta. Colour, crunch and flavour
are all retained, along with maximum nutritive value.

Almost all the recipes in this chapter can be cooked in
a very short time, making them perfect for quick after-
work suppers. Not all of them contain vegetables;
some simply consist of butter and herbs, cheese
and pepper, garlic and oil. These are the easiest of
all pasta sauces to make, and some of the best.

Traditional vegetable sauces come from the south
of Italy, where commercially dried pasta is favoured
more than fresh. Generally speaking, dried pasta does
seem to be the best choice for serving with vegetables,
but for extra nutritional value there is no reason why
fresh, egg-enriched pasta cannot be used.

Trenette with Pesto, French Beans and Potatoes

IN LIGURIA, IT IS TRADITIONAL to serve pesto with trenette, French beans and diced potatoes. The ingredients for making fresh pesto are quite expensive, so the French beans and potatoes are added to help make the pesto go further.

INGREDIENTS

about 40 fresh basil leaves
2 garlic cloves, thinly sliced
25ml/1 1/2 tbsp pine nuts
45ml/3 tbsp freshly grated Parmesan
  cheese, plus extra to serve
30ml/2 tbsp freshly grated Pecorino cheese,
  plus extra to serve
60ml/4 tbsp extra virgin olive oil
2 potatoes, total weight about 250g/9oz
100g/3 1/2oz French beans
350g/12oz dried trenette
salt and ground black pepper
Serves 4

1 Put the basil leaves, garlic, pine nuts and cheeses in a blender or food processor and process for about 5 seconds. Add half the olive oil and a pinch of salt and process for 5 seconds more. Stop the machine, remove the lid and scrape down the side of the bowl. Add the remaining oil and process for 5–10 seconds.

2 Cut the potatoes in half length-ways. Slice each half crossways into 5mm/1/4in thick slices. Top and tail the beans, then cut them into 2cm/3/4in pieces. Plunge the potatoes and beans into a large saucepan of salted boiling water and boil, uncovered, for 5 minutes.

3 Add the pasta, bring the water back to the boil, stir well, then cook for 5–7 minutes or until the pasta is al dente.

4 Meanwhile, put the pesto in a large bowl and add 45–60ml/3–4 tbsp of the water used for cooking the pasta. Mix well.

5 Drain the pasta and vegetables, add them to the pesto and toss well. Serve immediately on warmed plates, with extra grated Parmesan and Pecorino handed separately.

COOK'S TIPS

• Don't worry if the potatoes break up during cooking – this will add to the creaminess of the finished dish.
• The pesto can be made up to 2–3 days in advance and kept in a bowl in the fridge until needed. Pour a thin film of olive oil over the surface of the pesto and cover the bowl tightly with clear film before refrigerating.
• Trenette is the traditional Ligurian pasta that is served with pesto, but if you find it difficult to obtain you can use bavette or linguine instead. The two-coloured paglia e fieno would be another good choice.

Paglia e Fieno with Sun-dried Tomatoes and Radicchio

THIS IS A LIGHT, MODERN PASTA dish of the kind served in fashionable restaurants. It is the presentation that sets it apart, not the preparation, which is very quick and easy.

INGREDIENTS

45ml/3 tbsp pine nuts
350g/12oz dried paglia e fieno
45ml/3 tbsp extra virgin olive oil
30ml/2 tbsp sun-dried tomato paste
2 pieces drained sun-dried tomatoes in olive
*   oil, cut into very thin slivers*
40g/1½oz radicchio leaves, finely shredded
4–6 spring onions, thinly sliced into rings
salt and ground black pepper
Serves 4

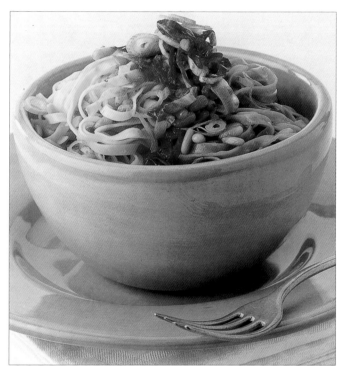

1 Put the pine nuts in a non-stick frying pan and toss over a low to medium heat for 1–2 minutes or until they are lightly toasted and golden. Remove and set aside.

2 Cook the pasta according to the packet instructions, keeping the colours separate by using two pans.

3 While the pasta is cooking, heat 15ml/1 tbsp of the oil in a medium skillet or saucepan. Add the sun-dried tomato paste and the sun-dried tomatoes, then stir in 2 ladlefuls of the water used for cooking the pasta. Simmer until the sauce is slightly reduced, stirring constantly.

4 Mix in the shredded radicchio, then taste and season if necessary. Keep on a low heat. Drain the paglia e fieno, keeping the colours separate, and return the noodles to the pans in which they were cooked. Add about 15ml/1 tbsp oil to each pan and toss over a medium to high heat until the pasta is glistening with the oil.

5 Arrange a portion of green and white pasta in each of four warmed bowls, then spoon the sun-dried tomato and radicchio mixture in the centre. Sprinkle the spring onions and toasted pine nuts decoratively over the top and serve immediately. Before eating, each diner should toss the sauce ingredients with the pasta to mix well.

COOK'S TIP

If you find the presentation too fiddly, you can toss the sun-dried tomato and radicchio mixture with the pasta in one large warmed bowl before serving, then serve it sprinkled with the spring onions and toasted pine nuts.

Penne with Artichokes

Artichokes are a very popular vegetable in Italy, and are often used in sauces for pasta. This sauce is garlicky and richly flavoured, the perfect dinner party first course during the globe artichoke season.

INGREDIENTS

juice of ¹/₂–1 lemon

2 globe artichokes

30ml/2 tbsp olive oil

1 small fennel bulb, thinly sliced, with feathery tops reserved

1 onion, finely chopped

4 garlic cloves, finely chopped

1 handful fresh flat leaf parsley, roughly chopped

400g/14oz can chopped Italian plum tomatoes

150ml/¹/₄ pint/²/₃ cup dry white wine

350g/12oz/3 cups dried penne

10ml/2 tsp capers, chopped

salt and ground black pepper

freshly grated Parmesan cheese, to serve

Serves 6

1 Have ready a bowl of cold water to which you have added the juice of half a lemon. Cut off the artichoke stalks, then discard the outer leaves until the pale inner leaves that are almost white at the base remain.

2 Cut off the tops of these leaves so that the base remains. Cut the base in half lengthways, then prise the hairy choke out of the centre with the tip of the knife and discard. Cut the artichokes lengthways into 5mm/¹/₄in slices, adding them immediately to the bowl of acidulated water.

3 Bring a large saucepan of water to the boil. Add a good pinch of salt, then drain the artichokes and add them immediately to the water. Boil for 5 minutes, drain and set aside.

4 Heat the oil in a large skillet or saucepan and add the fennel, onion, garlic and parsley. Cook over a low to medium heat, stirring frequently, for about 10 minutes until the fennel has softened and is lightly coloured.

5 Add the tomatoes and wine, with salt and pepper to taste. Bring to the boil, stirring, then lower the heat, cover the pan and simmer for 10–15 minutes. Stir in the artichokes, replace the lid and simmer for 10 minutes more. Meanwhile, cook the pasta in salted boiling water according to the instructions on the packet.

6 Drain the pasta, reserving a little of the cooking water. Stir the capers into the sauce, then taste for seasoning and add the remaining lemon juice if you like.

7 Tip the pasta into a warmed large bowl, pour the sauce over and toss well to mix, adding a little of the reserved cooking water if you like a runnier sauce. Serve immediately, garnished with the reserved fennel fronds. Hand around a bowl of grated Parmesan separately.

Spaghetti with Aubergines

THIS COMBINATION of ingredients is very popular in Italy, where it is known as *Spaghetti alla Norma*, after Bellini's opera.

INGREDIENTS

60ml/4 tbsp olive oil
1 garlic clove, roughly chopped
450g/1lb ripe Italian plum tomatoes, peeled
  and chopped
vegetable oil for shallow-frying
350g/12oz aubergines, diced small
400g/14oz fresh or dried spaghetti
1 handful fresh basil leaves, shredded
115g/4oz ricotta salata cheese,
  coarsely grated
salt and ground black pepper
Serves 4–6

1 Heat the olive oil, add the garlic and cook over a low heat, stirring constantly, for 1–2 minutes. Stir in the tomatoes, then add salt and pepper to taste. Cover and simmer for 20 minutes.

2 Meanwhile, pour oil into a deep frying pan to a depth of about 1cm/½in. Heat the oil until hot but not smoking, then fry the aubergine cubes in batches for 4–5 minutes until tender and lightly browned. Remove the aubergine with a slotted spoon and drain on kitchen paper.

3 Cook the pasta according to the instructions on the packet. Meanwhile, stir the fried aubergines into the tomato sauce and warm through. Taste for seasoning.

4 Drain the pasta and tip it into a warmed bowl. Add the sauce, with the shredded basil and a generous handful of the grated ricotta salata. Toss well and serve immediately, with the remaining ricotta sprinkled on top.

COOK'S TIP

Some cooks sprinkle aubergines with salt and leave them for 20–30 minutes. This is said to help remove any bitterness, but it is not necessary if the aubergines are young and fresh.

Farfalle with Fennel and Walnut

A SCRUMPTIOUS BLEND of walnuts and crisp steamed fennel.

INGREDIENTS

75g/3oz/¹/₂ cup walnuts, roughly chopped
1 garlic clove, chopped
25g/1oz fresh flat-leaf parsley, picked from
   the stalks
115g/4oz/¹/₂ cup ricotta cheese
450g/1lb/4 cups dried farfalle
450g/1lb fennel bulbs
chopped walnuts, to garnish
Serves 4

1 Place the chopped walnuts, garlic and parsley in a food processor. Process until roughly chopped. Transfer the mixture to a bowl and stir in the ricotta cheese.

2 Cook the pasta in a large saucepan of salted boiling water following the instructions on the packet until *al dente*. Drain thoroughly through a colander.

3 Slice the fennel thinly and steam for 4–5 minutes until just tender but still crisp.

4 Return the pasta to the pan and add the walnut mixture and the fennel. Toss well and sprinkle with the chopped walnuts to garnish. Serve the pasta immediately.

Pappardelle with Grilled Vegetables

A HEARTY DISH to be eaten with crusty bread and washed down with a robust red wine. Try barbecuing the vegetables for a really smoky flavour.

INGREDIENTS

1 aubergine
2 courgettes
1 red pepper
3 garlic cloves, unpeeled
about 150ml/¼ pint/⅔ cup extra virgin olive oil
450g/1lb fresh or dried pappardelle
salt and ground black pepper
a few sprigs fresh thyme, to garnish

Serves 4

1 Preheat the grill. With a sharp knife, trim then slice the aubergine and courgettes lengthways.

2 Halve the pepper; cut out the stalk and white pith and scrape out the seeds. Slice the pepper lengthways into eight pieces.

3 Line a grill pan with foil and arrange the vegetables and unpeeled garlic in a single layer over the foil. Brush liberally with olive oil and season with salt and ground black pepper.

4 Grill the vegetables until they are slightly charred on the surface, turning once. If you can't fit all the vegetables on the grill at once, cook them in two batches.

5 Once the garlic is cool enough to handle, remove the charred skins and halve. Toss all of the vegetables with the remaining olive oil and keep warm in a low oven.

6 Meanwhile cook the pasta in plenty of salted boiling water according to the instructions on the packet. Drain well and toss with the grilled vegetables. Serve immediately garnished with sprigs of fresh thyme.

Buckwheat Noodles with Cabbage, Potatoes and Cheese

THIS IS A VERY UNUSUAL PASTA dish from Valtellina in the Italian Alps. The buckwheat noodles are unique to this area, and have a slightly nutty flavour.

INGREDIENTS

400g/14oz Savoy cabbage, cut into
   1cm/½in strips
2 potatoes, total weight about 200g/7oz,
   cut into 5mm/¼in slices
400g/14oz dried pizzoccheri
75g/3oz/6 tbsp butter
1 generous bunch fresh sage
   leaves, shredded
2 garlic cloves
200g/7oz Fontina cheese, rind removed and
   thinly sliced
30–45ml/2–3 tbsp freshly grated
   Parmesan cheese, plus extra to serve
salt and ground black pepper
Serves 6

1 Bring a very large saucepan of salted water to the boil. Add the cabbage and potatoes and boil for 5 minutes.

2 Add the pasta, stir well and let the water return to the boil. Lower the heat and simmer for 15 minutes, or according to the instructions on the packet, until the pasta is al dente.

3 A few minutes before the pasta is ready, melt the butter in a small saucepan. Add the sage and whole garlic cloves and fry over a low to medium heat until the garlic is golden and sizzling. Lift the garlic out of the pan and discard it. Set the sage and garlic butter aside.

4 Drain the pasta and vegetables. Pour a quarter of the mixture into a warmed large bowl and arrange about a third of the Fontina slices on top. Repeat these layers until all the ingredients have been used, then sprinkle with the grated Parmesan. Pour the sage and garlic butter over the top and serve immediately, with extra Parmesan handed separately.

COOK'S TIPS

• Look for packets of dried pizzoccheri pasta in Italian delicatessens.
• Fontina is a mountain cheese with a sweet, nutty taste that is quite widely available, but if you cannot get it, look for Taleggio, Gruyère or Emmental – they are all similar cheeses. Cooks in the mountain regions of northern Italy would probably use either bitto or casera cheese, but these are not so easy to obtain outside the region.
• When in season, Swiss chard is used instead of cabbage, as is spinach.

Fettuccine with Butter and Parmesan

VERY FEW INGREDIENTS are needed to make up this incredibly simple dish. It comes from northern Italy, where butter and cheese are the most popular ingredients for serving with pasta. Children love it.

INGREDIENTS

400g/14oz fresh or dried fettuccine
50g/2oz/¼ cup unsalted butter, cubed
115g/4oz/1⅓ cups freshly grated
   Parmesan cheese
salt and ground black pepper
Serves 4

1 Cook the pasta in a pan of salted boiling water according to the instructions on the packet. Drain, then tip into a warmed bowl.

2 Add the butter and Parmesan a third at a time, tossing the pasta after each addition until it is evenly coated. Season to taste and serve.

Linguine with Sweet Pepper and Cream

THE SWEETNESS of red onion complements the peppers in this dish.

INGREDIENTS

1 orange pepper, quartered, cored and seeded
1 yellow pepper, quartered, cored and seeded
1 red pepper, quartered, cored and seeded
350g/12oz fresh or dried linguine
30ml/2 tbsp olive oil
1 red onion, sliced
1 garlic clove, chopped
30ml/2 tbsp chopped fresh rosemary
150ml/¼ pint/²⁄₃ cup double cream
salt and ground black pepper
fresh rosemary sprigs, to garnish
Serves 4

5 Heat the oil in a frying pan and
fry the onion and garlic for about
5 minutes until softened.

6 Stir in the sliced peppers and
chopped rosemary and fry gently
for about 5 minutes until heated
through stirring occasionally.

7 Stir in the cream and heat
through gently. Season to taste
with salt and pepper.

8 Drain the pasta thoroughly
and toss in the sauce. Serve
immediately in warmed bowls,
garnished with sprigs of fresh rosemary.

1 Preheat the grill to hot. Place the
peppers, skin-side up, on a grill rack.
Grill for 5–10 minutes until the skins
begin to blister and char, turning
occasionally.

2 Remove the peppers from the
heat, cover with a clean dish towel
and leave to stand for about 5 minutes.

3 Carefully peel away the skins from
the peppers and discard. Slice the
peppers into thin strips.

4 Cook the pasta in plenty of salted
boiling water according to the
instructions on the packet.

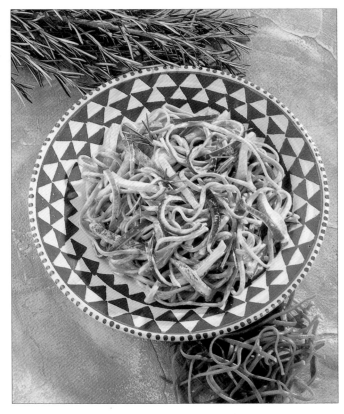

Macaroni Cheese with Mushrooms

MACARONI CHEESE is an all-time classic from the mid-week menu. Here it is served in a light creamy sauce with mushrooms and topped with pine nuts.

INGREDIENTS

450g/1lb/4 cups quick-cooking
  elbow macaroni
45ml/3 tbsp olive oil
225g/8oz button mushrooms, sliced
2 fresh thyme sprigs
60ml/4 tbsp plain flour
1 vegetable stock cube
600ml/1 pint/2½ cups milk
2.5ml/½ tsp celery salt
5ml/1 tsp Dijon mustard
175g/6oz/1½ cups grated Cheddar cheese
25g/1oz/¼ cup freshly grated
  Parmesan cheese
25g/1oz/2 tbsp pine nuts
salt and ground black pepper
Serves 4

1 Cook the macaroni in plenty of salted boiling water according to the instructions on the packet until *al dente*.

COOK'S TIP

Closed button mushrooms are best for white cream sauces. Open varieties can darken a pale sauce to an unattractive sludgy grey.

2 Heat the oil in a heavy-based saucepan. Add the mushrooms and thyme, cover and cook over a gentle heat for 2–3 minutes.

3 Stir in the flour and remove from the heat, add the stock cube and stir continuously until evenly blended. Pour over the milk, a little at a time, stirring after each addition. Add the celery salt, Dijon mustard and grated Cheddar cheese and season. Stir and simmer for 1–2 minutes until the sauce is thickened.

4 Preheat a grill. Drain the macaroni; toss into the sauce. Tip into four individual dishes or one large flameproof gratin dish. Scatter with grated Parmesan cheese and pine nuts; grill under a moderate heat until brown and bubbly.

Rigatoni with Wild Mushrooms

THIS IS A GOOD SAUCE to make from
storecupboard ingredients because
it doesn't rely on anything fresh,
apart from the fresh herbs.

INGREDIENTS

2 x 15g/¹/₂oz packets dried porcini
   mushrooms
175ml/6fl oz/³/₄ cup warm water
30ml/2 tbsp olive oil
2 shallots, finely chopped
2 garlic cloves, crushed
a few sprigs of fresh marjoram, leaves
   stripped and finely chopped, plus extra
   to garnish
1 handful fresh flat leaf parsley, chopped
25g/1oz/2 tbsp butter, diced
400g/14oz can chopped Italian
   plum tomatoes
400g/14oz/3¹/₂ cups dried rigatoni
25g/1oz/¹/₃ cup freshly grated Parmesan
   cheese, plus extra to serve
salt and ground black pepper
Serves 4–6

1   Put the dried mushrooms in a bowl,
pour the warm water over and
soak for 15–20 minutes. Tip into a fine
sieve set over a bowl and squeeze the
mushrooms to release as much liquid
as possible. Reserve the mushrooms
and the strained liquid.

2   Heat the oil in a medium skillet
and fry the shallots, garlic and
herbs over a low heat, stirring frequently, for about 5 minutes. Add the
mushrooms and butter and stir until
the butter has melted. Season well.

3   Stir in the tomatoes and the
reserved liquid from the soaked
mushrooms. Bring to the boil, then
cover, lower the heat and simmer for
about 20 minutes, stirring occasionally.
Meanwhile, cook the pasta according
to the instructions on the packet.

4   Taste the sauce for seasoning.
Drain the pasta, reserving some of
the cooking water, and tip it into a
warmed large bowl. Add the sauce and
the grated Parmesan and toss to mix.
Add a little cooking water if you prefer
a runnier sauce. Serve immediately,
garnished with marjoram and with
more Parmesan handed separately.

VARIATIONS

• If you have a bottle of wine open, add
a splash with the canned tomatoes.
• For a richer sauce, add a few spoonfuls
of panna da cucina, cream or mascarpone
to the sauce just before serving.

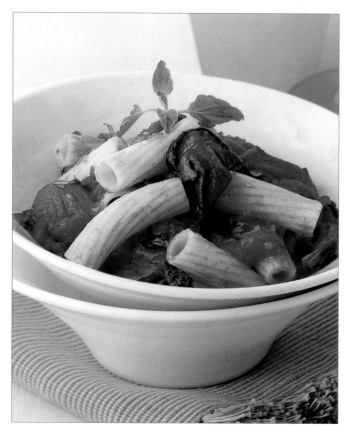

Eliche with Pesto

BOTTLED PESTO IS a useful stand-by, but if you have a food processor, it is very easy to make your own.

INGREDIENTS

50g/2oz/1¹/₃ cups fresh basil leaves, plus
    fresh basil sprigs, to garnish
2–4 garlic cloves
60ml/4 tbsp pine nuts
120ml/4fl oz/¹/₂ cup extra virgin olive oil
115g/4oz/1¹/₃ cups freshly grated
    Parmesan cheese, plus extra to serve
25g/1oz/¹/₃ cup freshly grated
    Pecorino cheese
400g/14oz/3¹/₂ cups dried eliche
salt and ground black pepper
Serves 4

1 Put the basil leaves, garlic and pine nuts in a blender or food processor. Add 60ml/4 tbsp of the olive oil. Process until the ingredients are finely chopped, then stop the machine, remove the lid and scrape down the sides of the bowl.

2 Turn the machine on again and slowly pour the remaining oil in a thin, steady stream through the feeder tube. You may need to stop the machine and scrape down the sides of the bowl once or twice to make sure everything is evenly mixed.

3 Scrape the mixture into a large bowl and beat in the cheeses with a wooden spoon. Taste and add salt and pepper if necessary.

4 Cook the pasta according to the instructions on the packet. Drain it well, then add it to the bowl of pesto and toss to mix. Serve immediately, garnished with the fresh basil leaves. Hand grated Parmesan separately.

COOK'S TIP

Pesto can be made up to 2–3 days in advance. To store pesto, transfer it to a small bowl and pour a thin film of olive oil over the surface. Cover the bowl tightly with clear film and keep it in the fridge.

Spaghetti with Garlic, Oil and Chilli

IN ROME THIS IS CALLED *Spaghetti Aglio e Olio*. Sometimes it is given its full name of *Spaghetti Aglio, Olio e Peperoncino* because chilli – *peperoncino* – is always used to give the dish some bite.

INGREDIENTS

400g/14oz fresh or dried spaghetti
90ml/6 tbsp extra virgin olive oil
2 – 4 garlic cloves, crushed
1 dried red chilli
1 small handful fresh flat leaf parsley,
  roughly chopped
salt
Serves 4

3 Drain the pasta and tip it into a warmed large bowl. Pour on the oil and garlic mixture, add the parsley and toss vigorously until the pasta glistens. Serve immediately.

COOK'S TIPS

• *Since the oil is such an important ingredient here, only use the very best cold-pressed extra virgin olive oil.*
• *Don't use salt in the oil and garlic mixture, because it will not dissolve sufficiently. This is why plenty of salt is recommended for cooking the pasta.*
• *In Rome, grated Parmesan is never served with Spaghetti Aglio e Olio, nor is the dish seasoned with pepper.*
• *In summer, Romans use fresh chillies, which they grow in pots on their terraces and window ledges.*

1 Cook the pasta according to the packet instructions, adding plenty of salt to the water. (See Cook's Tips.)

2 Meanwhile, heat the oil very gently in a small frying pan or saucepan. Add the crushed garlic and whole dried chilli and stir over a low heat until the garlic is just beginning to brown. Remove the chilli and discard.

Ruote with Mushrooms

THESE FUN PASTA SHAPES will appeal to the little people in your household – and that doesn't mean the Italians.

INGREDIENTS

15g/½oz dried porcini mushrooms
175ml/6fl oz/¾ cup warm water
45ml/3 tbsp olive oil
2 garlic cloves, finely chopped
1 handful fresh flat leaf parsley,
    roughly chopped
2 large pieces drained sun-dried tomato in
    olive oil, sliced into thin strips
120ml/4fl oz/½ cup dry white wine
225g/8oz/2 cups chestnut mushrooms,
    thinly sliced
475ml/16fl oz/2 cups vegetable stock
450g/1lb/4 cups dried ruote or other pasta
    shapes, such as penne, fusilli or eliche
salt and ground black pepper
rocket and/or fresh flat leaf parsley,
    to garnish

Serves 4

1 Put the dried porcini mushrooms in a bowl, pour the warm water over and leave to soak for 15–20 minutes. Tip into a fine sieve set over a bowl and squeeze the porcini with your hands to release as much liquid as possible. Reserve the strained soaking liquid. Chop the porcini finely.

2 Heat the oil and cook the garlic, parsley, sun-dried tomato strips and porcini over a low heat, stirring frequently, for about 5 minutes.

3 Stir in the wine, simmer for a few minutes until reduced, then stir in the chestnut mushrooms. Pour in the stock and simmer, uncovered, for 15–20 minutes more until the liquid has reduced and the sauce is quite thick and rich.

4 Cook the pasta according to the instructions on the packet.

5 Taste the mushroom sauce for seasoning. Drain the pasta, reserving a little of the cooking liquid, and tip it into a warmed large bowl. Add the mushroom sauce and toss well, thinning the sauce if necessary with some of the pasta cooking water. Serve immediately, sprinkled liberally with chopped rocket and/or parsley.

VARIATION

Fresh wild mushrooms can be used instead of chestnut mushrooms, but they are seasonal and often expensive. A cheaper alternative is to use a box of mixed wild mushrooms. These are sold in many supermarkets.

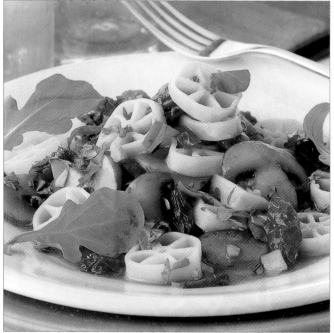

Tagliatelle with Walnut Sauce

AN UNUSUAL SAUCE which would make this a spectacular dinner party starter or satisfying supper.

INGREDIENTS

2 thick slices wholemeal bread

300ml/½ pint/1¼ cups milk

275g/10oz/2½ cups walnut pieces

1 garlic clove, crushed

50g/2oz/½ cup freshly grated
    Parmesan cheese

90ml/6 tbsp olive oil, plus extra for tossing
    the pasta

150ml/¼ pint/⅔ cup double
    cream (optional)

450g/1lb tagliatelle

salt and ground black pepper

30ml/2 tbsp chopped fresh parsley,
    to garnish

Serves 4–6

3 Place the bread, walnuts, garlic, Parmesan cheese and olive oil in a blender or food processor and blend until smooth. Season to taste with salt and pepper. Stir in the cream, if using.

4 Cook the pasta in plenty of salted boiling water according to the instructions on the packet, drain and toss with a little olive oil. Divide the pasta equally among four or six bowls and place a dollop of sauce on each portion. Sprinkle with parsley and serve immediately.

1 Cut the crusts off the bread and soak in the milk until all of the milk is absorbed.

2 Preheat the oven to 190°C/ 375°F/Gas 5. Spread the walnuts on a baking sheet and toast in the oven for 5 minutes. Leave to cool.

VARIATION

Replace the walnuts with pecans or hazelnuts if you prefer, and prepare as above.

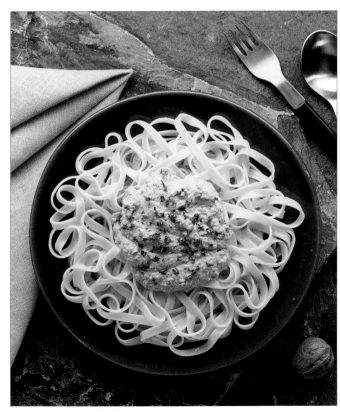

Eliche with Courgettes and Walnuts

THE VEGETABLES are softened slowly to release their flavours.

INGREDIENTS

65g/2¹/₂oz/5 tbsp butter
1 large Spanish onion, halved and
  thinly sliced
450g/1lb courgettes, very thinly sliced
375g/12oz/3 cups dried eliche
50g/2oz/¹/₂ cup walnuts, coarsely chopped
45ml/3 tbsp chopped fresh parsley
30ml/2 tbsp single cream
salt and ground black pepper
freshly grated Parmesan cheese, to serve
Serves 4

1 Melt the butter in a frying pan. Add the sliced onion, cover and sweat for 5 minutes until translucent, then add the courgettes.

2 Stir well, cover again and sweat until the vegetables are very soft, stirring occasionally.

3 Meanwhile, cook the pasta in plenty of salted boiling water, according to the instructions on the packet, until *al dente*.

4 While the pasta is cooking, add the walnuts, parsley and cream to the courgette mixture and stir well. Season with salt and pepper.

5 Drain the pasta and return to the pan. Add the courgette sauce and mix together well. Serve immediately in a warmed bowl, with freshly grated Parmesan handed separately.

Pappardelle with Beans and Mushrooms

A MIXTURE OF WILD and cultivated mushrooms help to give this dish a rich and nutty flavour.

INGREDIENTS

30ml/2 tbsp olive oil
50g/2oz/4 tbsp butter
2 shallots, chopped
2–3 garlic cloves, crushed
675g/1½lb mixed mushrooms,
    thickly sliced
4 sun-dried tomatoes in oil, drained
    and chopped
90ml/6 tbsp dry white wine
400g/14oz can borlotti beans, drained
350g/12oz/3 cups fresh or dried pappardelle
45ml/3 tbsp grated Parmesan cheese
salt and ground black pepper
chopped fresh parsley, to garnish

Serves 4

1 Heat the oil and butter in a frying pan and fry the shallots until they are soft but not coloured.

2 Add the garlic and mushrooms and fry for 3–4 minutes. Stir in the sun-dried tomatoes, wine and add seasoning to taste.

3 Stir in the borlotti beans and cook for 5–6 minutes, until most of the liquid has evaporated from the pan and the beans are warmed through.

4 Meanwhile, cook the pasta in a saucepan of salted boiling water according to the instructions on the packet.

5 Stir the grated Parmesan cheese. into the sauce.

6 As soon as the pasta is *al dente*, drain it through a colander and serve immediately with the sauce and a sprinkling of parsley.

Mushroom and Chilli Carbonara

FOR A RICHER mushroom flavour, use a small packet of dried Italian porcini mushrooms in this quick, eggy sauce as they have a really good, meaty taste. For an extra spicy zing, toss in some chilli flakes too.

INGREDIENTS

15g/¹/₂oz pack dried porcini mushrooms
300ml/¹/₂ pint/1¹/₄ cups hot water
225g/8oz dried spaghetti
25g/1oz/2 tbsp butter
1 garlic clove, crushed
225g/8oz button or chestnut mushrooms,
    thinly sliced
5ml/1 tsp dried red chilli flakes
2 eggs
300ml/¹/₂ pint/1¹/₄ cups single cream
salt and ground black pepper
freshly grated Parmesan cheese and
    chopped fresh parsley, to serve

Serves 4

1 Soak the dried mushrooms in the hot water for 15 minutes; drain and reserve the liquid.

2 Cook the spaghetti according to the instructions in plenty of salted boiling water. Drain and rinse in cold water.

3 In a large saucepan, heat the butter and oil together and lightly sauté the garlic for half a minute.

4 Add the mushrooms, including the soaked porcini, and the chilli flakes to the pan of garlic, and stir well. Cook for about 2 minutes.

5 Pour in the reserved soaking liquid from the mushrooms, give the mixture a good stir and then boil to reduce slightly.

6 Beat the eggs with the cream and season well. Tip the cooked spaghetti into the mushroom sauce in the pan and then toss in the eggs and cream. Reheat the mixture, without boiling, and serve hot, sprinkled with freshly grated Parmesan cheese and chopped parsley.

VARIATION

If you don't want to use mushrooms, try replacing them with finely sliced and sautéed leeks or perhaps coarsely shredded lettuce with peas. If chilli flakes are too hot and spicy for you, then try the delicious alternative of skinned and chopped tomatoes with torn, fresh basil leaves as a garnish.

Chitarra Spaghetti with Butter and Herbs

THIS IS A VERSATILE RECIPE. You can use just one favourite herb or several – basil, flat leaf parsley, rosemary, thyme, marjoram or sage would all work well. Square-shaped spaghetti is traditional for this type of sauce, but you can use ordinary spaghetti or spaghettini, or even linguine.

INGREDIENTS

400g/14oz fresh or dried spaghetti
*   alla chitarra*
2 good handfuls mixed fresh herbs, plus
*   extra herb leaves and flowers,*
*   to garnish*
115g/4oz/½ cup butter
salt and ground black pepper
freshly grated Parmesan cheese, to serve
Serves 4

VARIATION

If you like the flavour of garlic with herbs, add 1–2 crushed garlic cloves when melting the butter.

1 Cook the pasta according to the instructions on the packet.

2 Chop the herbs roughly or finely, whichever you prefer.

3 When the pasta is almost *al dente*, melt the butter in a large skillet or saucepan. As soon as it sizzles, drain the pasta and add it to the pan, then sprinkle in the herbs and salt and pepper to taste.

4 Toss over a medium heat until the pasta is coated in the oil and herbs. Serve immediately in warmed bowls, sprinkled with extra herb leaves and flowers. Hand around freshly grated Parmesan separately.

Spaghetti with Cheese and Pepper

THIS IS A ROMAN DISH, always made with spaghetti. It is remarkably easy to cook, and tastes wonderful.

INGREDIENTS

400g/14oz fresh or dried spaghetti
115g/4oz/1⅓ cup freshly grated Pecorino
*   (preferably Pecorino Romano) cheese*
5ml/1 tsp coarsely ground black pepper
extra virgin olive oil, to taste
salt
Serves 4

1 Cook the pasta according to the instructions on the packet.

2 As soon as the pasta is *al dente*, drain it through a colander, but leave it a little more moist than is usual, before tipping it into a large warmed bowl.

3 Add the cheese, pepper and salt to taste. Toss well to mix, then moisten with as much olive oil as you like. Serve immediately.

Chilli and Aubergine Pasta

FULL OF FLAVOUR, THIS EXCELLENT vegetarian sauce goes well with any short pasta shape. It can also be layered with sheets of pasta and béchamel or cheese sauce to make a delicious vegetarian lasagne.

INGREDIENTS

30ml/2 tbsp olive oil
1 small fresh red chilli
2 garlic cloves
2 handfuls fresh flat leaf parsley,
    roughly chopped
450g/1lb aubergines, roughly chopped
1 handful fresh basil leaves
200ml/7fl oz/scant 1 cup water
1 vegetable stock cube
8 ripe Italian plum tomatoes, peeled and
    finely chopped
60ml/4 tbsp red wine
5ml/1 tsp granulated sugar
1 sachet saffron powder
2.5ml/½ tsp ground paprika
salt and ground black pepper
Serves 4–6

1 Heat the oil in a large skillet or saucepan and add the whole chilli, whole garlic cloves and half the chopped parsley. Smash the garlic cloves with a wooden spoon to release their juice, then cover the pan and cook the mixture over a low to medium heat for about 10 minutes, stirring occasionally.

2 Remove and discard the chilli. Add the aubergines to the pan with the rest of the parsley and all the basil. Pour in half the water. Crumble in the stock cube and stir until it is dissolved, then cover and cook, stirring frequently, for about 10 minutes.

3 Add the tomatoes, wine, sugar, saffron and paprika, with salt and pepper to taste, then pour in the remaining water. Stir well, replace the lid and cook for 30–40 minutes more, stirring occasionally. Taste for seasoning and serve with pasta or use as suggested in a baked dish. If you like, garnish with extra chopped parsley.

COOK'S TIP

Italian cooks often sprinkle a little "all-purpose seasoning" into sauces like this one. It is very good for accentuating savoury flavours, and is well worth keeping in the storecupboard.

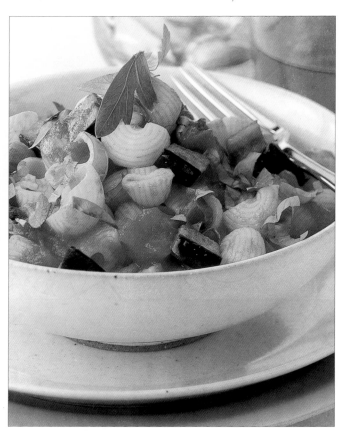

Orecchiette with Rocket

THIS HEARTY DISH IS FROM PUGLIA in the south-east of Italy. Serve it as a main course with fresh country bread. Some delicatessens and supermarkets sell a farmhouse-style Italian loaf called *pugliese*, which would be most appropriate.

INGREDIENTS

45ml/3 tbsp olive oil
1 small onion, finely chopped
300g/11oz canned chopped Italian plum
*   tomatoes or passata*
2.5ml/¹/₂ tsp dried oregano
pinch of chilli powder or cayenne pepper
about 30ml/2 tbsp red or white wine
*   (optional)*
2 potatoes, total weight about
*   200g/7oz, diced*
300g/11oz/2³/₄ cups dried orecchiette
2 garlic cloves, finely chopped
150g/5oz rocket leaves, stalks
*   removed, shredded*
90g/3¹/₂oz/scant ¹/₂ cup ricotta cheese
salt and ground black pepper
freshly grated Pecorino cheese, to serve
Serves 4–6

1 Heat 15ml/1 tbsp of the olive oil in a medium saucepan, add half the finely chopped onion and cook gently, stirring frequently, for about 5 minutes until softened. Add the canned tomatoes or passata, oregano and chilli powder or cayenne pepper to the onion. Pour the wine over, if using, and add a little salt and pepper to taste. Cover the pan and simmer for about 15 minutes, stirring occasionally.

2 Bring a large saucepan of salted water to the boil. Add the potatoes and pasta. Stir well and let the water return to the boil. Lower the heat and simmer for 15 minutes, or according to the instructions on the packet, until the pasta is cooked.

3 Heat the remaining oil in a large skillet or saucepan, add the rest of the onion and the garlic and fry for 2–3 minutes, stirring occasionally. Add the rocket, toss over the heat for about 2 minutes until wilted, then stir in the tomato sauce and the ricotta. Mix well.

4 Drain the pasta and potatoes, add both to the pan of sauce and toss to mix. Taste for seasoning and serve immediately in warmed bowls, with grated Pecorino handed separately.

COOK'S TIP

Orecchiette are always slightly chewy. When making this dish it is traditional to cook them in the same pan as the potatoes, but if you are unsure of getting the timing right, cook them separately.

Tagliolini with Asparagus

TAGLIOLINI ARE VERY THIN egg noodles, more delicate in texture than spaghetti. They go well with this subtle cream sauce, flavoured with fresh asparagus.

INGREDIENTS

450g/1lb fresh asparagus
egg pasta sheets made with 2 eggs, or
350g/12oz fresh tagliolini or other
egg noodles
50g/2oz/¼ cup butter
3 spring onions, finely chopped
3–4 fresh mint or basil leaves,
finely chopped
150ml/¼ pint/²⁄₃ cup double cream
50g/2oz/½ cup freshly grated
Parmesan cheese
salt and ground black pepper
Serves 4

1 Peel the asparagus by inserting a small sharp knife at the base of the stalks and pulling upwards towards the tips. Drop them into a pan of boiling water and boil until just tender, about 4–6 minutes.

2 Remove from the pan, reserving the cooking water. Cut the tips off, and then cut the stalks into 4cm/1½in pieces. Set aside.

3 Make the egg pasta sheets, if using, and fold and cut into thin noodles, or feed through the narrowest setting of a pasta-making machine. Open them out and dry for 5–10 minutes.

4 Melt the butter in a large frying pan. Add the spring onions and herbs, and cook for 3–4 minutes. Stir in the cream and asparagus, and heat gently, but do not boil. Season to taste.

5 Bring the asparagus cooking water back to the boil. Add salt. Drop the noodles in all at once. Cook until just tender (freshly made noodles will cook in about 30–60 seconds). Drain thoroughly through a colander.

6 Turn the pasta into the pan with the sauce, increase the heat slightly and mix well. Stir in the Parmesan cheese. Mix well and serve at once.

Magnificent Marrow

AT AUTUMN TIME, marrows – with their wonderful green and cream stripes – look so attractive and tempting. They make delicious, inexpensive main courses, just right for a satisfying family meal.

INGREDIENTS

250g/9oz2¼ cups dried conchiglie
1.5–1.75kg/3–4½lb marrow
45ml/3 tbsp sunflower oil
1 onion, chopped
1 pepper, seeded and chopped
15ml/1 tbsp fresh root ginger, grated
2 garlic cloves, crushed
4 large tomatoes, skinned and chopped
50g/2oz/½ cup pine nuts
15ml/1 tbsp chopped fresh basil
salt and ground black pepper
grated cheese, to serve (optional)
Serves 4–6

1 Preheat the oven to 190°C/375°F/ Gas 5. Cook the pasta in a large saucepan containing plenty of salted boiling water according to the instructions on the packet, slightly overcooking it so it is just a little soft. Drain well and reserve.

2 Cut the marrow in half length-ways and scoop out and discard the seeds. Use a small sharp knife and tablespoon to scoop out the marrow flesh. Chop the flesh roughly.

3 Heat the oil in a large saucepan and gently fry the onion, pepper, ginger and garlic for 5 minutes then add the marrow flesh, tomatoes and seasoning. Cover and cook for 10–12 minutes until the vegetables are soft.

4 Add the pasta, pine nuts and basil to the pan, stir well and set aside until required.

5 Meanwhile, place the marrow halves in a roasting tin, season lightly and pour a little water around the marrow, taking care it does not spill inside. Cover with foil and bake for 15 minutes.

6 Remove the foil, discard the water and fill the shells with the vegetable mixture. Cover with foil and return to the hot oven for a further 20–25 minutes.

7 Top with cheese, if using. To serve, scoop the filling out of the "shell" or cut the marrow into sections.

Pasta with Caponata

THE SICILIANS have an excellent
sweet-and-sour vegetable dish,
called *caponata*, which goes
wonderfully well with pasta.

INGREDIENTS

1 aubergine, cut into sticks
2 courgettes, cut into sticks
60ml/4 tbsp extra virgin olive oil
8 baby onions, peeled or 1 large
   onion, sliced
2 garlic cloves, crushed
1 large red pepper, cored, seeded and sliced
450ml/³/₄ pint/1³/₄ cups tomato juice
150ml/¹/₄ pint/²/₃ cup water
30ml/2 tbsp balsamic vinegar
juice of 1 lemon
15ml/1 tbsp sugar
30ml/2 tbsp sliced black olives
30ml/2 tbsp capers
400g/14oz fresh or dried tagliatelle or
   other ribbon pasta
salt and ground black pepper
Serves 4

1 Lightly salt the aubergine and
courgettes and leave them to drain
in a colander for 30 minutes. Rinse and
pat dry thoroughly with kitchen paper.

VARIATION

*Caponata is often made with the
addition of anchovies and pine nuts. It
also makes a delicious salad or side dish
when served at room temperature.*

2 Heat the olive oil in a large
saucepan, and lightly fry the onions,
garlic and pepper for 5 minutes, then
stir in the aubergine and courgettes
and fry for a further 5 minutes.

3 Stir in the tomato juice and the
water. Stir well, bring the mixture
to the boil, then add all the rest of the
ingredients except the pasta. Season to
taste and simmer for 10 minutes.

4 Meanwhile, cook the pasta
according to the instructions on
the packet, then drain. Serve the
caponata with the pasta.

Fusilli with Lentils and Cheese

THIS SURPRISING combination works extremely well.

INGREDIENTS

15ml/1 tbsp olive oil
1 onion, chopped
1 garlic clove, chopped
1 carrot, cut into matchsticks
350g/12oz/3 cups dried fusilli
*65g/2¹/₂oz/¹/₂ cup green lentils, boiled for
    25 minutes*
15ml/1 tbsp tomato purée
15ml/1 tbsp chopped fresh oregano
150ml/¹/₄ pint/²/₃ cup vegetable stock
225g/8oz/2 cups grated Cheddar cheese
salt and ground black pepper
freshly grated Cheddar cheese, to serve
Serves 4

1 Heat the oil in a large frying pan and fry the onion and garlic for 3 minutes. Add the carrot and cook for a further 5 minutes.

COOK'S TIP

Tomato purée is sold in small cans and tubes. If you use a can for this small amount, you can keep the remainder fresh by transferring it to a bowl, covering it with a thin layer of olive oil and then putting it in the fridge until needed.

2 Cook the pasta in plenty of salted boiling water according to the instructions on the packet.

3 Add the lentils, tomato purée and oregano to the frying pan, stirring to mix thoroughly, then cover and cook for 3 minutes.

4 Add the stock and salt and pepper to the pan. Cover and simmer for 10 minutes. Stir in the grated Cheddar cheese.

5 Drain the pasta thoroughly and stir into the sauce to coat. Serve in warmed bowls with plenty of extra grated cheese handed separately.

Spaghettini with Roasted Garlic

ROASTED GARLIC TASTES sweet and is milder than you would expect.

INGREDIENTS

1 whole head of garlic
400g/14oz fresh or dried spaghettini
120ml/4fl oz/½ cup extra virgin olive oil
salt and ground black pepper
coarsely shaved Parmesan cheese, to serve
Serves 4

1 Preheat the oven to 180°C/350°F/ Gas 4. Place the garlic in an oiled baking tin and roast it for 30 minutes.

2 Cook the pasta in a saucepan of salted boiling water according to the instructions on the packet.

3 Leave the garlic to cool, then lay it on its side and slice off the top third with a sharp knife.

4 Hold the garlic over a bowl and dig out the flesh from each clove with the point of the knife. When all the flesh has been added to the bowl, pour in the oil and add plenty of black pepper. Mix well.

5 Drain the pasta and return it to the clean pan. Pour in the oil and garlic mixture and toss the pasta vigorously over a medium heat until all the strands are thoroughly coated. Serve immediately, with shavings of Parmesan handed separately.

VARIATION

For a fiery finish, sprinkle crushed, dried red chillies over the pasta when tossing it with the oil and garlic.

COOK'S TIP

Although you can now buy roasted garlic in supermarkets, it is best to roast it yourself for this simple recipe, so that it melts into the olive oil and coats the strands of pasta beautifully.

Elicoidali with Cheese and Cream

ALTHOUGH THE INGREDIENTS for this dish are quite plain, the combination is very appetizing. It is very quick, so if you have a tub of ricotta in the fridge it makes a swift and simple evening meal.

INGREDIENTS

400g/14oz/3½ cups dried elicoidali
3 egg yolks
105ml/7 tbsp freshly grated
  Parmesan cheese
200g/7oz/scant 1 cup ricotta cheese
60ml/4 tbsp panna da cucina or
  double cream
nutmeg
40g/1½oz/3 tbsp butter
salt and ground black pepper
Serves 4

1 Cook the pasta according to the instructions on the packet.

2 Meanwhile, mix the egg yolks, grated Parmesan and ricotta together in a bowl. Add the cream and mix with a fork.

3 Grate in nutmeg to taste, then season with plenty of black pepper and a little salt. Drain the pasta thoroughly when cooked. Return the clean pan to the heat. Melt the butter, add the drained pasta and toss vigorously over a medium heat.

4 Turn off the heat under the pan and add the ricotta mixture. Stir well with a large spoon for 10–15 seconds until all the pasta is coated in sauce. Serve immediately, in warmed individual bowls.

COOK'S TIP

Elicoidali are a short tubular pasta with curved ridges. If you can't get them, use rigatoni, which have straight ridges.

Tagliatelle with "Hit-the-Pan" Salsa

IT IS POSSIBLE to make a hot, filling meal within just 15 minutes with this quick-cook salsa sauce. If you have no time don't peel the tomatoes.

INGREDIENTS

115g/4oz fresh or dried tagliatelle
45ml/3 tbsp extra virgin olive oil
3 large tomatoes
1 garlic clove, crushed
4 spring onions, sliced
1 green chilli, halved, seeded and sliced
juice of 1 orange (optional)
30ml/2 tbsp chopped fresh parsley
salt and ground black pepper
grated cheese, to serve (optional)

Serves 2

1 Cook the tagliatelle in plenty of salted boiling water until *al dente*. Drain and toss in a little of the oil. Season well.

2 Skin the tomatoes by dipping them in a bowl of boiling water for about 45 seconds and then into cold water. The skins should slip off easily. Roughly chop the flesh.

3 Heat the remaining oil until quite hot and stir-fry the garlic, onions and chilli for 1 minute.

4 Add the tomatoes, orange juice, if using, and parsley. Season well and stir in the tagliatelle to reheat. Serve with grated cheese, if desired.

COOK'S TIPS

• You could use any pasta shape for this recipe. It would be particularly good with large rigatoni or linguini, or as a sauce for fresh ravioli or tortellini.

• This sauce is so easy to prepare, you could save yourself some later later by preparing double the quantity and freezing the excess. Prepare for freezing as above, but omit the parsley. Add fresh parsley when you prepare to serve from frozen.

Campanelle with Yellow Pepper Sauce

ROASTED YELLOW PEPPERS make a deliciously sweet and creamy sauce to serve with pasta.

INGREDIENTS

2 yellow peppers
50g/2oz/¼ cup soft goat's cheese
115g/4oz/½ cup low-fat fromage blanc
450g/1lb dried campanelle
salt and ground black pepper
50g/2oz/½ cup toasted flaked almonds,
  to serve
Serves 4

1 After deseeding the peppers, place them under a preheated grill and turn them frequently until charred and blistered. Place in a plastic bag, seal and leave to cool. Then peel and remove all the pith and seeds.

2 Place the pepper flesh in a blender or food processor with the goat's cheese and fromage blanc. Process until well mixed and smooth. Season with salt and plenty of ground black pepper.

3 Cook the pasta in plenty of salted boiling water, according to the instructions on the packet, until *al dente*. Drain well.

4 Toss the pasta with the sauce and serve in warmed bowls sprinkled with the toasted flaked almonds.

Black Pasta with Ricotta

THIS IS DESIGNER PASTA at its most dramatic, the kind of dish you are most likely to see at a fashionable Italian restaurant. Serve it for a smart dinner party first course – it will be a great talking point.

INGREDIENTS

300g/11oz dried black pasta
60ml/4 tbsp ricotta cheese, as fresh
  as possible
60ml/4 tbsp extra virgin olive oil
1 small fresh red chilli, seeded and
  finely chopped
1 small handful fresh basil leaves
salt and ground black pepper
Serves 4

Cook the pasta in salted boiling water according to the instructions on the packet. Meanwhile, put the ricotta in a bowl, add salt and pepper to taste and use a little of the hot water from the pasta pan to mix it to a smooth, creamy consistency. Taste for seasoning.

2 Drain the pasta. Heat the oil gently in the clean pan and add the pasta with the chilli and salt and pepper to taste. Toss quickly over a high heat to combine.

3 Divide the pasta equally among four warmed bowls, then top with the ricotta. Sprinkle with the basil leaves and serve immediately. Each diner tosses their own portion of pasta and cheese.

COOK'S TIP

Black pasta is made with squid ink. If you prefer, use green spinach-flavoured pasta or red tomato-flavoured pasta.

Paglia e Fieno with Walnuts and Gorgonzola

CHEESE AND NUTS ARE popular ingredients for pasta sauces. The combination is very rich, so reserve this dish for a dinner party starter. It needs no accompaniment other than wine – a dry white would be good.

INGREDIENTS

275g/10oz dried paglia e fieno
25g/1oz/2 tbsp butter
5ml/1 tsp finely chopped fresh sage or
  2.5ml/1/2 tsp dried sage, plus fresh sage
  leaves, to garnish
115g/4oz torta di Gorgonzola
  cheese, diced
45ml/3 tbsp mascarpone cheese
75ml/5 tbsp milk
50g/2oz/1/2 cup walnut halves, ground
30ml/2 tbsp freshly grated Parmesan cheese
freshly ground black pepper
Serves 4

Cook the pasta in a large saucepan of salted boiling water, according to the instructions on the packet. Meanwhile, melt the butter in a large skillet or saucepan over a low heat, add the sage and stir it around. Sprinkle in the diced *torta di Gorgonzola* and then add the mascarpone. Stir the ingredients with a wooden spoon until the cheeses start to melt. Pour in the milk and keep stirring.

2 Sprinkle in the walnuts and grated Parmesan and add plenty of black pepper. Continue to stir over a low heat until the mixture forms a creamy sauce. Do not allow it to boil or the nuts will taste bitter, and do not cook the sauce for longer than a few minutes or the nuts will discolour it.

3 Drain the pasta, add it to the pan of sauce and toss well. Serve immediately, with more black pepper ground liberally on top. Garnish with the sage leaves.

COOK'S TIP

Ready-ground nuts are sold in packets in supermarkets, but you will get a better flavour if you buy walnut halves and grind them yourself in a food processor.

Tagliatelle with Peas, Asparagus and Beans

A CREAMY PEA SAUCE makes a wonderful combination with crunchy young vegetables.

INGREDIENTS

15ml/1 tbsp olive oil
1 garlic clove, crushed
6 spring onions, sliced
225g/8oz/2 cups frozen peas, thawed
350g/12oz fresh young asparagus
30ml/2 tbsp chopped fresh sage, plus extra
*   leaves to garnish*
finely grated rind of 2 lemons
450ml/¾ pint/1¾ cups vegetable stock
*   or water*
225g/8oz/2 cups frozen broad
*   beans, thawed*
450g/1lb fresh egg tagliatelle
60ml/4 tbsp low-fat natural yogurt
Serves 4

1 Heat the oil in a pan. Add the garlic and spring onions and cook gently for 2–3 minutes.

2 Add the peas and 115g/4oz of the asparagus, together with the sage, lemon rind and stock or water. Bring the mixture to the boil, reduce the heat and simmer for 10 minutes until tender. Purée in a blender or food processor until smooth.

3 Meanwhile remove the outer skins from the thawed broad beans and discard.

4 Cut the remaining asparagus into 5cm/2in lengths, trimming off any fibrous stems, and blanch in boiling water for 2 minutes.

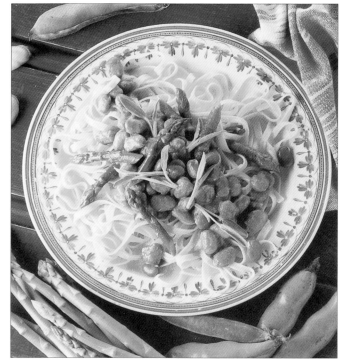

5 Cook the tagliatelle in plenty of salted boiling water according to the instructions on the packet until *al dente*. Drain well.

6 Add the cooked asparagus and shelled beans to the sauce and reheat. Stir in the yogurt and toss into the tagliatelle. Garnish with sage leaves and serve at once.

Conchiglie with Roasted Peppers

ADD OTHER VEGETABLES such as French beans or courgettes or even chick-peas if you like.

INGREDIENTS

2 red peppers
2 yellow peppers
45ml/3 tbsp olive oil
1 onion, sliced
2 garlic cloves, crushed
2.5ml/½ tsp mild chilli powder
400g/14oz can chopped tomatoes
450g/1lb/4 cups dried conchiglie or other
   pasta shapes, such as eliche or fusilli
salt and ground black pepper
freshly grated Parmesan cheese, to serve

Serves 4

1 Preheat the oven to 200°C/400°F/ Gas 6. Place the peppers on a baking sheet or in a roasting tin and bake for about 20 minutes or until they are beginning to char. Alternatively you could grill the peppers under a preheated grill, turning frequently until evenly blistered.

2 Rub the skins off the peppers under cold water. Halve, seed and roughly chop the flesh.

3 Heat the oil in a medium saucepan and add the onion and garlic. Cook gently for 5 minutes until soft and golden.

4 Stir in the chilli powder, cook for 2 minutes, then add the tomatoes and peppers. Bring to the boil and simmer for 10–15 minutes until the sauce is slightly thickened and reduced. Season to taste.

5 Cook the pasta in plenty of salted boiling water according to the instructions on the packet. Drain well through a colander and toss with the sauce. Serve piping hot with plenty of grated Parmesan cheese.

VARIATION

If you like, increase the strength of the chilli flavour by using a hotter blend of chilli powder.

Conchiglie with Roasted Vegetables

NOTHING COULD BE SIMPLER – or more delicious – than tossing freshly cooked pasta with roasted vegetables. The flavour is superb.

INGREDIENTS

1 red pepper, seeded and cut into
    1cm/½in squares
1 yellow or orange pepper, seeded and cut
    into 1cm/½in squares
1 small aubergine, roughly diced
2 courgettes, roughly diced
75ml/5 tbsp extra virgin olive oil
15ml/1 tbsp chopped fresh
    flat leaf parsley
5ml/1 tsp dried oregano or marjoram
250g/9oz baby Italian plum tomatoes,
    hulled and halved lengthways
2 garlic cloves, roughly chopped
350–400g/12–14oz/3–3½ cups
    dried conchiglie
salt and ground black pepper
4–6 fresh marjoram or oregano sprigs,
    to garnish
Serves 4–6

1 Preheat the oven to 190°C/375°F/ Gas 5. Rinse the prepared peppers, aubergine and courgettes in a sieve or colander under cold running water, drain, then tip the vegetables into a large roasting tin.

2 Pour 45ml/3 tbsp of the olive oil over the vegetables and sprinkle with the fresh and dried herbs. Add salt and pepper to taste and stir well. Roast for about 30 minutes, stirring two or three times.

3 Stir the halved tomatoes and chopped garlic into the vegetable mixture, then roast for 20 minutes more, stirring once or twice. Meanwhile, cook the pasta according to the instructions on the packet.

4 Drain the pasta and tip it into a warmed bowl. Add the roasted vegetables and the remaining oil and toss well. Serve the pasta and vegetables hot in warmed bowls, garnishing each portion with a herb sprig.

COOK'S TIP

Pasta and roasted vegetables are very good served cold, so if you have any of this dish left over, cover it tightly with clear film, chill in the fridge overnight and serve it the next day as a salad. It would also make a particularly good salad to take on a picnic.

Green Vegetable Sauce

ALTHOUGH DESCRIBED AS *SUGO* in Italian, this is not a true "sauce", because it does not have any liquid apart from the oil and melted butter. It is more a medley of vegetables. Tossed with freshly cooked pasta, it is ideal for a fresh and light lunch or supper. Allow about 450g/1lb dried pasta for this amount of sauce.

INGREDIENTS

2 carrots
1 courgette
75g/3oz French beans
1 small leek
2 ripe Italian plum tomatoes
1 handful fresh flat leaf parsley
25g/1oz/2 tbsp butter
45ml/3 tbsp extra virgin olive oil
2.5ml/¹/₂ tsp granulated sugar
115g/4oz/1 cup frozen peas
salt and ground black pepper
freshly cooked pasta, to serve

Serves 4

1 Dice the carrots and the courgette finely. Top and tail the French beans, then cut them into 2cm/³/₄in lengths. Slice the leek thinly. Peel and dice the tomatoes. Chop the flat leaf parsley and set aside.

2 Melt the butter in the oil in a medium skillet or saucepan. When the mixture sizzles, add the prepared leek and carrots. Sprinkle the sugar over and fry, stirring frequently, for about 5 minutes.

3 Stir in the courgette, French beans, peas and plenty of salt and pepper. Cover and cook over a low to medium heat for 5–8 minutes until the vegetables are tender, stirring occasionally.

4 Stir in the parsley and chopped plum tomatoes and adjust the seasoning to taste. Serve at once, tossed with freshly cooked pasta of your choice.

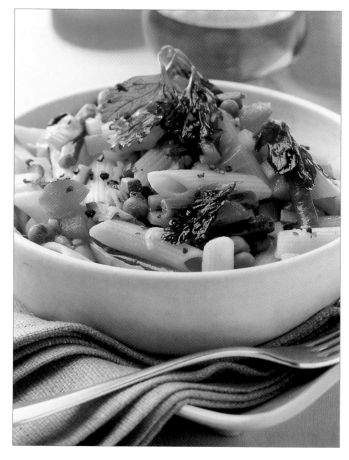

Penne with Aubergine and Mint Pesto

THIS SPLENDID VARIATION on the classic Italian pesto uses fresh mint rather than basil for a deliciously different flavour.

INGREDIENTS

2 large aubergines
450g/1lb/4 cups dried penne
50g/2oz/½ cup walnut halves
salt and ground black pepper

For the pesto
25g/1oz fresh mint
15g/½oz flat leaf parsley
40g/1½oz/scant ½ cup walnuts
40g/1½oz finely grated Parmesan cheese
2 garlic cloves
90ml/6 tbsp olive oil

Serves 4

1 Cut the aubergines lengthways into 1cm/½in slices.

2 Cut the slices again crossways to give short strips.

3 Layer the strips in a colander with salt and leave to stand for 30 minutes over a plate to catch any juices. Rinse well in cool water and then drain thoroughly.

4 Place all the pesto ingredients, except the oil, in a blender or food processor. Blend until very smooth, then gradually add the oil in a thin stream until the mixture amalgamates. Season to taste.

5 Cook the penne in plenty of boiling salted water according to the instructions on the packet for about 8 minutes or until *al dente*. Add the aubergine and cook for a further 3 minutes.

6 Drain the pasta well and mix in the mint pesto and walnut halves. Serve immediately.

Macaroni with Hazelnut and Coriander Sauce

THIS IS A VARIATION on pesto sauce, giving a smooth, herby flavour of coriander.

INGREDIENTS

350g/12oz/3 cups dried macaroni
50g/2oz/⅓ cup hazelnuts
2 garlic cloves
1 bunch fresh coriander
1 tsp salt
90ml/6 tbsp olive oil
fresh coriander sprigs, to garnish
Serves 4

1 Cook the pasta following the instructions on the packet, until *al dente*.

2 Meanwhile, finely chop the hazelnuts.

COOK'S TIP

To remove the skins from the hazelnuts, place them in a 180°C/350°F/Gas 4 oven for 20 minutes, then rub off the skins with a clean dish towel.

VARIATION

If you like the crunchy texture of the nuts, only process the nut and herb mixture briefly.

3 Place the nuts, garlic, coriander, salt and 75ml/5 tbsp of the olive oil in a food processor, or use a pestle and mortar and grind together to create the sauce.

4 Heat the remaining oil in a saucepan and add the sauce. Fry very gently for about 1 minute until heated through.

5 Drain the pasta thoroughly and stir it into the sauce. Toss well to coat. Serve immediately, garnished with fresh coriander.

Tagliatelle with Spinach and Garlic Cheese

IT'S FUN TO MIX ingredients from different cuisines and produce a delicious dish as a result. Italian coloured pasta and spinach combine with Chinese soy sauce and French garlic-and-herb cream cheese to create this mouthwatering and wonderfully rich dish.

INGREDIENTS

225g/8oz fresh egg tagliatelle
225g/8oz fresh leaf spinach
30ml/2 tbsp light soy sauce
75g/3oz garlic-and-herb cheese
45ml/3 tbsp milk
salt and ground black pepper
Serves 4

1 Cook the tagliatelle in plenty of salted boiling water according to the instructions on the packet. Drain and return to the pan.

2 Blanch the spinach in a tiny amount of water until just wilted, then drain well, squeezing dry with the back of a wooden spoon. Chop roughly with scissors.

3 Return the spinach to its pan and stir in the soy sauce, garlic-and-herb cheese and the milk. Bring slowly to the boil, stirring until smooth. Season to taste.

4 When the sauce is ready, pour over the pasta. Toss the pasta and sauce together and serve hot in warmed plates.

Tagliatelle with Greek Avocado Sauce

THIS IS AN UNUSUAL sauce with a pale green colour, studded with red tomato. It has a luxurious, velvety texture. The sauce is rather rich, so you don't need too much of it.

INGREDIENTS

3 ripe tomatoes
2 large ripe avocados
25g/1oz/2 tbsp butter, plus extra for tossing
   the pasta
1 garlic clove, crushed
350ml/12fl oz/1½ cups double cream
dash of Tabasco sauce
450g/1lb fresh egg tagliatelle
salt and ground black pepper
freshly grated Parmesan cheese, to garnish
60ml/4 tbsp soured cream, to garnish
Serves 6

1 Halve the tomatoes and remove the cores. Squeeze out the seeds and dice the flesh. Set the flesh aside until required.

2 Halve the avocados, remove the stones and peel. Roughly chop the flesh. If hard-skinned, scoop out the flesh with a spoon.

3 Melt the butter in a saucepan and add the garlic. Cook for 1 minute, then add the cream and chopped avocados. Increase the heat, stirring constantly and breaking up the avocado flesh with a spoon.

4 Add the diced tomatoes and season to taste with salt, pepper and a little Tabasco sauce. Keep the mixture warm.

5 Cook the pasta in plenty of salted boiling water according to the instructions on the packet. Drain well through a colander and toss with a knob of butter.

6 Divide the pasta among four warmed bowls and spoon the sauce on top. Sprinkle with grated Parmesan cheese and top with a spoonful of soured cream.

Fusilli with Peppers and Onions

PEPPERS ARE characteristic of southern Italy. When grilled and peeled they have a delicious smoky flavour, and are easier to digest.

INGREDIENTS

450g/1lb red and yellow peppers
90ml/6 tbsp olive oil
1 large red onion, thinly sliced
2 garlic cloves, minced
400g/14oz/3½ cups fresh or dried fusilli
45ml/3 tbsp finely chopped fresh parsley
salt and ground black pepper
freshly grated Parmesan cheese, to serve
Serves 4

1 Place the peppers under a hot grill and turn occasionally until they are blackened and blistered on all sides. Remove from the heat, place in a plastic bag, seal and put to one side for 5 minutes or so.

2 Peel the peppers. Cut them into quarters, remove the stems and seeds, and slice into thin strips.

3 Heat the oil in a large frying pan. Add the onion, and cook over a moderate heat until softened but not brown, about 5–8 minutes. Stir in the garlic, and cook for a further 2 minutes, stirring continuously.

4 Cook the pasta in a large saucepan with plenty of salted boiling water until just *al dente*. Do not drain yet.

5 Meanwhile, add the peppers to the onion, and mix together gently. Stir in about 45ml/3 tbsp of the pasta cooking water. Season with salt and pepper. Stir in the finely chopped fresh parsley.

6 Drain the pasta well through a colander. Tip it into the pan with the vegetables, and cook over a moderate heat for 3–4 minutes, stirring constantly to mix the pasta into the sauce. Serve immediately in warmed plates with the grated Parmesan cheese handed separately.

Fusilli with Cream and Cheese

SOURED CREAM and two cheeses make a lovely rich sauce.

INGREDIENTS

350g/12oz dried fusilli col buco
25g/1oz/2 tbsp butter
1 onion, chopped
1 garlic clove, chopped
15ml/1 tbsp chopped fresh oregano
300ml/½ pint/1¼ cups soured cream
75g/3oz/¾ cup grated mozzarella cheese
75g/3oz/¾ cup grated Bel Paese cheese
5 sun-dried tomatoes in oil, drained
   and sliced
salt and ground black pepper
Serves 4

1 Cook the pasta in plenty of salted boiling water according to the instructions on the packet.

2 Melt the butter in a large frying pan and fry the onion for about 10 minutes until softened. Add the garlic and cook for 1 minute.

3 Stir in the oregano and cream and heat gently until almost boiling. Stir in the mozzarella and Bel Paese cheese and heat gently, stirring occasionally, until melted. Add the sun-dried tomatoes and season to taste.

4 Drain the pasta twists well and turn into a serving dish. Pour over the sauce and toss well to coat. Serve immediately.

Mezze with Cheese and Coriander

A SPEEDY SUPPER dish, this is best served with a simple tomato and fresh basil salad.

INGREDIENTS

450g/1lb/4 cups dried mezze rigatoni
115g/4oz full-fat garlic-and-herb cheese
30ml/2 tbsp fresh coriander, very
   finely chopped
300ml/½ pint/1¼ cups single cream
115g/4oz/1 cup shelled peas, cooked
salt and ground black pepper
Serves 4

1 Cook the pasta in a large saucepan with plenty of salted boiling water according to the instructions on the packet.

2 Melt the cheese in a small pan over a low heat until smooth.

3 Stir in the coriander, cream and salt and pepper. Bring slowly to the boil, stirring occasionally, until well blended. Stir in the peas and continue cooking until heated through.

4 Drain the pasta and turn into a large serving dish. Pour over the sauce and toss well to coat thoroughly. Serve immediately.

COOK'S TIP

If you do not like the pronounced flavour of fresh coriander, substitute another fresh herb, such as basil leaves or flat leaf parsley.

Spaghetti with Pesto Sauce

DON'T STINT on the fresh basil – this is the most wonderful sauce in the world – and it tastes completely different from the ready-made pesto sold in jars.

INGREDIENTS

2 garlic cloves
50g/2oz/¹/₂ cup pine nuts
40g/1¹/₂oz/1 cup fresh basil leaves
150ml/¹/₄ pint/²/₃ cup olive oil
50g/2oz/4 tbsp unsalted butter, softened
60ml/4 tbsp freshly grated
    Parmesan cheese
450g/1lb fresh or dried spaghetti
salt and ground black pepper

Serves 4

1 Peel the garlic and place it in a blender or food processor. Add a little salt and the pine nuts and process the ingredients until broken up. Add the basil leaves to the mixture and continue to process until you have formed a thick paste.

2 Gradually add the olive oil, little by little, until the mixture is creamy, smooth and thick.

3 Beat in the butter and season with ground black pepper. Beat in the cheese. Alternatively, you can make the pesto by hand using a pestle and mortar to blend the ingredients.

4 Store the pesto sauce in a jar, with a layer of olive oil on top to exclude the air, in the fridge until you are ready to use it.

5 Cook the pasta in plenty of salted boiling water according to the instructions on the packet, until *al dente*. Drain well.

6 Toss the pasta with half the pesto and serve in warm bowls, with the remaining pesto sauce spooned over the top.

Spaghetti with Fresh Tomato Sauce

THE HEAT FROM the pasta will release the delicious flavours of this sauce. Only use the really red and soft tomatoes – large ripe beefsteak or Marmande tomatoes are ideal. Don't be tempted to use small hard tomatoes: they have very little flavour.

INGREDIENTS

4 large ripe tomatoes
2 garlic cloves, finely chopped
60ml/4 tbsp chopped fresh herbs, such as
    basil, marjoram, oregano or parsley
150ml/¼ pint/⅔ cup olive oil
450g/1lb dried spaghetti
salt and ground black pepper
Serves 4

1 Skin the tomatoes by placing them in a saucepan of boiling water for 1 minute. Lift out with a slotted spoon and plunge immediately into a bowl of cold water. You will then find that the skins peel off easily. Dry the tomatoes on kitchen paper.

2 Halve the peeled tomatoes and squeeze out the seeds. Chop into 5mm/¼in cubes and mix with the garlic, herbs, olive oil and seasoning in a non-metallic bowl. Cover and set aside to allow the flavours to mellow for at least 30 minutes.

3 Cook the pasta in plenty of salted boiling water, according to the instructions on the packet.

4 Drain the pasta and mix with the sauce. Cover with a lid and leave for 2–3 minutes, then toss again and serve immediately.

VARIATION

Mix 115g/4oz/1 cup stoned and chopped black Greek olives into the sauce just before serving.

Spaghetti with Aubergine and Tomato

A GREAT SUPPER RECIPE – serve this aubergine and tomato dish with freshly cooked mangetouts.

INGREDIENTS

3 small aubergines
olive oil, for frying
450g/1lb dried spaghetti
1 quantity Classic Tomato Sauce
  (see Curly Lasagne with Classic
  Tomato Sauce)
225g/8oz freshly grated Fontina cheese
salt and ground black pepper
Serves 4

1 Top and tail the aubergines and cut into thin, even slices. Arrange in a colander, sprinkling with plenty of salt between each layer. Leave to stand for about 30 minutes.

2 Rinse the aubergine slices under cold running water. Drain and pat dry on kitchen paper.

3 Heat plenty of oil in a large frying pan and fry the aubergine slices in batches for about 5 minutes, turning them once during the cooking time, until evenly browned.

4 Meanwhile, cook the pasta in a large saucepan with plenty of salted boiling water according to the instructions on the packet, until *al dente*.

5 Stir the tomato sauce into the pan with the aubergines and bring to the boil. Cover and then simmer for 5 minutes.

6 Stir in the Fontina cheese and salt and pepper. Continue stirring over a medium heat until the cheese melts.

7 Drain the pasta and stir into the sauce, tossing well to coat. Serve immediately on warmed plates.

Pasta Pumpkin Surprise

GLORIOUS PUMPKIN SHELLS summon up the delights of autumn and seem too good simply to throw away. Use one instead of a serving dish. Pumpkin and pasta make marvellous partners, especially as a main course served from the baked shell.

INGREDIENTS

1.75kg/4–4½lb pumpkin
1 onion, sliced
2.5cm/1in piece fresh root ginger
45ml/3 tbsp extra virgin olive oil
1 courgette, sliced
115g/4oz mushrooms, sliced
400g/14oz can chopped tomatoes
75g/3oz¾ cup dried conchiglie
450ml/¾ pint/1¾ cups stock
60ml/4 tbsp fromage frais
30ml/2 tbsp chopped fresh basil
salt and ground black pepper

Serves 4

1 Preheat the oven to 180°C/350°F/ Gas 4. Cut the top off the pumpkin with a large, sharp knife and scoop out and discard all of the pumpkin seeds.

2 Using a small sharp knife and a sturdy tablespoon, cut and scrape out as much flesh from the pumpkin shell as possible, then chop the flesh into rough chunks.

3 Bake the pumpkin with its lid on for 45 minutes–1 hour until the inside begins to soften.

4 Meanwhile, make the filling. Heat the olive oil in a pan and gently fry the onion, ginger and pumpkin flesh for about 10 minutes, stirring the mixture occasionally.

5 Add the sliced courgette and mushrooms and cook for a further 3 minutes, then stir in the tomatoes, pasta and stock. Season well, bring to the boil, then cover the pan and simmer gently for about 10 minutes.

6 Stir the fromage frais and basil into the pasta and spoon the mixture into the pumpkin. It may not be possible to fit all the filling into the pumpkin shell, so serve the rest separately if necessary.

Baked Pasta

Like Bolognese sauce, lasagne, macaroni cheese and cannelloni have become so popular outside Italy that we seldom stop to consider the origins of these delicious pasta dishes. A kind of layered pasta pie was mentioned by the Roman gastronome Apicius in the first century AD, so we know that lasagne, at least, has a very long history. In the Renaissance, sumptuous layered pasta dishes, often moulded into fanciful shapes, were popular with the wealthy. Nowadays, *pasta al forno*, as baked pasta dishes are called in Italy, are more often eaten at family meals, especially on occasions when large numbers must be catered for. Baked dishes can be prepared in advance and are easy to serve.

This chapter introduces classic dishes and regional favourites with modern adaptations. In calculating serving quantities, it is assumed the dish will be the main course, but smaller portions can be served as a first course, which is more traditional in Italy.

Chicken Cannelloni al Forno

A LIGHTER ALTERNATIVE to the usual beef-filled, béchamel-coated version. Fill with ricotta cheese, onion and mushroom for a vegetarian dish.

INGREDIENTS

450g/1lb skinless, boneless chicken
  breast, cooked
225g/8oz mushrooms
2 garlic cloves, crushed
30ml/2 tbsp chopped fresh parsley
15ml/1 tbsp chopped fresh tarragon
1 egg, beaten
freshly squeezed lemon juice
12–18 fresh or dried cannelloni tubes
1 quantity Classic Tomato Sauce (see Curly
  Lasagne with Classic Tomato Sauce)
50g/2oz/½ cup grated Parmesan cheese
salt and ground black pepper
fresh parsley sprig, to garnish
Serves 4–6

1 Preheat the oven to 200°C/
400°F/Gas 6. Place the chicken in a blender or food processor and process until finely minced. Transfer to a bowl.

2 Place the mushrooms, garlic, parsley and tarragon in the blender or food processor and process until finely minced.

3 Beat the mushroom mixture into the chicken with the egg, salt and ground black pepper and lemon juice to taste.

4 If necessary, cook the cannelloni in plenty of salted boiling water according to the instructions on the packet. Drain well and pat dry on a clean dish towel.

5 Place the filling in a piping bag fitted with a large plain nozzle. Use to fill each tube of cannelloni.

6 Lay the filled cannelloni tightly together in a single layer in a buttered shallow ovenproof dish. Spoon the tomato sauce over and sprinkle with Parmesan cheese. Bake in the oven for 30 minutes or until brown and bubbling. Serve the cannelloni garnished with a sprig of parsley.

Aubergine Lasagne

This delicious lasagne is also suitable for home freezing.

INGREDIENTS

3 aubergines, sliced
75ml/5 tbsp olive oil
2 large onions, finely chopped
2 x 400g/14oz cans chopped tomatoes
5ml/1 tsp dried mixed herbs
2–3 garlic cloves, crushed
6 sheets "no-need-to-pre-cook" dried
  lasagne sheets
salt and ground black pepper

For the cheese sauce

25g/1oz/2 tbsp butter
25g/1oz/2 tbsp plain flour
300ml/½ pint/1¼ cups milk
2.5ml/½ tsp hot mustard
115g/4oz/8 tbsp grated mature Cheddar
15g/½oz/1 tbsp grated Parmesan cheese

Serves 4

1 Layer the sliced aubergine in a colander, sprinkling lightly with salt between each layer. Leave to stand for 1 hour, then rinse and pat dry with kitchen paper.

COOK'S TIP

To save time, this recipe uses lasagne that does not need pre-cooking. Look in the supermarket, or ask at your delicatessen, for lasagne sheets marked "no need to pre-cook".

2 Heat 60ml/4 tbsp of the oil in a large pan, fry the aubergine and drain on kitchen paper. Add the remaining oil to the pan, cook the onions for 5 minutes, then stir in the tomatoes, herbs, garlic and seasoning. Bring to the boil and simmer, covered, for 30 minutes.

3 To make th sauce, melt the butter in a pan, stir in the flour and cook gently for 1 minute, stirring. Gradually stir in the milk. Bring to the boil, stirring, and cook for 2 minutes. Remove from the heat and stir in the mustard, cheeses and seasoning.

4 Preheat the oven to 200°C/400°F/Gas 6. Arrange half the aubergines in the base of an ovenproof dish, spoon half the tomato sauce over. Arrange three sheets of lasagne on top. Repeat.

5 Spoon the cheese sauce over, cover and bake for 30 minutes until lightly browned.

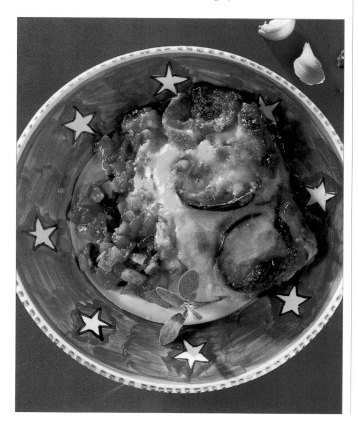

Mushroom and Courgette Lasagne

THIS IS THE PERFECT main-course lasagne for vegetarians. Adding dried porcini to fresh chestnut mushrooms intensifies the "mushroomy" flavour and gives the whole dish more substance. Serve with crusty Italian bread.

INGREDIENTS

15g/¹/₂oz dried porcini mushrooms
175ml/6fl oz/³/₄ cup warm water
30ml/2 tbsp olive oil
75g/3oz/6 tbsp butter
450g/1lb courgettes, thinly sliced
1 onion, finely chopped
450g/1lb/6 cups chestnut mushrooms,
    thinly sliced
2 garlic cloves, crushed
1 quantity Winter Tomato Sauce
10ml/2 tsp chopped fresh marjoram or
    5ml/1 tsp dried marjoram, plus extra
    fresh leaves, to garnish
6–8 "no-need-to-pre-cook" dried
    lasagne sheets
50g/2oz/²/₃ cup freshly grated
    Parmesan cheese
salt and ground black pepper

For the white sauce
40g/1¹/₂oz/3 tbsp butter
40g/1¹/₂oz/¹/₃ cup plain flour
900ml/1¹/₂ pints/3³/₄ cups hot milk
nutmeg
Serves 6

1   Put the dried porcini mushrooms in a bowl. Pour over the warm water and leave to soak for 15–20 minutes. Tip the porcini and liquid into a fine sieve set over a bowl and squeeze the mushrooms with your hands to release as much liquid as possible. Chop the mushrooms finely and set aside. Strain the soaking liquid through a fine sieve and reserve half for the sauce.

2   Preheat the oven to 190°C/375°F/ Gas 5. Heat the olive oil with 25g/1oz/2 tbsp of the butter in a large skillet or saucepan.

3   Add about half the courgette slices to the pan and season with salt and pepper to taste. Cook the courgettes over a medium heat, turning the slices frequently, for 5–8 minutes until they are lightly coloured on both sides. Remove the courgettes from the pan with a slotted spoon and allow to drain on kitchen paper. Repeat with the remaining courgettes.

4   Melt half the remaining butter in the fat remaining in the pan, then cook the finely chopped onion, stirring, for 1–2 minutes. Add half of the fresh mushrooms and the crushed garlic to the pan and sprinkle with a little salt and pepper to taste.

5   Toss the mushrooms over a high heat for 5 minutes or so until the mushrooms are juicy and tender. Transfer to a bowl with a slotted spoon, then repeat with the remaining butter and mushrooms.

6   Make the white sauce. Melt the butter in a large saucepan, add the flour and cook, stirring, over a medium heat for 1–2 minutes.

7   Add the hot milk a little at a time, whisking well after each addition. Bring to the boil and cook, stirring, until the sauce is smooth and thick. Grate in fresh nutmeg to taste and season with a little salt and pepper. Whisk well, then remove the sauce from the heat.

8   Place the tomato sauce in a blender or food processor with the reserved porcini soaking liquid and blend to a pureé. Add the courgettes to the bowl of fried mushrooms, then stir in the porcini and marjoram.

9   Adjust the seasoning to taste, then spread a third of the tomato sauce in a baking dish. Add half the vegetable mixture, spreading it evenly.

10 Top with about a third of the white sauce, then about half the lasagne sheets. Repeat these layers, then top with the remaining tomato sauce and white sauce and sprinkle with the grated Parmesan cheese.

11 Bake the lasagne for 35–40 minutes, or until the pasta feels tender when pierced with a skewer. Allow to stand for about 10 minutes before serving. If you like, sprinkle each serving with marjoram leaves.

COOK'S TIPS

• *The amount of pasta will depend on the size and shape of the pasta sheets and your baking dish; you may need to break the pasta to fit.*

• *This dish is time-consuming to prepare, but well worth the effort. You can make the tomato sauce in advance and chill it for up to 2 days until you are ready to assemble the lasagne, or you can freeze it. Make sure that you leave it to thaw completely before using.*

Baked Tortellini with Three Cheeses

SERVE THIS STRAIGHT out of the oven while the cheese is still runny. If smoked mozzarella cheese is not available, try using a smoked German cheese or even grated smoked Cheddar as an alternative.

INGREDIENTS

450g/1lb fresh tortellini
2 eggs
350g/12oz/1½ cups ricotta or curd cheese
25g/1oz/2 tbsp butter
25g/1oz fresh basil leaves
115g/4oz smoked mozzarella cheese
60ml/4 tbsp freshly grated
  Parmesan cheese
salt and ground black pepper
Serves 4–6

1 Preheat the oven to 190°C/375°F/ Gas 5. Cook the fresh tortellini in plenty of salted boiling water according to the instructions on the packet. Drain well.

2 Beat the eggs with the ricotta or curd cheese and season well with salt and pepper.

3 Use the butter to grease an ovenproof dish. Spoon in half the tortellini, pour half the cheese mixture over and cover with half the basil leaves.

4 Cover with the mozzarella and remaining basil. Top with the rest of the tortellini and spread the remaining ricotta or curd cheese mixture over.

5 Sprinkle evenly with the Parmesan cheese. Bake in the oven for 35–45 minutes or until golden brown and bubbling.

Cannelloni with Mixed Vegetables

THIS VERSION of a classic Italian dish introduces a variety of vegetables topped with cheese sauce.

INGREDIENTS

8 dried cannelloni tubes
115g/4oz spinach
tomatoes and green salad, to serve

For the filling

15ml/1 tbsp oil
175g/6oz/1½ cups minced beef
2 garlic cloves, crushed
25g/1oz/2 tbsp plain flour
120ml/4fl oz/½ cup beef stock
1 small carrot, finely chopped
1 small yellow courgette, chopped
salt and ground black pepper

For the sauce

25g/1oz/2 tbsp butter
25g/1oz/2 tbsp plain flour
250ml/8fl oz/1 cup milk
50g/2oz/½ cup freshly grated
   Parmesan cheese
Serves 4

1 Preheat the oven to 180°C/350°F/ Gas 4. For the filling, heat the oil in a large pan. Add the minced beef and garlic. Cook for 5 minutes.

2 Add the flour and cook for a further 1 minute. Slowly stir in the stock and bring to the boil.

3 Add the carrot and courgette and season. Cook for 10 minutes.

4 Spoon the mince mixture into the cannelloni tubes and place in an ovenproof dish.

5 Blanch the spinach in boiling water for 3 minutes. Drain well and place on top of the cannelloni tubes in the dish.

6 For the sauce melt the butter in a pan. Add the flour and cook for 1 minute. Pour in the milk, add the grated cheese and season well. Bring to the boil, stirring all the time. Pour over the cannelloni and spinach and bake for 30 minutes. Serve with tomatoes and a crisp green salad, if liked.

Vermicelli Omelette

A FRITTATA IS A FLAT BAKED omelette. Here it is made with vegetables and herbs, but you can put anything you fancy in it. Ham, sausage, salami, chicken, mushrooms, courgettes and aubergines are just a few suggestions, or you could simply add mixed herbs. Frittata is absolutely delicious cold. Cut into wedges, it is excellent food for picnics.

INGREDIENTS

50g/2oz dried vermicelli
6 eggs
60ml/4 tbsp panna da cucina or
    double cream
1 handful fresh basil leaves, shredded
1 handful fresh flat leaf parsley, chopped
75g/3oz/1 cup freshly grated
    Parmesan cheese
25g/1oz/2 tbsp butter
15ml/1 tbsp olive oil
1 onion, finely sliced
3 large pieces bottled roasted red pepper,
    drained, rinsed, dried and cut into strips
1 garlic clove, crushed
salt and ground black pepper
rocket leaves, to serve
Serves 4–6

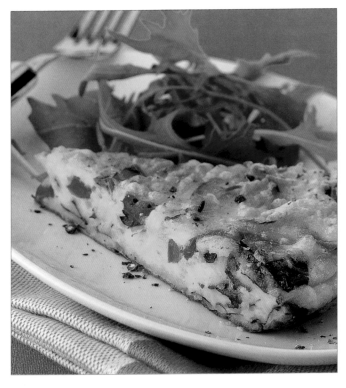

1 Preheat the oven to 190°C/375°F/ Gas 5. Cook the pasta in a saucepan of salted boiling water for 8 minutes.

2 Meanwhile, break the eggs into a bowl and add the cream and herbs. Whisk in about two-thirds of the grated Parmesan and add salt and pepper to taste.

3 Drain the pasta well and allow to cool; snip it into short lengths with scissors. Add to the egg mixture and whisk again. Set aside.

4 Melt the butter in the oil in a large, ovenproof non-stick frying pan. Add the onion and cook gently, stirring frequently, for 5 minutes until softened. Add the peppers and garlic.

5 Pour the egg and pasta mixture into the pan and stir well. Cook over a low to medium heat, without stirring, for 3–5 minutes or until the frittata is just set underneath. Sprinkle the remaining Parmesan over and bake in the oven for 5 minutes or until set. Before serving, leave to stand for at least 5 minutes. Cut into wedges and serve warm or cold, with rocket.

Lasagne 'Bolognese'

THIS IS THE CLASSIC *lasagne al forno.*
It is based on a rich, meaty filling, as
you would expect from an authentic
Bolognese recipe.

INGREDIENTS

1 quantity Bolognese Meat Sauce
150–250ml/5–8fl oz/²/₃–1 cup hot
   beef stock
12 "no-need-to-pre-cook" dried
   lasagne sheets
50g/2oz/²/₃ cup freshly grated
   Parmesan cheese

For the white sauce

50g/2oz/¹/₄ cup butter
50g/2oz/¹/₂ cup plain flour
900ml/1¹/₂ pints/3³/₄ cups hot milk
salt and ground black pepper
Serves 6

1 Preheat the oven to 190°C/375°F/
Gas 5. If the Bolognese sauce is
cold, reheat it. Once it is hot, stir in
enough stock to make it quite runny.

2 Make the white sauce. Melt the
butter in a medium saucepan,
add the flour and cook, stirring, for
1–2 minutes. Add the milk a little at a
time, whisking vigorously after each
addition. Bring to the boil and cook,
stirring, until the sauce is smooth and
thick. Add salt and pepper to taste,
whisk well, then remove from the heat.

3 Spread about a third of the
Bolognese sauce over the bottom
of a baking dish.

4 Cover the Bolognese sauce in the
bottom of the dish with about a
quarter of the white sauce, followed by
four sheets of lasagne. Repeat the
layers twice more, then cover the top
layer of lasagne with the remaining
white sauce and sprinkle the grated
Parmesan evenly over the top.

5 Bake for 40–45 minutes or until
the pasta feels tender when
pierced with a skewer. Allow to stand
for about 10 minutes before serving.

COOK'S TIPS

• The Bolognese sauce can be made up
to 3 days in advance and kept in a
covered container in the fridge.
• The lasagne is best baked straight after
layering or the pasta will begin to absorb
the sauces and dry out.
• To reheat leftover lasagne, prick it all
over with a skewer, then slowly pour a
little milk over to moisten. Cover with foil
and reheat in a 190°C/375°F/Gas 5
oven for 20 minutes, or until bubbling.

Baked Lasagne with Béchamel Sauce

THIS LASAGNE made from egg pasta uses a béchamel sauce flavoured with bay and mace to give it a lift.

INGREDIENTS

*2 quantities Bolognese sauce (see Tagliatelli
 with Bolognese Sauce)*
*12–16 fresh egg lasagne sheets or
 400g/14oz dried lasagne*
115g/4oz/1 cup grated Parmesan cheese
40g/1¹/₂oz/3 tbsp butter

For the béchamel sauce
750ml/1¹/₄ pints/3 cups milk
1 bay leaf
3 mace blades
115g/4oz/¹/₂ cup butter
75g/3oz/³/₄ cup plain flour
salt and ground black pepper

Serves 8–10

1 Prepare the meat sauce and set aside. Butter a large shallow baking dish, preferably rectangular or square.

COOK'S TIP

If you are using dried or bought pasta, follow step 4, but boil the lasagne in just two batches, and stop the cooking about 4 minutes before the recommended cooking time on the packet has elapsed. Rinse in cold water and lay the pasta out the same way as for the egg pasta.

2 Make the béchamel sauce by gently heating the milk with the bay leaf and mace in a small saucepan. Melt the butter in a medium heavy-based saucepan. Add the flour, and mix well with a wire whisk. Cook for 2–3 minutes, whisking constantly. Strain the hot milk into the flour and butter, and mix smoothly with the whisk. Bring the sauce to the boil, stirring constantly, and cook for a further 4–5 minutes. Season with salt and pepper and set aside.

3 If making your own fresh pasta, make sure it does not dry out. Cut it into rectangles measuring about 11cm/4¹/₂in wide and the same length as the baking dish (this will make it easier to assemble the dish later). Preheat the oven to 200°C/400°F/Gas 6.

4 Bring a very large pan of water to the boil. Place a large bowl of cold water near the cooker. Cover a large work surface with a tablecloth. Add salt to the rapidly boiling water. Drop in 3 or 4 of the egg pasta rectangles.

Cook very briefly, about 30 seconds. Remove the pasta from the pan, using a slotted spoon, and drop into the cold water for about 30 seconds. Pull them out of the water, shaking off the excess water. Lay them out flat without overlapping on the tablecloth. Repeat until all the pasta rectangles and the trimmings have been thoroughly drained on the tablecloth.

5 To assemble the lasagne, spread one large spoonful of the meat sauce over the base of the dish. Arrange a layer of pasta in the dish, cutting it with a sharp knife so that it covers the meat sauce.

6 Cover with another thin layer of meat sauce, then one of béchamel. Sprinkle with a little cheese. Repeat the layers in the same order, and ending with a layer of pasta coated with béchamel. Do not make more than about 6 layers of pasta. Use the pasta trimmings to patch any gaps in the pasta. Sprinkle the top with grated Parmesan cheese, and dot with butter.

7 Bake in the preheated oven for 20 minutes, or until brown on top. Remove from the oven and allow to stand for about 5 minutes before serving. Serve directly from the baking dish, cutting out rectangular or square sections for each helping.

Pasta Timbales

AN ALTERNATIVE WAY to serve pasta for a special occasion is to mix it with minced beef and tomato and bake it in a lettuce parcel.

INGREDIENTS

8 cos lettuce leaves
fresh basil leaves, to garnish

For the filling
15ml/1 tbsp oil
175g/6oz/1½ cups minced beef
15ml/1 tbsp tomato purée
1 garlic clove, crushed
115g/4oz/1 cup fresh or dried macaroni
salt and ground black pepper

For the sauce
25g/1oz/2 tbsp butter
25g/1oz/2 tbsp plain flour
250ml/8fl oz/1 cup double cream
30ml/2 tbsp chopped fresh basil

Serves 4

1 Preheat the oven to 180°C/350°F/ Gas 4. For the filling, heat the oil in a large pan and fry the minced beef for 7 minutes. Add the tomato purée and garlic and cook for a further 5 minutes.

2 Cook the macaroni in salted boiling water for 8–10 minutes or until al dente. Drain.

3 Mix together the pasta and minced beef mixture.

4 Line four 150ml/¼ pint/⅔ cup ramekin dishes with the cos lettuce leaves. Season the mince and spoon into the lettuce-lined ramekins.

5 Fold the lettuce leaves over the filling and place the ramekins in a roasting tin. Carefully pour boiling water to come halfway up the sides of the ramekins. Cover and cook for 20 minutes.

6 For the sauce, melt the butter in a pan. Add the flour and cook for 1 minute. Stir in the cream and fresh basil. Season and bring to the boil, stirring all the time. Turn out the timbales and serve on warmed plates with the creamy basil sauce, and garnish with fresh basil leaves.

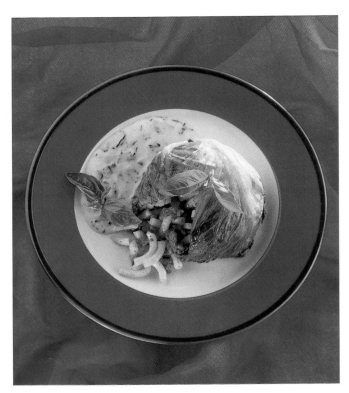

Broccoli and Ricotta Cannelloni

A DELICIOUS AND FILLING dish for
a meat-free dinner.

INGREDIENTS

12 dried cannelloni tubes, 7.5cm/3in long
450g/1lb/4 cups broccoli florets
75g/3oz/1½ cups fresh breadcrumbs
150ml/¼ pint/⅔ cup milk
60ml/4 tbsp olive oil, plus extra
    for brushing
225g/8oz/1 cup ricotta cheese
pinch of grated nutmeg
90ml/6 tbsp grated Parmesan or
    Pecorino cheese
salt and ground black pepper
30ml/2 tbsp pine nuts, for sprinkling

For the tomato sauce
30ml/2 tbsp olive oil
1 onion, finely chopped
1 garlic clove, crushed
2 x 400g/14oz cans chopped tomatoes
15ml/1 tbsp tomato purée
4 black olives, pitted and chopped
5ml/1 tsp dried thyme
Serves 4

1 Preheat the oven to 190°C/375°F/
Gas 5 and lightly grease an
ovenproof dish with olive oil. Bring a
large saucepan of water to the boil,
add a little olive oil and simmer the
cannelloni tubes, uncovered, for about
6–7 minutes, or until nearly cooked.

2 Meanwhile, steam or boil the
broccoli for 10 minutes, until
tender. Drain the pasta, rinse under
cold water and reserve. Drain the
broccoli and leave to cool, then place
in a blender or food processor and
process until smooth. Set aside.

3 Place the breadcrumbs in a bowl,
add the milk and oil and stir until
softened. Add the ricotta, broccoli
purée, nutmeg, 60ml/4 tbsp of the
Parmesan cheese and seasoning, then
set aside.

4 To make the sauce, heat the oil in
a frying pan; add the onion and
garlic. Fry for 5–6 minutes, until
softened but not brown.

5 Stir the tomatoes, tomato purée,
black olives, thyme and seasoning
into the sauce. Boil rapidly for
2–3 minutes, then pour into the base
of the dish.

6 Spoon the cheese mixture into a
piping bag fitted with a 1cm/½in
nozzle. Carefully open the cannelloni
tubes. Standing each one upright on a
board, pipe the filling into each tube.
Lay them in rows in the tomato sauce.

7 Brush the tops of the cannelloni
with a little olive oil and sprinkle
the remaining Parmesan cheese and
pine nuts over. Bake for about
25–30 minutes, until golden on top.

Cannelloni al Forno

THIS IS A RICH AND SUBSTANTIAL dish, which takes quite a long time to prepare. Serve it for a party — it can be made a day ahead up to the baking stage. Your guests are bound to appreciate your efforts, because the cannelloni tastes so good.

INGREDIENTS

15ml/1 tbsp olive oil
1 small onion, finely chopped
450g/1lb minced beef
1 garlic clove, finely chopped
5ml/1 tsp dried mixed herbs
120ml/4fl oz/½ cup beef stock
1 egg
75g/3oz cooked ham or mortadella
  sausage, finely chopped
45ml/3 tbsp fine fresh white
  breadcrumbs
150g/5oz/1⅔ cups freshly grated
  Parmesan cheese
18 "no-need-to-pre-cook" cannelloni tubes
salt and ground black pepper

For the tomato sauce

30ml/2 tbsp olive oil
1 small onion, finely chopped
½ carrot, finely chopped
1 celery stick, finely chopped
1 garlic clove, crushed
400g/14oz can chopped Italian
  plum tomatoes
a few sprigs of fresh basil
2.5ml/½ tsp dried oregano

For the white sauce

50g/2oz/¼ cup butter
50g/2oz/½ cup plain flour
900ml/1½ pints/3¾ cups milk
nutmeg
Serves 6

1 Heat the olive oil in a medium skillet or saucepan and cook the finely chopped onion over a gentle heat, stirring occasionally, for about 5 minutes until softened.

2 Add the minced beef and garlic and cook gently for 10 minutes, stirring and breaking up any lumps with a wooden spoon. Add the mixed herbs, and salt and pepper to taste, then moisten with half the stock. Cover the pan and simmer for 25 minutes, stirring from time to time and adding more stock as the mixture reduces. Spoon into a bowl and leave to cool.

3 Meanwhile, make the tomato sauce. Heat the olive oil in a medium saucepan, add the vegetables and garlic and cook over a medium heat, stirring frequently, for about 10 minutes. Add the canned tomatoes. Fill the empty can with water, pour it into the pan, then stir in the herbs, with salt and pepper to taste. Bring to the boil, lower the heat, cover and simmer for 25–30 minutes, stirring occasionally. Purée the tomato sauce in a blender or food processor.

4 Add the egg, ham or mortadella, breadcrumbs and 90ml/6 tbsp of the grated Parmesan to the meat and stir well to mix. Taste for seasoning.

5 Spread a little of the tomato sauce over the bottom of a baking dish. Using a teaspoon, fill the cannelloni tubes with the meat mixture and place them in a single layer in the dish on top of the tomato sauce. Pour the remaining tomato sauce over the top.

6 Preheat the oven to 190°C/375°F/ Gas 5. Make the white sauce. Melt the butter in a saucepan, add the flour and cook, stirring, for 1–2 minutes. Add the milk a little at a time, whisking vigorously after each addition.

7 Bring to the boil and cook, stirring, until the sauce is smooth and thick. Grate in fresh nutmeg to taste and season with a little salt and pepper. Whisk well, then remove from the heat.

8 Pour the white sauce over the stuffed cannelloni, then sprinkle with the remaining Parmesan. Place in the oven and bake for 40–45 minutes or until the cannelloni tubes feel tender when pierced with a skewer. Allow the cannelloni to stand for about 10 minutes before serving.

Baked Macaroni with Cheese

THIS DELICIOUS DISH is perhaps less common in Italy than other pasta dishes, but has become a family favourite around the world.

INGREDIENTS

475ml/16fl oz/2 cups milk
1 bay leaf
3 mace blades
50g/2oz/4 tbsp butter
40g/1½oz/⅓ cup flour
175g/6oz/1½ cups grated Parmesan or
    Cheddar cheese, or a combination
    of both
40g/½oz/⅓ cup breadcrumbs
450g/1lb/4 cups short-cut macaroni
salt and ground black pepper
Serves 6

1 Make a béchamel sauce by gently heating the milk with the bay leaf and mace, in a small saucepan. Do not let it boil.

2 In a separate medium, heavy-based saucepan, melt the butter. Add the flour, and mix it in well with a wire whisk. Cook for 2–3 minutes, but do not let the butter burn.

3 Strain the hot milk into the flour and butter mixture all at once, and mix smoothly with the whisk. Bring the sauce to the boil, stirring constantly, and cook for a further 4–5 minutes.

4 Season with salt and pepper. Add all but 30ml/2 tbsp of the cheese, and stir over a low heat until melted. Place a layer of clear film right on the surface of the sauce to prevent a skin forming and set aside while you prepare the pasta.

5 Preheat the oven to 200°C/ 400°F/Gas 6. Grease an ovenproof dish and sprinkle with some breadcrumbs. Cook the pasta in plenty of boiling salted water until *al dente*.

6 Drain the pasta, and combine it with the sauce. Pour it into the prepared dish. Sprinkle the top with the remaining breadcrumbs and grated cheese and bake in the centre of the oven for 20 minutes, until golden and bubbling.

Tagliatelle and Prawn Parcels

A QUICK AND IMPRESSIVE dish, easy to prepare in advance and cook at the last minute. When the paper packets are opened at the table, the filling smells wonderful.

INGREDIENTS

750g/1¾lb raw prawns in the shell
450g/1lb fresh egg tagliatelle
150ml/¼ pint/⅔ cup fresh or ready-made
    pesto sauce
20ml/4 tsp olive oil
1 garlic clove, crushed
120ml/4fl oz/½ cup dry white wine
salt and ground black pepper
Serves 4

1 Preheat the oven to 200°C/400°F/ Gas 6. Twist the heads off the prawns, remove the legs and discard.

2 Cook the tagliatelle in plenty of rapidly boiling salted water for 2 minutes only, then drain. Mix with half the pesto.

COOK'S TIP

Cooking in a paper parcel keeps the food moist and full of flavour, but care must be taken when opening the parcel because of the escaping steam.

3 Cut four 30cm/12in squares of greaseproof paper and place 5ml/1 tsp olive oil in the centre of each. Pile equal amounts of pasta in the middle of each square.

4 Top with equal amounts of prawns and spoon over the remaining pesto mixed with the garlic. Season with pepper; sprinkle each with the wine.

5 Brush the edges of the paper lightly with water and bring them loosely up around the filling, twisting to enclose. (The parcels should look like money bags.)

6 Place the parcels on a baking sheet. Bake in the oven for 10–15 minutes. Serve at once, allowing the diners to open their own packets at the table.

Macaroni with Four Cheeses

RICH AND CREAMY, this is a deluxe macaroni cheese that can be served for an informal lunch or supper party. It goes well with both a tomato and basil salad or a leafy green salad.

INGREDIENTS

250g/9oz/2¼ cups short-cut macaroni
50g/2oz/¼ cup butter
50g/2oz/½ cup plain flour
600ml/1 pint/2½ cups milk
100ml/3½ fl oz/scant ½ cup panna da
* cucina or double cream*
100ml/3½ fl oz/scant ½ cup dry
* white wine*
50g/2oz/½ cup grated Gruyère or
* Emmental cheese*
50g/2oz Fontina cheese, diced small
50g/2oz Gorgonzola cheese, crumbled
75g/3oz/1 cup freshly grated
* Parmesan cheese*
salt and ground black pepper
Serves 4

1 Preheat the oven to 180°C/350°F/ Gas 4. Cook the pasta according to the instructions on the packet.

2 Meanwhile, gently melt the butter in a medium saucepan, add the flour and cook, stirring, for 1–2 minutes. Add the milk a little at a time, whisking vigorously after each addition. Stir in the cream, followed by the dry white wine. Bring to the boil. Cook, stirring continuously, until the sauce thickens, then remove the sauce from the heat.

3 Add the Gruyère or Emmental, Fontina, Gorgonzola and about a third of the grated Parmesan to the sauce. Stir well to mix in the cheeses, then taste for seasoning and add salt and pepper if necessary.

4 Drain the pasta well and tip it into a baking dish. Pour the sauce over the pasta and mix well, then sprinkle the remaining Parmesan over the top. Bake for 25–30 minutes or until golden brown. Serve hot.

Sicilian Lasagne

LASAGNE IS NOT TRADITIONAL in Sicily as it is in northern Italy, but the Sicilians have their own version.

INGREDIENTS

1 small onion
$^1\!/_2$ carrot
$^1\!/_2$ celery stick
45ml/3 tbsp olive oil
250g/9oz diced boneless pork
60ml/4 tbsp dry white wine
400g/14oz can chopped Italian
    plum tomatoes or 400ml/14fl oz/
    $1^2\!/_3$ cups passata
200ml/7fl oz/scant 1 cup chicken stock
15ml/1 tbsp tomato purée
2 bay leaves
15ml/1 tbsp chopped fresh flat leaf parsley
250g/9oz fresh lasagne sheets, pre-cooked
    if necessary
2 hard-boiled eggs, sliced
125g/4$^1\!/_2$oz packet mozzarella cheese,
    drained and sliced
60ml/4 tbsp freshly grated Pecorino cheese
salt and ground black pepper
Serves 6

1 Chop the fresh vegetables finely, either in a food processor or by hand. Heat 30ml/2 tbsp of the oil in a large skillet or saucepan, add the chopped vegetables and cook over a medium heat, stirring frequently, for about 10 minutes.

2 Add the pork and fry for about 5 minutes, stirring occasionally, until well browned on all sides. Pour in the wine and let it bubble and reduce for a few minutes, then add the tomatoes or passata, the stock and the tomato purée. Make a tear in each bay leaf to release the flavour, then add to the pan with the parsley and salt and pepper to taste, mixing well. Cover and cook for 30–40 minutes until the pork is tender, stirring from time to time. Take the pan off the heat and remove and discard the bay leaves from the sauce.

3 Using a slotted spoon, lift the pieces of meat out of the sauce. Chop them roughly, then return them to the sauce. Stir well.

4 Preheat the oven to 190°C/375°F/ Gas 5. Bring a saucepan of salted water to the boil. Cut the lasagne sheets into 2.5cm/1in strips and add them to the boiling water. Cook for 3–4 minutes until just al dente. Drain well, then stir the strips into the sauce.

5 Spread out half the pasta and sauce mixture in a shallow baking dish and cover with half the egg and mozzarella slices and half the grated Pecorino. Repeat the layers, then drizzle the remaining oil over the top. Bake for 30–35 minutes until golden brown and bubbling. Allow to stand for about 10 minutes before serving.

Fusilli with Ham and Cheese

WITH ITS CRISPY CRUST and moist and creamy centre, this quick and easy pasta bake is both filling and nutritious. Serve it for a winter supper, with a salad on the side.

INGREDIENTS 3

300g/11oz/2¼ cups dried fusilli, eliche or
    other short pasta shapes
3 eggs
200ml/7fl oz/scant 1 cup milk
150ml/¼ pint/⅔ cup single cream
150g/5oz Gruyère cheese, grated
nutmeg
115g/4oz cooked ham, cut into strips
30ml/2 tbsp freshly grated Parmesan cheese
salt and ground black pepper
Serves 4

1 Preheat the oven to 190°C/375°F/ Gas 5. Bring a large saucepan of salted water to the boil. Add the pasta and cook for 5 minutes.

2 Meanwhile, beat the eggs in a jug with the milk, cream and half the grated Gruyère. Grate in a little fresh nutmeg and season to taste.

3 Drain the pasta and tip half of it into a buttered baking dish. Arrange half the strips of ham on top, then follow with the remaining pasta and ham. Pour the egg and cream mixture into the dish, stir to mix a little, then sprinkle the remaining Gruyère and the Parmesan over the top. Bake for 30 minutes or until golden brown.

Lasagne with Lamb

IT IS UNUSUAL TO MAKE lasagne with lamb, but the flavour is excellent.

INGREDIENTS

15ml/1 tbsp olive oil
1 small onion, finely chopped
450g/1lb minced lamb
1 garlic clove, crushed
45ml/3 tbsp dry white wine
5ml/1 tsp dried mixed herbs
5ml/1 tsp dried oregano
450ml/¾ pint/scant 2 cups passata
12–16 fresh lasagne sheets, pre-cooked
    if necessary
30ml/2 tbsp freshly grated Parmesan cheese
salt and ground black pepper

For the white sauce
50g/2oz/¼ cup butter
50g/2oz/½ cup plain flour
900ml/1½ pints/3¾ cups hot milk
30ml/2 tbsp freshly grated Parmesan cheese
nutmeg
Serves 4–6

1 Heat the oil in a saucepan and cook the onion over a gentle heat, stirring frequently, for about 5 minutes until softened. Add the minced lamb and garlic and cook gently for 10 minutes, stirring frequently. Stir in salt and pepper to taste, then add the wine and cook rapidly for about 2 minutes, stirring constantly. Stir in the herbs and passata. Simmer gently for 45 minutes to 1 hour, stirring occasionally.

2 Preheat the oven to 190°C/375°F/ Gas 5. Make the white sauce. Melt the butter in a saucepan, add the flour and cook, stirring, for 1–2 minutes. Add the milk a little at a time, whisking vigorously after each addition. Bring to the boil and cook, stirring, until the sauce is smooth and thick. Add the Parmesan, grate in fresh nutmeg to taste, season with a little salt and pepper and whisk well. Remove the pan from the heat.

3 Spread a few spoonfuls of meat sauce over the bottom of a baking dish and cover with three or four sheets of lasagne. Spread a quarter of the remaining meat sauce over the lasagne, then a quarter of the white sauce. Repeat the layers three times, finishing with white sauce.

4 Sprinkle the Parmesan over the surface and bake for 30–40 minutes or until the topping is golden brown and bubbling. Allow to stand for about 10 minutes before serving.

Lasagne al Forno

THE CLASSIC VERSION of this dish is pasta layered with meat sauce and creamy béchamel sauce. You can vary it by using mozzarella cheese instead of the béchamel sauce, or by mixing ricotta cheese, Parmesan and herbs together instead of the meat sauce.

INGREDIENTS

*12 dried lasagne sheets, pre-cooked
   if necessary*
*1 quantity Bolognese sauce (see Tagliatelli
   with Bolognese Sauce)*
*about 50g/2oz/¹/₂ cup freshly grated
   Parmesan cheese*
tomato slices and parsley sprig, to garnish

For the béchamel sauce
900ml/1¹/₂ pints/3³/₄ cups milk
sliced onion, carrot and celery
a few whole black peppercorns
50g/2oz/¹/₂ cup butter
75g/3oz/³/₄ cup plain flour
freshly grated nutmeg
salt and ground black pepper
Serves 4–6

1 First make the béchamel sauce. Pour the milk into a saucepan and add the vegetables and peppercorns. Bring to boiling point, remove from the heat and leave to infuse for at least 30 minutes for the milk to absorb the flavour.

2 Strain the milk into a jug. Then melt the butter in the same saucepan and stir in the flour. Cook, stirring, for 2 minutes.

3 Remove from the heat and add the milk all at once, whisk well and return to the heat. Bring to the boil, whisking all the time, then simmer for 2–3 minutes, stirring constantly until thickened. Season to taste with nutmeg, salt and ground black pepper.

4 Preheat the oven to 180°C/ 350°F/Gas 4. If necessary, cook the sheets of lasagne in plenty of boiling salted water according to the instructions on the packet. Lift out with a slotted spoon and drain on a clean dish towel. Spoon a third of the meat sauce into a buttered baking-dish.

5 Place four sheets of lasagne over the meat sauce. Spread with one-third of the béchamel sauce. Repeat twice more, finishing with a layer of béchamel sauce covering the top of the dish.

6 Sprinkle with Parmesan cheese and bake in the oven for about 45 minutes until brown and bubbling. Serve garnished with tomato slices and a sprig of parsley.

Leek and Chèvre Lasagne

AN UNUSUAL and lighter than average lasagne using a soft French goat's cheese. The pasta sheets are not so chewy if boiled briefly first, or you could use no-precook lasagne instead if you prefer.

INGREDIENTS

6–8 lasagne sheets
1 large aubergine, sliced
30ml/2 tbsp olive oil
3 leeks, thinly sliced
2 red peppers
200g/7oz chèvre, broken into pieces
50g/2oz/1½ cup freshly grated Pecorino or
   Parmesan cheese

For the sauce
65g/2½oz/9 tbsp plain flour
65g/2½oz/5 tbsp butter
900ml/1½ pints/3¾ cups milk
2.5ml/½ tsp ground bay leaves
freshly grated nutmeg
salt and ground black pepper
Serves 6

1 Blanch the pasta sheets in plenty of boiling water for just 2 minutes. Drain and place on a clean dish towel.

2 Lightly salt the aubergine slices and place in a colander to drain for 30 minutes, then rinse and pat dry with kitchen paper.

3 Preheat the oven to 190°C/ 375°F/Gas 5. Lightly fry the leeks in the oil until softened. Grill the peppers under a pre-heated grill until charred. Peel and cut into strips.

4 For the sauce, melt the butter in a saucepan and add the flour. Cook, stirring, for 2–3 minutes. Add the milk and bring to the boil, stirring constantly until thickened. Add the bay leaves, nutmeg and seasoning. Simmer for 2 minutes.

5 In a greased shallow casserole, layer the leeks, lasagne sheets, aubergine, chèvre and Pecorino or Parmesan. Trickle the sauce over the layers, ensuring that it is evenly distributed over the entire dish.

6 Finish with a layer of sauce and grated cheese. Bake in the oven for 30 minutes, or until bubbling and browned on top. Serve immediately.

Baked Seafood Spaghetti

IN THIS DISH, each portion is baked and served in an individual packet which is then opened at the table. Use baking parchment paper or foil to make the packets.

INGREDIENTS

450g/1lb fresh mussels
120ml/4fl oz/½ cup dry white wine
60ml/4 tbsp olive oil
2 garlic cloves, finely chopped
450g/1lb tomatoes, fresh or canned, peeled and finely chopped
400g/14oz fresh or dried spaghetti
225g/8oz/2 cups peeled and deveined prawns, fresh or frozen
30ml/2 tbsp chopped fresh parsley
salt and ground black pepper
Serves 4

1 Scrub the mussels well under cold running water, cutting off the "beards" with a small sharp knife. Discard any that do not close when tapped sharply. Place the mussels and the wine in a large saucepan, cover and heat until opened.

COOK'S TIP

Use mussels as soon as possible after purchasing, but if you have to keep them overnight, store them in cold water with 1 tbsp flour and 50g salt; fresh water will kill them.

2 Lift out the mussels and remove to a side dish. Discard any that do not open. Strain the cooking liquid through a sieve lined with kitchen paper into a bowl and reserve until needed. Preheat the oven to 150°C/300°F/Gas 2.

3 In a medium saucepan, heat the oil and garlic together for 1–2 minutes. Add the tomatoes and cook over a moderate to high heat until softened. Stir 175ml/6fl oz/¾ cup of the mussel cooking liquid into the tomato mixture in the saucepan.

4 Cook the pasta in plenty of salted boiling water until just *al dente*. Just before draining the pasta, add the prawns and parsley to the tomato sauce. Cook for 2 minutes. Taste for seasoning, adding salt and pepper if necessary. Remove the pan from the heat.

5 Prepare four pieces of baking parchment paper or foil about 30 x 45cm/12 x18in. Place each sheet in the centre of a shallow bowl for ease of handling. Tip the drained pasta into a mixing bowl. Add the tomato sauce and mix together well. Stir in the mussels.

6 Divide the pasta and seafood among the four pieces of paper or foil, placing a mound in the centre of each, and twisting the ends together to make a closed packet. Arrange on a large baking sheet and place in the centre of the oven. Bake for 8–10 minutes. Place the unopened packets on individual serving plates for each person to open on serving.

Smoked Trout Cannelloni

SMOKED TROUT can be bought already filleted or whole. If you buy fillets, you'll need 225g/8oz.

INGREDIENTS

1 large onion, finely chopped
1 garlic clove, crushed
60ml/4 tbsp vegetable stock
2 x 400g/14oz cans chopped tomatoes
2.5ml/¹/₂ tsp dried mixed herbs
1 smoked trout, about 400g/14oz
75g/3oz/³/₄ cup frozen peas, thawed
75g/3oz/1¹/₂ cups fresh breadcrumbs
16 cannelloni tubes
salt and ground black pepper
25ml/1¹/₂ tbsp freshly grated
   Parmesan cheese
mixed salad, to serve (optional)

For the cheese sauce
25g/1oz/2 tbsp margarine
25g/1oz/¹/₄ cup plain flour
350ml/12fl oz/1¹/₂ cups skimmed milk
freshly grated nutmeg
Serves 4–6

1 Simmer the onion, garlic and stock in a large covered saucepan for 3 minutes. Uncover and continue to cook, stirring the mixture occasionally, until the stock has reduced entirely from the other ingredients.

2 Stir the chopped tomatoes and dried herbs into the onion and garlic mixture. Simmer, uncovered, for a further 10 minutes, or until the mixture has reduced and is very thick.

3 Meanwhile, skin the smoked trout with a sharp knife. Carefully flake the flesh and discard the bones. Mix the fish together with the tomato mixture, peas, breadcrumbs, salt and ground black pepper.

4 Preheat the oven to 190°C/ 375°F/Gas 5. Spoon the filling into the cannelloni tubes and arrange them side by side in a lightly greased ovenproof dish.

5 For the sauce, melt the margarine in a saucepan, add the flour and cook for 2–3 minutes, whisking constantly. Pour in the milk and bring to the boil, whisking, until the sauce thickens. Simmer for 2–3 minutes, stirring all the time. Season to taste with salt, pepper and nutmeg.

6 Pour the sauce over the cannelloni and sprinkle with the grated Parmesan cheese. Bake in the oven for 35–40 minutes, or until the top is golden and bubbling. Serve with a mixed salad, if desired.

Tuna Lasagne

TUNA AND PASTA ARE always family favourites together and this version of lasagne will be no exception.

INGREDIENTS

12–16 fresh or dried lasagne sheets
15g/¹⁄₂oz butter
1 small onion, finely chopped
1 garlic clove, finely chopped
115g/4oz mushrooms, thinly sliced
60ml/4 tbsp dry white wine (optional)
600ml/1 pint/2¹⁄₂ cups white sauce
150ml/¹⁄₄ pint/²⁄₃ cup whipping cream
45ml/3 tbsp chopped parsley
2 x 200g/7oz cans tuna, drained
2 canned pimientos, cut into strips
65g/2¹⁄₂oz/generous ¹⁄₂ cup frozen
   peas, thawed
115g/4oz mozzarella cheese, grated
30ml/2 tbsp freshly grated
   Parmesan cheese
salt and ground black pepper
Serves 6

1 For fresh lasagne, cook in a pan of salted boiling water until *al dente*. For dried, soak in a bowl of hot water for 3–5 minutes.

2 Place the lasagne in a colander and rinse with cold water. Lay on a dish towel to drain.

3 Preheat the oven to 180°C/350°F/Gas 4. Melt the butter in a saucepan and cook the onion until soft.

4 Add the garlic and mushrooms, and cook until soft, stirring occasionally. Pour in the wine, if using. Boil for 1 minute. Add the white sauce, cream and parsley. Season.

5 Spoon a thin layer of sauce over the base of a 30 x 23cm/12 x 9in baking dish. Cover with a layer of lasagne sheets.

6 Flake the tuna. Scatter half the tuna, pimiento strips, peas and mozzarella over the lasagne. Spoon one-third of the remaining sauce over the top and cover with another layer of lasagne sheets.

7 Repeat the layers, ending with pasta and sauce. Sprinkle with the Parmesan. Bake for 30–40 minutes or until lightly browned.

Spaghetti and Turkey in Cheese Sauce

AN AMERICAN-ITALIAN RECIPE, this dish makes an excellent family meal. It is quite filling and rich, so serve it with a tossed green salad.

INGREDIENTS

75g/3oz/6 tbsp butter

350g/12oz turkey breast fillet, cut into thin strips

2 pieces bottled roasted pepper, drained, rinsed, dried and cut into thin strips

175g/6oz dried spaghetti

50g/2oz/1/2 cup plain flour

900ml/11/2 pints/32/3 cups hot milk

115g/4oz/11/3 cups freshly grated Parmesan cheese

1.25–2.5ml/1/4–1/2 tsp mustard powder

salt and ground black pepper

Serves 4–6

1 Melt about a third of the butter in a saucepan, add the turkey and sprinkle with a little salt and plenty of pepper. Toss the turkey over a medium heat for about 5 minutes until the meat turns white, then add the roasted pepper strips and toss to mix. Remove with a slotted spoon and set aside.

2 Preheat the oven to 180°C/350°F/ Gas 4. Cook the pasta according to the instructions on the packet.

3 Meanwhile, melt the remaining butter over a low heat in the pan in which the turkey was cooked. Sprinkle in the flour and cook, stirring, for 1–2 minutes, then increase the heat to medium.

4 Add the hot milk a little at a time, whisking vigorously after each addition. Bring to the boil and cook, stirring, until the sauce is smooth and thick. Add two thirds of the grated Parmesan, then whisk in mustard, salt and pepper to taste. Remove the sauce from the heat.

5 Drain the pasta and return it to the clean pan. Mix in half the cheese sauce, then spoon the mixture around the edge of a baking dish. Stir the turkey mixture into the remaining cheese sauce and spoon into the centre of the dish. Sprinkle the remaining Parmesan evenly over the dish and bake for 15–20 minutes until the cheese topping is just crisp. Serve hot.

Shellfish Lasagne

THIS IS A LUXURY LASAGNE suitable for an informal supper or lunch party. It is quite expensive to make, but the flavour is superb.

INGREDIENTS

4–6 fresh scallops

450g/1lb peeled raw tiger prawns

1 garlic clove, crushed

75g/3oz/6 tbsp butter

50g/2oz/1/2 cup plain flour

600ml/1 pint/21/2 cups hot milk

100ml/31/2fl oz/scant 1/2 cup panna da cucina or double cream

100ml/31/2fl oz/1/2 cup dry white wine

2 sachets saffron powder

good pinch of cayenne pepper

130g/41/2oz Fontina cheese, thinly sliced

75g/3oz/1 cup freshly grated Parmesan cheese

6–8 fresh lasagne sheets, pre-cooked if necessary

salt and ground black pepper

Serves 4–6

1 Preheat the oven to 190°C/375°F/ Gas 5. Cut the scallops, corals and prawns into bite-size pieces and spread out in a dish. Sprinkle with the garlic and salt and pepper to taste. Melt about a third of the butter in a medium saucepan, add the scallops, corals and prawns and toss over a medium heat for 1–2 minutes or just until the prawns turn pink. Remove the shellfish with a slotted spoon and set aside.

2 Add the remaining butter to the pan and melt over a low heat. Sprinkle in the flour and cook, stirring, for 1–2 minutes, then increase the heat to medium and add the hot milk a little at a time, whisking vigorously after each addition. Bring to the boil and cook, stirring, until the sauce is smooth and very thick. Whisk in the cream, wine, saffron powder, cayenne and salt and pepper to taste, then remove the sauce from the heat.

3 Spread about a third of the sauce over the bottom of a baking dish. Arrange half the Fontina slices over the sauce and sprinkle with about a third of the grated Parmesan. Scatter about half the shellfish evenly on top, then cover with half the lasagne sheets. Repeat the layers, then cover with the remaining sauce and Parmesan.

4 Bake the lasagne for 30–40 minutes or until the topping is golden brown and bubbling. Allow to stand for 10 minutes before serving.

Turkey Pastitsio

A TRADITIONAL Greek pastitsio is made with minced lamb, but this lighter version is just as tasty.

INGREDIENTS

450g/1lb/4 cups lean minced turkey
1 large onion, finely chopped
60ml/4 tbsp tomato purée
250ml/8fl oz/1 cup red wine or stock
5ml/1 tsp ground cinnamon
300g/11oz/2¾ cups dried macaroni
25g/1oz/2 tbsp sunflower margarine
25g/1oz/3 tbsp plain flour
300ml/½ pint/1¼ cups skimmed milk
5ml/1 tsp grated nutmeg
2 tomatoes, sliced
60ml/4 tbsp wholemeal breadcrumbs
salt and ground black pepper
green salad, to serve

Serves 4–6

1 Preheat the oven to 220°C/425°F/Gas 7. Fry the turkey and onion in a non-stick pan without any fat, stirring until lightly browned and the turkey fat has reduced.

2 Stir in the tomato purée, red wine or stock and cinnamon. Season, then cover and simmer for about 5 minutes.

3 Cook the macaroni in plenty of salted boiling water according to the instructions on the packet, until *al dente*, then drain.

4 Layer the macaroni with the turkey mixture in a wide ovenproof dish.

5 Heat the margarine in a saucepan and add the flour, stirring. Cook for 2–3 minutes then gradually add the milk and whisk over a moderate heat until thickened and smooth.

6 Whisk the nutmeg and seasoning to taste into the sauce, then pour evenly over the pasta. Arrange the tomato slices on top and sprinkle with lines of breadcrumbs.

7 Bake for 30–35 minutes, or until golden brown.

Chicken Lasagne

BASED ON THE Italian beef lasagne, this is an excellent dish for entertaining guests of all ages. Serve simply with a green salad.

INGREDIENTS

30ml/2 tbsp olive oil
900g/2lb/8 cups minced raw chicken
225g/8oz rindless streaky bacon
    rashers, chopped
2 garlic cloves, crushed
450g/1lb leeks, sliced
225g/8oz carrots, diced
30ml/2 tbsp tomato purée
450ml/3/4 pint/1 3/4 cups chicken stock
12 sheets "no-need-to-pre-cook" dried
    lasagne sheets

For the cheese sauce

50g/2oz/4 tbsp butter
50g/2oz/4 tbsp plain flour
600ml/1 pint/2 1/2 cups milk
115g/4oz/1 cup grated mature
    Cheddar cheese
1.5ml/1/4 tsp English mustard powder
salt and ground black pepper

Serves 8

1 Heat the oil in a large flameproof casserole and brown the minced chicken and bacon briskly, separating the pieces with a wooden spoon. Add the crushed garlic cloves, chopped leeks and diced carrots and cook for about 5 minutes until softened. Add the tomato purée, stock and seasoning. Bring to the boil, cover and simmer for 30 minutes.

2 For the sauce, melt the butter in a saucepan, add the flour and gradually blend in the milk, stirring until smooth. Bring to the boil, stirring all the time until thickened, and simmer for several minutes. Add half the grated Cheddar cheese and the mustard and season to taste.

3 Preheat the oven to 190°C/375°F/Gas 5. Layer the chicken mixture, lasagne and half the cheese sauce in a 2.5 litre/5 pint/12 cup ovenproof dish, starting and finishing with the chicken mixture.

4 Pour the remaining cheese sauce over, sprinkle with the remaining cheese and bake in the preheated oven for 1 hour, or until lightly browned on top.

Pasta Pie

THIS IS AN EXCELLENT SUPPER dish for vegetarians, and children absolutely love it. All the ingredients will probably already be in your storecupboard or fridge, so it makes a good "standby" meal if you have guests at short notice.

INGREDIENTS

30ml/2 tbsp olive oil
1 small onion, finely chopped
400g/14oz can chopped Italian
  plum tomatoes
15ml/1 tbsp sun-dried tomato paste
5ml/1 tsp dried mixed herbs
5ml/1 tsp dried oregano or basil
5ml/1 tsp sugar
175g/6oz/1½ cups dried conchiglie
  or rigatoni
30ml/2 tbsp freshly grated
  Parmesan cheese
30ml/2 tbsp dried breadcrumbs
salt and ground black pepper

For the white sauce
25g/1oz/2 tbsp butter
25g/1oz/¼ cup plain flour
600ml/1 pint/2½ cups milk
1 egg
Serves 4

1 Heat the olive oil in a large skillet or saucepan and cook the finely chopped onion over a gentle heat, stirring frequently, for about 5 minutes until softened. Stir in the tomatoes. Fill the empty can with water and add it to the tomato mixture, with the tomato paste, herbs and sugar.

2 Add salt and pepper to taste and bring to the boil, stirring. Cover the pan, lower the heat and simmer, stirring occasionally, for 10–15 minutes.

3 Meanwhile, preheat the oven to 190°C/375°F/Gas 5. Cook the pasta according to the instructions on the packet.

4 Meanwhile, make the white sauce. Melt the butter in a pan, add the flour and cook, stirring, for 1 minute.

5 Add the milk a little at a time, whisking well after each addition. Bring to the boil and cook, stirring, until the sauce is smooth and thick. Season, then remove the pan from the heat.

6 Drain the pasta and tip it into a baking dish. Taste the tomato sauce and add salt and pepper. Pour the sauce into the dish and stir well to mix with the pasta.

7 Beat the egg into the white sauce, then pour the sauce over the pasta mixture. With a fork, separate the pasta in several places so that the white sauce fills the gaps.

8 Level the surface, sprinkle it with grated Parmesan and breadcrumbs and bake for 15–20 minutes or until the topping is golden brown and the cheese is bubbling. Allow to stand for about 10 minutes before serving.

VARIATIONS

• *If you don't have any dried bread-crumbs, you can cheat by crushing a packet of crisps and sprinkling them over the pie instead. Children love this crisp topping, especially if you use their favourite flavour.*
• *You could add chunks of roasted vegetables, such as courgettes, peppers or aubergines to the tomato sauce if you like. This will add extra flavour and make a more substantial meal.*
• *For meat eaters, Bolognese sauce can be used instead of the tomato sauce.*

Cheesy Pasta Bolognese

MOZZARELLA GIVES the cheese sauce a particularly creamy taste.

INGREDIENTS

30ml/2 tbsp olive oil
1 onion, chopped
1 garlic clove, crushed
1 carrot, diced
2 celery sticks, chopped
2 rashers streaky bacon, finely chopped
5 button mushrooms, chopped
450g/1lb lean minced beef
120ml/4fl oz/½ cup red wine
15ml/1 tbsp tomato purée
200g/7oz can chopped tomatoes
fresh thyme sprig
225g/8oz/2 cups dried penne
25g/1oz/2 tbsp butter
25g/1oz/2 tbsp flour
300ml/½ pint/1¼ cups milk
150g/5oz/1 cup cubed mozzarella cheese
60ml/4 tbsp grated Parmesan cheese
salt and ground black pepper
fresh basil sprigs, to garnish
Serves 4

1 Heat the oil in a pan and fry the onion, garlic, carrot and celery for 6 minutes, until the onions have softened.

2 Add the bacon and continue frying for 3–4 minutes. Stir in the mushrooms, fry for 2 minutes, then add the beef. Fry over a high heat until well browned all over.

3 Pour in the red wine, the tomato purée dissolved in 45ml/3 tbsp water, and the tomatoes, then add the thyme and season well. Bring to the boil, cover the pan and simmer gently for about 30 minutes.

4 Preheat the oven to 200°C/ 400°F/Gas 6. Bring a pan of water to the boil, add a little oil. Cook the pasta for 10 minutes.

5 Meanwhile, melt the butter in a saucepan and add the flour. Cook, stirring for 2 minutes then gradually add the milk and whisk constantly with a balloon whisk until the mixture is thickened. Stir in the cubed mozzarella cheese, half the Parmesan and season lightly.

6 Drain the pasta and stir into the cheese sauce. Uncover the tomato sauce and boil rapidly for about 2 minutes to reduce.

7 Spoon the sauce into an ovenproof dish, top with the pasta mixture and sprinkle the remaining Parmesan cheese evenly over the top. Bake for 25 minutes until golden. Garnish with basil and serve hot.

Rotolo di Pasta

A GIANT SWISS ROLL of pasta with a spinach filling, which is poached, sliced and baked with béchamel or tomato sauce. Use fresh homemade pasta for this recipe, or ask your local Italian deli to make a large sheet of pasta for you.

INGREDIENTS

700g/1½lb frozen chopped
   spinach, thawed
50g/2oz/4 tbsp butter
1 onion, chopped
100g/4oz ham or bacon, diced
225g/8oz ricotta or curd cheese
1 egg
freshly grated nutmeg
6 fresh spinach lasagne sheets
1.2 litres/2 pints/5 cups béchamel
   sauce, warmed (see Baked Lasagne with
   Béchamel Sauce)
50g/2oz/1/2 cup freshly grated
   Parmesan cheese
salt and ground black pepper

Serves 6

1   Squeeze the excess moisture from the spinach and set aside.

2   Melt the butter in a saucepan and fry the onion until golden. Add the ham and fry until beginning to brown. Take off the heat and stir in the spinach. Cool slightly, then beat in the ricotta or curd cheese and the egg. Season with salt, pepper and nutmeg.

3   Roll the pasta out to a rectangle about 30 × 40cm/12 × 16in. Spread the filling all over, leaving a 1cm/½in border all round the edge of the rectangle.

4   Roll up the pasta and filling from the shorter end and wrap in muslin to form a sausage shape, tying the ends securely with string.

5   Poach the pasta roll in a very large pan (or fish kettle) of simmering water for about 20 minutes or until firm. Carefully remove, drain and then unwrap. Leave to cool.

6   When you are ready to finish the dish, preheat the oven to 200°C/400°F/Gas 6. Cut the pasta roll into 2.5cm/1in slices. Spoon a little béchamel sauce over the base of a shallow baking dish and arrange the slices on top, slightly overlapping.

7   Spoon the remaining sauce over the roll slices, sprinkle with the cheese and bake for 15–20 minutes or until browned on top and bubbling. Allow to stand for a few minutes before serving.

Lasagne with Meatballs

THIS IS AN UNUSUAL RECIPE for lasagne in that there is both a meat sauce and meatballs. The result is very rich and satisfying, making it an ideal dish for an informal winter lunch or supper party. It takes a long time to make, so prepare it the day before and bake it on the day.

INGREDIENTS

300g/11oz minced beef
300g/11oz minced pork
1 large egg
50g/2oz/1 cup fresh white breadcrumbs
75ml/5 tbsp freshly grated Parmesan cheese
30ml/2 tbsp chopped fresh flat leaf parsley
2 garlic cloves, crushed
60ml/4 tbsp olive oil
1 onion, finely chopped
1 carrot, finely chopped
1 celery stick, finely chopped
2 x 400g/14oz cans chopped Italian
    plum tomatoes
10ml/2 tsp dried oregano or basil
6–8 fresh lasagne sheets, pre-cooked
    if necessary
salt and ground black pepper

For the béchamel sauce
750ml/1¼ pints/3 cups milk
1 bay leaf
1 fresh thyme sprig
50g/2oz/¼ cup butter
50g/2oz/½ cup plain flour
nutmeg
Serves 6–8

1 First make the meatballs. Put 175g/6oz each of the minced beef and pork in a large bowl. Add the egg, breadcrumbs, 30ml/2 tbsp of the grated Parmesan, half the parsley and garlic and plenty of salt and pepper.

2 Mix everything together with a wooden spoon, then use your hands to squeeze and knead the mixture so that it becomes smooth and quite sticky.

3 Wash your hands, rinse under the cold tap, then pick up small pieces of the mixture and roll them between your palms to make about 60 very small balls. Place the balls on a tray and chill in the fridge for about 30 minutes.

4 Meanwhile, put the milk for the béchamel sauce in a saucepan. Make a tear in the bay leaf, then add the leaf and thyme sprig to the milk and bring it to the boil. Remove from the heat, cover and leave to infuse.

5 Make the meat sauce. Heat half the oil in a medium skillet or saucepan, add the onion, carrot, celery and remaining garlic and stir over a low heat for about 5 minutes until softened. Add the remaining minced beef and pork and cook gently for 10 minutes, stirring frequently and breaking up any lumps in the meat.

6 Stir in salt and pepper to taste, then add the tomatoes, remaining parsley and the oregano or basil. Stir well, cover and simmer gently for 45 minutes to 1 hour, stirring occasionally.

7 Meanwhile, heat the remaining oil in a large, non-stick frying pan. When hot, cook the meatballs in batches over a medium to high heat for 5–8 minutes until browned on all sides. Shake the pan from time to time so that the meatballs roll around. As they cook, transfer the meatballs to kitchen paper to drain.

8 Preheat the oven to 190°C/375°F/Gas 5. Make the béchamel sauce. Strain the milk to remove the bay leaf and thyme sprig. Melt the butter in a medium saucepan, add the flour and cook, stirring, for 1–2 minutes.

9 Add the milk a little at a time, whisking vigorously after each addition. Bring to the boil and cook, stirring constantly, until the sauce is smooth and thick. Grate in a little nutmeg to taste and season with salt and pepper. Whisk well, then remove from the heat.

10 Spread about a third of the meat sauce in the bottom of a large, shallow baking dish.

11   Add half the meatballs, spread with a third of the béchamel and cover with half the lasagne sheets. Repeat these layers, then top with the remaining meat sauce and béchamel.

12   Sprinkle the remaining grated Parmesan evenly over the surface and bake for 30–40 minutes or until golden brown and bubbling. Allow the lasagne to stand for 10 minutes before serving. If you like, garnish each serving with extra chopped parsley.

VARIATION

In the south of Italy, where this type of lasagne is popular, they often add salami, chopped hard-boiled eggs, mozzarella and ricotta cheese to the layers.

COOK'S TIPS

• *Home-made lasagne does not need pre-cooking, but if you have bought fresh pasta check the instructions on the packet.*

• *To prevent cooked lasagne sheets from sticking together, rinse them under cold running water, then return to the pan with enough cold water to cover. Drain well on kitchen paper before using.*

Macaroni Soufflé

THIS IS GENERALLY a great favourite with children, and is rather like a light and fluffy macaroni cheese. Make sure you serve the soufflé immediately after it is cooked or it will sink dramatically.

INGREDIENTS

75g/3oz/1¾ cup dried short-cut macaroni
melted butter, to coat
25g/1oz/3 tbsp dried breadcrumbs
50g/2oz/4 tbsp butter
5ml/1 tsp ground paprika
40g/1½oz/⅓ cup plain flour
300ml/½ pint/1¼ cups milk
75g/3oz Cheddar or Gruyère
   cheese, grated
50g/2oz Parmesan cheese, grated
3 eggs, separated
salt and ground black pepper
Serves 3–4

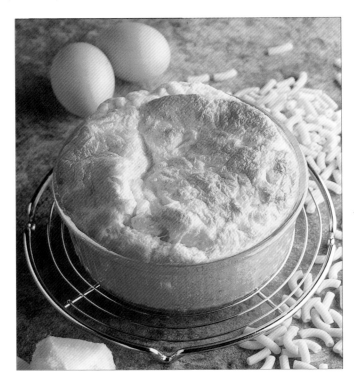

1 Cook the macaroni in plenty of boiling salted water according to the instructions on the packet. Drain well and set aside. Preheat the oven to 150°C/300°F/Gas 2.

2 Brush a 1.2 litre/2 pint/5 cup soufflé dish with melted butter, then coat evenly with the bread-crumbs, shaking out any excess from the dish.

3 Melt the butter in a pan and add the paprika and flour and cook, stirring for 1–2 minutes. Add the milk and bring to the boil, whisking until smooth and thick.

4 Simmer the sauce for 1 minute, then remove from the heat and stir in the cheeses until melted. Season well and mix with the cooked and drained macaroni.

5 Beat in the egg yolks. Whisk the egg whites until they form soft peaks and spoon a quarter of the beaten whites into the sauce mixture to lighten it slightly.

6 Using a large metal spoon, carefully fold the rest of the egg white into the sauce and transfer to the prepared soufflé dish.

7 Bake in the centre of the oven for about 40–45 minutes until the soufflé is risen and golden brown. The middle should wobble very slightly and the soufflé should be lightly creamy inside. Serve immediately.

Pastitsio

THIS IS A CLASSIC GREEK dish which makes an excellent main meal. The recipe is both economical and filling.

INGREDIENTS

15ml/1 tbsp oil
450g/1lb/4 cups minced lamb
1 onion, chopped
2 garlic cloves, crushed
30ml/2 tbsp tomato purée
25g/1oz/2 tbsp plain flour
300ml/½ pint/1¼ cups lamb stock
2 large tomatoes, sliced
115g/4oz/1 cup dried pasta shapes, such as fusilli or conchiglie
450g/1lb tub Greek yogurt
2 eggs, lightly beaten
salt and ground black pepper
radicchio and sliced cucumber, to serve

Serves 4

1 Preheat the oven to 190°C/375°F/ Gas 5. Heat the oil in a large pan and fry the lamb for 5 minutes, breaking up the meat with a spoon. Add the onion and garlic and continue to fry for a further 5 minutes.

2 Stir the tomato purée and flour into the pan. Cook for a further 1 minute, stirring occasionally.

3 Stir in the stock and season to taste. Bring to the boil and cook for 20 minutes.

4 Place the meat in an ovenproof dish, spreading it evenly and arrange the sliced tomatoes on top.

5 Cook the pasta shapes in salted boiling water for about 8–10 minutes or until al dente. Drain thoroughly through a colander.

6 Mix together the pasta, yogurt and eggs. Spoon on top of the tomatoes and then cook in the preheated oven for 1 hour. Serve with crisp radicchio leaves and slices of cucumber.

Cannelloni Sorrentina-style

THERE'S MORE THAN ONE way of making cannelloni. For this fresh-tasting dish, sheets of cooked lasagne are rolled around a tomato filling to make a delicious main course for a summer dinner party. The ingredients are similar to those used on a Neapolitan pizza.

INGREDIENTS

60ml/4 tbsp olive oil
1 small onion, finely chopped
900g/2lb ripe Italian plum tomatoes, peeled and finely chopped
2 garlic cloves, crushed
1 large handful fresh basil leaves, shredded, plus extra basil leaves, to garnish
250ml/8fl oz/1 cup vegetable stock
250ml/8fl oz/1 cup dry white wine
30ml/2 tbsp sun-dried tomato paste
2.5ml/½ tsp sugar
16–18 fresh or dried lasagne sheets
250g/9oz/generous 1 cup ricotta cheese
130g/4½oz packet mozzarella cheese, drained and diced small
8 bottled anchovy fillets in olive oil, drained and halved lengthways
50g/2oz/⅔ cup freshly grated Parmesan cheese
salt and ground black pepper
Serves 4–6

1 Heat the oil in a medium saucepan, add the onion and cook gently, stirring frequently, for about 5 minutes until softened. Stir in the tomatoes, garlic and half the basil. Season with salt and pepper to taste and toss over a medium to high heat for 5 minutes.

2 Scoop about half the tomato mixture out of the pan, place in a bowl and set it aside to cool.

3 Stir the vegetable stock, white wine, tomato paste and sugar into the tomato mixture remaining in the pan and simmer for about 20 minutes, stirring occasionally.

4 Meanwhile, cook the lasagne sheets in batches in a saucepan of salted boiling water, according to the instructions on the packet. Drain and separate the sheets of lasagne and lay them out flat on a clean dish towel.

VARIATION

For vegetarians, use 8 pitted black olives instead of the anchovies. Chop them roughly and sprinkle them in a line along the length of the cannelloni filling.

5 Preheat the oven to 190°C/ 375°F/Gas 5. Add the ricotta and mozzarella to the tomato mixture in the bowl. Stir in the remaining basil and season to taste with salt and pepper.

6 Spread a little of the mixture over each lasagne sheet. Place an anchovy fillet across the width of each sheet, close to one of the short ends. Starting from the end with the anchovy, roll each lasagne sheet up like a Swiss roll.

7 Purée the tomato sauce in a blender or food processor. Spread a little of the tomato sauce over the bottom of a large baking dish. Arrange the cannelloni seam-side down in a single layer in the dish and spoon the remaining sauce over them.

8 Sprinkle the Parmesan over the top and bake for 20 minutes or until the topping is golden brown and bubbling. Serve hot, garnished with basil leaves.

Macaroni and Blue Cheese

THE BLUE CHEESE gives this simple
dish a new twist.

INGREDIENTS

450g/1lb/4 cups dried macaroni
900ml/1½ pints/3¾ cups milk
50g/2oz/4 tbsp butter
75g/3oz/6 tbsp plain flour
1.5ml/¼ tsp salt
225g/8oz blue cheese, crumbled
ground black pepper
Serves 6

1 Preheat the oven to 180°C/350°F/
Gas 4. Lightly grease a 33 × 23cm/
12 × 9in baking dish.

2 Cook the macaroni in plenty of
salted boiling water according to
the instructions on the packet, or until
al dente. Drain and rinse under cold
water. Place in a large bowl and set
aside until required.

3 In another pan, bring the milk to
the boil and set aside.

4 Melt the butter in a heavy-based
saucepan over a low heat. Whisk
in the flour and cook for 5 minutes,
whisking continuously. Be careful not to
let the mixture brown.

5 Remove from the heat and whisk
the hot milk into the butter and
flour mixture. When smoothly blended,
return to a medium heat and continue
cooking for about 5 minutes, whisking
constantly until the sauce is smooth
and thick. Add the salt.

6 Add the sauce to the macaroni.
Add three-quarters of the
crumbled blue cheese and stir well.
Transfer the macaroni mixture to the
prepared baking dish and spread in an
even layer.

7 Sprinkle the remaining cheese
evenly over the surface. Bake for
25 minutes, until bubbling hot.

8 If desired, lightly brown the top of
the macaroni and cheese under a
preheated grill for 3–4 minutes. Serve
hot, sprinkled with ground black
pepper to taste.

Tortellini with Cream, Butter and Cheese

THIS IS AN INDULGENT but quick alternative to macaroni cheese. Stir in some ham or pepperoni if you wish, though it's quite delicious as it is.

INGREDIENTS

450g/1lb fresh tortellini
50g/2oz/4 tbsp butter
300ml/½ pint/1¼ cups double cream
115g/4oz Parmesan cheese
freshly grated nutmeg
salt and ground black pepper
Serves 4–6

3 Grate the Parmesan cheese and stir 75g/3oz/¾ cup of it into the sauce, stirring continuously over a moderate heat, until all of it has melted. Season to taste with salt, ground black pepper and nutmeg. Preheat the grill.

4 Drain the pasta well and spoon into a buttered heatproof serving dish. Pour the sauce over, sprinkle the remaining cheese over and place under a preheated grill until brown and bubbling on top. Serve the tortellini and sauce immediately.

1 Cook the pasta in plenty of salted boiling water according to the instructions on the packet.

2 Meanwhile melt the butter in a medium saucepan and stir in the cream. Bring to the boil and cook for 2–3 minutes until the mixture is slightly thickened, stirring frequently.

Lasagne with Three Cheeses

RICH AND FILLING, this is the type of lasagne that is popular in America. It was invented by Italian immigrants who made full use of the abundant ingredients available to them.

INGREDIENTS

25g/1oz/2 tbsp butter
15ml/1 tbsp olive oil
225–250g/8–9oz/2–2¼ cups button
    mushrooms, quartered lengthways
30ml/2 tbsp chopped fresh flat
    leaf parsley
1 quantity Bolognese Sauce with
    Red Wine
250–350ml/8–12fl oz/1–1½ cups hot
    beef stock
9–12 fresh lasagne sheets, pre-cooked
    if necessary
450g/1lb/2 cups ricotta cheese
1 large egg
3 x 130g/4½oz packets mozzarella
    cheese, drained and thinly sliced
115g/4oz/1⅓ cups freshly grated
    Parmesan cheese
salt and ground black pepper
Serves 6–8

Preheat the oven to 190°C/375°F/ Gas 5. Melt the butter in the oil in a frying pan. Add the mushrooms, with salt and pepper to taste, and toss over a medium to high heat for 5–8 minutes until the mushrooms are tender and quite dry. Remove the pan from the heat and stir in the parsley.

2 Make the Bolognese sauce or, if it is cold, reheat it. Once it is hot, stir in enough hot beef stock to make the sauce quite runny.

3 Stir in the mushroom and parsley mixture, then spread about a quarter of this sauce over the bottom of a baking dish. Cover with three or four sheets of lasagne.

4 Beat together the ricotta and egg in a bowl, with salt and pepper to taste, then spread about a third of the mixture over the lasagne sheets. Cover with a third of the mozzarella slices, then sprinkle with about a quarter of the grated Parmesan.

5 Repeat these layers twice, using half the remaining Bolognese sauce each time, and finishing with the remaining Parmesan.

6 Bake the lasagne for 30–40 minutes or until the cheese topping is golden brown and bubbling. Allow to stand for about 10 minutes before serving.

VARIATIONS

• For a spicier alternative version of this recipe, replace the meat sauce with the sauce used for Spaghetti with Minced Beef Sauce.
• Grated mature Cheddar cheese is very good in lasagne. Use it instead of some, or all, of the grated Parmesan. It is a good deal less expensive than Parmesan.

COOK'S TIP

If you have made the lasagne yourself, there is no need to pre-cook it, but if you have bought fresh lasagne, check whether it needs to be boiled briefly before being layered. Packets of fresh lasagne from the supermarket usually need to be boiled for 2 minutes before use.

Baked Conchiglie

THIS MAKES AN EXCELLENT dinner party starter for six, or a vegetarian main course for four, in which case you should fill 20 shells, rather than 18.

INGREDIENTS

18 large pasta shells for stuffing
25g/1oz/2 tbsp butter
1 small onion, finely chopped
275g/10oz fresh spinach leaves, trimmed, washed and shredded
1 garlic clove, crushed
1 sachet of saffron powder
nutmeg
250g/9oz/generous 1 cup ricotta cheese
1 egg
1 quantity Winter Tomato Sauce (see Rigatoni with Winter Tomato Sauce)
about 150ml/¼ pint/⅔ cup dry white wine, vegetable stock or water
100ml/3½fl oz/scant ½ cup panna da cucina or double cream
50g/2oz/⅔ cup freshly grated Parmesan cheese
salt and ground black pepper
Serves 6

1 Preheat the oven to 190°C/375°F/ Gas 5. Bring a large saucepan of salted water to the boil. Add the pasta shells and cook for 10 minutes. Drain the shells, half fill the pan with cold water and place the shells in the water.

2 Melt the butter in a saucepan, add the onion and cook gently, stirring, for about 5 minutes until softened. Add the spinach, garlic and saffron, then grate in plenty of nutmeg and add salt and pepper to taste. Stir well, increase the heat to medium and cook for 5–8 minutes, stirring frequently, until the spinach is wilted and tender.

3 Increase the heat to high and stir until the water is driven off and the spinach is quite dry. Tip the spinach into a bowl, add the ricotta and beat well to mix. Taste for seasoning, then add the egg and beat well again.

4 Purée the tomato sauce in a blender or food processor, pour it into a measuring jug and make it up to 750ml/1¼ pints/3 cups with wine, stock or water. Add the cream, stir well to mix and taste for seasoning.

5 Spread about half the sauce over the bottom of six individual gratin dishes. Remove the pasta shells one at a time from the water, shake them well and fill them with the spinach and ricotta mixture, using a teaspoon. Arrange three shells in the centre of each dish, spoon the remaining sauce over them, then cover with the grated Parmesan. Bake in the oven for 10–12 minutes or until hot. Leave to stand for about 5 minutes before serving.

Mixed Meat Cannelloni

A CREAMY, RICH FILLING and sauce
make this an unusual cannelloni.

INGREDIENTS

60ml/4 tbsp olive oil
1 onion, finely chopped
1 carrot, finely chopped
2 garlic cloves, crushed
2 ripe Italian plum tomatoes, peeled and
    finely chopped
130g/4¹/₂oz minced beef
130g/4¹/₂oz minced pork
250g/9oz minced chicken
30ml/2 tbsp brandy
25g/1oz/2 tbsp butter
90ml/6 tbsp panna da cucina or
    double cream
16 dried cannelloni tubes
75g/3oz/1 cup freshly grated
    Parmesan cheese
salt and ground black pepper
green salad, to serve

For the white sauce

50g/2oz/¹/₄ cup butter
50g/2oz/¹/₂ cup plain flour
900ml/1¹/₂ pints/3³/₄ cups milk
nutmeg

Serves 4

1 Heat the oil in a medium skillet, add
the onion, carrot, garlic and tomatoes
and cook over a low heat, stirring, for
about 10 minutes or until very soft.

COOK'S TIP

Instead of pasta tubes you could roll
fresh lasagne sheets around the filling.

2 Add all the minced meats to the
pan and cook gently for about
10 minutes, stirring frequently to break
up any lumps. Add the brandy, increase
the heat and stir until it has reduced,
then add the butter and cream and
cook gently, stirring occasionally, for
about 10 minutes. Allow to cool.

3 Preheat the oven to 190°C/375°F/
Gas 5. Make the white sauce. Melt
the butter in a medium saucepan, add
the flour and cook, stirring, for 1–2
minutes. Add the milk a little at a time,
whisking vigorously after each addition.
Bring to the boil and cook, stirring, until
the sauce is smooth and thick. Grate
in fresh nutmeg to taste, then season
with salt and pepper and whisk well.
Remove the pan from the heat.

4 Spoon a little of the white sauce
into a baking dish. Fill the cannelloni tubes with the meat mixture and
place in a single layer in the dish. Pour
the remaining white sauce over them,
then sprinkle with the Parmesan. Bake
for 35–40 minutes or until the pasta
feels tender when pierced with a
skewer. Allow to stand for 10 minutes
before serving with green salad.

Baked Vegetable Lasagne

FOLLOWING THE PRINCIPLES of the classic meat sauce lasagne, other combinations of ingredients can be used most effectively. This vegetarian lasagne uses tomatoes and wild and cultivated mushrooms.

INGREDIENTS

8 fresh lasagne sheets, pre-cooked
30ml/2 tbsp olive oil
1 onion, very finely chopped
500g/1¼lb tomatoes, fresh or canned, chopped
675g/1½lb cultivated or wild mushrooms, or a combination of both
75g/3oz/⅓ cup butter
2 garlic cloves, finely chopped
juice of ½ lemon
1 litre/1¾ pints/4 cups béchamel sauce (see Baked Lasagne with Béchamel Sauce)
175g/6oz/1½ cups freshly grated Parmesan or Cheddar cheese
salt and ground black pepper
Serves 8

1 Butter a large shallow baking dish, rectangular or square in shape.

2 If you are making the pasta, do not let it dry out before cutting into rectangles measuring about 11cm/4½in wide and the same length as the baking dish (this will make it easier to assemble).

3 In a small frying pan heat the oil and sauté the onion until soft but not coloured. Add the chopped tomatoes and cook for about 6–8 minutes, stirring frequently. Season with salt and pepper and set aside until required.

4 Wipe the mushrooms carefully with a damp cloth. Slice finely. Heat 40g/1½oz/3 tbsp of the butter in a frying pan and, when it is bubbling, add the mushrooms. Cook until the mushrooms start to exude their juices. Add the garlic and lemon juice, and season with salt and pepper. Cook until the liquids have almost all evaporated and the mushrooms are starting to brown. Set aside.

5 Preheat the oven to 200°C/400°F/Gas 6. Bring a very large pan of water to the boil. Place a large bowl of cold water near the cooker. Cover a large work surface with a tablecloth. Add salt to the rapidly boiling water. Drop in three or four of the egg pasta rectangles. Cook very briefly, about 30 seconds.

6 Once cooked, remove the pasta from the pan using a slotted spoon and then drop into the cold water for about 30 seconds. Remove and lay out to dry. Continue with the remaining pasta.

7 To assemble the lasagne, spread one large spoonful of the béchamel sauce over the base of the dish. Arrange a layer of pasta in the dish, cutting it with a sharp knife to fit. Cover with a thin layer of mushrooms, then one of béchamel sauce. Sprinkle with a little of the freshly grated Parmesan or Cheddar cheese.

8 Make another layer of pasta, spread with a thin layer of tomatoes, and then one of béchamel. Sprinkle with cheese. Repeat the layers in the same order, ending with a layer of pasta coated with béchamel. Do not make more than about six layers of pasta. Use the pasta trimmings to patch any gaps in the pasta. Sprinkle with more cheese and dot with butter.

9 Bake for 20 minutes. Remove from the oven and allow to stand for 5 minutes before serving.

Spinach and Hazelnut Lasagne

A VEGETARIAN DISH which is hearty
enough to satisfy meat-eaters too.
Use frozen spinach – you will need
450g/1lb – if you're short of time.

INGREDIENTS
900g/2lb fresh spinach
300ml/¹/₂ pint/1¹/₄ cups vegetable or
    chicken stock
1 onion, finely chopped
1 garlic clove, crushed
75g/3oz/³/₄ cup hazelnuts
30ml/2 tbsp chopped fresh basil
6 "no-need-to-pre-cook" dried lasagne sheets
400g/14oz can chopped tomatoes
200g/7oz/scant 1 cup low-fat fromage frais
flaked hazelnuts and chopped parsley,
    to garnish
Serves 4

1 Preheat the oven to 200°C/400°F/
   Gas 6. Wash the fresh spinach and
place in a pan with just the water that
clings to the leaves. Cook the spinach
over a fairly high heat for 2 minutes
until wilted. Drain well.

2 Heat 30ml/2 tbsp of the stock in a
   large pan and simmer the onion
and garlic until soft. Stir in the spinach,
hazelnuts and basil.

3 In a large ovenproof dish, layer the
   spinach, lasagne and the tomatoes.
Season well between the layers. Pour
over the remaining stock. Spread the
low-fat fromage frais over the top.

4 Bake the lasagne for about
   45 minutes, or until golden brown.
Serve hot, sprinkled with lines of flaked
hazelnuts and chopped parsley.

Cannelloni with Tuna

CHILDREN LOVE THIS pasta dish.
Fontina cheese has a sweet, nutty
flavour and very good melting
qualities. Look for it in large supermarkets and Italian delicatessens.

INGREDIENTS

50 g/2 oz/4 tbsp cup butter
50 g/2 oz/¹/₂ cup plain flour
about 900 ml/1¹/₂ pints/3³/₄ cups
    hot milk
2 x 200 g/7 oz cans tuna, drained
115 g/4 oz/1 cup Fontina cheese, grated
1.5 ml/¹/₄ tsp grated nutmeg
12 "no-need-to-pre-cook" cannelloni tubes
50 g/2 oz/²/₃ cup grated Parmesan cheese
salt and freshly ground black pepper
fresh herbs, to garnish
Serves 4–6

1 Melt the butter in a heavy-based
saucepan, add the flour and stir
over a low heat for 1–2 minutes.
Remove the pan from the heat and
gradually add 350 ml/12 fl oz/1¹/₂ cups
of the milk, beating vigorously after
each addition. Return the pan to the
heat and whisk for 1–2 minutes until
the sauce is very thick and smooth.
Remove from the heat.

2 Mix the drained tuna with about
120 ml/4 fl oz/¹/₂ cup of the warm
white sauce in a bowl. Add salt and
black pepper to taste. Preheat the oven
to 180°C/350°F/Gas 4.

3 Gradually whisk the remaining
milk into the rest of the sauce,
return to the heat and simmer,
whisking, until thickened. Add the
grated Fontina and nutmeg, and season
to taste. Simmer for a few minutes,
stirring frequently. Pour one-third of
the sauce into a baking dish.

4 Fill the cannelloni tubes with the
tuna mixture, pushing it in with
the handle of a teaspoon. Place the
cannelloni in a single layer in the dish.
Thin the remaining sauce with a little
more milk if necessary, then pour it
over the cannelloni. Sprinkle with
Parmesan cheese and bake for
30 minutes or until golden. Serve hot,
garnished with herbs.

Stuffed Pasta

The recipes in this chapter are for a variety of different shapes, and the majority of them involve making your own pasta which is easier than you think, especially if you have a pasta machine. You can make pasta by hand, but the machine will save you time and effort, and make the whole process much more interesting and fun. They all use the same basic pasta dough, but the dough is always made with eggs for stuffed pasta, which strengthens it. This helps to hold the filling in during cooking. Stuffed pasta originated in the north of Italy, but now every Italian town seems to have its own speciality, often associated with a particular day in the calendar, such as a feast day or New Year. Home-made stuffed pasta is therefore a special-occasion dish, and it is usually served very simply, either drizzled with melted butter or oil, or floating in *brodo*. Practice makes perfect when it comes to making anything by hand, but much of the charm of home-made pasta lies in its imperfections, so don't try too hard to make every shape the same size. After all, you want your guests to know you have made it yourself!

Stuffed Pasta Half-moons

THESE STUFFED EGG PASTA half-moons are filled with a delicate mixture of cheeses. They make an elegant first course as well as a good supper.

INGREDIENTS
1 quantity Pasta with Eggs

For the filling
*225g/8oz/1¼ cups fresh ricotta or
    curd cheese
225g/8oz/1¼ cups mozzarella cheese
115g/4oz/1 cup freshly grated
    Parmesan cheese
2 eggs
45ml/3 tbsp finely chopped fresh basil
salt and ground black pepper*

For the sauce
*450g/1lb fresh tomatoes
30ml/2 tbsp olive oil
1 small onion, very finely chopped
90ml/6 tbsp cream*
Serves 6–8

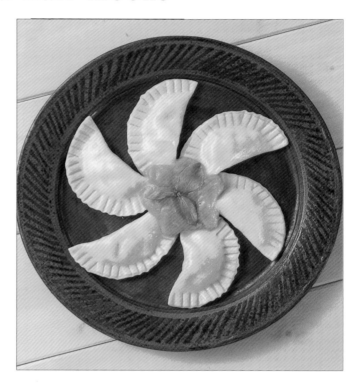

1 Make the filling. Press the ricotta or curd cheese through a sieve or strainer. Chop the mozzarella into very small cubes. Combine all three cheeses in a bowl. Beat in the eggs and basil, season and set aside.

2 Make the sauce by dropping the tomatoes into a small pan of boiling water for 1 minute. Remove, and peel. Chop the tomatoes finely. Heat the oil in a medium saucepan. Add the onion and cook over a moderate heat until softened. Add the tomatoes and cook until soft, about 15 minutes. Season with salt and pepper. Set aside.

3 Prepare the sheets of egg pasta. Roll out very thinly by hand or machine. Do not let the pasta dry out before filling.

4 Using a glass or pastry cutter, cut out rounds approximately 10cm/4in in diameter. Spoon one large tablespoon of the cheese filling on to one half of each pasta round and fold the other pasta half over.

5 Press the edges closed with the tines of a fork. Re-roll any trimmings and use to make more rounds. Allow the half-moons to dry for at least 10–15 minutes. Turn them over so they dry evenly.

6 Bring a large pan of salted water to the boil. Meanwhile, place the tomato sauce in a small saucepan and heat gently. Stir in the cream. Do not allow to boil.

7 Gently drop the stuffed pasta into the boiling water, and stir carefully to prevent them from sticking. Cook for 5–7 minutes. Scoop them out of the water, drain carefully, and arrange in individual dishes. Spoon over some sauce and serve.

Spinach and Dolcelatte Ravioli

THE ITALIAN DOLCELATTE cheese used
in this recipe gives it a unique and
strong taste so it is best served
simply, with olive oil and Parmesan.

INGREDIENTS

350g/12oz/3 cups strong white flour
4ml/¾ tsp salt
2 eggs
15ml/1 tbsp olive oil

For the filling

225g/8oz fresh spinach
40g/1½oz/½ cup butter
1 small onion, finely chopped
25g/1oz Parmesan cheese, grated
40g/1½oz dolcelatte cheese, crumbled
15ml/1 tbsp chopped fresh parsley
salt and ground black pepper
freshly grated Parmesan cheese, to serve
Serves 4

1 To make the pasta dough, mix
together the flour and salt in a large
bowl or food processor. Add the eggs,
olive oil and about 45ml/3 tbsp of cold
water or enough to make a pliable
dough. If working by hand, mix the
ingredients together and then knead
the dough fo about 15 minutes until it
has become very smooth. Or, process
the dough for about 1 minute or so in
a food processor. Place the dough in a
plastic bag and chill in the fridge for at
least 12 hours (or overnight if this is
more convenient).

2 Cook the spinach in a large,
covered saucepan for about
3-4 minutes, until the leaves have
wilted. Strain and press out the excess
liquid. Set aside to cool a little and then
chop the spinach finely.

3 Melt half the butter in a small
saucepan and fry the onion over a
gentle heat for about 5-6 minutes until
soft. Place in a bowl with the chopped
spinach, the Parmesan and dolcelatte
cheeses and seasoning. Mix all the
ingredients together well.

4 Grease a ravioli tin. Roll out half
or a quarter of the pasta dough
to a thickness of about 3mm/⅛ in. Lay
the dough over the ravioli tin, pressing
it well into each of the squares.

5 Spoon a little spinach mixture into
each cavity, then roll out a second
piece of dough and lay it on top. Press
a rolling pin evenly over the top of the
tin to seal all the edges and then cut
the ravioli into neat squares using a
pastry cutter.

6 Place the ravioli in a large
saucepan of boiling water and
simmer for about 4-5 minutes until
cooked through but al dente. Drain
well and then toss with the remaining
butter and the parsley.

7 Divide between four serving
plates and serve scattered with
shavings of Parmesan cheese.

Meat-filled Agnolotti with Vodka Sauce

DAINTY HALF-MOON SHAPES are filled with spiced minced meat and bacon and served with a cream and blue-cheese sauce spiked with vodka. This is a very special dish for a dinner party first course.

INGREDIENTS

1 quantity Pasta with Eggs
freshly grated Parmesan cheese, to serve

For the filling
15ml/1 tbsp olive oil
75g/3oz pancetta, streaky bacon or ham,
*   finely diced*
250g/9oz minced pork or veal
2 garlic cloves, crushed
good pinch of ground cinnamon
120ml/4fl oz/½ cup red wine
60ml/4 tbsp chopped fresh flat leaf parsley
1 small egg
salt and ground black pepper

For the sauce
50g/2oz/¼ cup butter
250ml/8fl oz/1 cup panna da cucina or
*   double cream*
115g/4oz Gorgonzola cheese, diced
45ml/3 tbsp vodka
Serves 6–8

1 Make the filling. Heat the oil in a medium saucepan, add the pancetta, bacon or ham and stir-fry for a few minutes until lightly coloured. Add the minced pork, the garlic, cinnamon and salt and pepper to taste and cook gently for 5–6 minutes, stirring frequently and breaking up any lumps.

2 Pour in the wine and stir well to mix, then simmer gently, stirring occasionally, for 15–20 minutes until the meat is cooked and quite dry. Transfer the meat to a bowl with a slotted spoon and leave to cool.

3 Add the parsley and egg to the meat mixture and stir well to mix.

4 Using a pasta machine, roll out one-quarter of the pasta into a 90cm–1 metre/36in–3 foot strip. Cut the strip with a sharp knife into two 45–50cm/18–20in lengths (you can do this during rolling if the strip gets too long to manage).

5 Using a teaspoon, put 8–10 little mounds of the filling along one side of one of the pasta strips, spacing them evenly. Brush a little water around each mound, then fold the plain side of the pasta strip over the filling.

6 Starting from the folded edge, press down gently with your fingertips around each mound, pushing the air out at the unfolded edge.

7 Using only half of a 5cm/2in fluted round ravioli or biscuit cutter, cut around each mound of filling to make a half-moon shape. The folded edge should be the straight edge. If you like, press the cut edges of the agnolotti with the tines of a fork to give a decorative effect.

8 Put the agnolotti on floured dish towels, spreading them out in a single layer, so that they don't stick together. Sprinkle them lightly with flour and leave to dry while repeating the process with the remaining pasta to get 64–80 agnolotti altogether.

9 Drop the agnolotti into a large pan of salted boiling water, bring back to the boil and boil for 4–5 minutes.

10 Meanwhile, make the sauce. Melt the butter in a medium saucepan, add the cream and cheese and heat through, stirring, until the cheese has melted. Add the vodka, season to taste with pepper and stir well to mix.

|| Drain the agnolotti and divide
them among six or eight
warmed bowls. Spoon the sauce over
them and sprinkle liberally with grated
Parmesan. Serve immediately.

• *Instead of the pancetta, bacon or ham,
you could use a spicy salami for the
agnolotti filling. Buy the salami in one
very thick piece, peel off the skin, and
then chop it finely.*

• *Agnolotti are also often made with
prosciutto crudo (Parma ham), which
gives them a more delicate flavour than
the streaky pancetta.*

*Gorgonzola is a sharp-tasting blue
Italian cheese with a soft and creamy
consistency. Gorgonzola piccante is a
particularly strong variety, while
gorgonzola dolce — better known as
dolcelatte — is creamier and less sharp in
flavour. Supermarkets, specialist cheese
shops and delicatessens usually sell both
types of Gorgonzola.*

Ravioli with Pumpkin

THIS IS A VERY SIMPLE VERSION of a Christmas Eve speciality from Lombardy. In traditional recipes the pumpkin filling is flavoured with *mostarda di frutta* (a kind of sweet fruit pickle), crushed amaretti biscuits and sugar. Here the pumpkin is seasoned with Parmesan and nutmeg. It is quite sweet enough for most tastes.

INGREDIENTS

1 quantity Pasta with Eggs
115g/4oz/½ cup butter
freshly grated Parmesan cheese,
*   to serve*

For the filling
450g/1lb piece of pumpkin
15ml/1 tbsp olive oil
40g/1½oz/scant ¼ cup freshly grated
*   Parmesan cheese*
nutmeg
salt and ground black pepper
Serves 8

1 Make the filling. Preheat the oven to 220°C/425°F/Gas 7. Cut the piece of pumpkin into chunks and remove the seeds and fibres. Put the chunks, skin side down, in a roasting tin and drizzle the oil over the pumpkin flesh. Roast in the oven for 30 minutes, turning the pieces over once or twice.

2 Leave the roasted pumpkin until it is cool enough to handle, then scrape the flesh out into a bowl and discard the pumpkin skin.

3 Mash the roasted pumpkin flesh with a fork, then add the grated Parmesan and freshly grated nutmeg and salt and pepper to taste. Stir well to mix, then set aside until cold.

4 Using a pasta machine, roll out one-quarter of the pasta into a 90cm–1 metre/36in–3 foot strip. Cut the strip with a sharp knife into two 45–50cm/18–20in lengths (you can do this during rolling if the strip gets too long to manage).

5 Using a teaspoon, put 10–12 little mounds of the filling along one side of one of the pasta strips, spacing them evenly.

6 Brush a little water around each mound, then fold the plain side of the pasta strip over the mounds of filling. Starting from the folded edge, press down gently with your fingertips around each mound, pushing the air out at the unfolded edge. Sprinkle lightly with flour.

7 With a fluted pasta wheel, cut along each long side, then in between each mound to make small square shapes. Put the ravioli on floured dish towels, sprinkle lightly with flour and leave to dry, while repeating the process with the remaining pasta to get 80–96 ravioli altogether.

8 Drop the ravioli into a large pan of salted boiling water, bring back to the boil and boil for 4–5 minutes. Meanwhile, melt the butter in a small saucepan until it is sizzling.

9 Drain the ravioli and divide them equally among eight warmed dinner plates or large bowls. Drizzle the sizzling butter over the ravioli and serve immediately, sprinkled with grated Parmesan. Hand more grated Parmesan separately.

VARIATION

You can buy mostarda di frutta *at Italian delicatessens, especially at Christmas time. If you would like to try some in the filling, add about 45ml/3 tbsp, together with a few crushed amaretti.*

Spinach and Ricotta Ravioli

THE ITALIAN NAME FOR this dish is *ravioli di magro* which means lean ravioli. It is used to describe meat-less ravioli, usually those with a spinach and ricotta filling. *Ravioli di magro* are served on Christmas Eve, a time when meat-filled pasta should not be eaten.

INGREDIENTS

1 quantity Pasta with Eggs
freshly grated Parmesan cheese, to serve

For the filling

40g/1½oz/3 tbsp butter
175g/6oz fresh spinach leaves, trimmed, washed and shredded
200g/7oz/scant 1 cup ricotta cheese
25g/1oz/⅓ cup freshly grated Parmesan cheese
nutmeg
1 small egg
salt and ground black pepper

For the sauce

50g/2oz/¼ cup butter
250ml/8fl oz/1 cup panna da cucina or double cream
50g/2oz/⅔ cup freshly grated Parmesan cheese

Serves 8

1 Make the filling. Melt the butter in a medium saucepan, add the spinach and salt and pepper to taste and cook over a medium heat for 5–8 minutes, stirring frequently, until the spinach is wilted and tender. Increase the heat to high and stir until the water is driven off and the spinach is quite dry.

2 Tip the spinach into a bowl and leave until cold, then add the ricotta, grated Parmesan and freshly grated nutmeg to taste. Beat well to mix, taste for seasoning, then add the egg and beat well again.

3 Using a pasta machine, roll out one-quarter of the pasta into a 90cm–1 metre/36in–3 foot strip. Cut the strip with a sharp knife into two 45–50cm/18–20in lengths (you can do this during rolling if the strip gets too long to manage).

4 Using a teaspoon, put 10–12 little mounds of the filling along one side of one of the pasta strips, spacing them evenly. Brush a little water around each mound, then fold the plain side of the pasta strip over the filling.

5 Starting from the folded edge, press down gently with your fingertips around each mound of filling, pushing the air out at the unfolded edge. Sprinkle lightly with flour.

6 With a fluted pasta wheel, cut along each long side, then in between each mound to make small square shapes.

7 Put the ravioli on floured dish towels, sprinkle lightly with flour and leave to dry while repeating the process with the remaining pasta to get 80–96 ravioli altogether.

8 Drop the ravioli into a large pan of salted boiling water, bring back to the boil and boil for 4–5 minutes.

9 Meanwhile, make the sauce. Gently heat the butter, cream and Parmesan in a medium saucepan until the butter and Parmesan have melted.

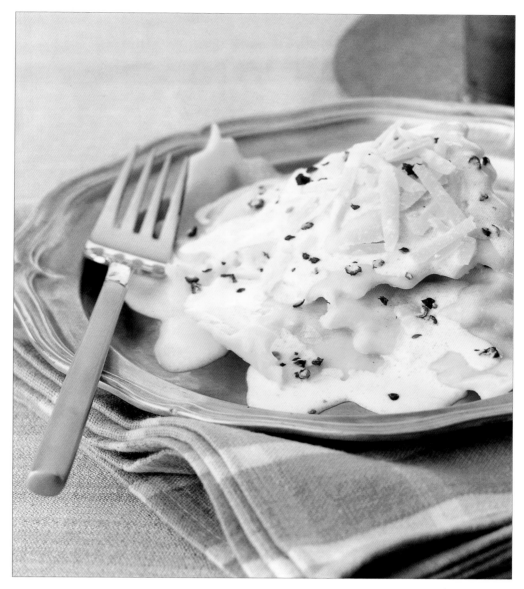

10 Increase the heat and simmer for a minute or two until the sauce is slightly reduced, then add salt and pepper to taste.

11 Drain the ravioli and divide them equally among 8 warmed large bowls. Drizzle the sauce over them and serve immediately, sprinkled with grated Parmesan.

VARIATION

If you prefer, serve the ravioli with sizzling sage butter. Melt 50g/2oz/¹⁄4 cup butter in a small pan, add a handful of fresh sage leaves and stir constantly over a medium to high heat until sizzling. This will be slightly less rich than the cream sauce suggested here.

COOK'S TIP

To prevent the pasta sticking when working with it, lightly flour the work surface and your cutting tools and use more flour as necessary.

Coriander Ravioli with Pumpkin Filling

THIS STUNNING HERB PASTA is served with a superb creamy pumpkin and roast garlic filling.

INGREDIENTS

200g/7oz/scant 1 cup strong white flour
2 eggs
pinch of salt
45ml/3 tbsp chopped fresh coriander
coriander sprigs, to garnish

For the filling
4 garlic cloves, unpeeled
450g/1lb pumpkin, peeled and seeded
115g/4oz/¹/₂ cup ricotta cheese
4 sun-dried tomatoes in olive oil, drained
  and finely chopped, and
  30ml/2 tbsp of the oil
ground black pepper
Serves 4–6

1 Place the flour, eggs, salt and chopped fresh coriander into a blender or food processor and process until combined.

COOK'S TIP

To get the best out of your pasta machine, start rolling your pasta on the widest roller setting, then fold the pasta and roll again. Re-roll the piece three or four times, without folding, making the roller setting thinner each time.

2 Place the dough on a lightly floured board and knead well for 5 minutes, until smooth. Press your finger in the dough: if it is still sticky, add a little more flour. Wrap in clear film and leave to rest in the fridge for at least 20 minutes.

3 Preheat the oven to 200°C/ 400°F/Gas 6. Place the garlic cloves on a baking sheet and bake for 10 minutes until soft. Steam the pumpkin for 5–8 minutes until tender and drain well. Peel the garlic cloves and mash into the pumpkin together with the ricotta cheese and drained sun-dried tomatoes. Season with lots of ground black pepper.

4 Divide the pasta into four pieces and flatten slightly. Using a pasta machine, on its thinnest setting, roll out each piece. Leave the sheets of pasta on a lightly floured clean dish towel until they are slightly dried, about 1 hour.

5 Using a 7.5cm/3in crinkle-edged round cutter, stamp out about 36 rounds of pasta.

6 Top half of the rounds with a teaspoonful of filling, brush the edges with water and place another round of pasta on top. Press firmly around the edges to seal. Bring a large pan of water to the boil, add the ravioli and cook for 3–4 minutes. Drain well and toss into the reserved tomato oil. Serve at once garnished with fresh coriander sprigs.

Stuffed Pasta Roll

THIS IS A DINNER PARTY first course to impress. It takes quite a long time to make, but it can be made up to the baking stage the day before.

INGREDIENTS

75g/3oz/6 tbsp butter
1 small onion, finely chopped
150g/5oz fresh spinach leaves, washed and trimmed
250g/9oz/generous 1 cup ricotta cheese
1 egg
60ml/4 tbsp freshly grated Parmesan cheese
60ml/4 tbsp freshly grated Pecorino cheese
nutmeg
²⁄₃ quantity Pasta with Eggs
salt and ground black pepper

For the tomato sauce
60ml/4 tbsp olive oil
1 garlic clove, thinly sliced
1 onion, finely chopped
1 carrot, finely chopped
1 celery stick, finely chopped
a few leaves each fresh basil, thyme and oregano or marjoram, plus extra basil leaves, to garnish
2 x 400g/14oz cans chopped Italian plum tomatoes
15ml/1 tbsp sun-dried tomato paste
5ml/1 tsp sugar
75–105ml/5–7 tbsp dry white wine
Serves 6

1 Melt 25g/1oz/2 tbsp of the butter in a medium saucepan, add the finely chopped onion and cook gently, stirring frequently, for about 5 minutes until softened.

2 Add the spinach and salt and pepper to taste and cook over a medium heat for 5–8 minutes, stirring frequently, until the spinach is wilted and tender. Increase the heat to high and stir until the water is driven off and the spinach is quite dry.

3 Finely chop the spinach mixture in a food processor or by hand. Transfer to a bowl and add the ricotta, egg and half the grated Parmesan and Pecorino. Season to taste with freshly grated nutmeg and salt, and add plenty of pepper. Beat well to mix.

4 Roll out the pasta dough to a 50 x 40cm /20 x 16in rectangle. Place the rectangle on a large piece of muslin, with one of the short sides nearest you.

5 Spread the spinach mixture thinly over the pasta, leaving a 2cm/³⁄₄in margin along the two long sides and a 5cm/2in margin along the short side that is furthest away from you. Moisten the two long sides with water.

6 Starting from the short side that is nearest you, pick up the muslin and roll the pasta away from you as you would a Swiss roll. Don't press it, just let it roll until you have a 40cm/16in long "sausage". Press the two open ends to seal the pasta, then roll the muslin around the roll a couple of times and tie the two ends tightly with string.

7 Half fill a fish kettle or large oval flameproof casserole with water and bring it to the boil. Add a large pinch of salt, then the pasta roll. Half cover with a lid and simmer for 45 minutes, turning the roll over twice. Remove the roll from the water and place it on a board near the sink. Prop the board up at one end to allow the excess water to drain away from the roll, then leave to cool.

8 Make the tomato sauce for serving with the pasta roll. Heat the oil in a saucepan, add the garlic slices and stir over a very low heat for 1–2 minutes. Add the chopped vegetables and the fresh herbs. Cook over a low heat, stirring continuously for 5–7 minutes until the vegetables have softened and are lightly coloured but not browned.

9 Add the tomatoes, tomato paste and sugar, then add salt and pepper to taste. Bring to the boil, stirring all the time, then lower the heat and simmer gently, uncovered, for about 45 minutes, stirring occasionally.

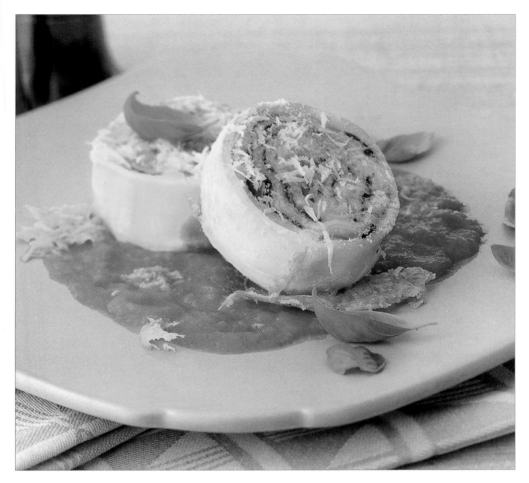

10 Preheat the oven to 200°C/ 400°F/ Gas 6. Unwrap the pasta roll and cut it into 12 thick slices. Melt the remaining butter and brush a little of it over the inside of six individual ovenproof dishes or a large shallow baking dish.

11 Arrange the pasta roll slices slightly overlapping in the dishes or dish and drizzle the remaining butter over them. Sprinkle with the remaining Parmesan and Pecorino and bake in the oven for 10–15 minutes or until golden brown.

12 Meanwhile, blend the tomato sauce in a food processor until smooth. Transfer to a pan and add enough wine to thin it down to a pouring consistency, then heat until bubbling. Serve the pasta roll slices on individual plates, on a pool of tomato sauce, sprinkled with basil leaves.

COOK'S TIP

If you have a pasta machine, roll out half the dough into a 90cm–1 metre/ 36in–3 foot strip. Cut the strip with a sharp knife into two 50cm/20in lengths (you can do this during rolling if the strip gets too long to manage). Brush the long edge of one of the strips with water, then overlap the other strip on top by about 1cm/¹/₂in. Dust lightly with flour and press together, then seal the join by rolling over it with a rolling pin. Repeat with the remaining dough, then join the two pieces of pasta together in the same way so that you have a large rectangle.

Cheese Cappellacci with Bolognese Sauce

In Emilia-Romagna it is traditional to serve these *cappellacci* with a rich meat sauce, but if you prefer you can serve them with a tomato sauce, or just melted butter.

INGREDIENTS

1 quantity Pasta with Eggs
2 litres/3½ pints/8 cups beef stock
    made with stock cubes or diluted
    canned consommé
basil leaves, to garnish
freshly grated Parmesan cheese,
    to serve

For the filling

250g/9oz/generous 1 cup ricotta cheese
90g/3½oz taleggio cheese, rind removed,
    diced very small
60ml/4 tbsp freshly grated Parmesan cheese
1 small egg
nutmeg
salt and ground black pepper

For the Bolognese meat sauce

25g/1oz/2 tbsp butter
15ml/1 tbsp olive oil
1 onion, finely chopped
2 carrots, finely chopped
2 celery sticks, finely chopped
2 garlic cloves, finely chopped
130g/4½oz pancetta or rindless streaky
    bacon, diced
250g/9oz lean minced beef
250g/9oz lean minced pork
120ml/4fl oz/½ cup dry white wine
2 x 400g/14oz cans crushed Italian
    plum tomatoes
475–750ml/16fl oz–1¼ pints/2–3 cups
    beef stock
100ml/3½fl oz/scant ½ cup panna da
    cucina or double cream

Serves 6

1 Make the filling. Put the ricotta, taleggio and grated Parmesan in a bowl and mash together with a fork.

2 Add the egg and freshly grated nutmeg and salt and pepper to taste and stir well to mix.

3 Using a pasta machine, roll out one-quarter of the pasta into a 90cm–1 metre/36in–3 foot strip. Cut the strip with a sharp knife into two 45–50cm/18–20in lengths (you can do this during rolling if the strip gets too long to manage).

4 Using a 6–7.5cm/2½–3in square ravioli cutter, cut 6–7 squares from one of the pasta strips. Using a teaspoon, put a mound of filling in the centre of each square. Brush a little water around the edge of each square, then fold the square diagonally in half over the filling to make a triangular shape. Press to seal.

5 Wrap the triangle around one of your index fingers, bringing the bottom two corners together. Pinch the ends together to seal, then press with your fingertip around the top edge of the filling to make an indentation so that the "hat" looks like a bishop's mitre.

6 Place the *cappellacci* on floured dish towels, sprinkle them lightly with flour and leave to dry while repeating the process with the remaining dough to make 48–56 *cappellacci* altogether.

7 Make the meat sauce. Heat the butter and oil in a large skillet or saucepan until sizzling. Add the vegetables, garlic, and the pancetta or bacon and cook over a medium heat, stirring frequently, for 10 minutes or until the vegetables have softened.

8 Add the minced beef and pork, lower the heat and cook gently for 10 minutes, stirring frequently and breaking up any lumps in the meat with a wooden spoon. Stir in salt and pepper to taste, then add the wine and stir again. Simmer for about 5 minutes, or until reduced.

9 Add the tomatoes and 250ml/ 8fl oz/1 cup of the stock and bring to the boil. Stir well, then lower the heat, half cover the pan with a lid and leave to simmer very gently for 2 hours. Stir occasionally during this time and add more stock as it becomes absorbed.

10 Add the *panna da cucina* or double cream to the meat sauce. Stir well to mix, then simmer the sauce, without a lid, for another 30 minutes, stirring frequently.

11 Bring the stock to the boil in a large saucepan.

12 Drop the *cappellacci* into the stock, bring back to the boil and boil for 4–5 minutes; drain the *cappellacci* and divide them equally among six warmed bowls. Spoon the hot Bolognese sauce over the *cappellacci* and sprinkle with grated Parmesan and basil leaves. Serve immediately.

COOK'S TIP

The exact shape of cappellacci *varies from one cook to another. Some are made from discs rather than squares of pasta, although these are more often called tortellini or tortelloni. It all depends on the region in which they are made. If you prefer a party-hat shape to a bishop's mitre, don't make an indentation above the filling in Step 5, but instead turn up the bottom edge of each "hat" so that they have brims. Cappelletti are the same shape as cappellacci but are made from smaller squares of pasta (about 5cm/2in square). Not surprisingly, because of their size, cappelletti are very fiddly to make.*

Cheese and Ham Ravioli with Tomato Sauce

TYPICAL OF SOUTHERN ITALIAN cuisine, these ravioli are very tasty. They are substantial enough for a main course, served with a green or mixed salad. If you prefer them as a first course, there are enough ravioli for 8 servings.

INGREDIENTS

I quantity Pasta with Eggs
60ml/4 tbsp freshly grated Pecorino cheese,
*   plus extra to serve*

For the filling

175g/6oz/³⁄₄ cup ricotta cheese
30ml/2 tbsp freshly grated Parmesan cheese
115g/4oz prosciutto, finely chopped
150g/5oz packet mozzarella cheese,
*   drained and finely chopped*
I small egg
15ml/1 tbsp chopped fresh flat
*   leaf parsley, plus extra to garnish*

For the tomato sauce

30ml/2 tbsp olive oil
I onion, finely chopped
400g/14oz can chopped Italian
*   plum tomatoes*
15ml/1 tbsp sun-dried tomato paste
5–10ml/1–2 tsp dried oregano, to taste
salt and ground black pepper
Serves 4–6

I Make the sauce. Heat the oil in a medium saucepan, add the onion and cook gently, stirring frequently, for about 5 minutes until softened.

2 Add the tomatoes. Fill the empty can with water, pour it into the pan, then stir in the tomato paste, oregano and salt and pepper to taste. Bring to the boil and stir well, then cover the pan and simmer gently for 30 minutes, stirring occasionally and adding more water if the sauce becomes too thick.

3 Meanwhile, make the filling and the ravioli. Put all the filling ingredients in a bowl with salt and pepper to taste. Mix well with a fork, breaking up any lumps in the ricotta.

4 Using a pasta machine, roll out one-quarter of the pasta into a 90cm–1 metre/36in–3 foot strip. Cut the strip with a sharp knife into two 45–50cm/18–20in lengths (you can do this during rolling if the strip gets too long to manage).

5 Using 2 teaspoons, put 10–12 little mounds of the filling along one side of one of the pasta strips, spacing them evenly. The filling will be quite moist. Brush a little water around each mound, then fold the plain side of the pasta strip over the filling.

6 Starting from the folded edge, press down gently with your fingertips around each mound, pushing the air out at the unfolded edge.

7 Sprinkle lightly with flour. With a fluted pasta wheel, cut along each long side, then in between each mound to make small square shapes.

8 Put the ravioli on floured dish towels; sprinkle lightly with flour.

9 Leave the ravioli to dry while repeating the process with the remaining pasta to get 80–96 ravioli altogether. Drop the ravioli into a large pan of salted boiling water, bring back to the boil and boil for 4–5 minutes.

10 Drain the ravioli well and pour about a third of them into a warmed bowl. Sprinkle 15ml/1 tbsp freshly grated Pecorino over the ravioli. Pour over a third of the tomato sauce.

11 Repeat the layers twice, then top with the remaining grated Pecorino. Serve immediately, garnished with chopped parsley. Hand around more grated Pecorino separately.

VARIATION

If you like the flavour of garlic with tomatoes, gently cook 1–2 crushed garlic cloves, with the onion when making the tomato sauce.

Agnolotti with Taleggio and Marjoram

THE FILLING FOR THESE LITTLE half-moons is very simple – only two ingredients – but the combination of flavours is absolutely delicious.

INGREDIENTS

1 quantity Pasta with Eggs
350–400g/12–14oz taleggio cheese
about 30ml/2 tbsp finely chopped
*   fresh marjoram, plus extra to garnish*
115g/4oz/¹/₂ cup butter
salt and ground black pepper
freshly grated Parmesan cheese, to serve
Serves 6–8

1 Using a pasta machine, roll out a quarter of the pasta into a 90cm–1 metre/36in–3 foot strip. Cut the strip with a sharp knife into two 45–50cm/18–20in lengths (you can do this during rolling if the strip gets too long to manage).

2 Cut 8–10 little cubes of taleggio and place them along one side of one of the pasta strips, spacing them evenly. Sprinkle each taleggio cube with a little chopped marjoram and pepper to taste.

3 Brush a little water around each cube of cheese, then fold the plain side of the pasta strip over them.

4 Starting from the folded edge, press down gently with your fingertips around each cube, pushing the air out at the unfolded edge. Sprinkle lightly with flour.

5 Using only half of a 5cm/2in fluted round ravioli or biscuit cutter, cut around each cube of cheese to make a half-moon shape. The folded edge should be the straight edge.

6 If you like, press the cut edges of the agnolotti with the tines of a fork to give a decorative effect.

7 Put the agnolotti on floured dish towels, sprinkle lightly with flour and leave to dry while repeating the process with the remaining pasta, cheese, marjoram and pepper to get 64–80 agnolotti altogether.

8 Drop the agnolotti into a large saucepan of salted boiling water, bring back to the boil and boil for 4–5 minutes until *al dente*.

9 Meanwhile, melt the butter in a small saucepan until it is sizzling.

10 Drain the agnolotti and divide them equally among six or eight warmed large bowls. Drizzle the sizzling butter over them and serve immediately, sprinkled with freshly grated Parmesan and chopped fresh marjoram. Hand around more grated Parmesan separately.

COOK'S TIPS

• *Taleggio is a square-shaped, semi-soft cheese from Lombardy. It is quite easy to get in large supermarkets, or any Italian delicatessen. It has a mild, slightly nutty flavour and good melting qualities. For this recipe, make sure that you remove the rind, which tends to be quite tough and salty.*
• *If you are unable to get taleggio, use fontina cheese instead, or a strongly flavoured blue cheese, such as Gorgonzola. If you use a blue cheese, substitute sage for the marjoram.*

VARIATION

Marjoram is traditional with the taleggio cheese in this recipe, both for the filling and the sizzling butter, but you can use other fresh herbs, such as sage, basil or flat leaf parsley.

Pansotti with Herbs and Cheese

In Liguria, the dough for *pansotti* is flavoured with white wine, and the stuffing is made of cheese and *pre-boggion*, a mixture of many different types of fresh herbs and wild leaves. The dish is traditionally served with a kind of pesto made from walnuts, making it very rich and quite complex. The recipe given here is a simple version.

INGREDIENTS

1 quantity Herb-flavoured Pasta
   with Eggs
50g/2oz/¼ cup butter
freshly grated Parmesan cheese,
   to serve

For the filling

250g/9oz/generous 1 cup ricotta cheese
150g/5oz/1⅔ cups freshly grated
   Parmesan cheese
1 large handful fresh basil leaves,
   finely chopped
1 large handful fresh flat leaf parsley,
   finely chopped
a few sprigs fresh marjoram or oregano,
   leaves removed and finely chopped
1 garlic clove, crushed
1 small egg
salt and ground black pepper

For the sauce

90g/3½oz shelled walnuts
1 garlic clove
60ml/4 tbsp extra virgin olive oil
125ml/4fl oz/½ cup panna da cucina or
   double cream
Serves 6–8

1 First make the filling and sauce. Put the ricotta, Parmesan, herbs, garlic and egg in a bowl with salt and pepper to taste and beat well to mix.

2 To make the sauce, put the walnuts, garlic clove and oil in a food processor and process to a paste, adding up to 125ml/4fl oz/½ cup warm water through the feeder tube to slacken the consistency. Spoon the mixture into a large bowl and add the cream. Beat well to mix, then add salt and pepper to taste.

3 Using a pasta machine, roll out one-quarter of the pasta into a 90cm–1 metre/36in–3 foot strip. Cut the strip with a sharp knife into two 45–50cm/18–20in lengths (you can do this during rolling if the strip gets too long to manage).

4 Using a 5cm/2in square ravioli cutter, cut 8–10 squares from one of the pasta strips. Using a teaspoon, put a mound of filling in the centre of each square.

5 Brush a little water around the edge of each square, then fold the square diagonally in half over the filling to make a triangular shape. Press gently to seal.

6 Spread out the *pansotti* on clean floured dish towels, sprinkle lightly with flour and leave to dry, while repeating the process with the remaining dough to make 64–80 *pansotti* altogether.

7 Cook the *pansotti* in a large saucepan of salted boiling water for 4–5 minutes. Meanwhile, put the walnut sauce in a large warmed bowl and add a ladleful of the pasta cooking water to thin it down. Melt the butter in a small saucepan until sizzling.

8 Drain the *pansotti* and tip them into the bowl of walnut sauce. Drizzle the butter over them, toss well, then sprinkle with grated Parmesan. Alternatively, toss the pansotti in the melted butter, spoon into warmed individual bowls and drizzle the sauce over. Serve immediately, with more grated Parmesan handed separately.

COOK'S TIP

Try not to overfill the pansotti, *or they will burst open during cooking.*

Tortellini from Emilia-Romagna

THESE ARE THE TORTELLINI that are served on the day after Christmas in Emilia-Romagna. Traditionally they were made with minced leftover capon from Christmas Day, but nowadays turkey or chicken is often used.

INGREDIENTS

I quantity Pasta with Eggs
2 litres/3¹/₂ pints/8 cups beef stock made
  with stock cubes or diluted canned
  consommé
freshly grated Parmesan cheese,
  to serve

For the filling

25g/Ioz/2 tbsp butter
250g/9oz minced turkey or chicken
5ml/I tsp chopped fresh rosemary
5ml/I tsp chopped fresh sage
nutmeg
250ml/8fl oz/I cup chicken stock
60ml/4tbsp freshly grated Parmesan cheese
90g/3¹/₂oz mortadella sausage, very
  finely chopped
I small egg, lightly beaten
salt and ground black pepper
Serves 6–8

1 Make the filling. Melt the butter in a medium skillet, then add the minced turkey or chicken and chopped herbs.

2 Grate in a little nutmeg and add salt and pepper to taste. Cook gently for 5–6 minutes, stirring frequently and breaking up any lumps in the meat with a wooden spoon.

3 Add the stock and stir well to mix, then simmer gently, uncovered, for 15–20 minutes until the meat is cooked and quite dry. Transfer the meat to a bowl with a slotted spoon and leave to cool. Add the grated Parmesan, mortadella and egg to the meat and stir well to mix.

4 Using a pasta machine, roll out one-quarter of the pasta into a 90cm–I metre/36in–3 foot strip. Cut the strip with a sharp knife into two 45–50cm/18–20in lengths (you can do this during rolling if the strip gets too long to manage).

5 With a 5cm/2in fluted ravioli or biscuit cutter, cut out 8–10 discs from one of the pasta strips. Using a teaspoon, put a little mound of filling in the centre of each disc. Brush a little water around the edge of each disc.

6 Fold the disc in half over the filling so that the edges do not quite meet. Press to seal. Wrap the tortellini shape around your index finger and pinch the bottom corners together to seal.

7 Put the tortellini in a single layer on floured dish towels, sprinkle lightly with flour and leave to dry while repeating the process with the remaining dough to make 64–80 tortellini altogether. If you have any stuffing left, re-roll the pasta trimmings and make more tortellini.

8 Bring the beef stock to the boil in a large saucepan. Drop in the tortellini, then bring back to the boil and boil for 4–5 minutes. Taste the stock and season with salt and pepper if necessary.

9 Pour the tortellini and stock into a warmed large soup tureen, sprinkle with a little grated Parmesan and serve immediately. Hand more Parmesan separately.

COOK'S TIP

In Emilia-Romagna, cooked leftover meat is minced by hand for these tortellini, or raw meat is cooked in the piece and then minced. For speed and convenience in this recipe, raw minced poultry is cooked with herbs and seasonings before being used in the filling.

Spinach and Ricotta Conchiglioni

LARGE PASTA SHELLS are designed to hold a variety of delicious stuffings. Few are more pleasing than this mixture of spinach and ricotta.

INGREDIENTS

350g/12oz large fresh or dried conchiglioni
450ml/³⁄₄ pint/1³⁄₄ cups passata or
*   tomato pulp*
275g/10oz frozen chopped
*   spinach, thawed*
50g/2oz crustless white bread, crumbled
120ml/4fl oz/¹⁄₂ cup milk
45ml/3 tbsp olive oil
250g/9oz ricotta cheese
pinch of grated nutmeg
1 garlic clove, crushed
15ml/1 tsbp olive oil
2.5ml/¹⁄₂ tsp black olive paste (optional)
Parmesan cheese, for sprinkling
25g/1oz/2 tbsp pine nuts
salt and ground black pepper
Serves 4

2 Pour the passata or tomato pulp into a nylon sieve over a bowl and strain the liquids to thicken. Place the thawed spinach in another sieve and press out any excess liquid with the back of a spoon.

5 Spoon the spinach mixture into a piping bag fitted with a large plain nozzle and fill the pasta shells (alternatively fill with a spoon). Arrange the pasta shells over the sauce in the dish.

3 Place the bread, milk and oil in a blender or food processor and process to combine. Add the spinach and ricotta cheese and season with salt, pepper and grated nutmeg. Process again to combine.

6 Preheat the grill to a moderate heat. Heat the pasta through in the microwave on a high power for 4 minutes. Scatter with Parmesan cheese and pine nuts, and finish under the grill to brown the cheese until bubbling.

1 Cook the pasta shells in plenty of salted boiling water according to the instructions on the packet. Rinse under cold water, drain and reserve until needed.

4 Combine the passata or tomato pulp with the garlic, olive oil and olive paste, if using. Pour the sauce into the base of an ovenproof dish spreading it out to the corners.

Ravioli with Vegetables and Nuts

IT IS A PLEASURE to make your own fresh pasta and you might be surprised at just how easy it is to fill and shape ravioli, although it does take a little time. A blender or food processor will save you time and effort in making and kneading the dough. A pasta-making machine helps with the rolling out, but both these jobs can be done by hand if necessary.

INGREDIENTS

200g/7oz/1¾ cups strong plain flour
5ml/½ tsp salt
15ml/1 tbsp olive oil
2 eggs, beaten

For the filling
15ml/1 tbsp olive oil
1 small red onion, finely chopped
1 small green pepper, finely chopped
1 carrot, coarsely grated
50g/2oz/½ cup walnuts, chopped
115g/4oz/½ cup ricotta cheese
30ml/2 tbsp freshly grated Parmesan or
    Pecorino cheese, plus extra to serve
15ml/1 tbsp chopped fresh marjoram
    or basil
salt and ground black pepper
extra oil or melted butter, to serve

Serves 6

1 Sift the flour and salt together into a blender or food processor. With the machine running, trickle in the oil and eggs and blend to a stiff but smooth dough.

2 Allow the machine to run for at least 1 minute if possible, otherwise remove the dough and knead by hand for 5 minutes.

3 If you are using a pasta machine, break off small balls of dough and feed them through the rollers, several times, according to the instructions that come with the machine.

4 If rolling the pasta by hand, divide the dough into two and roll out on a lightly floured surface to a thickness of about 5mm/¼in.

5 Fold the pasta into three and re-roll. Repeat this up to six times until the dough is smooth and no longer sticky. Roll the pasta slightly more thinly each time.

6 Keep the rolled dough under clean, dry dish towels, to prevent it drying out, while you complete the rest and make the filling. You should aim to have an even number of pasta sheets, all the same size.

7 Heat the oil in a frying pan and cook the onion, pepper and carrot for 5 minutes, then allow to cool. Mix with the walnuts, cheeses, herbs and lots of seasoning.

8 Lay out a pasta sheet and place small scoops of the filling in neat rows about 5cm/2in apart. Brush between the mounds of filling with a little water.

9 Carefully place another pasta sheet of a similar size on the top, making sure that you cover all the mounds of filling.

10 Press down well in between the rows then, using a ravioli or pastry cutter, cut into squares. If the edges pop open, press them back gently with your fingers or the tines of a fork.

11 Leave the ravioli to dry in the fridge, then boil in plenty of lightly salted water for just 5 minutes. Drain thoroughly.

12 Toss the cooked ravioli in a little oil or melted butter before serving with extra cheese.

Ravioli with Pork and Turkey

THIS ROMAN-STYLE RAVIOLI stuffed with minced meat and cheese is scented with fresh herbs. It makes a substantial first course.

INGREDIENTS

1 quantity Pasta with Eggs
50g/2oz/¼ cup butter
a large bunch of fresh sage, leaves removed and roughly chopped
60ml/4 tbsp freshly grated Parmesan cheese, plus extra, to serve
sage leaves, to garnish

For the filling
25g/1oz/2 tbsp butter
150g/5oz minced pork
115g/4oz minced turkey
4 fresh sage leaves, finely chopped
1 sprig of fresh rosemary, leaves removed and finely chopped
30ml/2 tbsp dry white wine
65g/2½oz/generous ¼ cup ricotta cheese
45ml/3 tbsp freshly grated Parmesan cheese
1 egg, lightly beaten
nutmeg
salt and ground black pepper
Serves 8

1 Make the filling. Melt the butter in a medium saucepan, add the minced pork and turkey and the herbs and cook gently for 5–6 minutes, stirring frequently and breaking up any lumps in the meat with a wooden spoon. Add salt and pepper to taste and stir to mix.

2 Add the wine to the pan and stir again. Simmer for 1–2 minutes until reduced slightly, then cover the pan and simmer gently for about 20 minutes, stirring occasionally. With a slotted spoon, transfer the meat to a bowl and leave to cool.

3 Add the ricotta and Parmesan cheeses to the bowl with the egg and freshly grated nutmeg to taste. Stir well to mix the ingredients thoroughly.

4 Using a pasta machine, roll out one-quarter of the pasta into a 90cm–1 metre/35in–3 foot strip. Cut the strip with a sharp knife into two 45–50cm/18–20in lengths (you can do this during rolling if the strip gets too long to manage).

5 Using a teaspoon, put 10–12 little mounds of the filling along one side of one of the pasta strips, spacing them evenly. Brush a little water on to the pasta strip around each mound, then fold the plain side of the pasta strip over the filling.

6 Starting from the folded edge, press down gently with your fingertips around each mound of filling, pushing the air out at the unfolded edge. Sprinkle lightly with flour.

7 With a fluted pasta wheel, cut along each long side, then in between each mound to make small square shapes. Dust lightly with flour.

8 Put the ravioli in a single layer on floured dish towels and leave to dry while repeating the process with the remaining pasta to make 80–96 ravioli altogether.

9 Drop the ravioli into a large pan of salted boiling water, bring back to the boil and boil for 4–5 minutes.

COOK'S TIP

Minced pork and turkey are widely available at supermarkets, but if you cannot get one or the other you can use just one type of meat, or substitute minced veal, beef or lamb to use in the ravioli filling.

10 While the ravioli are cooking, melt the butter in a small saucepan, add the fresh sage leaves and stir over a medium to high heat until the sage leaves are sizzling in the butter.

11 Drain the ravioli and pour half into a warmed large bowl. Sprinkle with half the grated Parmesan, then half the sage butter. Repeat with the remaining ravioli, Parmesan and sage butter. Serve immediately, garnished with fresh sage leaves. Hand more grated Parmesan separately.

Ravioli with Crab

This modern recipe for a dinner party starter uses chilli-flavoured pasta, which looks and tastes good with crab, but you can use plain pasta if you prefer.

INGREDIENTS

1 quantity Chilli-flavoured Pasta
    with Eggs
90g/3¹/₂oz/ 6 tbsp butter
juice of 1 lemon

For the filling

175g/6oz/³/₄ cup mascarpone cheese
175g/6oz/³/₄ cup crabmeat
30ml/2 tbsp finely chopped fresh
    flat leaf parsley
finely grated rind of 1 lemon
pinch of crushed dried chillies (optional)
salt and ground black pepper
Serves 4

COOK'S TIP

You can use all white crabmeat or a mixture of white and dark. If you use dark meat, the flavour will be stronger.

1 Make the filling. Put the mascarpone in a bowl and mash it with a fork. Add the crabmeat, parsley, lemon rind, crushed dried chillies (if using) and salt and pepper to taste. Stir well.

2 Using a pasta machine, roll out one-quarter of the pasta into a 90cm–1 metre/36in–3 foot strip. Cut the strip with a sharp knife into two 45–50cm/18–20in lengths (you can do this during rolling if the strip gets too long to manage).

3 With a 6cm/2¹/₂in fluted biscuit cutter, cut out 8 squares from each pasta strip.

4 Using a teaspoon, put a mound of filling in the centre of half the discs. Brush a little water around the edge of the filled discs, then top with the plain discs and press the edges to seal. For a decorative finish, press the edges with the tines of a fork.

5 Put the ravioli on floured dish towels, sprinkle lightly with flour and leave to dry while repeating the process with the remaining dough to make 32 ravioli altogether. If you have any stuffing left, you can re-roll the pasta trimmings and make more ravioli.

6 Cook the ravioli in a large saucepan of salted boiling water for 4–5 minutes. Meanwhile, melt the butter and lemon juice in a small saucepan until sizzling.

7 Drain the ravioli and divide them equally among four warmed bowls. Drizzle the lemon butter over the ravioli and serve immediately.

Sardinian Ravioli

THESE RAVIOLI, with their unusual mashed potato and mint filling, are from northern Sardinia. Here they are gratinéed in the oven with butter and cheese, but they are often served dressed with a tomato sauce.

INGREDIENTS

1 quantity Pasta with Eggs
50g/2oz/¼ cup butter
50g/2oz/⅔ cup freshly grated
  Pecorino cheese

For the filling

2 potatoes, each about 200g/7oz, diced
65g/2½oz/generous ⅔ cup freshly grated
  hard salty Pecorino cheese
75g/3oz soft fresh Pecorino cheese
1 egg yolk
1 large bunch fresh mint, leaves removed
  and chopped
good pinch of saffron powder
salt and ground black pepper
Serves 4–6

1 Make the filling. Cook the diced potatoes in salted boiling water for 15–20 minutes or until soft. Drain the potatoes and tip into a bowl, then mash until smooth. Leave until cold. Add the cheeses, egg yolk, mint, saffron and salt and pepper to taste and stir well to mix.

2 Using a pasta machine, roll out one-quarter of the pasta into a 90cm–1 metre/36in–3 foot strip. Cut the strip with a sharp knife into two 45–50cm/18–20in lengths.

3 With a fluted 10cm/4in biscuit cutter, cut out 4–5 discs from one of the pasta strips. Using a heaped teaspoon, put a mound of filling to one side of each disc. Brush a little water around the edge of each disc, then fold the plain side of the disc over the filling to make a half-moon shape. Pleat the curved edge to seal.

4 Put the culurgiones on floured dish towels, sprinkle with flour and leave to dry. Repeat the process with the remaining dough to make 32–40 culurgiones altogether. If you have any stuffing left, re-roll the pasta trimmings and make more culurgiones.

5 Preheat the oven to 190°C/375°F/ Gas 5. Cook the culurgiones in a large saucepan of salted boiling water for 4–5 minutes. Meanwhile, melt the butter in a small saucepan.

6 Drain the culurgiones, tip them into a large baking dish and pour the melted butter over them. Sprinkle with the grated Pecorino and bake in the oven for 10–15 minutes until golden and bubbly. Allow to stand for 5 minutes before serving.

COOK'S TIP

There is quite an art to pleating the curved edge of culurgiones, but each cook has his or her own way of doing it, so don't worry about getting a precise finish. Do whatever you think looks best — some culurgiones look like miniature Cornish pasties, others more like Chinese wontons. If you prefer, simply make square or round ravioli, or plain half-moons.

Fresh
and
Healthy

Chargrilled vegetables, designer salad leaves and pesto made with rocket are just a few of the new ingredients being introduced to pasta by today's chefs. To call these sauces is stretching the point a little: many of them consist of little more than a handful of fresh ingredients tossed with hot pasta, but the results are simply sensational.

These are not traditional pasta dishes. Many of them originated in restaurants, in response to the current taste for lighter, healthier food, but they are so quick and easy to make at home that you will find there's no need to go out to eat them.

The recipes in this chapter are tried and tested, but there are no hard-and-fast rules. Half the fun is in inventing your own combinations, using fresh vegetables and herbs according to the season. The key to success lies in the quality of these ingredients, and only the best will do. This goes for the pasta as much as anything else. Buy Italian brands of pasta to be sure of good texture and taste or, if you have the inclination and time, make your own fresh egg pasta.

Pasta is a natural, additive-free food, packed with protein, vitamins and minerals – the perfect partner for other healthy ingredients to make a high-energy meal.

Spaghetti with Herb Sauce

HERBS MAKE a wonderfully aromatic
sauce – the heat from the pasta
releases their flavours.

INGREDIENTS

50g/2oz chopped fresh mixed herbs, such
   as parsley, basil and thyme
2 garlic cloves, crushed
60ml/4 tbsp pine nuts, toasted
150ml/¼ pint/⅔ cup olive oil
350g/12oz dried spaghetti
60ml/4 tbsp freshly grated
   Parmesan cheese
salt and ground black pepper
basil leaves, to garnish
Serves 4

1 Put the herbs, garlic and half the
pine nuts into a blender or food
processor. With the machine running
slowly, add the oil and process to form
a thick purée.

2 Cook the spaghetti in plenty of
salted boiling water for about
8 minutes until *al dente*. Drain.

3 Transfer the herb purée to a large
warmed serving dish, then add
the spaghetti and Parmesan. Toss well
to coat the pasta with the sauce.
Sprinkle the remaining pine nuts and
the basil leaves over the top and
serve immediately.

Capellini with Rocket and Mangetouts

A LIGHT BUT FILLING pasta dish with the added pepperiness of fresh rocket leaves.

INGREDIENTS

250g/9oz dried capellini
225g/8oz mangetouts
75g/3oz rocket leaves
50g/2oz/¹/₄ cup pine nuts, roasted
*30ml/2 tbsp finely grated Parmesan cheese
    (optional)*
30ml/2 tbsp olive oil (optional)

Serves 4

1   Cook the capellini in a large saucepan with plenty of salted boiling water, according to the instructions on the packet, until just *al dente*.

2   Meanwhile, carefully top and tail the mangetouts, and discard any that are damaged.

3   As soon as the pasta is cooked, drop in the rocket and mangetouts. Drain immediately.

4   Toss the pasta with the roasted pine nuts, and Parmesan and olive oil if using. Serve at once.

Tagliatelle with Broccoli and Spinach

This is an excellent vegetarian supper dish. It is nutritious and filling, and needs no accompaniment. If you like, you can use tagliatelle flecked with herbs.

INGREDIENTS

2 heads of broccoli
450g/1lb fresh spinach,
   stalks removed
nutmeg
450g/1lb fresh or dried egg tagliatelle
about 45ml/3 tbsp extra virgin olive oil
juice of ½ lemon, or to taste
salt and ground black pepper
freshly grated Parmesan cheese,
   to serve
Serves 4

1 Put the broccoli in the basket of a steamer, cover and steam over boiling water for 10 minutes. Add the spinach to the broccoli, cover and steam for 4–5 minutes or until both are tender. Towards the end of the cooking time, sprinkle the vegetables with freshly grated nutmeg and salt and pepper to taste. Lift out the steamer and put to one side.

2 Add salt to the water already in the steamer and fill up with more boiling water, then add the pasta and cook according to the instructions on the packet. Meanwhile, chop the broccoli and spinach in the colander.

3 Drain the pasta. Heat 45ml/3tbsp oil in the pasta pan, add the pasta and chopped vegetables and toss over a medium heat until evenly mixed. Sprinkle in the lemon juice and plenty of black pepper, then taste and add more lemon juice, oil, salt and nutmeg if you like. Serve immediately, sprinkled liberally with freshly grated Parmesan and black pepper.

VARIATIONS

• If you like, add a sprinkling of crushed dried chillies with the black pepper in Step 3.
• To add both texture and protein, garnish the finished dish with one or two handfuls of toasted pine nuts. They are often served with broccoli and spinach in Italy.

Conchiglie from Pisa

NOTHING COULD BE MORE simple than hot pasta tossed with fresh ripe tomatoes, ricotta and sweet basil. Serve it on hot summer days – it is surprisingly cool and refreshing.

INGREDIENTS

350g/12oz/3 cups dried conchiglie
125g/4¹/₂oz/generous ¹/₂ cup
   ricotta cheese
6 ripe Italian plum tomatoes, diced
2 garlic cloves, crushed
1 handful fresh basil leaves, shredded, plus
   extra basil leaves to garnish
60ml/4 tbsp extra virgin olive oil
salt and ground black pepper
Serves 4–6

1 Cook the pasta in salted boiling water according to the instructions on the packet.

COOK'S TIP

If you like, peel the tomatoes before you dice them. It won't take long if the tomatoes are ripe.

2 Meanwhile, put the ricotta in a large bowl and mash with a fork.

3 Add the tomatoes, garlic and basil, with salt and pepper to taste, and mix well. Add the olive oil and whisk thoroughly. Taste for seasoning.

4 Drain the cooked pasta, tip it into the ricotta mixture and toss well to mix. Garnish with basil leaves and serve immediately.

VARIATION

• You can use diced mozzarella instead of ricotta cheese and call the dish Conchiglie Caprese, after the salad of tomatoes, mozzarella and basil known as Caprese.

• An avocado is the ideal ingredient for adding extra colour and flavour to this pasta dish. Halve, stone and peel, then dice the flesh. Toss it with the hot pasta at the last minute.

Conchiglie with Tomatoes and Rocket

THIS PRETTY-COLOURED pasta dish relies for its success on the salad green, rocket. Available in large supermarkets, it is a leaf easily grown in the garden or a window-box and tastes slightly peppery.

INGREDIENTS

450g/1lb conchiglie rigate
450g/1lb ripe cherry tomatoes
75g/3oz fresh rocket leaves
45ml/3 tbsp olive oil
salt and ground black pepper
Parmesan cheese shavings, to serve

Serves 4

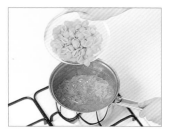

1 Cook the pasta in plenty of salted boiling water according to the instructions on the packet, until *al dente*. Drain well.

2 Halve the tomatoes. Trim, wash and dry the rocket leaves.

3 Heat the oil in a large saucepan, add the tomatoes and cook for barely 1 minute. The tomatoes should only just heat through and not disintegrate or brown.

4 Add the pasta, then the rocket. Carefully stir to mix and heat through. Season well with salt and ground black pepper. Serve immediately with plenty of Parmesan cheese shavings.

Eliche with Low-fat Pesto Sauce

TRADITIONALLY MADE with lashings of olive oil, this simple pesto sauce is still packed with flavour.

INGREDIENTS

225g/8oz/2 cups dried eliche
50g/2oz/1 cup fresh basil leaves
25g/1oz/¹/₂ cup parsley sprigs
1 garlic clove, crushed
25g/1oz/¹/₄ cup pine nuts
115g/4oz/¹/₂ cup curd cheese
30ml/2 tbsp freshly grated
  Parmesan cheese
salt and ground black pepper
fresh basil sprigs, to garnish

Serves 4

1 Cook the pasta in plenty of salted boiling water in a large saucepan for 8–10 minutes, or until *al dente*. Drain well through a colander.

2 Meanwhile put half the basil and half the parsley, the garlic clove, pine nuts and curd cheese into a blender or food processor fitted with a metal blade and process until smooth. Scrape down the sides.

3 Add the remaining basil and parsley together with the Parmesan cheese and seasoning. Continue to process until the herbs are finely chopped.

4 Toss the pasta with the pesto and serve on warmed plates. Garnish with fresh basil sprigs.

Pipe with Ricotta, Saffron and Spinach

TOSSING PASTA IN RICOTTA is popular in Sicily and Sardinia, where this cheese is widely used in cooking. For best results, use fresh white ricotta, which is sold by weight in Italian delicatessens. Serve this rich dish in small quantities. Omit the saffron, with its quite strong flavour, if preferred.

INGREDIENTS

1 small pinch of saffron threads
300g/11oz/2¾ cups dried pipe
300–350g/11–12oz fresh spinach,
  stalks removed
nutmeg
250g/9oz/generous 1 cup ricotta cheese
salt and ground black pepper
freshly grated Pecorino cheese, to serve
Serves 4–6

1 Soak the saffron threads in 60ml/ 4 tbsp warm water. Cook the pasta according to the packet instructions.

2 Meanwhile, wash the spinach and put the leaves in a saucepan with only the water clinging to the leaves. Season with freshly grated nutmeg, salt and pepper to taste.

3 Cover the pan and cook over a medium to high heat for about 5 minutes, shaking the pan occasionally, until the spinach is wilted and tender. Tip into a colander, press to extract as much liquid as possible, then roughly chop letting the water drain through.

4 Put the ricotta in a large bowl. Strain in the saffron water. Add the spinach, beat well to mix, then add a ladleful or two of the pasta cooking water to loosen the mixture. Season.

5 Drain the pasta, reserving some of the cooking water. Add the pasta to the ricotta mixture and toss well, adding a little of the water if necessary. Serve at once, sprinkled with Pecorino.

Tagliarini with White Truffle

THERE IS NOTHING QUITE like the fragrance and flavour of the Italian white truffle. It is one of the rarest and therefore most expensive of truffles, which comes from around the towns of Alba and Asti in Piedmont. This simple style of serving it is one of the best ways to enjoy it.

INGREDIENTS

350g/12oz fresh tagliarini
75g/3oz/6 tbsp unsalted butter, diced
60ml/4 tbsp freshly grated Parmesan cheese
nutmeg
1 small white truffle, about
  25–40g/1–1½oz
salt and ground black pepper
Serves 4

1 Cook the pasta in salted boiling water according to the instructions on the packet.

2 Drain the cooked pasta thoroughly and tip it into a warmed large bowl. Add the diced butter, grated Parmesan, freshly grated nutmeg and a little salt and pepper to taste. Toss well until the pasta is coated in melted butter.

3 Divide the pasta equally among four warmed bowls and shave paper-thin slivers of the white truffle on top. Serve immediately.

COOK'S TIPS

• *White Italian truffles can be bought during the months of September and October from specialist food shops and delicatessens. They are very expensive, however, and there are some alternative ways of getting the flavour of truffles without the expense. Some Italian delicatessens sell "truffle cheese", which is a mountain cheese with shavings of truffle in it, and this can be used instead of the Parmesan and truffle in this recipe. Another alternative is to toss hot pasta in truffle oil and serve it with freshly grated Parmesan.*

• *In Piedmont a very thin home-made egg pasta called tagliarin or tajarin is used for this dish. Tagliarini are the nearest equivalent, or you could use tagliatellini or tagliolini instead, or even fettuccine if you like.*

Spaghetti with Rocket Pesto

THIS IS THE PESTO for real rocket lovers. It is sharp and peppery, and delicious for a summer pasta meal with a glass of chilled dry white wine.

INGREDIENTS

4 garlic cloves
90ml/6 tbsp pine nuts
2 large handfuls rocket, total weight about
  150g/5oz, stalks removed
50g/2oz/²⁄₃ cup Parmesan cheese,
  freshly grated
50g/2oz/²⁄₃ cup Pecorino cheese,
  freshly grated
90ml/6 tbsp extra virgin olive oil
400g/14oz fresh or dried spaghetti
salt and ground black pepper
freshly grated Parmesan and Pecorino cheese,
  to serve

Serves 4

1 Put the garlic and pine nuts in a blender or food processor and process until finely chopped.

2 Add the rocket, Parmesan and Pecorino, oil and salt and pepper to taste and process for 5 seconds. Stop and scrape down the side of the bowl. Process for 5–10 seconds more until a smooth paste is formed.

3 Cook the spaghetti in a saucepan of salted boiling water according to the packet instructions.

4 Tip the pesto into a large bowl. Just before the pasta is ready, add 1–2 ladlefuls of the cooking water to the pesto and stir well to mix.

5 Drain the pasta, tip it into the bowl of pesto and toss well to mix. Serve immediately, with the grated cheeses handed separately.

VARIATION

To temper the flavour of the rocket and make the pesto milder, add 115g/4oz/¹⁄₂ cup ricotta or mascarpone cheese to the pesto in Step 4 and mix well before adding the water.

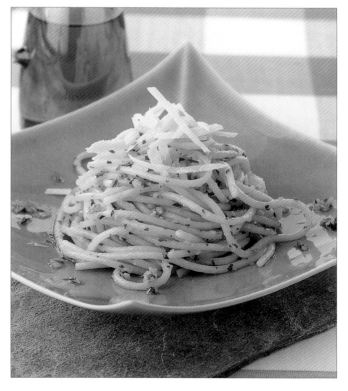

Spaghetti with Lemon

THIS IS THE DISH TO MAKE when you get home and find there's nothing to eat. If you keep spaghetti and olive oil in the storecupboard and garlic and lemons in the vegetable rack, you can prepare the most delicious meal in minutes.

INGREDIENTS

350g/12oz dried spaghetti
90ml/6 tbsp extra virgin olive oil
juice of 1 large lemon
2 garlic cloves, cut into very thin slivers
salt and ground black pepper
freshly grated Parmesan cheese, to serve

Serves 4

1 Cook the pasta in a saucepan of salted boiling water according to the instructions on the packet, then drain well and return to the pan.

2 Pour the olive oil and lemon juice over the cooked pasta, sprinkle in the slivers of garlic and add salt and pepper to taste.

3 Toss the pasta over a medium to high heat for 1–2 minutes. Serve immediately in four warmed bowls, with freshly grated Parmesan.

COOK'S TIP

Spaghetti is the best type of pasta for this recipe, because the olive oil and lemon juice cling to its long thin strands – even more so if you serve it with freshly grated Parmesan. If you are out of spaghetti, use another dried long pasta shape instead, such as spaghettini, linguine or tagliatelle.

Orecchiette with Broccoli

PUGLIA, IN SOUTHERN ITALY, specializes in imaginative pasta and vegetable combinations. Using the broccoli cooking water for boiling the pasta gives it more of the vegetable's lovely fresh flavour.

INGREDIENTS

800g/1¾lb broccoli
450g/1lb/4 cups fresh or dried orecchiette
90ml/6 tbsp olive oil
3 garlic cloves, finely chopped
6 anchovy fillets in oil
salt and ground black pepper
Serves 6

1 Peel the stems of the broccoli, starting from the base and pulling up towards the florets with a knife. Discard the woody parts of the stem. Cut the florets and stems into 5cm/2in pieces.

2 Bring a large pan of water to the boil. Drop in the broccoli and boil until barely tender, about 5–8 minutes. Remove the broccoli pieces from the pan to a serving bowl. Do not discard the broccoli cooking water.

3 Add salt to the broccoli cooking water and bring back to the boil. Drop in the pasta, stir well, and cook until al dente.

4 While the pasta is boiling, heat the oil in a small saucepan. Add the garlic and, after 2–3 minutes, the anchovy fillets. Using a fork, mash the anchovies and garlic to a smooth paste. Then cook for a further 3–4 minutes.

5 Before draining the pasta, ladle 1–2 cupfuls of the cooking water over the broccoli. Add the drained pasta and the hot anchovy and oil mixture. Mix well, and season with salt and pepper if necessary. Serve at once.

Pasta Napoletana

THE SIMPLE CLASSIC cooked tomato
sauce with no adornments.

INGREDIENTS

900g/2lb fresh ripe red tomatoes or
750g/1¾lb canned plum tomatoes with
their juice
1 onion, chopped
1 carrot, diced
1 celery stick, diced
150ml/¼ pint/⅔ cup dry white
wine (optional)
1 sprig fresh parsley
pinch of caster sugar
15ml/1 tbsp chopped fresh oregano or
5ml/1 tsp dried
450g/1lb pasta, any variety
salt and ground black pepper
freshly grated Parmesan cheese, to serve
Serves 4

1 Roughly chop the tomatoes and
place in a medium saucepan.

2 Add the vegetables, wine if using,
parsley and sugar and bring to
the boil. Simmer, half-covered, for
45 minutes until thick. Strain through
a sieve.

3 Stir the oregano into the sauce.
Taste and adjust the seasoning
if necessary.

4 Cook the pasta in plenty of
salted boiling water according to
the instructions on the packet, until
al dente. Drain well.

5 Toss the pasta with the sauce.
Serve with plenty of freshly grated
Parmesan cheese.

Spaghetti Olio e Aglio

THIS IS ANOTHER VERSION of the classic recipe from Rome. Originally the food of the poor, involving nothing more than pasta, olive oil (*olio*) and garlic (*aglio*), this is a quick and filling dish which is fast becoming fashionable the world over.

INGREDIENTS

2 garlic cloves
25g/¹/₄oz fresh parsley
120ml/4fl oz/¹/₂ cup olive oil
450g/1lb spaghetti
salt and ground black pepper
Serves 4

VARIATION

Although spaghetti is the traditional accompaniment to this sauce, this method works well with spaghettini, capellini or capellini d'angelo.

1 Using a sharp knife, peel and chop the two cloves of garlic as finely as possible.

2 Using a nylon chopping board and a sharp knife, roughly chop the fresh parsley.

3 Heat the olive oil in a medium saucepan and add the garlic and a pinch of salt. Cook gently, stirring all the time, until golden. If the garlic becomes too brown, it will taste bitter and spoil the dish.

4 Meanwhile cook the spaghetti in plenty of salted boiling water according to the instructions on the packet until *al dente*. Drain well through a colander.

5 Toss with the warm – not sizzling – garlic and oil and add plenty of black pepper and the parsley. Serve the dish immediately.

Pasta Rapido with Parsley Pesto

HERE IS A FRESH and lively sauce that will appeal to even the most jaded of appetites.

INGREDIENTS

450g/1lb dried pasta, any shape
75g/3oz/³⁄₄ cup whole almonds
50g/2oz/½ cup flaked almonds
25g/1oz/¼ cup freshly grated
  Parmesan cheese
pinch of salt

For the sauce

40g/1½oz fresh parsley
2 garlic cloves, crushed
45ml/3 tbsp olive oil
45ml/3 tbsp lemon juice
5ml/1 tsp sugar
250ml/8fl oz/1 cup boiling water

Serves 4

2 For the sauce, chop the parsley finely in a blender or food processor. Add the whole almonds; reduce to a fine consistency. Add the garlic, oil, lemon juice, sugar and water. Combine to a sauce.

3 Drain the pasta and combine with half the sauce. (The remainder of the sauce will keep in a screw-top jar in the fridge for up to ten days.) Top with Parmesan and flaked almonds.

1 Cook the pasta in plenty of salted boiling water, according to the instructions on the packet, until *al dente*. Toast the whole and flaked almonds separately under a moderate grill until golden brown. Set the flaked almonds aside.

Eliche with Turkey

BROCCOLI COMBINES with the other ingredients to make a one-pan meal.

INGREDIENTS

675g/1½lb ripe, firm plum
   tomatoes, quartered
90ml/6 tbsp olive oil
5ml/1 tsp dried oregano
350g/12oz broccoli florets
1 small onion, sliced
5ml/1 tsp dried thyme
450g/1lb skinless, boneless turkey
   breast, cubed
3 garlic cloves, crushed
15ml/1 tbsp fresh lemon juice
450g/1lb/4 cups eliche
salt and ground black pepper
Serves 4

1 Preheat the oven to 200°C/
400°F/Gas 6. Place the plum tomatoes in a baking dish. Add 15ml/ 1 tbsp of the oil, the oregano and 2.5ml/½ tsp salt and stir.

2 Bake for 30–40 minutes, until the tomatoes are just browned; do not stir.

3 Meanwhile, bring a large saucepan of salted water to the boil. Add the broccoli florets and cook until just tender, about 5 minutes. Drain and set aside. (Alternatively, steam the broccoli until tender.)

4 Heat 30ml/2 tbsp of the oil in a large non-stick frying pan. Add the onion, thyme, turkey and 2.5ml/½ tsp salt. Cook over a high heat, stirring often, until the meat is cooked and beginning to brown, about 5–7 minutes. Add the garlic and cook for a further 1 minute, stirring frequently.

5 Remove from the heat. Stir in the lemon juice and season with ground black pepper. Set aside and keep warm.

6 Cook the pasta in plenty of salted boiling water according to the instructions on the packet until *al dente*. Drain and place in a large bowl. Toss the pasta with the remaining oil.

7 Add the broccoli to the turkey mixture, then stir into the fusilli. Add the tomatoes and stir gently to blend. Serve immediately.

Penne with Broccoli and Chilli

FOR A MILDER FLAVOUR, remove the seeds from the chilli. Take care, when handling chilli, to wash your hands thoroughly afterwards.

INGREDIENTS

350g/12oz/3 cups fresh or dried penne
450g/1lb small broccoli florets
30ml/2 tbsp stock
1 garlic clove, crushed
1 small red chilli, sliced,
  or 2.5ml/½ tsp chilli sauce
60ml/4 tbsp natural low-fat yogurt
30ml/2 tbsp toasted pine nuts or
  cashew nuts
salt and ground black pepper

Serves 4

1 Add the pasta to a large pan of lightly salted boiling water and return to the boil. Then place the broccoli in a steamer basket over the top. Cover and cook for about 8–10 minutes until the penne are *al dente* and the broccoli are just tender. Drain them both through a colander once cooked.

2 Heat the stock in a large pan and add the crushed garlic and chilli or chilli sauce. Stir over a low heat for 2–3 minutes.

3 Stir in the broccoli, pasta and yogurt. Adjust the seasoning, sprinkle with nuts and serve hot in warmed bowls.

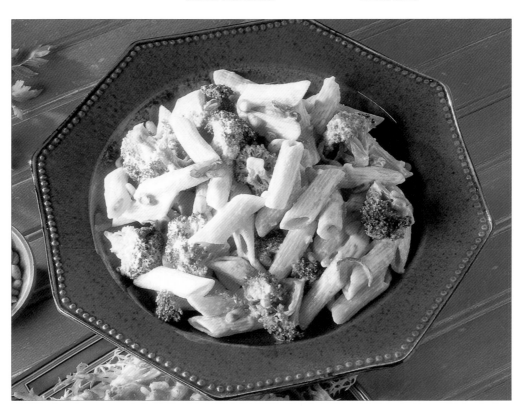

Spaghetti with Mixed Mushrooms

THIS COMBINATION of mixed mushrooms and freshly chopped sweet basil tossed with spaghetti would be well complemented by a simple tomato salad drizzled with extra virgin olive oil and whole fresh basil leaves.

INGREDIENTS

50g/2oz/¹/₄ cup butter
I onion, chopped
350g/I2oz spaghetti
350g/I2oz mixed mushrooms, such as
   brown, flat and button, sliced
I garlic clove, chopped
300ml/¹/₂ pint/I¹/₄ cups soured cream
30ml/2 tbsp chopped fresh basil
50g/2oz/¹/₂ cup freshly grated
   Parmesan cheese
salt and ground black pepper
torn flat leaf parsley, to garnish
freshly grated Parmesan cheese, to serve
Serves 4

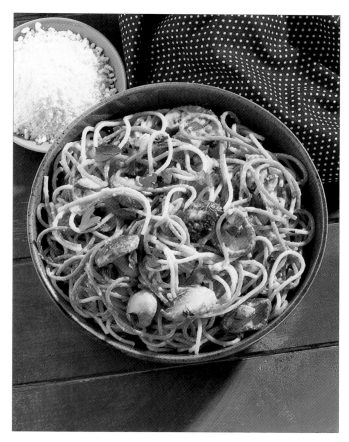

1   Melt the butter in a large frying pan and fry the chopped onion for 10 minutes until softened.

2   Cook the pasta in plenty of boiling salted water according to the instructions on the packet.

3   Stir the mushrooms and garlic into the onion mixture and fry for 10 minutes until softened.

4   Add the soured cream, basil, grated Parmesan cheese and salt and pepper to taste. Cover and heat through over a low heat.

5   Drain the pasta thoroughly and toss with the sauce. Serve immediately, garnished with torn flat leaf parsley, and with plenty of grated Parmesan cheese.

VARIATION

For a low-fat alternative, substitute the soured cream for plain yogurt.

Tagliatelle with Herbs

THIS IS A LOVELY dish for summer when fresh herbs are plentiful. It is quick and ideal for vegetarians.

INGREDIENTS

3 rosemary sprigs
1 small handful fresh flat leaf parsley
5–6 fresh mint leaves
5–6 fresh sage leaves
8–10 large fresh basil leaves
30ml/2 tbsp extra virgin olive oil
50g/2oz/¼ cup butter
1 shallot, finely chopped
2 garlic cloves, finely chopped
pinch of chilli powder, to taste
400g/14oz fresh egg tagliatelle
1 bay leaf
120ml/4fl oz/½ cup dry white wine
90–120ml/6–8 tbsp vegetable stock
salt and ground black pepper
Serves 4

1 Strip the rosemary and parsley leaves from their stalks and chop them together with the fresh mint, sage and basil.

2 Heat the olive oil and half the butter in a large skillet or saucepan. Add the shallot and garlic and the chilli powder, and cook over a very low heat, stirring frequently, for 2–3 minutes.

3 Cook the pasta in salted boiling water according to the packet instructions.

4 Add the chopped herbs and the bay leaf to the shallot mixture and stir for 2–3 minutes, then add the wine and increase the heat. Boil rapidly for 1–2 minutes until the wine reduces. Lower the heat, add the stock and simmer gently for 1–2 minutes.

5 Drain the pasta and add it to the herb mixture. Toss well to mix and remove and discard the bay leaf.

6 Put the remaining butter in a warmed large bowl, tip the dressed pasta into it and toss well to mix. Serve immediately.

Garganelli with Spring Vegetables

YOUNG FRESH VEGETABLES both look and taste good with pasta. Butter is used to marry the two together, but you can use extra virgin olive oil if you prefer.

INGREDIENTS

1 bunch asparagus, about 350g/12oz
4 young carrots
1 bunch spring onions
130g/4½oz shelled fresh peas
350g/12oz/3 cups dried garganelli
60ml/4 tbsp dry white wine
75g/3oz/6 tbsp unsalted butter, diced
a few sprigs each fresh flat leaf parsley,
*   mint and basil, leaves stripped*
*   and chopped*
salt and ground black pepper
freshly grated Parmesan cheese, to serve
Serves 4

1 Trim off and discard the woody part of each asparagus stem, then cut off the tips on the diagonal. Cut the stems on the diagonal into 4cm/1½in pieces. Cut the carrots and spring onions on the diagonal into similar pieces.

2 Plunge the asparagus stems, carrots and peas into a saucepan of salted boiling water. Bring back to the boil and simmer for 5–8 minutes, adding the asparagus tips for the last 3 minutes.

3 Meanwhile, cook the pasta in salted boiling water according to the instructions on the packet.

4 Drain the vegetables and return them to the pan. Add the wine, butter and salt and pepper to taste, then toss over a medium to high heat until the wine has reduced and the vegetables glisten with melted butter.

5 Drain the pasta and tip it into a warmed large bowl. Add the vegetables, spring onions and herbs and toss well. Serve immediately, with freshly grated Parmesan.

COOK'S TIP

Garganelli are rolled short pasta shapes made with egg. If you can't get garganelli, use another short shape made with egg.

Linguine with Rocket

THIS IS A FIRST COURSE THAT you will find in many a fashionable restaurant in Italy. It is very quick and easy to make at home and is worth trying for yourself.

INGREDIENTS

350g/12oz fresh or dried linguine
120ml/4fl oz/1/2 cup extra virgin olive oil
1 large bunch rocket, about 150g/5oz,
*   stalks removed, leaves shredded*
75g/3oz/1 cup freshly grated
*   Parmesan cheese*
salt and ground black pepper
Serves 4

1 Cook the pasta in a large saucepan of salted boiling water according to the instructions on the packet, then drain thoroughly.

2 Heat about 60ml/4 tbsp of the olive oil in the pasta pan, then add the drained pasta, followed by the rocket. Toss over a medium to high heat for 1–2 minutes or until the rocket is just wilted, then remove the pan from the heat.

3 Tip the pasta and rocket into a warmed large bowl. Add half the freshly grated Parmesan and the remaining olive oil. Add a little salt and black pepper to taste.

4 Toss the mixture quickly to mix. Serve immediately, sprinkled with the remaining Parmesan.

COOK'S TIP

Buy rocket by the bunch from the green-grocer. The type sold in small cellophane packets in supermarkets is very expensive for this kind of dish. Always check when buying rocket that all the leaves are bright green. In hot weather, rocket leaves quickly turn yellow.

Strozzapreti with Courgette Flowers

THIS PRETTY, SUMMERY DISH is strewn with courgette flowers, but you can make it even if you don't have the flowers. In Italy, bunches of courgette flowers are a common sight on vegetable stalls in summer, and are frequently used for stuffing and cooking.

INGREDIENTS

50g/2oz/¼ cup butter
30ml/2 tbsp extra virgin olive oil
1 small onion, thinly sliced
200g/7oz small courgettes, cut into
    thin julienne
1 garlic clove, crushed
10ml/2 tsp finely chopped fresh marjoram
350g/12oz/3 cups dried strozzapreti
1 large handful courgette flowers,
    thoroughly washed and dried
salt and ground black pepper
thin shavings of Parmesan cheese, to serve
Serves 4

1 Heat the butter and half the olive oil in a medium skillet or saucepan, add the sliced onion and cook gently, stirring frequently, for about 5 minutes until softened. Add the courgettes to the pan and sprinkle with the crushed garlic, chopped marjoram and salt and pepper to taste. Cook for 5–8 minutes until the courgettes have softened but are not coloured, turning them over from time to time.

2 Meanwhile, cook the pasta in a saucepan of salted boiling water according to the packet instructions.

3 Set aside a few whole courgette flowers for the garnish, then roughly shred the rest and add them to the courgette mixture. Stir to mix and taste for seasoning.

4 Drain the pasta, tip it into a warmed large bowl and add the remaining oil. Toss, add the courgette mixture and toss again. Top with Parmesan and the reserved flowers.

COOK'S TIP

Strozzapreti or "priest stranglers" are a special kind of short pasta shape from Modena. You can buy packets of them in Italian delicatessens, or use gemelli, a similar kind of twisted pasta.

Paglia e Fieno

THE TITLE OF THIS DISH translates as "straw and hay" which refers to the yellow and green colours of the pasta when mixed together. Fresh peas make all the difference to this dish.

INGREDIENTS

50g/2oz/4 tbsp butter

350g/12oz/3 cups frozen petits pois or 900g/2lb fresh peas, shelled

150ml/¼ pint/⅔ cup double cream, plus 60ml/4 tbsp extra

450g/1lb dried tagliatelle (plain and green mixed)

50g/2oz/½ cup freshly grated Parmesan cheese, plus extra to serve

freshly grated nutmeg

salt and ground black pepper

Serves 4

1 Melt the butter in a heavy saucepan and add the peas. Sauté for 2–3 minutes, then add the cream, bring to the boil and simmer for 1 minute until the mixture is slightly thickened.

2 Cook the plain and green mixed tagliatelle in plenty of salted boiling water according to the instructions on the packet, but for 2 minutes less time, until *al dente*.

3 Drain well and then tip the tagliatelle into the saucepan containing the cream and pea sauce.

4 Place the pan on the heat and turn the pasta in the sauce to coat. Pour in the extra cream, the cheese, salt and pepper to taste and a little grated nutmeg. Toss until well coated and heated through. Serve immediately with extra freshly grated Parmesan cheese.

COOK'S TIP

Sautéed mushrooms and narrow strips of cooked ham also make good additions to this dish.

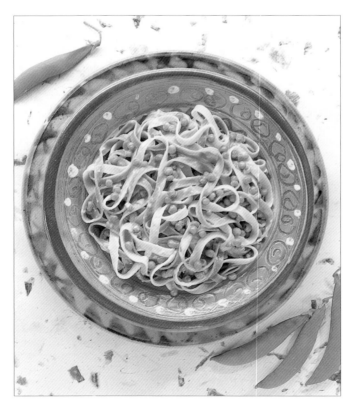

Spaghetti with Olives and Mushrooms

A RICH, PUNGENT SAUCE topped with sweet cherry tomatoes.

INGREDIENTS

15ml/1 tbsp olive oil
1 garlic clove, chopped
225g/8oz mushrooms, chopped
150g/5oz/scant 1 cup black olives, pitted
30ml/2 tbsp chopped fresh parsley
1 red chilli, seeded and chopped
450g/1lb fresh or dried spaghetti
225g/8oz cherry tomatoes
Parmesan cheese shavings, to
*   serve (optional)*
Serves 4

1 Heat the oil in a large pan. Add the garlic and cook for 1 minute, stirring. Add the chopped mushrooms, cover, and cook over a medium heat for 5 minutes.

2 Place the mushrooms in a blender or food processor with the olives, parsley and red chilli. Process the mixture until smooth.

3 Cook the pasta in plenty of salted boiling water, according to the instructions on the packet, until *al dente*. Drain well and return to the pan. Add the olive mixture and toss together until the pasta is well coated. Cover and keep warm.

4 Heat an ungreased frying pan and shake the cherry tomatoes around until they start to split, about 2–3 minutes. Serve the pasta topped with the tomatoes and garnished with Parmesan cheese shavings, if desired.

Penne with Rocket and Mozzarella

LIKE A WARM SALAD, this pasta dish is very quick and easy to make – perfect for an *al fresco* summer lunch. Its success depends on the very best Italian ingredients, so make sure they are as fresh as possible and in tip-top condition.

INGREDIENTS

400g/14oz/3½ cups fresh or dried penne

6 ripe Italian plum tomatoes, peeled, seeded and diced

2 x 150g/5oz packets mozzarella cheese, drained and diced

2 large handfuls of rocket, total weight about 150g/5oz

75ml/5 tbsp extra virgin olive oil

salt and ground black pepper

Serves 4

1 Cook the pasta in a large saucepan of salted boiling water according to the packet instructions.

2 Meanwhile, put the tomatoes, mozzarella, rocket and olive oil into a large bowl with a little salt and pepper to taste and toss well to mix.

3 Drain the cooked pasta and tip it into the bowl. Toss well to mix and serve immediately.

VARIATION

For a less peppery taste, use basil leaves instead of rocket, or a mixture of the two.

Eliche with Chargrilled Peppers

CHARGRILLED PEPPERS ARE GOOD with pasta because they have a soft juicy texture and a wonderful smoky flavour. This is a dish for high summer when peppers and tomatoes are plentiful and ripe. It is equally good cold as a salad.

INGREDIENTS

3 large peppers (red, yellow and orange)

350g/12oz/3 cups fresh or dried eliche or fusilli

1–2 garlic cloves, to taste, finely chopped

60ml/4 tbsp extra virgin olive oil

4 ripe Italian plum tomatoes, peeled, seeded and diced

50g/2oz/½ cup pitted black olives, halved or quartered lengthways

1 handful of fresh basil leaves

salt and ground black pepper

Serves 4

1 Put the whole peppers under a hot grill and grill them for about 10 minutes, turning them frequently until they are charred on all sides. Put the hot peppers in a plastic bag, seal the bag and set aside until the peppers are cold.

2 Remove the peppers from the bag and hold them one at a time under cold running water. Peel off the charred skins with your fingers, split the peppers open and pull out the cores. Rub off all the seeds under the running water, then pat the peppers dry on kitchen paper.

3 Cook the pasta in a large saucepan of salted boiling water according to the instructions on the packet until *al dente*.

4 Meanwhile, thinly slice the peppers and place them in a large bowl with the remaining ingredients and salt and pepper to taste.

5 Drain the cooked pasta and tip it into the bowl. Toss well to mix and serve immediately.

VARIATION

Add a few slivers of bottled or canned anchovy fillets in Step 4.

Penne with Spring Vegetables

Don't be tempted to use dried herbs in this flavoursome dish.

INGREDIENTS
115g/4oz broccoli florets
115g/4oz baby leeks
225g/8oz asparagus
1 small fennel bulb
115g/4oz/1 cup fresh or frozen peas
40g/1½oz/3 tbsp butter
1 shallot, chopped
45ml/3 tbsp chopped fresh mixed herbs,
    such as parsley, thyme and sage
300ml/½ pint/1¼ cups double cream
350g/12oz/3 cups dried penne
salt and ground black pepper
freshly grated Parmesan cheese, to serve

Serves 4

1 Divide the broccoli florets into tiny sprigs. Cut the leeks and asparagus diagonally into 5cm/2in lengths. Trim the fennel bulb and remove any tough outer leaves. Cut into wedges, leaving the layers attached at the root ends so the pieces stay intact.

2 Cook each vegetable, including the peas, separately in boiling salted water until just tender – use the same water for each vegetable. Drain well and keep warm.

3 Melt the butter in a separate pan, add the chopped shallot and cook, stirring occasionally, until softened but not browned. Stir in the herbs and cream and cook for a few minutes, until slightly thickened.

4 Meanwhile, cook the pasta in plenty of salted boiling water for 10 minutes until al dente. Drain well and add to the sauce with the vegetables. Toss gently and season with plenty of ground black pepper.

5 Serve the pasta immediately with a sprinkling of freshly grated Parmesan cheese on top.

Spaghetti with Feta Cheese

WE THINK OF PASTA as being essentially Italian but, in fact, the Greeks have a great appetite for it too. It complements tangy, full-flavoured feta cheese beautifully in this simple but effective dish.

INGREDIENTS

115g/4oz fresh or dried spaghetti
1 garlic clove
30ml/2 tbsp extra virgin olive oil
8 cherry tomatoes, halved
a little freshly grated nutmeg
75g/3oz feta cheese, crumbled
15ml/1 tbsp chopped fresh basil
salt and ground black pepper
a few black olives, to serve (optional)
Serves 2–3

1 Cook the spaghetti in plenty of salted boiling water according to the instructions on the packet, then drain well.

2 In the same pan gently heat the garlic clove in the olive oil for 1–2 minutes, then add the halved cherry tomatoes.

3 Increase the heat to fry the tomatoes lightly for 1 minute, then remove the garlic and discard.

4 Toss in the spaghetti, season with the nutmeg and salt and pepper to taste, then stir in the crumbled feta cheese and basil.

5 Check the seasoning, remembering that feta can be quite salty, and serve the spaghetti hot topped with black olives, if using.

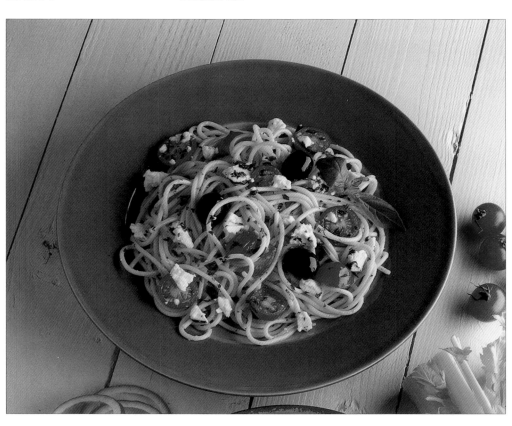

Three-colour Tagliatelle

COURGETTES AND CARROTS are cut into delicate ribbons so that when they are cooked and tossed with tagliatelle they look like coloured pasta. Serve as a side dish, or sprinkle with freshly grated Parmesan cheese for a light starter or vegetarian main course.

INGREDIENTS

2 large courgettes
2 large carrots
250g/9oz fresh egg tagliatelle
60ml/4 tbsp extra virgin olive oil
flesh of 2 roasted garlic cloves, plus extra
roasted garlic cloves, to serve (optional)
salt and ground black pepper
Serves 4

1 With a vegetable peeler, cut the courgettes and carrots into long thin ribbons. Bring a large pan of salted water to the boil, then add the courgette and carrot ribbons. Bring the water back to the boil and boil for 30 seconds, then drain and set aside.

2 Cook the pasta according to the instructions on the packet.

3 Drain the pasta and return it to the pan. Add the vegetable ribbons, oil, garlic and salt and pepper and toss over a medium to high heat until the pasta and vegetables are glistening with oil. Serve immediately, with extra roasted garlic, if you like.

COOK'S TIP

To roast garlic, put a whole head of garlic on a lightly oiled baking sheet. Place in a 180°C/350°F/Gas 4 oven and roast for about 30 minutes. Remove the garlic from the oven and set aside. When cool enough to handle, dig out the flesh from the cloves with the point of a knife. If you don't want to go to the trouble of roasting garlic, you can use crushed raw garlic but the flavour will be stronger.

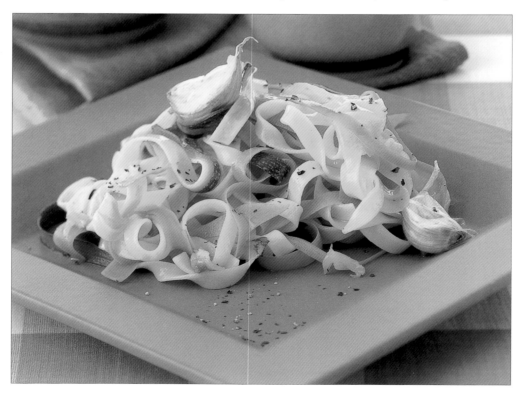

Macaroni with Broccoli and Cauliflower

THIS IS A SOUTHERN ITALIAN DISH, full of flavour. Without the anchovies, it can be served to vegetarians.

INGREDIENTS

175g/6oz cauliflower florets, cut into
    small sprigs
175g/6oz broccoli florets, cut into
    small sprigs
350g/12oz/3 cups short-cut macaroni
45ml/3 tbsp extra virgin olive oil
1 onion, finely chopped
45ml/3 tbsp pine nuts
1 sachet of saffron powder, dissolved in
    15ml/1 tbsp warm water
15–30ml/1–2 tbsp raisins, to taste
30ml/2 tbsp sun-dried tomato paste
4 bottled or canned anchovies in olive oil,
    drained and chopped, plus extra
    anchovies to serve (optional)
salt and ground black pepper
freshly grated Pecorino cheese,
    to serve

Serves 4

1 Cook the cauliflower sprigs in a large saucepan of salted boiling water for 3 minutes. Add the broccoli and boil for another 2 minutes. Remove the vegetables from the pan with a large slotted spoon and set aside.

2 Add the pasta to the vegetable cooking water and bring the water back to the boil. Cook the pasta according to the instructions on the packet until it is al dente.

3 Meanwhile, heat the olive oil in a large skillet or saucepan, add the finely chopped onion and cook over a low to medium heat, stirring frequently, for 2–3 minutes or until golden. Add the pine nuts, the cooked broccoli and cauliflower, and the saffron water. Add the raisins, sun-dried tomato paste and a couple of ladlefuls of the pasta cooking water until the vegetable mixture has the consistency of a sauce. Finally, add plenty of pepper.

4 Stir well, cook for 1–2 minutes, then add the chopped anchovies. Drain the pasta and tip it into the vegetable mixture. Toss well, then taste for seasoning and add salt if necessary. Serve the pasta immediately in four warmed bowls, sprinkled with freshly grated Pecorino. If you like the flavour of anchovies, add 1–2 whole anchovies to each serving.

Pasta Salads

Although not traditionally Italian, pasta salads have earned their place in the Italian cook's repertoire. They are extremely versatile in that they can be served as part of an antipasto, as a first course or a main course. Salads can be prepared well in advance, so make marvellous party food, and are popular for picnics, because they are so easy to transport.

Freshly cooked pasta soaks up oil, lemon juice, vinegar and seasonings so that when the pasta cools down, the shapes are separate, moist and full of flavour. Never soak pasta in cold water after cooking; this makes the pasta waterlogged and soggy, especially with shapes like shells and tubes that trap liquid. Simply cook the pasta until it is *al dente*, then drain it thoroughly and toss it in extra virgin olive oil or dressing until it glistens. This method works well for any vinaigrette-type dressing, but if you are using mayonnaise it is best to wait until the pasta has cooled down before tossing, or the mayonnaise may spoil.

Any pasta shape can be used in a salad, although shells and tubes are particularly good, because they trap the dressing so well. Many Italians prefer egg pasta to plain durum wheat pasta, because it has a good colour, holds its shape well and does not stick.

Pasta Salade Niçoise

ALONG THE MEDITERRANEAN coast,
where Italy meets France, the
cuisines of both countries have
many similarities. In this salad the
ingredients of a classic French
salade niçoise are given a modern
Italian twist.

INGREDIENTS

115g/4oz French beans, topped and tailed
    and cut into 5cm/2in lengths
250g/9oz/2¼ cups dried penne rigate
105ml/7 tbsp extra virgin olive oil
2 fresh tuna steaks, total weight
    350–450g/12oz–1lb
6 baby Italian plum tomatoes, quartered
    lengthways
50g/2oz/½ cup pitted black olives,
    halved lengthways
6 bottled or canned anchovies in olive oil,
    drained and chopped
30–45ml/2–3 tbsp chopped fresh flat leaf
    parsley, to taste
juice of ½–1 lemon, to taste
2 heads of chicory, leaves
    separated
salt and ground black pepper
lemon wedges, to serve
Serves 4

1 Cook the beans in a large pan of
salted boiling water for 5–6 minutes.
Remove the beans with a large slotted
spoon and refresh under the cold tap.

2 Add the pasta to the pan of
bean cooking water, bring back
to the boil and cook according to the
instructions on the packet.

3 Meanwhile, heat a ridged cast-iron
pan over a low heat. Dip a wad of
kitchen paper in the oil, wipe it over
the surface of the pan and heat gently.
Brush the tuna steaks on both sides
with oil and sprinkle liberally with
pepper; add to the pan and cook over
a medium to high heat for 1–2 minutes
on each side. Remove and set aside.

4 Drain the cooked pasta well and
tip into a large bowl. Add the
remaining oil, the beans, tomato
quarters, black olives, anchovies,
parsley, lemon juice and salt and
pepper to taste. Toss well to mix, then
leave to cool.

5 Flake or slice the tuna into large
pieces, discarding the skin, then
fold it into the salad. Taste the salad for
seasoning. Arrange the chicory leaves
around the insides of a large shallow
bowl. Spoon the pasta salad into the
centre and serve with lemon wedges.

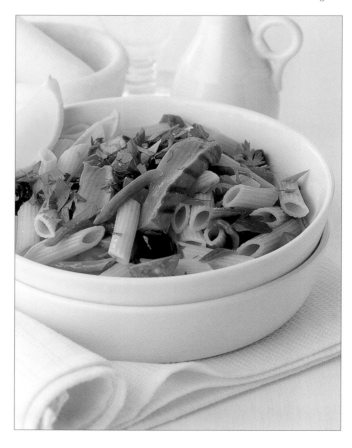

Chargrilled Pepper Salad

THIS IS A GOOD SIDE SALAD to serve with plain grilled or barbecued chicken or fish. The ingredients are simple and few, but the overall flavour is quite intense.

INGREDIENTS

2 large peppers (red and green)
250g/9oz/2¼ cups dried fusilli tricolore
1 handful fresh basil leaves
1 handful fresh coriander leaves
1 garlic clove
salt and ground black pepper

For the dressing
30ml/2 tbsp bottled pesto
juice of ½ lemon
60ml/4 tbsp extra virgin olive oil
Serves 4

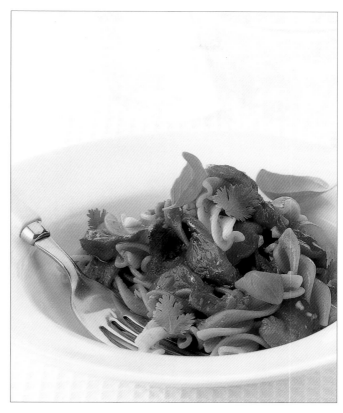

Put the peppers under a hot grill and grill them for about 10 minutes, turning them frequently until they are charred on all sides. Put the hot peppers in a plastic bag, seal the bag and set aside until the peppers are cool. Meanwhile, cook the pasta according to the instructions on the packet.

2 Whisk all the dressing ingredients together in a large bowl. Drain the cooked pasta well and tip it into the bowl of dressing. Toss well to mix and set aside to cool.

COOK'S TIP

Serve the salad at room temperature or chilled, whichever you prefer.

3 Remove the peppers from the bag and hold them one at a time under cold running water. Peel off the charred skins with your fingers, split the peppers open and pull out the cores. Rub off all the seeds under the running water, then pat the peppers dry on kitchen paper.

4 Chop the peppers and add them to the pasta. Put the basil, coriander and garlic on a board and chop them all together. Add to the pasta and toss to mix, then taste for seasoning and serve.

Roquefort and Walnut Pasta Salad

THIS IS A SIMPLE earthy salad, relying totally on the quality of the ingredients. There is no real substitute for Roquefort – a blue-veined ewe's-milk cheese which comes from south-western France.

INGREDIENTS

225g/8oz pasta shapes
mixed salad leaves, such as rocket, curly
   endive, lamb's lettuce, baby spinach,
   radicchio, etc
30ml/2 tbsp walnut oil
60ml/4 tbsp sunflower oil
30ml/2 tbsp red wine vinegar or
   sherry vinegar
225g/8oz Roquefort cheese,
   roughly crumbled
115g/4oz/1 cup walnut halves
salt and ground black pepper

Serves 4

1 Cook the pasta in plenty of salted boiling water according to the instructions on the packet until *al dente*. Drain well and cool. Wash and dry the salad leaves and place them in a large bowl.

COOK'S TIP

Try toasting the walnuts under the grill for a couple of minutes to release the flavour before adding to the salad.

2 Whisk together the walnut oil, sunflower oil, vinegar and salt and pepper to taste.

3 Pile the pasta in the centre of the leaves, scatter the crumbled Roquefort over and pour the dressing on top.

4 Scatter the walnuts over the salad. Toss just before serving.

Conchiglie and Beetroot Salad

COLOUR IS VITAL at a party table, and this salad is certainly eye-catching. Prepare the egg and avocado at the last moment to avoid discoloration.

INGREDIENTS

2 uncooked beetroots, scrubbed
225g/8oz/2 cups fresh or dried conchiglie
45ml/3 tbsp vinaigrette dressing
2 celery sticks, thinly sliced
3 spring onions, sliced
75g/3oz/¾ cup walnuts or hazelnuts, roughly chopped
1 eating apple, cored, halved and sliced
salt and ground black pepper

For the dressing

60ml/4 tbsp mayonnaise
45ml/3 tbsp natural yogurt or fromage frais
30ml/2 tbsp milk
10ml/2 tsp creamed horseradish

To serve

curly lettuce leaves
3 eggs, hard-boiled and chopped
2 ripe avocados
1 box salad cress
Serves 8

1 Boil the beetroots, without peeling, in lightly salted water until they are just tender, about 1 hour. Drain, cool, then peel and chop. Set aside.

2 Cook the pasta in plenty of salted boiling water according to the instructions on the packet. Drain, toss in the vinaigrette and season well. Leave to cool then mix with the beetroot, celery, onions, nuts and apple in a bowl.

3 Stir all the dressing ingredients together and then mix into the pasta. Chill well.

4 To serve, line a salad bowl with the lettuce and spoon in the salad. Scatter the chopped egg over. Peel and slice the avocados and arrange them on top then sprinkle the cress over.

Tuna Pasta Salad

THIS EASY PASTA SALAD uses canned beans and tuna for a quick main course dish.

INGREDIENTS

450g/1lb short pasta, such as rotelle or farfalle
60ml/4 tbsp olive oil
2 x 200g/7oz cans tuna, drained and flaked
2 x 400g/14oz cans cannellini or borlotti beans, rinsed and drained
1 small red onion, very thinly sliced
2 celery sticks, very thinly sliced
juice of 1 lemon
30ml/2 tbsp chopped fresh parsley
salt and ground black pepper
Serves 6–8

1 Cook the pasta in plenty of salted boiling water according to the packet instructions until *al dente*. Drain, and rinse under cold water to stop the cooking. Drain well and tip into a large bowl. Toss with the olive oil and set aside. Allow to cool completely.

2 Mix the flaked tuna and the beans into the cooked pasta. Add the onion and celery slices to the pasta and toss gently to mix.

3 Combine the lemon juice with the parsley. Mix into the other ingredients. Season with salt and pepper. Allow the salad to stand for at least 1 hour before serving.

Chicken Pasta Salad

THIS SALAD USES leftover chicken from a roast or a cold poached chicken breast if you prefer.

INGREDIENTS

350g/12oz short pasta, such as rigatoni, fusilli or penne
45ml/3 tbsp olive oil
225g/8oz cold cooked chicken
2 small red and yellow peppers, seeded and chopped
50g/2oz/1/2 cup pitted green olives
4 spring onions, chopped
45ml/3 tbsp mayonnaise
5ml/1 tsp Worcestershire sauce
15ml/1 tbsp white wine vinegar
salt and ground black pepper
a few fresh basil leaves, to garnish
Serves 4

1 Cook the pasta in plenty of salted boiling water according to the packet instructions until *al dente*. Drain, and rinse under cold water to stop the cooking. Drain well and tip into a large bowl. Toss with the olive oil and set aside. Allow to cool completely.

2 Cut the chicken into bite-size pieces, removing any bones.

3 Combine all the ingredients except the pasta in a medium bowl. Taste for seasoning, then mix into the pasta. Serve well chilled, garnished with basil leaves.

Warm Pasta Salad with Ham and Egg

IN THE SUMMER months when the weather is hot, warm pasta salad makes a perfect supper dish. Here it is served with ham, eggs and asparagus. A mustard dressing made from the thick part of asparagus provides a rich accompaniment.

INGREDIENTS

450g/1lb asparagus
450g/1lb dried tagliatelle
225g/8oz sliced cooked ham, 5mm/¼in
   thick, cut into fingers
2 eggs, hard-boiled and sliced
50g/2oz Parmesan cheese, shaved
salt and ground black pepper

For the dressing
50g/2oz cooked potato
75g/5 tbsp olive oil, preferably Sicilian
15ml/1 tbsp lemon juice
10ml/2 tsp Dijon mustard
120ml/4fl oz/½ cup vegetable stock

Serves 4

1 Bring a saucepan of salted water to the boil. Trim and discard the tough woody parts of the asparagus. Cut the asparagus in half and boil the thicker halves for 12 minutes. After 6 minutes throw in the tips. Refresh under cold water until warm, then drain.

2 Finely chop 150g/5oz of the thicker section of the asparagus. Place in a blender or food processor with the dressing ingredients and process until smooth and creamy. Season to taste with salt and pepper.

3 Cook the pasta in plenty of salted boiling water according to the instructions on the packet. Refresh under cold water until warm, then drain. Dress with the asparagus sauce and turn out on to four pasta plates. Top the pasta with the ham, hard-boiled eggs and asparagus tips. Finish with Parmesan cheese shavings.

Chicken and Eliche Salad

THIS IS A DELICIOUS WAY to use up leftover cooked chicken, and makes a really filling meal.

INGREDIENTS

225g/8oz/2 cups tri-coloured dried eliche
30ml/2 tbsp ready-made pesto sauce
15ml/1 tbsp olive oil
1 beefsteak tomato
12 stoned black olives
225g/8oz cooked French beans, cut into
    4cm/1 1/2in lengths
350g/12oz cooked chicken, cubed
salt and ground black pepper
fresh basil, to garnish

Serves 4

1 Cook the pasta in plenty of salted boiling water according to the instructions on the packet.

2 Drain the pasta and rinse in plenty of cold running water.

3 Place the cooked pasta in a large bowl and pour in the pesto sauce and olive oil. Mix well to combine.

4 Skin the tomato by placing it in a pan of boiling water for about 45 seconds. Remove it with a slotted spoon and plunge it immediately into a bowl of cold water, to loosen the skin.

5 Cut the tomato into small cubes and add to the pasta mixture in the bowl with the olives, seasoning and French beans. Add the cubed chicken. Toss gently together and transfer to a serving platter or individual bowls. Garnish with fresh basil.

Chicken and Broccoli Salad

GORGONZOLA MAKES A tangy dressing that goes well with both chicken and broccoli. Serve for a lunch or supper dish, with crusty Italian bread.

INGREDIENTS

175g/6oz broccoli florets, divided into
  small sprigs
225g/8oz/2 cups dried farfalle
2 large cooked chicken breasts

For the dressing
90g/3½oz Gorgonzola cheese
15ml/1 tbsp white wine vinegar
60ml/4 tbsp extra virgin olive oil
2.5–5ml/½–1 tsp finely chopped fresh
  sage, plus extra sage sprigs to garnish
salt and ground black pepper

Serves 4

1 Cook the broccoli florets in a large saucepan of salted boiling water for 3 minutes. Remove with a slotted spoon and rinse under cold running water, then spread out on kitchen towels to drain and dry.

2 Add the pasta to the broccoli cooking water, then bring back to the boil and cook according to the packet instructions. When cooked, drain the pasta into a colander, rinse under cold running water until cold, then leave to drain and dry, shaking the colander occasionally.

3 Remove the skin from the cooked chicken breasts and cut the meat into bite-size pieces.

4 Make the dressing. Put the cheese in a large bowl and mash with a fork, then whisk in the wine vinegar followed by the oil and sage and salt and pepper to taste.

5 Add the pasta, chicken and broccoli. Toss well, then season to taste and serve, garnished with sage.

Pasta Salad with Salami and Olives

GARLIC AND HERB DRESSING gives a Mediterranean flavour to a handful of ingredients from the store-cupboard and fridge, making this an excellent salad for winter. There are many different types of Italian salami that can be used. *Salame napoletano* is coarse cut and peppery, while *salame milanese* is fine cut and mild in flavour.

INGREDIENTS

225g/8oz/2 cups dried gnocchi
or conchiglie
50g/2oz/¹⁄₂ cup pitted black olives,
quartered lengthways
75g/3oz thinly sliced salami, any skin
removed, diced
¹⁄₂ small red onion, finely chopped
1 large handful fresh basil leaves, shredded

For the dressing
60ml/4 tbsp extra virgin olive oil
good pinch of sugar, to taste
juice of ¹⁄₂ lemon
5ml/1 tsp Dijon mustard
10ml/2 tsp dried oregano
1 garlic clove, crushed
salt and ground black pepper
Serves 4

1 Cook the pasta in a pan of salted boiling water according to the packet instructions.

2 Meanwhile, make the dressing for the pasta. Put all the ingredients for the dressing in a large bowl with a little salt and pepper to taste, and whisk well to mix.

3 Drain the pasta thoroughly, add it to the bowl of dressing and toss well to mix. Leave the dressed pasta to cool, stirring occasionally.

4 When the pasta is cold, add the remaining ingredients and toss well to mix again. Taste for seasoning, then serve immediately.

Tuna and Sweetcorn Salad

THIS IS AN EXCELLENT main course salad for a summer lunch outside. It travels very well, so it is good for picnics, too.

INGREDIENTS

175g/6oz/1 1/2 cups dried conchiglie
175g/6oz can tuna in olive oil, drained
  and flaked
175g/6oz can sweetcorn, drained
75g/3oz bottled roasted red pepper, rinsed,
  dried and finely chopped
1 handful of fresh basil leaves, chopped
salt and ground black pepper

For the dressing
60ml/4 tbsp extra virgin olive oil
15ml/1 tbsp balsamic vinegar
5ml/1 tsp red wine vinegar
5ml/1 tsp Dijon mustard
5–10ml/1–2 tsp honey, to taste
Serves 4

1 Cook the pasta according to packet instructions. Drain it into a colander, and rinse under cold running water. Leave to drain until cold and dry, shaking the colander occasionally.

2 Make the dressing. Put the oil in a large bowl, add the two kinds of vinegar and whisk well together until emulsified. Add the mustard, honey and salt and pepper to taste and whisk again until thick.

3 Add the pasta to the dressing and toss well to mix, then add the tuna, sweetcorn and roasted pepper and toss again. Mix in about half the basil and taste for seasoning. Serve at room temperature or chilled, with the remaining basil sprinkled on top.

VARIATION

To save time, you could use canned sweetcorn with peppers.

Pink and Green Salad

SPIKED WITH A LITTLE fresh chilli, this pretty salad makes a delicious light lunch served with hot ciabatta rolls and a bottle of sparkling dry Italian white wine. Prawns and avocado are a winning combination, so it's also a good choice for a buffet party.

INGREDIENTS

225g/8oz/2 cups dried farfalle
juice of 1/2 lemon
1 small fresh red chilli, seeded and very
  finely chopped
60ml/4 tbsp chopped fresh basil
30ml/2 tbsp chopped fresh coriander
60ml/4 tbsp extra virgin olive oil
15ml/1 tbsp mayonnaise
250g/9oz/1 1/2 cups peeled cooked prawns
1 avocado
salt and ground black pepper
Serves 4

1 Cook the pasta in a large saucepan of salted boiling water according to the packet instructions.

2 Meanwhile, put the lemon juice and chilli in a bowl with half the basil and coriander and salt and pepper to taste. Whisk well to mix, then whisk in the oil and mayonnaise until thick. Add the prawns and gently stir to coat in the dressing.

3 Drain the pasta into a colander, and rinse under cold running water until cold. Leave to drain and dry, shaking the colander occasionally.

4 Halve, stone and peel the avocado, then cut the flesh into neat dice. Add to the prawns and dressing with the pasta, toss well to mix and taste for seasoning. Serve immediately, sprinkled with the remaining basil and coriander.

COOK'S TIP

This pasta salad can be made several hours ahead of time, without the avocado. Cover the bowl with clear film and chill in the fridge. Prepare the avocado and add it to the salad just before serving or it will discolour.

Smoked Trout Pasta Salad

BULB FENNEL gives this salad a lovely aniseed flavour.

INGREDIENTS

15ml/1 tbsp butter
115g/4oz minced bulb fennel
6 spring onions, 2 very finely chopped
    and 4 thinly sliced
225g/8oz skinless smoked trout
    fillets, flaked
45ml/3 tbsp chopped fresh dill
115g/4oz/½ cup mayonnaise
10ml/2 tsp fresh lemon juice
30ml/2 tbsp whipping cream
450g/1lb small pasta shapes, such as shells
salt and ground black pepper
fresh dill sprigs, to garnish

Serves 6

2 Add the sliced spring onions, trout, dill, mayonnaise, lemon juice and cream to the bowl with the fennel. Mix gently until well blended.

3 Cook the pasta in plenty of boiling salted water according to the instructions on the packet until *al dente*. Drain thoroughly in a colander and leave to cool.

4 Add the pasta to the vegetable and trout mixture and toss to coat evenly. Taste for seasoning and adjust if necessary.

5 Serve the salad lightly chilled or at room temperature, garnished with dill.

1 Melt the butter in a small non-stick frying pan. Add the fennel and finely chopped spring onions and season lightly with salt and black pepper. Cook over a medium heat for 3–5 minutes, or until just softened. Transfer to a large bowl and leave to cool slightly.

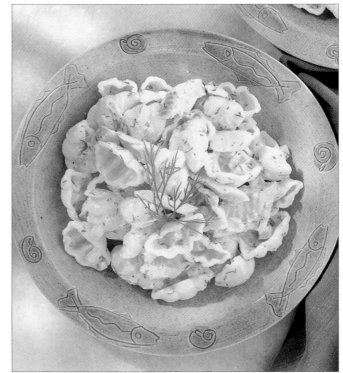

Pasta, Asparagus and Potato Salad

A MEAL IN ITSELF, this is a real treat when made with fresh asparagus just in season.

INGREDIENTS

225g/8oz wholemeal pasta shapes
60ml/4 tbsp extra virgin olive oil
350g/12oz baby new potatoes
225g/8oz fresh asparagus
115g/4oz Parmesan cheese
salt and ground black pepper

Serves 4

1 Cook the pasta in salted boiling water according to the instructions on the packet. Drain well and toss with the olive oil and salt and pepper while still warm.

2 Wash the potatoes and cook in salted boiling water for about 12–15 minutes or until just tender. Drain the potatoes and gently toss with the pasta.

3 Trim any woody ends off the asparagus and halve the stalks if very long. Blanch in salted boiling water for 6 minutes until bright green and still crunchy. Drain, refresh in cold water and allow to cool. Drain well and pat dry with kitchen paper.

4 Toss the asparagus with the potatoes and pasta, season and transfer to a shallow bowl. Using a rotary vegetable peeler, shave the Parmesan over. Serve immediately.

Seafood Salad

THIS IS A VERY SPECIAL SALAD which can be served as a first course or main meal. The choice of pasta shape is up to you, but one of the unusual "designer" shapes would suit it well.

INGREDIENTS

450g/1lb mussels
250ml/8fl oz/1 cup dry white wine
2 garlic cloves, roughly chopped
1 handful of fresh flat leaf parsley
175g/6oz/1 cup prepared squid rings
175g/6oz/1½ cups small dried
  pasta shapes
175g/6oz/1 cup peeled cooked prawns

For the dressing
90ml/6 tbsp extra virgin olive oil
juice of 1 lemon
5–10ml/1–2 tsp capers, to taste,
  roughly chopped
1 garlic clove, crushed
1 small handful fresh flat leaf parsley,
  finely chopped
salt and ground black pepper

Serves 4–6

1 Scrub the mussels under cold running water to remove the beards. Discard any that are open or that do not close when sharply tapped against the work surface.

2 Pour half the wine into a large saucepan, add the garlic, parsley and mussels. Cover the pan tightly and bring to the boil over a high heat. Cook for about 5 minutes, shaking the pan frequently, until the mussels are open.

3 Tip the mussels and their liquid into a colander set over a bowl. Leave the mussels until cool enough to handle. Reserve a few mussels for garnishing, then remove the rest from their shells, tipping the liquid from the mussels into the bowl of cooking liquid. Discard any closed mussels.

4 Return the mussel cooking liquid to the pan and add the remaining wine and the squid rings. Bring to the boil, cover and simmer gently, stirring occasionally, for 30 minutes or until the squid is tender. Leave the squid to cool in the cooking liquid.

5 Meanwhile, cook the pasta according to packet instructions and whisk all the dressing ingredients in a large bowl, adding a little salt and pepper to taste.

6 Drain the cooked pasta well, add it to the bowl of dressing and toss well to mix. Leave to cool.

7 Tip the cooled squid into a sieve and drain well, then rinse it lightly under the cold tap. Add the squid, mussels and prawns to the dressed pasta and toss well to mix. Cover the bowl tightly with clear film and chill in the fridge for about 4 hours. Toss well and adjust the seasoning to taste before serving.

COOK'S TIP

For a quick and easy short cut, buy ready-prepared seafood salad from an Italian delicatessen and toss it with the pasta and dressing.

Roasted Cherry Tomato and Rocket Salad

THIS IS A GOOD SIDE SALAD to
accompany barbecued chicken,
steaks or chops. Roasted tomatoes
are very juicy, with an intense,
smoky-sweet flavour.

INGREDIENTS

225g/8oz/2 cups dried chifferini or pipe
450g/1lb ripe baby Italian plum tomatoes,
    halved lengthways
75ml/5 tbsp extra virgin olive oil
2 garlic cloves, cut into thin slivers
30ml/2 tbsp balsamic vinegar
2 pieces sun-dried tomato in olive oil,
    drained and chopped
large pinch of sugar, to taste
1 handful rocket, about 65g/2½oz
salt and ground black pepper
Serves 4

Preheat the oven to 190°C/375°F/
Gas 5. Meanwhile, cook the pasta in
salted boiling water according to the
instructions on the packet.

2 Arrange the halved tomatoes cut
side up in a roasting tin, drizzle
30ml/2tbsp of the oil over them and
sprinkle with the slivers of garlic and
salt and pepper to taste. Roast in the
oven for 20 minutes, turning once.

3 Put the remaining oil in a large
bowl with the vinegar, sun-dried
tomatoes, sugar and a little salt and
pepper to taste. Stir well to mix. Drain
the pasta, add it to the bowl of
dressing and toss to mix. Add the
roasted tomatoes and mix gently.

4 Before serving, add the chopped
rocket, toss lightly and taste for
seasoning. Serve either at room
temperature or chilled.

VARIATIONS

• If you are in a hurry and don't have
time to roast the tomatoes, you can
make the salad with halved raw
tomatoes instead.
• If you like, add 150g/5oz mozzarella
cheese, drained and diced, with the rocket
in Step 4.

Summer Salad

RIPE RED TOMATOES, mozzarella and olives make a good base for a fresh and tangy salad that is perfect for a light summer lunch.

INGREDIENTS

350g/12oz/3 cups dried penne
3 ripe tomatoes, diced
150g/5oz packet mozzarella di bufala,
    drained and diced
10 pitted black olives, sliced
10 pitted green olives, sliced
1 spring onion, thinly sliced on the diagonal
30ml/2 tbsp chopped fresh flat leaf parsley
a few fresh basil leaves

For the dressing
90ml/6 tbsp extra virgin olive oil
15ml/1 tbsp balsamic vinegar or lemon juice
salt and ground black pepper
Serves 4

1 Cook the pasta according to the instructions on the packet. Tip it into a colander and rinse under cold running water, then shake the colander to remove as much water as possible. Leave the pasta to drain.

2 Make the dressing. Whisk the olive oil and balsamic vinegar or lemon juice in a large bowl with a little salt and pepper to taste.

3 Add the pasta, mozzarella, tomatoes, olives and spring onion to the dressing and toss together well. Taste for seasoning before serving, sprinkled with basil leaves.

VARIATION

Make the salad more substantial by adding other ingredients, such as sliced peppers, flaked tuna, bottled or canned anchovy fillets or diced ham.

COOK'S TIP

Mozzarella made from buffalo milk has more flavour than the type made with cow's milk. It is sold in most delicatessens and supermarkets.

Country Pasta Salad

COLOURFUL, TASTY and nutritious, this is the ideal pasta salad for a summer picnic.

INGREDIENTS

300g/11oz/2¾ cups dried fusilli
150g/5oz French beans, topped and tailed
    and cut into 5cm/2in lengths
1 potato, about 150g/5oz, diced
200g/7oz baby tomatoes, hulled and halved
2 spring onions, finely chopped
90g/3½oz Parmesan cheese, diced or
    coarsely shaved
6–8 pitted black olives, cut into rings
15–30ml/1–2 tbsp capers, to taste

For the dressing
90ml/6 tbsp extra virgin olive oil
15ml/1 tbsp balsamic vinegar
15ml/1 tbsp chopped fresh flat leaf parsley
salt and ground black pepper
Serves 6

1 Cook the pasta according to the instructions on the packet. Drain it into a colander, rinse under cold running water until cold, then shake the colander to remove as much water as possible. Leave to drain and dry, shaking the colander occasionally.

2 Cook the beans and diced potato in a saucepan of salted boiling water for 5–6 minutes or until tender. Drain and leave to cool.

3 Make the dressing. Put all the ingredients in a large bowl with salt and pepper to taste and whisk well to mix.

4 Add the baby tomatoes, spring onions, Parmesan, olive rings and capers to the dressing, then the cold pasta, beans and potato. Toss well to mix. Cover and leave to stand for about 30 minutes. Taste for seasoning before serving.

COOK'S TIP

Buy a piece of fresh Parmesan from the delicatessen. This is the less mature, softer type, which is sold as a table cheese, rather than the hard, mature Parmesan used for grating.

Pasta, Melon and Prawn Salad

ORANGE CANTALOUPE or Charentais melon look spectacular in this salad. Or try a mixture of ogen, cantaloupe and water melon.

INGREDIENTS

175g/6oz pasta shapes
225g/8oz/2 cups frozen prawns, thawed
*   and drained*
1 large or 2 small melons
60ml/4 tbsp olive oil
15ml/1 tbsp tarragon vinegar
30ml/2 tbsp snipped fresh chives or
*   chopped parsley*
herb sprigs, to garnish
Chinese leaves, to serve
Serves 4–6

1 Cook the pasta in salted boiling water according to the instructions on the packet. Drain well in a colander and allow to cool.

2 Break the heads off the prawns, peel them and discard the shells.

3 Halve the melon and remove the seeds with a spoon. Carefully scoop the flesh into balls with a melon baller and toss in a large bowl with the prawns and pasta.

4 Whisk the oil, vinegar and chopped herbs together. Pour on to the pasta and prawn mixture and turn to coat with the dressing. Cover and chill for at least 30 minutes.

5 Meanwhile shred the Chinese leaves and use to line a shallow bowl or the empty melon halves.

6 Pile the prawn mixture on to the Chinese leaves, garnish with sprigs of herbs and serve.

Pasta Salad with Olives

THIS DELICIOUS SALAD combines all the flavours of the Mediterranean. It is an excellent way of serving pasta and is particularly suitable for a hot summer's day.

INGREDIENTS

450g/1lb dried short pasta, such as farfalle or penne
60ml/4 tbsp extra virgin olive oil
10 sun-dried tomatoes, thinly sliced
30ml/2 tbsp capers, in brine or salted
115g/4oz/1 cup pitted black olives
2 garlic cloves, finely chopped
45ml/3 tbsp balsamic vinegar
45ml/3 tbsp chopped fresh parsley
salt and ground black pepper

Serves 6

1 Cook the pasta in plenty of salted boiling water until *al dente*. Drain and rinse under cold water to stop the cooking. Drain well and tip into a large bowl. Toss with the olive oil and set aside until required.

2 Soak the tomatoes in a bowl of hot water for 10 minutes. Do not discard the water. Rinse the capers well. If they have been preserved in salt, soak them in a little hot water for 10 minutes. Rinse again.

3 Combine the olives, tomatoes, capers, garlic and vinegar in a small bowl. Season with salt and ground black pepper.

4 Stir the olive mixture into the cooked pasta and toss well. Add 30–45ml/2–3 tbsp of the tomato soaking water if the salad seems too dry. Toss with the parsley and allow to stand for 15 minutes before serving.

Wholemeal Pasta Salad

THIS SUBSTANTIAL vegetarian salad is easily assembled from any combination of seasonal vegetables. Use raw or lightly blanched vegetables, or a mixture of both.

INGREDIENTS

450g/1lb short wholemeal pasta, such as
   fusilli or penne
45ml/3 tbsp olive oil
2 carrots
1 small bunch broccoli
175g/6oz/1½ cups shelled peas, fresh
   or frozen
1 red or yellow pepper
2 celery sticks
4 spring onions
1 large tomato
75g/3oz/¾ cup pitted olives
115g/4oz/1 cup diced Cheddar or
   mozzarella cheese or a combination
   of both
salt and ground black pepper

For the dressing
45ml/3 tbsp white wine or
   balsamic vinegar
60ml/4 tbsp olive oil
15ml/1 tbsp Dijon mustard
15ml/1 tbsp sesame seeds
10ml/2 tsp chopped mixed fresh herbs,
   such as parsley, thyme and basil
Serves 8

1 Cook the pasta in plenty of salted boiling water until *al dente*. Drain, and rinse under cold water to stop the cooking. Drain well and tip into a large bowl. Toss with 45ml/3 tbsp of the olive oil and set aside. Allow the pasta to cool completely.

2 Lightly blanch the carrots, broccoli and peas in a large pan of boiling water. Refresh under cold water. Drain well through a colander.

3 Chop the carrots and broccoli into bite-size pieces and add to the pasta with the peas. Slice the pepper, celery, spring onions and tomato into small pieces. Add them to the salad with the olives.

4 To make the dressing combine the vinegar with the oil and mustard. Stir in the sesame seeds and herbs.

5 Pour the dressing into the salad and toss gently to mix. Taste for seasoning, adding salt, pepper or more olive oil and vinegar if necessary. Stir in the cheese, then allow the salad to stand for about 15 minutes before serving.

Artichoke Pasta Salad

THE EXQUISITE TASTE of the artichokes
adds a sweetness to this salad.

INGREDIENTS

105ml/7 tbsp olive oil
1 red pepper, quartered, seeded, and
   thinly sliced
1 onion, halved and thinly sliced
5ml/1 tsp dried thyme
45ml/3 tbsp sherry vinegar
450g/1lb pasta shapes, such as penne
   or fusilli
2 x 175g/6oz jars marinated artichoke
   hearts, drained and thinly sliced
150g/5oz cooked broccoli, chopped
20–25 salt-cured black olives, pitted
   and chopped
30ml/2 tbsp chopped fresh parsley
salt and ground black pepper

Serves 4

1   Heat 30ml/2 tbsp of the olive oil in
a non-stick frying pan. Add the red
pepper and onion and cook over a low
heat until just soft, about 10 minutes,
stirring from time to time.

2   Stir in the thyme, 1.5ml/¼ tsp salt
and the vinegar. Cook, stirring, for
a further 30 seconds, then set aside
until required.

3   Cook the pasta in plenty of salted
boiling water according to the
instructions on the packet until al
dente. Drain, rinse with hot water, then
drain again. Transfer to a large bowl.
Add 30ml/2 tbsp of the oil and toss to
coat thoroughly.

4   Add the artichokes, broccoli,
olives, parsley, onion mixture and
remaining oil to the pasta. Season with
salt and pepper. Stir to blend. Leave to
stand for at least 1 hour before serving
or chill overnight. Serve the salad at
room temperature.

Avocado, Tomato and Mozzarella Salad

THIS SALAD is made from ingredients representing the colours of the Italian flag – a sunny cheerful dish!

INGREDIENTS

175g/6oz/1½ cups dried farfalle
6 ripe red tomatoes
225g/8oz mozzarella cheese
1 large ripe avocado
30ml/2 tbsp chopped fresh basil
30ml/2 tbsp pine nuts, toasted
fresh basil sprig, to garnish

For the dressing

90ml/6 tbsp olive oil
30ml/2 tbsp wine vinegar
5ml/1 tsp balsamic vinegar (optional)
5ml/1 tsp wholegrain mustard
pinch of sugar
salt and ground black pepper

Serves 4

1 Cook the pasta in plenty of salted boiling water according to the instructions on the packet. Drain well and cool.

2 Using a sharp knife slice the tomatoes thinly. Repeat for the mozzarella cheese, slicing it into thin, even rounds.

3 Halve the avocado, remove the stone and peel off the skin. Slice the flesh lengthways.

4 Place all the dressing ingredients together in a small bowl and whisk until well blended.

5 Arrange the sliced tomato, mozzarella cheese and avocado overlapping one another around the edge of a flat serving plate.

6 Toss the pasta with half the dressing and the chopped basil. Pile into the centre of the plate. Pour the remaining dressing over, scatter the pine nuts over and garnish with a sprig of fresh basil. Serve immediately.

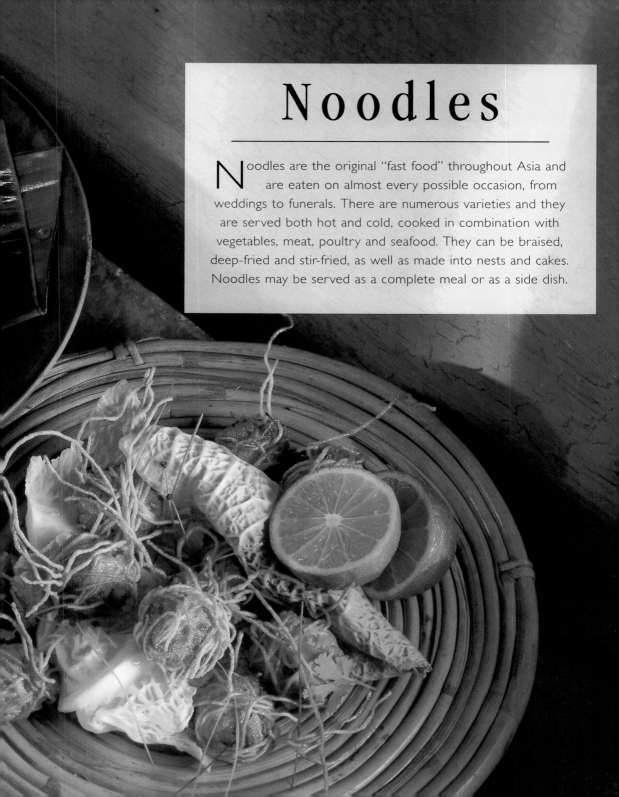

Noodles

Noodles are the original "fast food" throughout Asia and are eaten on almost every possible occasion, from weddings to funerals. There are numerous varieties and they are served both hot and cold, cooked in combination with vegetables, meat, poultry and seafood. They can be braised, deep-fried and stir-fried, as well as made into nests and cakes. Noodles may be served as a complete meal or as a side dish.

Introduction

Noodles have universal appeal. Although thousands of words have been written on the subject, it is the Italian influence that prevails in most pasta cookbooks; scant mention is made of the ever-growing popularity of noodle dishes from China, Japan, Thailand and other Asian countries.

There has been much speculation about whether the Chinese invented noodles before the Italians discovered spaghetti. One theory is that when Marco Polo journeyed overland to China late in the thirteenth century, he brought the secret of pasta-making back to his native Italy. This seems a plausible scenario: noodles were certainly known in China before the start of the Christian era. Soon after the Chinese learned how to grind grains into flour, they discovered that by adding liquid they could make dough which could be kneaded and rolled into thin sheets. It was a short step to cutting the sheets into ribbons and cooking them in boiling water. Noodles rapidly became a staple food, in China and the entire Far East.

Noodles play an important role in many traditional festivities. In China they are a symbol of longevity and are often eaten at birthday celebrations and as "crossing of the threshold of the year" food. They are eaten at happy and sad occasions, between meals, standing up or sitting down. You could say noodles are the oldest form of fast food in the East. Asian pasta includes a wide variety of noodles, ranging from fine and thin to coarse and thick. Many are made with wheat flour, with or without egg. Most of these varieties are softer and starchier than their Italian counterparts, and are sold fresh or dried. Other varieties, such as glass noodles, are based on vegetable starch, such as that derived from mung beans. Rice flour is used for rice sticks or vermicelli and also paper-thin rice sheets. Of the many varieties of Asian pasta, the most familiar ones are the Chinese wontons and Japanese udon, soba and somen noodles. The range of noodle types is extensive, although the Asians have never felt the need to produce as many varied shapes of pasta as the Italians.

Noodles can be cooked, mixed and combined with just about every variety of meat, seafood and vegetables. Eaten hot or cold, they are used in soups, salads and stir-fries. They can also be braised, deep fried or made into cakes. In short, noodles can be served in innumerable ways, as side dishes, snacks, garnishes or complete meals.

Left: Rice vermicelli noodles are deep fried until crisp, then tossed in a piquant sauce.

Equipment

No elaborate equipment is required to prepare the dishes in this book. A cleaver, chopping block, spatula and chopsticks are basic utensils that all Asian kitchens have. You would find a draining spoon useful and will certainly need a wok.

Wok

This all-purpose cooking pan, round in shape with high sides, distributes the heat evenly and allows ingredients to be stirred and tossed without spilling. Woks come in a range of sizes and are made from various metals. Traditional woks are made of thin metal and work best on gas cookers, but you can also purchase flat-bottomed woks for electric cookers. The wok's versatility is limitless. It is ideal for both stir-frying and deep frying because of its shape. It requires less oil than a flat-bottomed deep fryer and has more depth and cooking surface. It can also be used for shallow frying, poaching, boiling and, with the lid, for steaming and braising.

Draining spoons

For deep frying you will need either a large twisted wire draining spoon with a wooden handle, or a metal spider to lift food out of the hot oil.

Cleaver knife

This all-purpose Chinese cutting tool looks like a butcher's cleaver. There are several kinds: stainless steel looks good; carbon steel holds a better edge and is easier to sharpen, but will rust; wooden handled cleavers are also available in different sizes. Lightweight cleavers are used only for slicing. Heavier cleavers are more versatile and can also be used to chop bones. The handle is useful for pounding or mashing.

Chopsticks

These can be used to replace spoons, forks and whisks. Wooden chopsticks are best for cooking because they can with-

Noodle equipment, clockwise from top left: large twisted wire draining spoon, wok and chopsticks, heavy cleaver knife and metal spider.

stand high temperatures. They are also nicer to eat with than plastic ones.

SAFETY FIRST

Oil catches fire easily when overheated and can inflict serious burns. Never fill a pan more than one-third full, keep the handle out of the way and never leave a pan of hot oil unsupervised. Oil for deep frying should cover the food by at least 2cm/3/4in and should be heated to 190°C/375°F/Gas 5 (or until a cube of dry bread, added to the oil, browns in 30 seconds). Food should always be fried in small batches to avoid overcrowding the pan, which causes the temperature to drop. Always lower food carefully into the fat, using a wire basket or slotted spoon.

The food should be as dry as possible, as hot oil will spatter on contact with water. Never pour water on an oil fire. In the event of a fire, do not panic. Turn off the heat if it is safe to do so, and cover the pan tightly to exclude air; a fire blanket is ideal for this, but a large pan lid or a baking sheet would do. If you have not already turned off the heat, do so as soon as the flames have been smothered sufficiently. Do not move the pan.

Types of Noodles

Cellophane noodles

Made from ground mung beans, these are commonly called bean thread, transparent or glass noodles. Dried noodles must be soaked in hot water before cooking.

Egg noodles

Egg noodles are made from wheat flour, egg and water. The dough is flattened and then shredded or extruded through a

Fresh Ingredients

Beancurd

Beancurd is also known as tofu or dofu and is highly nutritious. The flavourless curd blends beautifully with other ingredients. Fresh, long-life and deep-fried varieties are available.

Beansprouts

High in protein and very nutritious, these can be eaten raw or cooked.

Bok choy

This Chinese cabbage has thick white stalks and dark green leaves.

Chinese chives

Better known as garlic chives, these are sometimes sold with their flowers.

Coriander

Also known as Chinese parsley or cilantro, this leafy green herb is often an accompaniment to meat and fish.

Ginger

An aromatic rhizome widely available in supermarkets. It gives a subtle piquancy to fish, meat and vegetables.

Lemon grass

An aromatic tropical grass that characterizes Thai and Vietnamese cuisine, lemon grass gets its name from its very distinctive scent and flavour. Crush lemon grass lightly before slicing or chopping to release more flavour.

pasta machine to the chosen shape and correct thickness.

Rice noodles

Banh Trang are made from ground rice and water. They range in thickness from very thin to wide ribbons and sheets. Dried ribbon rice noodles are usually sold tied up in bundles. Fresh rice noodles are also available. Rinse rice noodles in warm water and drain before use.

Rice vermicelli

These thin, brittle noodles look like white hair, and are sold in large bundles. Rice vermicelli cooks almost instantly in hot liquid, provided the noodles are first soaked in warm water. They can also be deep fried.

Soba noodles

Made from a mixture of buckwheat and wheat flour these noodles are very popular in Japan. They are traditionally cooked in simmering water, then drained and served hot in winter or cold in summer with a dipping sauce.

Somen noodles

These delicate, thin white Japanese noodles made from wheat flour come in dried form, usually tied in bundles,

Udon noodles

Wheat flour and water are used to make these Japanese noodles. They are usually round, but can also be flat and are available fresh, pre-cooked or dried.

Fresh noodles

Wonton wrappers

Shanghai noodles

Thin egg noodles

Ribbon noodles

Medium egg noodles

Fresh rice noodles

Wheat noodles

Sometimes called Shanghai noodles, these are made from wheat, water and salt. They are made in the same way as ordinary egg noodles but are whiter in colour.

Wonton wrappers

Small square sheets rolled from egg noodle dough, these are available in packets from Chinese food markets.

Noodle know-how

All dried noodles should be stored in airtight containers where they can be kept for many months.

Fresh noodles can be chilled for several days in the plastic bag in which they were purchased (check use-by dates).

Allow 5–115g/3–4oz noodles per person.

Many recipes call for noodles to be cooked twice – first par-boiled and then stir-fried or simmered in a soup or sauce. Where this is the case, the preliminary cooking should be brief. Remove the noodles from the heat when they are barely tender, immediately drain them in a colander and rinse under cold running water to arrest the cooking process. Separate the noodles with a fork and add a dash of oil if not using at once. Par-boiled noodles can be prepared in advance. They will keep for several days if stored in a tightly sealed container in the fridge.

Dried noodles, clockwise from top left: ribbon noodles (two bundles), somen noodles, udon noodles, soba noodles, egg ribbon noodles, medium egg noodles, cellophane noodles, rice sheets, rice vermicelli, egg noodles, and, centre, rice ribbon noodles.

Storecupboard Ingredients

Hoisin sauce

Also known as barbecue sauce, hoisin sauce is thick, dark-brown, savoury/sweet and tangy.

Dried mushrooms

Dried Chinese black mushrooms, cloud ears and wood ears become meaty and succulent when soaked in water.

Oyster sauce

This thickish, slightly sweet and salty brown sauce is made from oyster extract, soy sauce, sugar and vinegar. It is used to flavour all sorts of meat, fish and vegetable dishes.

Rice wine

Made from fermented glutinous rice, this golden wine is used for both drinking and cooking.

Sesame oil

Extracted from toasted sesame seeds, this aromatic oil has a nutty flavour.

Soy sauce

Essential for Chinese cooking, soy sauce enhances the flavour of meat, fish and vegetable dishes and sauces. It ranges in colour from pale to dark, the light soy sauce having more flavour than the sweeter dark variety.

Seafood Wontons

THESE TASTY WONTONS resemble tortellini. Water chestnuts add a light crunch to the filling.

INGREDIENTS

225g/8oz raw prawns, peeled and deveined
115g/4oz white crabmeat, picked over
4 canned water chestnuts, finely diced
1 spring onion, finely chopped
1 small green chilli, seeded and
 finely chopped
1.25ml/½ tsp grated fresh root ginger
1 egg, separated
20–24 wonton wrappers
salt and freshly ground black pepper
coriander leaves, to garnish

For the coriander dressing
30ml/2 tbsp rice vinegar
15ml/1 tbsp chopped pickled ginger
90ml/6 tbsp olive oil
15ml/1 tbsp soy sauce
45ml/3 tbsp chopped coriander
30ml/2 tbsp finely diced red pepper
Serves 4

1 Finely dice the prawns and place them in a bowl. Add the crabmeat, water chestnuts, spring onion, chilli, ginger and egg white. Season with salt and pepper and stir well to combine.

2 Place a wonton wrapper on a board. Put about 5ml/1 tsp of the filling just above the centre of the wrapper. With a pastry brush, moisten the edges of the wrapper with a little of the egg yolk. Bring the bottom of the wrapper up over the filling. Press gently to expel any air, then seal the wrapper neatly in a triangle.

3 For a more elaborate shape, bring the two side points up over the filling, overlap the points and pinch the ends firmly together. Space the filled wontons on a large baking sheet lined with greaseproof paper, so that they do not stick together.

4 Half fill a large saucepan with water. Bring to simmering point. Add the filled wontons, a few at a time, and simmer for 2–3 minutes. The wontons will float to the surface. When ready the wrappers will be translucent and the filling should be cooked. Remove the wontons with a large slotted spoon, drain them briefly, then spread them on trays. Keep warm while cooking the remaining wontons.

5 Make the coriander dressing by whisking all the ingredients together in a bowl. Divide the wontons among serving dishes, drizzle with the dressing and serve garnished with a handful of coriander leaves.

Clay Pot of Chilli Squid and Noodles

INGREDIENTS

675g/1½ lb fresh squid
30ml/2 tbsp vegetable oil
3 slices fresh root ginger,
    finely shredded
2 garlic cloves, finely chopped
1 red onion, finely sliced
1 carrot, finely sliced
1 celery stick, diagonally sliced
50g/2oz sugar snap peas, topped
    and tailed
5ml/1 tsp sugar
15ml/1 tbsp chilli bean paste
2.5ml/½ tsp chilli powder
75g/3oz dried cellophane noodles, soaked in
    hot water until soft
120ml/4fl oz/½ cup chicken stock
    or water
15ml/1 tbsp soy sauce
15ml/1 tbsp oyster sauce
5ml/1 tsp sesame oil
pinch of salt
coriander leaves, to garnish

Serves 4

1 Prepare the squid. Holding the body in one hand, gently pull away the head and tentacles. Discard the head; trim and reserve the tentacles. Remove the transparent "quill" from inside the body of the squid. Peel off the brown skin on the outside of the body. Rub a little salt into the squid and wash thoroughly under cold running water. Cut the body of the squid into rings or split it open lengthways, score criss-cross patterns on the inside of the body and cut it into even 5 × 4cm/ 2 × 1½ in pieces.

2 Heat the oil in a large clay pot or flameproof casserole. Add the ginger, garlic and onion, and fry for 1–2 minutes. Add the squid, carrot, celery and sugar snap peas. Fry until the squid curls up. Season with salt and sugar, and stir in the chilli bean paste and powder. Transfer the mixture to a bowl and set aside until required.

3 Drain the soaked noodles and add them to the clay pot or casserole. Stir in the stock or water, soy sauce and oyster sauce. Cover and cook over a medium heat for about 10 minutes or until the noodles are tender.

4 Return the squid and vegetables to the pot. Cover and cook for about 5–6 minutes more, until all the flavours are combined. Season to taste.

5 Just before serving, drizzle with the sesame oil and sprinkle with the coriander leaves.

COOK'S TIP

These noodles have a smooth, light texture that readily absorbs the other flavours in the dish. To vary the flavour, the vegetables can be altered according to what is available.

Fresh Salad with Wonton Crisps

INGREDIENTS

8 wonton wrappers
oil for frying
2 Little Gem lettuces, separated
　　into leaves
½ cucumber, halved, seeded and cut into
　　1cm/½ in dice
2 ripe tomatoes, peeled, seeded and cut
　　into 1cm/½ in dice
1 hard-boiled egg,
　　roughly chopped
50g/2oz roasted peanuts,
　　roughly chopped

For the peanut dressing
15ml/1 tbsp smooth
　　peanut butter
120ml/4fl oz/½ cup coconut milk
5ml/1 tsp sugar
juice of 1 lime
few drops of Tabasco sauce
salt and ground black pepper
Serves 4

1 Make the peanut dressing by combining the peanut butter, coconut milk and sugar together in a small saucepan. Stir over a low heat just until blended.

2 Remove the pan from the heat, stir in the lime juice and Tabasco sauce, then season with salt and pepper to taste. Set aside and leave to cool to room temperature before using.

3 Separate the wonton wrappers; restack them and cut into four.

4 Heat the oil in a deep saucepan or wok. When hot, add the wontons a few at a time and fry until browned. Lift them out of the oil using a slotted spoon and drain on kitchen paper. (The wontons will colour very quickly; take care not to burn them.)

5 Prepare the remaining ingredients for the salad in a large bowl. Toss with the dressing and serve in bowls, topped with wonton crisps.

Somen Noodles with Baked Cherry Tomatoes

THIS SUMMERY DISH is bursting with flavour. Baking the cherry tomatoes slowly strengthens their taste. If you can find yellow tomatoes, use half and half – the dish will look extra special.

INGREDIENTS

1kg/2¼ lb cherry tomatoes, halved
3 garlic cloves, finely sliced
1 bunch basil leaves, stripped
120ml/4fl oz/½ cup extra virgin
　　olive oil
450g/1lb somen noodles
salt and ground black pepper
shavings of Parmesan cheese and tiny basil
　　sprigs, to garnish (optional)
Serves 4–6

1 Preheat the oven to 180°C/350°F/ Gas 4. Arrange the tomatoes, cut side up, in a single layer in a baking dish. Season with salt and pepper and sprinkle with sliced garlic. Sprinkle half the basil leaves over the tomatoes; drizzle the olive oil over the top. Bake the tomatoes for 1–1½ hours. Set aside in a cool place until ready to serve.

2 Just before serving, cook the somen noodles in a saucepan of boiling salted water until just tender, following the directions on the packet. Drain well, tip into a bowl and toss lightly with the baked tomatoes and their juices. Add the remaining basil, with more olive oil and seasoning. Serve at once, garnished with Parmesan shavings and a few basil sprigs, if liked.

Cheese Fritters

THESE CRISP FRITTERS owe their inspiration to Italy. A note of caution – do be careful not to burn your mouth when you take your first bite, as the soft, rich cheese filling will be very hot.

INGREDIENTS

115g/4oz ricotta cheese
50g/2oz Fontina cheese, grated
25g/1oz Parmesan cheese, finely grated
pinch of cayenne pepper
1 egg, beaten, plus a little extra to seal
    the wontons
15–16 wonton wrappers
oil for deep frying
Makes 15–16

1 Line a large baking sheet with greaseproof paper or sprinkle it lightly with flour. Set aside. Combine the cheeses in a bowl, then add the cayenne and beaten egg and mix well.

2 Place one wonton wrapper at a time on a board. Brush the edges with egg. Spoon a little filling in the centre; pull the top corner down to the bottom corner, to make a triangle.

3 Transfer the filled wontons to the prepared baking sheet.

4 Heat the oil in a deep-fryer or large saucepan. Slip in as many wontons at one time as can be accommodated without overcrowding. Fry them for 2–3 minutes on each side or until the fritters are golden. Remove with a slotted spoon. Drain on kitchen paper and serve at once.

Chilled Soba Noodles with Nori

THE JAPANESE INGREDIENTS used in this recipe should be available in specialist shops and in larger supermarkets.

INGREDIENTS

350g/12oz dried soba noodles
1 sheet nori seaweed

For the dipping sauce

300ml/½ pint/1¼ cups bonito stock
120ml/4fl oz/½ cup dark soy sauce
60ml/4 tbsp mirin
5ml/1 tsp sugar
10g/1/4oz loose bonito flakes

Flavourings

4 spring onions, finely chopped
30ml/2 tbsp grated daikon
wasabi paste
4 egg yolks (optional)
Serves 4

1 Make the dipping sauce. Place the stock, soy sauce, mirin and sugar in a saucepan and stir to combine. Bring rapidly to the boil, add the bonito flakes, then remove from the heat. When cool, strain the sauce into a bowl and cover. (This can be done in advance and the sauce kept chilled for up to a week.)

2 Cook the soba noodles in a saucepan of lightly salted boiling water for 6–7 minutes or until just tender, following the manufacturer's directions on the packet.

3 Drain and then rinse the noodles under cold running water, agitating gently to remove the excess starch. Then drain again.

4 Toast the nori over a high gas flame or under a hot grill, then crumble into thin strips. Divide the noodles among four serving dishes and top with the nori. Serve each portion with an individual bowl of dipping sauce and offer the flavourings, handed separately.

Prawn Noodle Salad with Herbs

A LIGHT, REFRESHING SALAD with all the tangy flavour of the sea. Instead of prawns, try squid or scallops.

INGREDIENTS

115g/4oz dried cellophane noodles, soaked
   in hot water until soft
16 cooked prawns, peeled
1 small green pepper, seeded and cut
   into strips
½ cucumber, cut into strips
1 tomato, cut into strips
2 shallots, finely sliced
salt and ground black pepper
coriander leaves, to garnish

For the dressing
15ml/1 tbsp rice vinegar
30ml/2 tbsp fish sauce
30ml/2 tbsp fresh lime juice
pinch of salt
2.5ml/½ tsp grated fresh root ginger
1 lemon grass stalk, finely chopped
1 red chilli, seeded and finely sliced
30ml/2 tbsp roughly chopped mint
few sprigs tarragon, roughly chopped
15ml/1 tbsp snipped chives
Serves 4

1 Make the dressing by placing all the ingredients in a small bowl or jug; whisk well to combine thoroughly.

2 Drain the noodles, then plunge in a saucepan of boiling water for 1 minute. Drain, rinse and drain again.

3 In a large bowl, combine the noodles with the prawns, pepper, cucumber, tomato and shallots. Lightly season with salt and pepper, then toss with the dressing.

4 Spoon the noodles on to individual plates, arranging the prawns on top. Garnish with a few coriander leaves and serve at once.

COOK'S TIP

Prawns are available ready-cooked and often shelled. To cook prawns, boil them for 5 minutes. Leave them to cool in the cooking liquid, then gently pull off the tail shell and twist off the head.

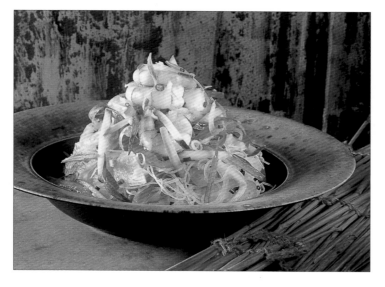

Smoked Trout and Noodle Salad

IT IS IMPORTANT to use ripe juicy tomatoes for this fresh salad. For a special occasion you could replace the smoked trout with smoked salmon.

INGREDIENTS

225g/8oz dried somen noodles
2 smoked trout, skinned and boned
2 hard-boiled eggs, coarsely chopped
30ml/2 tbsp snipped chives
lime halves, to serve (optional)

For the dressing
6 ripe plum tomatoes
2 shallots, finely chopped
30ml/2 tbsp tiny capers, rinsed
30ml/2 tbsp chopped fresh tarragon
finely grated rind and juice of ¹⁄₂ orange
60ml/4 tbsp extra virgin olive oil
salt and ground black pepper
Serves 4

1 To make the dressing, cut the tomatoes in half, remove the cores, and cut the flesh into chunks.

2 Place in a bowl with the shallots, capers, tarragon, orange rind, orange juice and olive oil. Season with salt and pepper, and mix well to combine. Leave the dressing to marinate at room temperature for 1–2 hours.

3 Cook the noodles in a large saucepan of boiling water until just tender. Drain through a colander and rinse under cold running water. Drain again.

5 Flake the smoked trout over the noodles, then sprinkle the coarsely chopped eggs and snipped chives over the top. Serve the lime halves on the side if liked.

COOK'S TIP

Choose tomatoes that are firm, bright in colour and have a matt texture, avoiding any with blotched or cracked skins.

4 Toss the noodles with the dressing, then adjust the seasoning to taste. Arrange the noodles on a large serving platter or individual plates.

Spicy Szechuan Noodles

INGREDIENTS

350g/12oz thick, dried noodles
175g/6oz cooked chicken,
    shredded
50g/2oz roasted cashew nuts

For the dressing

4 spring onions, chopped
30ml/2 tbsp chopped coriander
2 garlic cloves, chopped
30ml/2 tbsp smooth peanut butter
30ml/2 tbsp sweet chilli sauce
15ml/1 tbsp soy sauce
15ml/1 tbsp sherry vinegar
15ml/1 tbsp sesame oil
30ml/2 tbsp olive oil
30ml/2 tbsp chicken stock
    or water
10 toasted Szechuan peppercorns, ground
Serves 4

1 Cook the noodles in a large saucepan of salted boiling water until just tender, according to the instructions on the packet. Drain, rinse under cold running water and drain again.

2 While the noodles are cooking combine all the ingredients for the dressing in a large bowl and whisk together.

3 Add the noodles, shredded chicken and cashew nuts to the dressing, toss gently to coat and adjust the seasoning to taste. Serve at once.

COOK'S TIP

You could substitute cooked turkey or pork for the chicken for a change.

Sesame Noodles with Spring Onions

THIS SIMPLE BUT very tasty warm salad can be prepared and cooked in just a few minutes.

INGREDIENTS

2 garlic cloves, roughly chopped
30ml/2 tbsp Chinese sesame paste
15ml/1 tbsp dark sesame oil
30ml/2 tbsp soy sauce
30ml/2 tbsp rice wine
15ml/1 tbsp honey
pinch of five-spice powder
350g/12oz fresh or dried soba or
    buckwheat noodles
4 spring onions, finely
    sliced diagonally
50g/2oz beansprouts
7.5cm/3in piece of cucumber, cut
    into matchsticks
toasted sesame seeds
salt and freshly ground black pepper
Serves 4

1 Process the garlic, sesame paste, oil, soy sauce, rice wine, honey and five-spice powder with a pinch each of salt and pepper in a blender or food processor until they form a smooth paste.

2 Cook the noodles in a saucepan of boiling water until just tender, according to the instructions on the packet. Drain the noodles immediately and tip them into a bowl.

3 Toss the hot noodles with the dressing and the spring onions. Top with the beansprouts, cucumber and sesame seeds and serve.

COOK'S TIP

If you can't find Chinese sesame paste, then use either tahini paste or smooth peanut butter instead.

Fried Pork and Rice Vermicelli Salad

PORK CRACKLING adds a delicious crunch to this popular salad.

INGREDIENTS

225g/8oz lean pork
2 garlic cloves, finely chopped
2 slices fresh root ginger,
    finely chopped
30–45ml/2–3 tbsp rice wine
45ml/3 tbsp vegetable oil
2 lemon grass stalks, finely chopped
10ml/2 tsp curry powder
175g/6oz beansprouts
225g/8oz dried rice vermicelli,
    soaked in warm water until soft
½ lettuce, finely shredded
30ml/2 tbsp mint leaves
lemon juice and fish sauce, to taste
salt and ground black pepper
2 spring onions, chopped, 25g/1oz
    roasted peanuts, chopped, and
    pork crackling (optional), to garnish

Serves 4

1 Cut the pork into thin strips. Place in a shallow dish with half the garlic and ginger. Season with salt and pepper; pour 30ml/2 tbsp rice wine over and marinate for at least 1 hour.

2 Heat the oil in a frying pan. Add the remaining garlic and ginger and fry for a few seconds until fragrant. Stir in the pork, with the marinade, and add the lemon grass and curry powder. Fry until the pork is golden and cooked through, adding more rice wine if the mixture seems too dry.

3 Place the beansprouts in a sieve. Lower the sieve into a saucepan of boiling water for 1 minute, then drain and refresh under cold running water. Drain again. Using the same water, cook the drained rice vermicelli for 3–5 minutes until tender, drain and rinse under cold running water. Drain well and tip into a bowl.

4 Add the beansprouts, shredded lettuce and mint leaves to the rice vermicelli. Season with the lemon juice and fish sauce. Toss lightly.

5 Divide the noodle mixture among individual serving plates, making a nest on each plate. Arrange the pork mixture on top. Garnish with spring onions, roasted peanuts and pork crackles, if using.

Potato and Cellophane Noodle Salad

INGREDIENTS

2 medium potatoes, peeled and cut into eighths
175g/6oz cellophane noodles, soaked in hot
    water until soft
60ml/4 tbsp vegetable oil
1 onion, finely sliced
5ml/1 tsp ground turmeric
60ml/4 tbsp gram flour
5ml/1 tsp grated lemon rind
60–75ml/4–5 tbsp lemon juice
45ml/3 tbsp fish sauce
4 spring onions, finely sliced
salt and ground black pepper
Serves 4

1 Place the potatoes in a saucepan. Add water to cover, bring to the boil and cook for about 15 minutes until tender but firm. Drain the potatoes and set them aside to cool.

2 Meanwhile, cook the drained noodles in a saucepan of salted boiling water for 3 minutes. Drain well through a colander and rinse under cold running water. Then drain again.

VARIATION

This healthy salad would easily convert to a vegetarian dish by substituting soy sauce for the fish sauce.

3 Heat the oil in a frying pan. Add the onion and turmeric and fry for about 5 minutes until golden brown. Drain the onion, reserving the oil.

4 Heat a small frying pan. Add the gram flour and stir for about 4 minutes until it turns light golden brown in colour.

5 Mix the potatoes, noodles and fried onion in a large bowl. Add the reserved oil and the toasted gram flour with the lemon rind and juice, fish sauce and spring onions. Mix together well and adjust the seasoning to taste if necessary. Serve at once.

Noodles with Pineapple and Mango

INGREDIENTS

275g/10oz dried udon noodles
½ pineapple, peeled, cored and sliced into
    4cm/1½ in rings
45ml/3 tbsp soft light brown sugar
60ml/4 tbsp fresh lime juice
60ml/4 tbsp coconut milk
30ml/2 tbsp fish sauce
30ml/2 tbsp grated fresh root ginger
2 garlic cloves, finely chopped
1 ripe mango or 2 peaches,
    finely diced
ground black pepper
2 spring onions, finely sliced, 2 red chillies,
    seeded and finely shredded,
    plus mint leaves, to garnish
Serves 4

1 Cook the noodles in a large saucepan of boiling water until tender, following the directions on the packet. Drain, refresh under cold water and drain again.

2 Place the pineapple rings on a flameproof dish, sprinkle with 30ml/2 tbsp of the sugar and grill for about 5 minutes or until lightly golden. Cool slightly and then cut into small dice.

3 Mix the lime juice, coconut milk and fish sauce in a salad bowl. Add the remaining brown sugar, with the ginger and garlic, and whisk well to combine. Add the noodles and pineapple.

4 Add the mango or peaches and pepper to taste, and toss. Garnish with spring onions, chillies and mint leaves.

Buckwheat Noodles with Smoked Salmon

YOUNG PEA SPROUTS are only available for a short time. You can substitute watercress, mustard cress, young leeks or your favourite green vegetable or herb in this dish.

INGREDIENTS

225g/8oz fresh or dried buckwheat or
    soba noodles
15ml/1 tbsp oyster sauce
juice of ½ lemon
30–45ml/2–3 tbsp light olive oil
115g/4oz smoked salmon, cut into
    fine strips
115g/4oz young pea sprouts
2 ripe tomatoes, peeled, seeded and cut
    into strips
15ml/1 tbsp snipped chives
ground black pepper
Serves 4

1 Cook the buckwheat or soba noodles in a large saucepan of boiling water, following the directions on the packet. Drain, then rinse under cold running water and drain well.

2 Tip the noodles into a large bowl. Add the oyster sauce and lemon juice and season with pepper to taste. Moisten with the olive oil.

3 Add the smoked salmon, pea sprouts, tomatoes and chives. Mix well and serve at once.

Egg Noodle Salad with Sesame Chicken

INGREDIENTS

400g/14oz fresh thin egg noodles
1 carrot, cut into long fine strips
50g/2oz mangetouts, topped, tailed,
    cut into fine strips and blanched
115g/4oz beansprouts, blanched
30ml/2 tbsp olive oil
225g/8oz skinless, boneless chicken
    breasts, finely sliced
30ml/2 tbsp sesame seeds, toasted
salt and freshly ground black pepper
2 spring onions, finely sliced diagonally
    and coriander leaves, to garnish

For the dressing

45ml/3 tbsp sherry vinegar
75ml/5 tbsp soy sauce
60ml/4 tbsp sesame oil
90ml/6 tbsp light olive oil
1 garlic clove, finely chopped
5ml/1 tsp grated fresh root ginger
Serves 4–6

1 To make the dressing. Combine all the ingredients in a small bowl with a pinch of salt and mix together well using a whisk or a fork.

2 Cook the noodles in a saucepan of boiling water. Stir them occasionally to separate. They only take a few minutes to cook: be careful not to overcook them. Drain, rinse under cold running water and drain well. Tip into a bowl.

3 Add the vegetables to the noodles. Pour in half the dressing, then toss the mixture and adjust the seasoning.

4 Heat the oil in a large frying pan. Add the chicken and stir-fry for 3 minutes, or until cooked and golden. Remove from the heat. Add the sesame seeds and drizzle in some of the remaining dressing.

5 Arrange the noodles on individual serving plates, making a nest on each plate. Spoon the chicken on top. Sprinkle with the sliced spring onions and the coriander leaves and serve any remaining dressing separately.

Thai Noodle Salad

THE ADDITION OF coconut milk and sesame oil gives an unusual nutty flavour to the dressing for this colourful noodle salad.

INGREDIENTS

350g/12oz dried somen noodles
1 large carrot, cut into thin strips
1 bunch asparagus, trimmed and cut into
    4cm/1½ in lengths
1 red pepper, seeded and cut into
    fine strips
115g/4oz mangetouts, topped, tailed
    and halved
115g/4oz baby corn cobs, halved lengthways
115g/4oz beansprouts
115g/4oz can water chestnuts, drained and
    finely sliced
1 lime, cut into wedges, 50g/2oz roasted
    peanuts, roughly chopped, and coriander
    leaves, to garnish

For the dressing

45ml/3 tbsp roughly torn basil
75ml/5 tbsp roughly chopped mint
250ml/8fl oz/1 cup coconut milk
30ml/2 tbsp dark sesame oil
15ml/1 tbsp grated fresh root ginger
2 garlic cloves, finely chopped
juice of 1 lime
2 spring onions, finely chopped
salt and cayenne pepper
Serves 4–6

COOK'S TIP

Shredded omelette or sliced hard-boiled eggs are also popular garnishes, and tuna noodle salad is a children's favourite.

1 Make the dressing. Combine the basil, mint, coconut milk, sesame oil, ginger, garlic, lime juice and spring onions in a bowl and mix well. Season to taste with salt and cayenne pepper.

2 Cook the noodles in a saucepan of boiling water until just tender, following the directions on the packet. Drain, rinse under cold running water and drain again.

3 Cook all the vegetables in separate saucepans of boiling lightly salted water until tender but still crisp. Drain, plunge them immediately into cold water and drain again.

4 Toss the noodles, vegetables and dressing together. Arrange on individual serving plates and garnish with the lime wedges, peanuts and coriander leaves.

Thai Chicken Soup

THIS CLASSIC ORIENTAL soup now enjoys worldwide popularity.

INGREDIENTS

15ml/1 tbsp vegetable oil
1 garlic clove, finely chopped
2 boneless chicken breasts, about
    175g/6oz each, skinned and chopped
2.5ml/½ tsp ground turmeric
1.5ml/¼ tsp hot chilli powder
75g/3oz creamed coconut
900ml/1½ pints/3¾ cups hot
    chicken stock
30ml/2 tbsp lemon or lime juice
30ml/2 tbsp crunchy peanut butter
50g/2oz dried thread egg noodles, broken
    into small pieces
15ml/1 tbsp spring onions, finely chopped
15ml/1 tbsp chopped fresh coriander
salt and ground black pepper
30ml/2 tbsp desiccated coconut and
    ½ fresh red chilli, seeded and finely
    chopped, to garnish

Serves 4

1 Heat the oil in a large pan and fry the garlic for 1 minute until lightly golden. Add the chicken and spices and stir-fry for a further 3–4 minutes.

2 Heat the chicken stock in a large saucepan. Crumble the creamed coconut into the hot chicken stock and stir until dissolved. Pour on to the chicken then add the lemon or lime juice, peanut butter and egg noodles.

3 Cover the pan and simmer for about 15 minutes. Add the spring onions and fresh coriander, then season well and continue to cook for a further 5 minutes.

4 Meanwhile, place the desiccated coconut and chilli in a small frying pan and heat for 2–3 minutes, stirring frequently, until the coconut is golden and lightly browned.

5 Serve the soup in warmed bowls sprinkled with the fried coconut and chilli.

Chinese-style Vegetable Soup

INGREDIENTS

1.2 litres/2 pints/5 cups vegetable or
   chicken stock

1 garlic clove, lightly crushed

2.5cm/1in piece fresh root ginger, peeled
   and cut into fine matchsticks

30ml/2 tbsp soy sauce

15ml/1 tbsp cider vinegar

75g/3oz fresh shiitake or button
   mushrooms, stalks removed and
   thinly sliced

2 large spring onions, thinly sliced on
   the diagonal

40g/1½ oz dried rice vermicelli or other
   fine noodles, soaked in warm water
   until soft

175g/6oz Chinese leaves, shredded

a few fresh coriander leaves

Serves 4

1 Pour the stock into a saucepan. Add the garlic, root ginger, soy sauce and vinegar. Bring to the boil, then cover the pan and reduce the heat to very low. Leave to simmer gently for 10 minutes. Remove the garlic clove from the pan and discard.

COOK'S TIP

The flavour of a home-made chicken or vegetable stock is vastly superior to stock cubes, so prepare this soup when you have fresh stock to hand.

2 Add the sliced mushrooms and spring onions and bring the soup back to the boil. Simmer for 5 minutes, uncovered, stirring occasionally. Add the noodles and shredded Chinese leaves. Simmer for 3–4 minutes, or until the noodles and vegetables are just tender. Stir in the coriander leaves. Simmer for a final 1 minute. Serve the soup hot.

Seafood Wonton Soup

THIS IS A VARIATION on the popular wonton soup that is traditionally prepared using pork.

INGREDIENTS

50g/2oz raw tiger prawns
50g/2oz queen scallops
75g/3oz skinless cod fillet, roughly chopped
15ml/1 tbsp finely chopped chives
5ml/1 tsp dry sherry
1 small egg white, lightly beaten
2.5ml/½ tsp sesame oil
1.5ml/¼ tsp salt
large pinch of ground white pepper
900ml/1½ pints/3¾ cups fish stock
20 wonton wrappers
2 cos lettuce leaves, shredded
fresh coriander leaves and garlic chives,
   to garnish
Serves 4

COOK'S TIP

The filled wonton wrappers can be made ahead, then frozen for several weeks and cooked straight from the freezer.

1 Peel and devein the prawns. Rinse them well, pat them dry on kitchen paper and cut them into small pieces.

2 Rinse the scallops. Pat them dry, using kitchen paper. Chop them into small pieces roughly the same size as the prawns.

3 Place the cod in a food processor and process until a paste is formed. Scrape into a bowl and stir in the prawns, scallops, chives, sherry, egg white, sesame oil, salt and pepper. Mix thoroughly, cover and leave in a cool place to marinate for 20 minutes.

4 Heat the fish stock gently in a saucepan. Make the wontons. Place a teaspoonful of the seafood filling in the centre of a wonton wrapper, then bring the corners together to meet at the top. Twist them together to enclose the filling. Fill the remaining wonton wrappers in the same way.

5 Bring a saucepan of water to the boil. Drop in the wontons. When the water returns to the boil, lower the heat and simmer for 5 minutes. Drain and divide among four bowls.

6 Add a portion of lettuce to each bowl. Bring the fish stock to the boil. Ladle it into each bowl, garnish with coriander leaves and garlic chives.

Noodle Soup with Pork and Pickle

USE SZECHUAN HOT pickle to give this soup a real kick.

INGREDIENTS

1 litre/1¾ pints/4 cups chicken stock
350g/12oz fresh or dried egg noodles
15ml/1 tbsp dried shrimps, soaked
  in water
30ml/2 tbsp vegetable oil
225g/8oz lean pork,
  finely shredded
15ml/1 tbsp yellow bean paste
15ml/1 tbsp soy sauce
115g/4oz Szechuan hot pickle, rinsed,
  drained and shredded
pinch of sugar
2 spring onions, finely sliced,
  to garnish
Serves 4

1 Bring the stock to the boil in a large saucepan. Add the noodles and cook until almost tender. Drain the dried shrimps, rinse them under cold water, drain again and add to the stock. Lower the heat and simmer for a further 2 minutes. Keep hot. Heat the oil in a frying pan or wok. Add the pork and stir-fry over a high heat for about 3 minutes.

2 Add the bean paste and soy sauce to the pork; stir-fry for 1 minute more. Add the hot pickle with a pinch of sugar. Stir-fry for 1 minute more.

3 Divide the noodles and soup among individual serving bowls. Spoon the pork mixture on top, then sprinkle with the spring onions and serve at once.

Snapper and Tamarind Noodle Soup

TAMARIND GIVES this light, fragrant noodle soup a slightly sour taste.

INGREDIENTS

2 litres/3½ pints/8 cups water
1kg/2¼lb red snapper (or other red fish
  such as mullet)
1 onion, sliced
50g/2oz tamarind pods
15ml/1 tbsp fish sauce
15ml/1 tbsp sugar
30ml/2 tbsp vegetable oil
2 garlic cloves, finely chopped
2 lemon grass stalks, very
  finely chopped
4 ripe tomatoes, roughly chopped
30ml/2 tbsp yellow bean paste
225g/8oz dried rice vermicelli, soaked in
  warm water until soft
115g/4oz beansprouts
8–10 basil or mint sprigs
25g/1oz roasted peanuts, ground
salt and ground black pepper
Serves 4

1 Bring the water to the boil in a saucepan. Lower the heat and add the fish and onion, with 2.5ml/½ tsp salt. Simmer gently until the fish is cooked through. Remove and set aside.

2 Add the tamarind, fish sauce and sugar to the stock. Cook for 5 minutes, then strain the stock into a large jug or bowl. Carefully remove all of the bones from the fish, keeping the flesh in big pieces.

3 Heat the oil in a large frying pan. Add the garlic and lemon grass and fry for a few seconds. Stir in the tomatoes and bean paste. Cook gently for 5–7 minutes, until the tomatoes are soft. Add the stock, bring back to a simmer and adjust the seasoning.

4 Drain the vermicelli. Plunge it into a saucepan of boiling water for a few minutes, drain and divide among individual serving bowls. Add the beansprouts, fish, basil or mint, and sprinkle the ground peanuts on top. Top up each bowl with the hot soup.

Hanoi Beef and Noodle Soup

INGREDIENTS

I onion
1.5kg/3–3½ lb beef shank
  with bones
2.5cm/1in fresh root ginger
1 star anise
1 bay leaf
2 whole cloves
2.5ml/½ tsp fennel seeds
1 piece of cassia bark or
  cinnamon stick
3 litres/5 pints/12½ cups water
fish sauce, to taste
juice of 1 lime
150g/5oz fillet steak
450g/1lb fresh flat rice noodles

Accompaniments

1 small red onion, sliced into rings
115g/4oz beansprouts
2 red chillies, seeded and sliced
2 spring onions, finely sliced
handful of coriander leaves
lime wedges
Serves 4–6

1 Cut the onion in half. Grill under a high heat, cut side up, until the exposed sides are caramelized, and deep brown. Put to one side.

2 Cut the meat into large chunks and place with the bones in a stock pot. Add the caramelized onion, ginger, star anise, bay leaf, cloves, fennel seeds and cassia bark or cinnamon stick.

3 Add the water, bring to the boil, reduce the heat and simmer gently for 2–3 hours, skimming off the fat and scum from time to time.

4 Using a slotted spoon, remove the meat from the stock; when cool enough to handle, cut into small pieces, discarding the bones. Strain the stock and return to the pan or stock pot together with the meat. Bring the mixture back to the boil and then season with the fish sauce and lime juice.

5 Slice the fillet steak very thinly and then chill until required. Place the accompaniments in separate bowls.

6 Cook the noodles in a large saucepan of boiling water until just tender. Drain and divide among individual serving bowls. Arrange the thinly sliced steak over the noodles, pour the hot stock on top and serve, offering the accompaniments separately so that each person may garnish their soup as they like.

Seafood Laksa

FOR A SPECIAL OCCASION serve creamy
rice noodles in a spicy coconut-
flavoured soup, topped with seafood.
There is a fair amount of work involved
in the preparation but you can make the
soup base ahead.

INGREDIENTS

4 red chillies, seeded and
   roughly chopped
1 onion, roughly chopped
1 piece blacan, the size of a stock cube
1 lemon grass stalk, chopped
1 small piece fresh root ginger,
   roughly chopped
6 macadamia nuts or almonds
60ml/4 tbsp vegetable oil
5ml/1 tsp paprika
5ml/1 tsp ground turmeric
475ml/16fl oz/2 cups stock or water
600ml/1 pint/2½ cups coconut milk
fish sauce, to taste
12 king prawns, peeled and deveined
8 scallops
225g/8oz prepared squid, cut
   into rings
350g/12oz dried rice vermicelli or
   rice noodles, soaked in warm water
   until soft
salt and ground black pepper
lime halves, to serve

For the garnish

¼ cucumber, cut into matchsticks
2 red chillies, seeded and finely sliced
30ml/2 tbsp mint leaves
30ml/2 tbsp fried shallots or onions
Serves 4

COOK'S TIP

Blacan is dried shrimp or prawn paste. It is
sold in small blocks and you will find it in
oriental supermarkets.

1 In a blender or food processor, process
the chillies, onion, blacan, lemon grass,
ginger and nuts until smooth in texture.

2 Heat 45ml/3 tbsp of the oil in a large
saucepan. Add the chilli paste and fry
for 6 minutes. Stir in the paprika and
turmeric and fry for about 2 minutes more.

3 Add the stock or water and the
coconut milk to the pan. Bring to the
boil, reduce the heat and simmer gently for
15–20 minutes. Season the mixture to
taste with fish sauce.

4 Season the seafood. Heat the
remaining oil in a frying pan, add the
seafood and fry quickly for 2–3 minutes.

5 Add the drained noodles to the soup
and heat through. Divide among
individual serving bowls. Place the fried
seafood on top, then garnish with the
cucumber, chillies, mint and fried shallots
or onions. Serve with the limes.

Hot-and-Sour Soup

THIS SPICY, WARMING soup really whets the appetite and is the perfect introduction to a simple Chinese meal.

INGREDIENTS

10g/¼oz dried cloud ears
8 fresh shiitake mushrooms
75g/3oz beancurd (tofu)
50g/2oz/½ cup sliced, drained, canned
  bamboo shoots
900ml/1½ pints/3¾ cups vegetable stock
15ml/1 tbsp caster sugar
45ml/3 tbsp rice vinegar
15ml/1 tbsp light soy sauce
1.5ml/¼ tsp chilli oil
2.5ml/½ tsp salt
large pinch of ground white pepper
15ml/1 tbsp cornflour
15ml/1 tbsp cold water
1 egg white
5ml/1 tsp sesame oil
2 spring onions, cut into fine rings
Serves 4

COOK'S TIP

To transform this tasty soup into a nutritious light meal, add extra mushrooms, beancurd and bamboo shoots.

1 Soak the cloud ears in hot water for 30 minutes or until soft. Drain well, trim off and discard the hard base from each and chop the cloud ears roughly.

2 Remove and discard the stalks from the shiitake mushrooms. Cut the caps into thin strips. Cut the beancurd into 1cm/½ in cubes and shred the bamboo shoots finely.

3 Place the stock, mushrooms, beancurd, bamboo shoots and cloud ears in a large saucepan. Bring the stock to the boil, lower the heat and simmer for about 5 minutes.

4 Stir in the sugar, vinegar, soy sauce, chilli oil, salt and pepper. Mix the cornflour to a paste with the water. Add the mixture to the soup, stirring constantly until it thickens slightly.

5 Lightly beat the egg white, then pour it slowly into the soup in a steady stream, stirring constantly. Cook, stirring, until the egg white changes colour.

6 Add the sesame oil just before serving. Ladle into heated bowls and top each portion with spring onion rings.

Cheat's Shark's Fin Soup

SHARK'S FIN SOUP is a renowned delicacy. In this poor man's vegetarian version cellophane noodles, cut into short lengths, mimic shark's fin needles.

INGREDIENTS

4 dried Chinese mushrooms
25ml/1½ tbsp dried wood ears
115g/4oz cellophane noodles
30ml/2 tbsp vegetable oil
2 carrots, cut into fine strips
115g/4oz canned bamboo shoots, rinsed,
    drained and cut into fine strips
1 litre/1¾ pints/4 cups vegetable stock
15ml/1 tbsp soy sauce
15ml/1 tbsp arrowroot or potato flour
30ml/2 tbsp water
1 egg white, beaten (optional)
5ml/1 tsp sesame oil
salt and ground black pepper
2 spring onions, finely chopped,
    to garnish
Chinese red vinegar, to serve (optional)
Serves 4–6

1 Soak the mushrooms and wood ears separately in warm water for 20 minutes. Drain well. Remove and discard stems from the mushrooms and slice the caps thinly. Cut the wood ears into fine strips, discarding any hard bits. Soak the noodles in hot water until soft. Drain and cut into short lengths. Leave until required.

2 Heat the oil in a large saucepan. Add the mushrooms and stir-fry for 2 minutes. Add the wood ears, stir-fry for 2 minutes, then stir in the carrots, bamboo shoots and noodles.

3 Add the stock to the pan. Bring to the boil, reduce the heat and simmer gently for 15–20 minutes. Season with salt, pepper and soy sauce.

4 Blend the arrowroot or potato flour with a little water. Pour into the soup, stirring all the time to prevent lumps from forming as the soup continues to simmer.

5 Remove the pan from the heat. Stir in the egg white if using, so that it sets to form small threads in the hot soup. Stir in the sesame oil, then pour the soup into individual serving bowls. Sprinkle each portion with chopped spring onions and offer the Chinese red vinegar handed separately, if using.

Tomato and Beef Soup

USE REALLY FRESH tomatoes and spring onions to give this light beef broth a superb flavour.

INGREDIENTS

75g/3oz rump steak, trimmed of fat
900ml/1½ pints/3¾ cups beef stock
30ml/2 tbsp tomato purée
6 tomatoes, halved, seeded and chopped
10ml/2 tsp caster sugar
15ml/1 tbsp cornflour
15ml/1 tbsp cold water
1 egg white
2.5ml/½ tsp sesame oil
2 spring onions, finely shredded
salt and ground black pepper
Serves 4

1 Cut the beef into thin strips and place it in a large saucepan. Pour over boiling water to cover. Cook for 2 minutes, then drain thoroughly and set aside.

2 Bring the stock to the boil in a clean pan. Stir in the tomato purée, tomatoes and sugar. Add the beef strips, allow the stock to boil, lower the heat and simmer for 2 minutes.

3 Mix the cornflour to a paste with the water. Add the mixture to the soup, stirring constantly until it thickens slightly. Lightly beat the egg white in a separate cup.

COOK'S TIP

Try the soup topped with thin strips of fresh basil instead of spring onions for a more Mediterranean taste.

4 Pour the egg white into the soup in a steady stream, stirring all the time. As soon as the egg white changes colour, add salt and pepper, stir the soup and pour it into heated bowls. Drizzle each portion with a few drops of sesame oil, sprinkle with the spring onions and serve.

Seafood Soup Noodles

AUDIBLE SOUNDS of enjoyment are traditionally a compliment to the Chinese cook, so slurping this superb soup is not only permissible, but positively desirable.

INGREDIENTS

175g/6oz tiger prawns, peeled
*   and deveined*
225g/8oz monkfish fillet, cut into chunks
225g/8oz salmon fillet, cut into chunks
5ml/1 tsp vegetable oil
15ml/1 tbsp dry white wine
225g/8oz dried egg vermicelli
1.2 litres/2 pints/5 cups fish stock
1 carrot, thinly sliced
225g/8oz asparagus, cut into
*   5cm/2in lengths*
30 ml/2 tbsp dark soy sauce
5 ml/1 tsp sesame oil
salt and ground black pepper
2 spring onions, cut into thin rings,
*   to garnish*
Serves 4

VARIATION

Try this simple recipe using rice vermicelli for a slightly different texture and taste.

1 Mix the prawns and fish in a bowl. Add the vegetable oil and wine with 1.5 ml/¼ tsp salt and a little pepper. Mix lightly, cover and marinate in a cool plate for 15 minutes.

2 Bring a large saucepan of water to the boil and cook the noodles for 4 minutes until just tender, or according to the instructions on the packet. Drain the noodles thoroughly through a colander and divide among four serving bowls. Keep hot.

3 Bring the fish stock to the boil in a separate pan. Add the prawns and monkfish, cook for 1 minute, add the salmon and cook for 2 minutes.

4 Using a slotted spoon, carefully lift the fish and prawns out of the stock, add to the noodles in the serving bowls and keep hot.

5 Strain the stock through a sieve lined with muslin or cheesecloth into a clean pan. Bring to the boil and cook the carrot and asparagus for 2 minutes, then stir in the soy sauce and sesame oil, with salt to taste. Stir well.

6 Pour the stock and vegetables over the noodles and seafood, garnish with the spring onions and serve hot.

Chicken Vermicelli Soup with Egg Shreds

THIS SOUP is very quick and easy –
you can add all sorts of extra
ingredients to vary the taste, using
up leftovers such as spring onions,
mushrooms, a few prawns or
chopped salami.

INGREDIENTS

3 eggs
30ml/2 tbsp chopped fresh coriander
    or parsley
1.5 litres/2½ pints/6¼ cups good chicken
    stock or canned consommé
115g/4oz dried rice vermicelli or angel
    hair pasta
115g/4oz cooked chicken breast, sliced
salt and ground black pepper
Serves 4–6

1 First make the egg shreds. Whisk
the eggs together in a small bowl
and stir in the coriander or parsley
until well combined.

2 Heat a small non-stick frying pan
and pour in 30–45ml/2–3 tbsp
egg, swirling to cover the base evenly.
Cook until set. Repeat until all the
mixture is used up.

3 Roll each pancake up and slice
thinly into shreds. Set aside.

4 Bring the stock or consommé to
the boil and add the pasta,
breaking it up into short lengths. Cook
for 3–5 minutes until tender.

5 Add the chicken, and salt and
pepper to taste. Heat through for
about 2–3 minutes, then stir in the egg
shreds. Serve immediately.

VARIATION

*To make a Thai variation, use Chinese
rice noodles instead of pasta. Stir
1.5ml/½ tsp dried lemon grass, 2 small
whole fresh chillies and 60ml/4 tbsp
coconut milk into the stock. Add 4 sliced
spring onions and plenty of chopped
fresh coriander.*

Chicken and Buckwheat Noodle Soup

BUCKWHEAT OR SOBA noodles are widely enjoyed in Japan. The simplest way of serving them is in hot seasoned broth. Almost any topping can be added and the variations are endless.

INGREDIENTS

225g/8oz skinless, boneless
 chicken breasts
120ml/4fl oz/½ cup soy sauce
15ml/1 tbsp saké
1 litre/1¾ pints/4 cups chicken stock
2 pieces young leek, cut into 2.5cm/1in pieces
175g/6oz spinach leaves
300g/11oz fresh or dried buckwheat or
 soba noodles
sesame seeds, toasted, to garnish
Serves 4

1 Slice the chicken diagonally into bite-size pieces. Combine the soy sauce and saké in a saucepan. Bring to a simmer. Then add the chicken and cook gently for about 3 minutes until it is tender. Keep hot.

2 Bring the stock to the boil in a saucepan. Add the leek and simmer for 3 minutes, then add the spinach. Remove from the heat but keep warm.

3 Cook the noodles in a large saucepan of boiling water until just tender, according to the instructions on the packet.

4 Drain the noodles and divide among individual serving bowls. Ladle the hot soup into the bowls, then add a portion of chicken to each. Serve at once, sprinkled with sesame seeds.

COOK'S TIP

Home-made chicken stock makes the world of difference to noodle soup. Make a big batch of stock, use as much as you need and freeze the rest until required. Put about 1.5kg/3–3½lb meaty chicken bones into a large saucepan, add 3 litres/5 pints/ 12½ cups water and slowly bring to the boil, skimming off any foam that rises to the top. Add 2 slices fresh root ginger, 2 garlic cloves, 2 celery sticks, 4 spring onions, a handful of coriander stalks and about 10 peppercorns, crushed, then reduce the heat and simmer the stock for 2–2½ hours. Remove from the heat and leave to cool, uncovered and undisturbed. Strain the stock into a clean bowl, leaving the last dregs behind as they tend to cloud the soup. Use as required, removing any fat that congeals on top.

Buckwheat Noodles with Smoked Trout

THE LIGHT, CRISP texture of the pak choi balances the earthy flavours of the mushrooms and the smokiness of the trout.

INGREDIENTS

350g/12oz fresh or dried
    buckwheat noodles
30ml/2 tbsp vegetable oil
115g/4oz fresh shiitake
    mushrooms, quartered
2 garlic cloves, finely chopped
15ml/1 tbsp grated fresh
    root ginger
225g/8oz pak choi, shredded
1 spring onion, finely
    sliced diagonally
15ml/1 tbsp dark sesame oil
30ml/2 tbsp mirin
30ml/2 tbsp soy sauce
2 smoked trout, skinned and boned
salt and ground black pepper
30ml/2 tbsp coriander leaves and
    10ml/2 tsp sesame seeds, toasted,
    to garnish
Serves 4

1 Cook the buckwheat noodles according to the instructions on the packet.

2 Meanwhile heat the oil in a large frying pan. Add the mushrooms and sauté over a medium heat for 3 minutes. Add the garlic, ginger and pak choi, and sauté for 2 minutes.

3 Drain the noodles and add to the mushroom mixture with the spring onion, sesame oil, mirin and soy sauce. Toss and season with salt and pepper to taste.

4 Break the smoked trout in bite-size pieces. Arrange the noodle mixture on individual serving plates. Place the smoked trout on top of the noodles.

5 Garnish the noodles with coriander leaves and sesame seeds and serve them immediately.

COOK'S TIP

Mirin, or rice wine, is easily available but if you don't want to buy it specially for this dish, use sweet sherry, or omit altogether.

Noodles with Ginger and Coriander

HERE IS A SIMPLE noodle dish that
goes well with most Oriental dishes.
It can also be served as a snack for
2–3 people.

INGREDIENTS

handful of fresh coriander sprigs
225g/8oz/2 cups dried egg noodles
45ml/3 tbsp groundnut oil
5cm/2in piece fresh root ginger, cut into
  fine shreds
6–8 spring onions, cut into shreds
30ml/2 tbsp light soy sauce
salt and ground black pepper
Serves 4–6

1 Strip the leaves from the coriander
  stalks by hand. Put them in a pile
on a chopping board and coarsely
chop them using a cleaver or large
sharp knife.

2 Cook the noodles according to
  the instructions on the packet.
Rinse under cold water and drain well.
Toss in 15ml/1 tbsp of the oil.

3 Heat a wok until hot, add the
  remaining oil and swirl it around.
Add the ginger and stir-fry for a few
seconds, then add the noodles and
spring onions. Stir-fry for 3–4 minutes
until hot.

4 Sprinkle the soy sauce, coriander
  and seasoning over. Toss well,
then serve at once.

COOK'S TIP

*Many of the dried egg noodles available
are sold packed in layers. As a guide
allow 1 layer of noodles per person as
an average portion for a main dish.*

Noodles with Asparagus and Saffron

A RATHER ELEGANT summery dish
with fragrant saffron cream. The
delicate fresh flavour of the
asparagus is enhanced by the wine
and lemon.

INGREDIENTS

450g/1lb young asparagus
pinch of saffron threads
30ml/2 tbsp hot water
25g/1oz butter
2 shallots, finely chopped
30ml/2 tbsp white wine
250ml/8fl oz/1 cup double cream
grated rind and juice of ½ lemon
115g/4oz peas
350g/12oz dried somen noodles
½ bunch chervil, roughly chopped
salt and ground black pepper
grated Parmesan cheese (optional)
Serves 4

1 Cut off the asparagus tips (about
5cm/2in in length), then slice the
remaining spears into short rounds. Steep
the saffron in the hot water in a cup or a
small bowl.

2 Melt the butter in a saucepan, add the
shallots and cook over a low heat for
3 minutes until soft. Add the white wine,
cream and saffron infusion. Bring to the
boil, reduce the heat and simmer gently for
5 minutes or until the sauce thickens to a
coating consistency. Add the grated lemon
rind and juice, and season to taste.

3 Bring a saucepan of lightly salted water
to the boil. Blanch the asparagus tips,
scoop them out and add to the sauce, then
cook the peas and short asparagus rounds
in the boiling water until just tender. Scoop
them out and add to the sauce.

4 Cook the somen noodles in the same
water until just tender, following the
directions on the packet. Drain, place in a
wide pan and pour the sauce over the top.

5 Toss the noodles with the sauce and
vegetables, adding the chervil and
more salt and pepper if needed. Finally,
sprinkle with the grated Parmesan, if using,
and serve hot.

Noodles with Sun-dried Tomatoes

INGREDIENTS

350g/12oz dried somen noodles
45ml/3 tbsp olive oil
20 uncooked king prawns, peeled
    and deveined
2 garlic cloves, finely chopped
45–60ml/3–4 tbsp sun-dried
    tomato paste
salt and ground black pepper

For the garnish
handful of basil leaves
30ml/2 tbsp sun-dried tomatoes in oil, drained
    and cut into strips
Serves 4

COOK'S TIP

*Ready-made sun-dried tomato paste is
readily available, however you can make your
own simply by processing bottled sun-dried
tomatoes with their oil. You could also add
a couple of anchovy fillets and some capers
if you like.*

1 Cook the noodles in a large saucepan of boiling water until tender, following the directions on the packet. Drain.

2 Heat half the oil in a large frying pan. Add the prawns and garlic and fry them over a medium heat for 3–5 minutes, until the prawns turn pink and are firm to the touch.

3 Stir in 15ml/1 tbsp of the sun-dried tomato paste and mix well. Using a slotted spoon, transfer the prawns to a bowl and keep hot.

4 Add the remaining oil and reheat the pan. Stir in the remaining sun-dried tomato paste. You may need to add a spoonful of water to thin the mixture.

5 When the mixture starts to sizzle, toss in the noodles. Season and mix.

6 Return the prawns to the pan and toss to combine. Serve at once in plates or bowls garnished with the basil and strips of sun-dried tomatoes.

Crispy Fried Rice Vermicelli in a Garlic Sweet-and-sour Sauce

THIS DISH IS USUALLY served at celebration meals. It is a crisp tangle of fried rice vermicelli, which is tossed in a piquant sauce.

INGREDIENTS

60ml/4 tbsp oil
175g/6oz/1 1/2 cups dried rice vermicelli
2 garlic cloves, crushed
4-6 dried chillies, seeded and chopped
30ml/2 tbsp shallots, chopped
15ml/1 tbsp dried shrimps, soaked in
    water and rinsed
115g/4oz lean pork, finely shredded
115g/4oz raw peeled prawns, thawed if
    frozen, chopped
30ml/2 tbsp brown bean sauce
30ml/2 tbsp rice wine vinegar
45ml/3 tbsp fish sauce
75g/3oz palm sugar
30ml/2 tbsp tamarind juice or lime juice
115g/4oz/2 1/2 cups beansprouts

For the garnish
2 spring onions, shredded
30ml/2 tbsp fresh coriander leaves
2-egg omelette, rolled and sliced
2 fresh red chillies, chopped
Serves 4

1 Heat the oil in a wok. Cut or break the rice vermicelli into small handfuls about 7.5cm/3in long. Deep-fry these in the hot oil until they puff up. Lift out with a spider or slotted spoon and drain on kitchen paper.

2 Ladle off all but 30ml/2 tbsp of the oil, pouring it into a pan and setting aside to cool. Reheat the oil in the wok and fry the garlic, chillies, shallots and shrimps for 1 minute.

3 Add the pork and stir-fry for 3-4 minutes, until no longer pink. Add the prawns and fry for 2 minutes. Spoon into a bowl and set aside.

4 Add the brown bean sauce, vinegar, fish sauce and sugar. Heat gently, stirring in any sediment. Bring to a gentle boil, stir to dissolve the sugar and cook until thick and syrupy.

5 Add the tamarind or lime juice to the sauce and adjust the seasoning as necessary. The sauce should be sweet, sour and salty. Lower the heat, then return the pork and prawn mixture to the wok. Add the beansprouts and stir them into the sauce.

6 Add the fried rice noodles and toss gently to coat them with the sauce without breaking them up too much. Transfer the mixture to a large serving platter. Garnish with shredded spring onions, coriander leaves, omelette strips and fresh red chillies.

COOK'S TIP

Pickled garlic can also be used as a garnish. Thai garlic is smaller than European garlic; the heads are pickled whole, in sweet and sour brine.

Fried Singapore Noodles

THAI FISHCAKES vary in their size and their spiciness. They are available from Oriental supermarkets.

INGREDIENTS

175g/6oz dried rice vermicelli
60ml/4 tbsp vegetable oil
2.5ml/½ tsp salt
75g/3oz/¾ cup cooked prawns
175g/6oz cooked pork, cut
    into matchsticks
1 green pepper, seeded and cut
    into matchsticks
2.5ml/½ tsp sugar
10ml/2 tsp curry powder
75g/3oz Thai fishcakes
10ml/2 tsp dark soy sauce
Serves 4

1 Soak the rice noodles in warm water for about 10 minutes, drain well through a colander, then pat dry with kitchen paper.

2 Heat a wok, then add half the oil. When the oil is hot, add the noodles and half the salt and stir-fry for 2 minutes. Transfer to a warmed serving dish and keep warm.

3 Heat the remaining oil and add the prawns, pork, pepper, sugar, curry powder and remaining salt. Stir-fry for 1 minute.

4 Return the noodles to the pan and stir-fry with the Thai fishcakes for 2 minutes. Stir in the soy sauce and serve immediately.

Chow Mein

ONE OF THE MOST well-known
Chinese noodle dishes.

INGREDIENTS

225g/8oz fresh or dried egg noodles
30ml/2 tbsp oil
1 onion, chopped
1cm/½in piece fresh root ginger, chopped
2 garlic cloves, crushed
30ml/2 tbsp soy sauce
50ml/2fl oz/¼ cup dry white wine
10ml/2 tsp Chinese five-spice powder
450g/1lb/4 cups minced pork
4 spring onions, sliced
50g/2oz oyster mushrooms
75g/3oz bamboo shoots
15ml/1 tbsp sesame oil
prawn crackers, to serve

Serves 4

1 Cook the noodles in boiling water
for 4 minutes and drain.

2 Meanwhile, heat the oil in a wok
or frying pan and add the onion,
ginger, garlic, soy sauce and wine. Stir-
fry for 1 minute. Stir in the Chinese
five-spice powder.

3 Add the minced pork and cook
for 10 minutes, stirring constantly.
Add the spring onions, oyster
mushrooms and bamboo shoots
and continue to cook for a further
5 minutes still stirring.

4 Stir in the noodles and sesame
oil. Mix all the ingredients
together well and serve in bowls at
once with prawn crackers.

Spicy Fried Rice Sticks with Prawns

THIS RECIPE IS BASED on the classic Thai noodle dish called Pad Thai. Popular all over Thailand, it is enjoyed morning, noon and night.

INGREDIENTS

15g/½oz dried shrimps
15ml/1 tbsp tamarind pulp
60ml/4 tbsp hot water
45ml/3 tbsp Thai fish sauce (nam pla)
15ml/1 tbsp sugar
2 garlic cloves, chopped
2 fresh red chillies, seeded and chopped
45ml/3 tbsp groundnut oil
2 eggs, beaten
225g/8oz dried rice sticks, soaked in warm
    water for 30 minutes, refreshed under
    cold running water and drained
225g/8oz cooked peeled king prawns
3 spring onions, cut into 2.5cm/1in lengths
75g/3oz/scant½ cup beansprouts
30ml/2 tbsp roughly chopped, roasted
    unsalted peanuts
30ml/2 tbsp chopped fresh coriander
lime slices, to garnish
Serves 4

VARIATION

For a vegetarian dish omit the dried shrimps and replace the king prawns with cubes of deep-fried tofu.

1 Put the dried shrimps in a small bowl and pour over enough warm water to cover. Leave to soak for 30 minutes until soft; drain.

2 Put the tamarind pulp in a bowl with the hot water. Blend together, then press through a sieve to extract 30 ml/2 tbsp thick tamarind water. Mix the tamarind water with the fish sauce and sugar.

3 Using a mortar and pestle, pound the garlic and chillies to form a paste. Heat a wok over a medium heat, add 15 ml/1 tbsp of the oil, then add the beaten eggs and stir for 1–2 minutes until scrambled. Remove and set aside. Wipe the wok clean.

4 Reheat the wok, until hot, add the remaining oil, then the chilli paste and soaked shrimps and stir-fry for 1 minute. Add the rice sticks and tamarind mixture and continue to stir-fry for 3–4 minutes.

5 Add the scrambled eggs, prawns, spring onions, beansprouts, peanuts and coriander, then stir-fry for 2 minutes until well mixed. Serve at once, garnishing each portion with lime slices.

Stir-fried Turkey with Broccoli and Mushrooms

THIS IS A REALLY easy, tasty supper dish which works just as well if you use chicken instead of turkey.

INGREDIENTS

115g/4oz broccoli florets
4 spring onions
5ml/1 tsp cornflour
45ml/3 tbsp oyster sauce
15ml/1 tbsp dark soy sauce
120ml/4fl oz/½ cup chicken stock
10ml/2 tsp lemon juice
45ml/3 tbsp groundnut oil
450g/1lb turkey steaks, cut into strips,
    about 5mm x 5cm/¼ x 2in
1 small onion, chopped
2 garlic cloves, crushed
10ml/2 tsp grated fresh root ginger
115g/4oz/1 cup fresh shiitake
    mushrooms, sliced
75g/3oz baby sweetcorn, halved lengthways
15ml/1 tbsp sesame oil
salt and ground black pepper
egg noodles, to serve

Serves 4

1 Divide the broccoli florets into smaller sprigs and cut the stalks into thin diagonal slices.

2 Finely chop the white parts of the spring onions and slice the green parts into thin shreds.

3 In a bowl, blend together the cornflour, oyster sauce, soy sauce, stock and lemon juice. Set aside.

4 Heat a wok until hot, add 30 ml/ 2 tbsp of the groundnut oil and swirl it around. Add the turkey and stir-fry for about 2 minutes until golden and crispy at the edges. Remove the turkey from the wok and keep warm while you cook the vegetables.

5 Add the remaining groundnut oil to the wok and stir-fry the chopped onion, garlic and ginger over a medium heat for about 1 minute. Increase the heat to high, add the broccoli, mushrooms and sweetcorn and stir-fry for 2 minutes.

6 Return the turkey to the wok, then add the sauce with the chopped white spring onion and seasoning. Cook, stirring, until the sauce has thickened. Stir in the sesame oil. Serve on a bed of egg noodles with the shredded spring onion.

Lemon Grass Pork

CHILLIES AND LEMON GRASS flavour this simple stir-fry, while peanuts add crunch.

INGREDIENTS

675g/1½lb boneless loin of pork
2 lemon grass stalks, finely chopped
4 spring onions, thinly sliced
5ml/1 tsp salt
12 black peppercorns, coarsely crushed
30ml/2 tbsp groundnut oil
2 garlic cloves, chopped
2 fresh red chillies, seeded and chopped
5ml/1 tsp light brown soft sugar
30ml/2 tbsp Thai fish sauce (nam pla),
    or to taste
25g/1oz/¼ cup roasted unsalted
    peanuts, chopped
salt and ground black pepper
roughly torn coriander leaves, to garnish
rice noodles, to serve
Serves 4

COOK'S TIP

*If you can't get hold of lemon grass
stalks, use powdered, which is readily
available in most supermarkets.*

2 Heat a wok until hot, add the oil and swirl it around. Add the pork mixture and stir-fry for 3 minutes.

4 Add the sugar, fish sauce and peanuts, and toss to mix. Taste and adjust the seasoning, if necessary. Serve at once on a bed of rice noodles, garnished with roughly torn coriander leaves.

3 Add the garlic and chillies and stir-fry for a further 5–8 minutes.

1 Trim any excess fat from the pork. Cut the meat across into 5mm/¼in thick slices, then cut each slice into 5mm/¼in strips. Put the pork into a bowl with the lemon grass, spring onions, salt and crushed peppercorns; mix well. Cover and leave to marinate for 30 minutes.

Oriental Vegetable Noodles

THE SUPERIOR TASTE of balsamic
vinegar makes this dish really special.

INGREDIENTS

500g/1¼lb thin egg noodles
1 red onion
115g/4oz shiitake mushrooms
45ml/3 tbsp sesame oil
45ml/3 tbsp dark soy sauce
15ml/1 tbsp balsamic vinegar
10ml/2 tsp caster sugar
5ml/1 tsp salt
celery leaves, to garnish

Serves 6

1 Cook the noodles in plenty of
salted boiling water according to
the instructions on the packet until
al dente.

2 Cut the red onion and the
shiitake mushrooms into thin
slices, using a sharp knife.

3 Heat a wok, then add 15ml/
1 tbsp of the sesame oil. When
the oil is hot, stir-fry the onion and
mushrooms for about 2 minutes.

4 Drain the noodles, then add to
the wok with the soy sauce,
balsamic vinegar, sugar and salt. Stir-fry
for 1 minute, then add the remaining
sesame oil, and serve garnished with
celery leaves.

Rice Noodles with Vegetable Chilli Sauce

INGREDIENTS

15ml/1 tbsp sunflower oil
1 onion, chopped
2 garlic cloves, crushed
1 fresh red chilli, seeded and
    finely chopped
1 red pepper, seeded and diced
2 carrots, finely chopped
175g/6oz baby sweetcorn, halved
225g/8oz can sliced bamboo shoots, rinsed
    and drained
400g/14oz can red kidney beans, rinsed
    and drained
300ml/½ pint/1¼ cups passata or
    sieved tomatoes
15ml/1 tbsp gluten-free soy sauce
5ml/1 tsp ground coriander
250g/9oz/2¼ cups dried rice noodles
30ml/2 tbsp chopped fresh coriander
    or parsley
salt and ground black pepper
fresh parsley sprigs, to garnish

Serves 4

1 Heat the oil, add the onion, garlic, chilli and red pepper and cook for 5 minutes, stirring. Stir in the carrots, sweetcorn, bamboo shoots, kidney beans, passata or sieved tomatoes, soy sauce and ground coriander.

2 Bring to the boil, then cover, reduce the heat, and simmer gently for 30 minutes until the vegetables are tender, stirring occasionally. Season with salt and pepper to taste.

3 Meanwhile, place the noodles in a bowl and cover with boiling water. Stir with a fork and leave to stand for 3–4 minutes, or according to the instructions on the packet. Rinse with boiling water and drain.

4 Stir the coriander or parsley into the sauce. Spoon the noodles on to warmed serving plates and top with the sauce. Garnish with parsley and serve.

COOK'S TIP

After handling chillies, wash your hands. Chillies contain volatile oils that can irritate and burn sensitive areas, such as the eyes, if they are touched.

Vegetable and Egg Noodle Ribbons

SERVE THIS ELEGANT, colourful dish with a tossed green salad as a light lunch or as a starter dish for six to eight people.

INGREDIENTS

1 large carrot, peeled
2 courgettes
50g/2oz butter
15ml/1 tbsp olive oil
6 fresh shiitake mushrooms,
    finely sliced
50g/2oz frozen peas, thawed
350g/12oz fresh or dried broad egg
    ribbon noodles
10ml/2 tsp chopped mixed herbs (such as
    marjoram, chives and basil)
salt and ground black pepper
25g/1oz Parmesan cheese, to
    serve (optional)
Serves 4

1 Using a vegetable peeler, carefully slice thin strips from the carrot and from the courgettes to form ribbons.

2 Heat the butter with the olive oil in a large frying pan. Stir in the carrots and shiitake mushrooms; fry for 2 minutes. Add the courgettes and peas and stir-fry until the courgettes are cooked, but still crisp. Season with salt and pepper.

3 Meanwhile, cook the noodles in a large saucepan of boiling water until just tender. Drain the noodles well and tip them into a bowl. Add the vegetables and toss to mix.

4 Sprinkle the fresh herbs over and season to taste. If using the Parmesan cheese, grate or shave it over the top. Toss lightly and serve.

Buckwheat Noodles with Goat's Cheese

WHEN YOU DON'T FEEL like doing a lot of cooking, try this good fast supper dish. The earthy flavour of buckwheat goes well with the nutty, peppery taste of rocket leaves, offset by the deliciously creamy goat's cheese.

INGREDIENTS

350g/12oz fresh or dried
    buckwheat noodles
50g/2oz butter
2 garlic cloves, finely chopped
4 shallots, sliced
75g/3oz hazelnuts, lightly roasted and
    roughly chopped
large handful rocket leaves
175g/6oz goat's cheese
salt and ground black pepper
Serves 4

1 Cook the noodles in a large saucepan of boiling water until just tender according to the instructions on the packet. Drain well.

2 Heat the butter in a large frying pan. Add the garlic and shallots and cook for 2–3 minutes, stirring all the time, until the shallots are soft.

3 Add the hazelnuts and fry for about 1 minute. Add the rocket leaves and, when they start to wilt, toss in the noodles and heat through.

4 Season with salt and pepper. Crumble in the goat's cheese and serve immediately.

Chinese Mushrooms with Noodles

RED FERMENTED beancurd adds a unique flavour to this hearty vegetarian dish. It is brick red in colour, with a very strong, cheesy flavour, and is made by fermenting beancurd (tofu) with salt, red rice and rice wine.

INGREDIENTS

115g/4oz dried Chinese mushrooms
25g/1oz dried wood ears
115g/4oz dried beancurd
30ml/2 tbsp vegetable oil
2 garlic cloves, finely chopped
2 slices fresh root ginger,
   finely chopped
10 Szechuan peppercorns, crushed
15ml/1 tbsp red fermented
   beancurd
½ star anise
pinch of sugar
15–30ml/1–2 tbsp soy sauce
50g/2oz cellophane noodles, soaked
   in hot water until soft
salt

Serves 4

2 Strain the mushrooms, reserving the liquid. Squeeze as much liquid from the mushrooms as possible, then discard the mushroom stems. Cut the cups in half if they are large.

1 Soak the Chinese mushrooms and wood ears separately in bowls of hot water for about 30 minutes. Break the dried beancurd into small pieces and soak in water according to the instructions on the packet.

3 The wood ears should swell to five times their original size. Drain them, rinse thoroughly and drain again. Cut off any gritty parts, then cut each wood ear into two or three pieces.

4 Heat the oil in a heavy-based pan. Add the garlic, ginger and Szechuan peppercorns. Fry for a few seconds, then add the mushrooms and red fermented beancurd. Mix lightly and fry for 5 minutes.

5 Add the reserved mushroom liquid to the pan, with sufficient water to completely cover the mushrooms. Add the star anise, sugar and soy sauce, then cover and simmer for 30 minutes.

6 Add the chopped wood ears and reconstituted beancurd pieces to the pan. Cover and cook for about 10 minutes.

7 Drain the cellophane noodles, add them to the mixture and cook for a further 10 minutes until tender, adding more liquid if necessary. Add salt to taste and serve.

COOK'S TIP

If you can't find Szechuan peppercorns, then use ordinary black ones instead.

Toasted Noodles with Vegetables

SLIGHTLY CRISP NOODLE cakes topped with vegetables make a fabulous dinner party dish.

INGREDIENTS

175g/6oz/1½ cups dried egg vermicelli
15ml/1 tbsp vegetable oil
2 garlic cloves, finely chopped
115g/4oz/1 cup baby corn cobs
115g/4oz/1 cup fresh shiitake
  mushrooms, halved
3 celery sticks, sliced
1 carrot, diagonally sliced
115g/4oz/1 cup mangetouts
75g/3oz/¾ cup sliced, drained, canned
  bamboo shoots
15ml/1 tbsp cornflour
15ml/1 tbsp cold water
15ml/1 tbsp dark soy sauce
5ml/1 tsp caster sugar
300ml/½ pint/1¼ cups vegetable stock
salt and ground white pepper
spring onion curls, to garnish
Serves 4

1 Bring a saucepan of water to the boil. Add the egg vermicelli and cook according to instructions on the packet until just tender. Drain, refresh under cold water, drain again, then dry thoroughly on kitchen paper.

2 Heat 2.5ml/½ tsp oil in a non-stick frying pan or wok. Fry half the noodles for 2–3 minutes until lightly toasted. Turn and fry the other side, then slide on to a heated serving plate. Repeat with the remaining noodles to make two cakes. Keep hot.

3 Heat the remaining oil in the clean pan, then fry the garlic for a few seconds. Cut the corn cobs in half lengthways, add to the pan with the mushrooms, then stir-fry for 3 minutes, adding a little water, if needed, to prevent the mixture burning. Then add the celery, carrot, mangetouts and bamboo shoots. Stir-fry the mixture for 2 minutes or until the vegetables are tender-crisp.

4 Mix the cornflour to a paste with the water. Add the mixture to the pan with the soy sauce, sugar and stock. Cook, stirring, until the sauce thickens. Season with salt and white pepper. Divide the vegetable mixture between the noodle cakes, garnish with the spring onion curls and serve immediately. Each noodle cake serves two people.

Tomato Noodles with Fried Egg

THIS DISH MAKES a good brunch or supper dish; if you are cooking for children, omit the chilli.

INGREDIENTS

350g/12oz medium-thick
   dried noodles
60ml/4 tbsp vegetable oil
2 garlic cloves, very
   finely chopped
4 shallots, chopped
2.5ml/½ tsp chilli powder
5ml/1 tsp paprika
2 carrots, finely diced
115g/4oz button mushrooms, quartered
50g/2oz peas
15ml/1 tbsp tomato ketchup
10ml/2 tsp tomato purée
butter for frying
4 eggs
salt and ground black pepper
Serves 4

1 Cook the noodles in a saucepan of boiling water according to the instructions on the packet until just tender. Drain, rinse under cold running water and drain well.

2 Heat the oil in a wok or large frying pan. Add the garlic, shallots, chilli powder and paprika. Stir-fry for about 1 minute, then add the diced carrots, mushrooms and peas. Continue to stir-fry until the vegetables are cooked.

3 Stir the tomato ketchup and purée into the vegetable mixture in the wok. Add the noodles and cook over a medium heat until the noodles are heated through and have taken on the reddish tinge of the paprika and tomato.

4 Meanwhile melt the butter in a frying pan and fry each of the eggs. Season the noodle mixture, divide it among four serving plates and top each portion with one of the fried egg.

Curry Fried Noodles

ON ITS OWN, beancurd (tofu) has a fairly bland flavour, but by soaking up the flavour of the curry spices it takes on a wonderful flavour.

INGREDIENTS

60ml/4 tbsp vegetable oil
30–45ml/2–3 tbsp curry paste
225g/8oz smoked beancurd, cut into
   2.5cm/1in cubes
225g/8oz green beans, cut into 2.5cm/
   1in lengths
1 red pepper, seeded and cut into
   fine strips
350g/12oz dried rice vermicelli, soaked in
   warm water until soft
15ml/1 tbsp soy sauce
salt and ground black pepper
2 spring onions, finely sliced, 2 red chillies,
   seeded and chopped, and
   1 lime, cut into wedges, to garnish
Serves 4

1 Heat half the oil in a wok or large frying pan. Add the curry paste and stir-fry for a few minutes, then add the beancurd and continue to fry until golden brown. Using a slotted spoon remove the cubes from the pan and set aside until required.

2 Add the remaining oil to the wok or pan. When hot, add the green beans and red pepper. Stir-fry until the vegetables are cooked. You may need to moisten them with a little water.

3 Drain the noodles and add them to the wok or frying pan. Stir-fry until the noodles are heated through making sure they do not stick to the pan, then return the curried beancurd to the wok. Season with soy sauce, salt and pepper.

4 Transfer the mixture to a serving dish. Sprinkle with the spring onions and chillies and serve the lime wedges on the side for squeezing over.

Somen Noodles with Courgettes

A COLOURFUL DISH with lots of flavour. Pumpkin or patty pan squashes can be used as an alternative to courgettes.

INGREDIENTS

2 yellow courgettes
2 green courgettes
60ml/4 tbsp pine nuts
60ml/4 tbsp extra virgin olive oil
2 shallots, finely chopped
2 garlic cloves, finely chopped
30ml/2 tbsp capers, rinsed
4 sun-dried tomatoes in oil, drained and
    cut into strips
300g/11oz dried somen noodles
60ml/4 tbsp chopped mixed herbs (such
    as chives, thyme and tarragon)
grated rind of 1 lemon
50g/2oz Parmesan cheese, finely grated
salt and ground black pepper
Serves 4

1 Slice the courgettes diagonally into rounds the same thickness as the noodles. Cut the courgette slices into matchsticks. Toast the pine nuts in an ungreased frying pan over a medium heat until golden in colour.

2 Heat half the oil in a large frying pan. Add the shallots and garlic and fry until fragrant. Push the shallot mixture to one side of the pan, add the remaining oil and, when hot, stir-fry the courgettes until soft.

3 Stir thoroughly to incorporate the shallot mixture and add the capers, sun-dried tomatoes and pine nuts. Remove the pan from the heat.

4 Cook the noodles in a large saucepan of salted boiling water until just tender, following the directions on the packet. Drain well and toss into the courgette mixture, adding the herbs, lemon rind and Parmesan, with salt and pepper to taste. Serve at once.

Noodles Primavera

INGREDIENTS

225g/8oz dried rice noodles
115g/4oz broccoli florets
1 carrot, finely sliced
225g/8oz asparagus, cut into
    5cm/2in lengths
1 red or yellow pepper, seeded and cut
    into strips
50g/2oz baby corn cobs
50g/2oz sugar mantetouts, topped
    and tailed
45ml/3 tbsp olive oil
15ml/1 tbsp chopped fresh root ginger
2 garlic cloves, chopped
2 spring onions, finely chopped
450g/1lb tomatoes, chopped
1 bunch rocket leaves
soy sauce, to taste
salt and freshly ground black pepper
Serves 4

1 Soak the noodles in hot water for about 30 minutes until soft. Drain.

2 Blanch the broccoli florets, sliced carrot, asparagus, pepper strips, baby corn cobs and mangetouts separately in boiling, salted water. Drain them through a colander, rinse under cold water, then drain again and set aside.

3 Heat the olive oil in a frying pan. Add the ginger, garlic and onions. Stir-fry for 30 seconds, then add the tomatoes and stir-fry for 2–3 minutes.

4 Add the noodles and stir-fry for 3 minutes. Toss in the blanched vegetables and rocket leaves. Season with soy sauce, salt and pepper and cook until the vegetables are tender.

Fried Wontons

THESE DELICIOUS wontons have
a vegetarian filling.

INGREDIENTS

30 wonton wrappers
1 egg, beaten
oil for deep frying

For the filling
10ml/2 tsp vegetable oil
15ml/1 tbsp grated fresh root ginger
2 garlic cloves, finely chopped
225g/8oz firm beancurd
6 spring onions, finely chopped
10ml/2 tsp sesame oil
15ml/1 tbsp soy sauce
salt and ground black pepper

For the dipping sauce
30ml/2 tbsp soy sauce
15ml/1 tbsp sesame oil
15ml/1 tbsp rice vinegar
2.5ml/½ tsp chilli oil
2.5ml/½ tsp honey
30ml/2 tbsp water
Makes 30

1 Line a large baking sheet with greaseproof paper or sprinkle lightly with flour, then set aside. To make the filling, heat the oil in a frying pan. Add the root ginger and garlic cloves and fry for 30 seconds. Crumble in the beancurd and continue to stir-fry for a few minutes.

2 Add the spring onions, sesame oil and soy sauce to the pan. Stir well and taste for seasoning. Remove from the heat and set aside to cool.

3 Make the dipping sauce by combining all the ingredients in a separate bowl and mixing to combine well.

4 Place a wonton wrapper on a board in a diamond position. Brush the edges lightly with beaten egg. Spoon 5ml/1 tsp of the filling on the centre of each wrapper.

5 Pull the top corner down to the bottom corner, folding the wrapper over the filling to make a triangle. Press firmly to seal. Place on the prepared baking sheet as you go. Repeat with the rest of the wonton wrappers.

6 Heat the oil in a deep fryer or large saucepan. Carefully drop in the wontons, a few at a time, and cook for a few minutes until golden brown all over. Drain on kitchen paper, then serve at once with the dipping sauce to the side.

Vegetarian Fried Noodles

WHEN MAKING this dish for non-vegetarians, add a piece of blacan (compressed shrimp paste). A small chunk about the size of a stock cube, mashed with the chilli paste, will add a deliciously rich, aromatic flavour.

INGREDIENTS

2 eggs

5ml/1 tsp chilli powder

5ml/1 tsp turmeric

60ml/4 tbsp vegetable oil

1 large onion, finely sliced

2 red chillies, seeded and
    finely sliced

15ml/1 tbsp soy sauce

2 large cooked potatoes, cut into
    small cubes

6 pieces fried beancurd, sliced

225g/8oz beansprouts

115g/4oz green beans, blanched

350g/12oz fresh thick egg noodles

salt and ground black pepper

sliced spring onions, to garnish

Serves 4

1 Beat the eggs lightly, then strain them into a bowl. Heat a lightly greased omelette pan. Pour in half of the egg to cover the bottom of the pan thinly. When the egg is just set, turn the omelette over and fry the other side briefly. Slide on to a plate, blot with kitchen paper, roll up and cut into narrow strips. Make a second omelette in the same way and slice. Set the omelette strips aside for the garnish.

COOK'S TIP

Always be very careful when handling chillies. Keep your hands away from your eyes as chillies will sting them. Wash your hands thoroughly after touching them.

2 In a cup, mix together the chilli powder and turmeric. Form a paste by stirring in a little water.

3 Heat the oil in a wok or large frying pan. Fry the onion until soft. Reduce the heat and add the chilli paste, sliced chillies and soy sauce. Fry for 2–3 minutes.

4 Add the potatoes and fry for about 2 minutes, mixing well to combine. Add the beancurd, then the beansprouts, green beans and noodles.

5 Gently stir-fry until the noodles are evenly coated and heated through. Take care not to break up the potatoes or the bean curd. Season with salt and pepper. Serve hot, garnished with the reserved omelette strips and spring onion slices.

Singapore Rice Vermicelli

SIMPLE AND SPEEDILY prepared, this lightly curried rice noodle dish is a full meal in a bowl.

INGREDIENTS

225g/8oz/2 cups dried rice vermicelli
15ml/1 tbsp vegetable oil
1 egg, lightly beaten
2 garlic cloves, finely chopped
1 large fresh red or green chilli, seeded and finely chopped
15ml/1 tbsp medium curry powder
1 red pepper, seeded and thinly sliced
1 green pepper, seeded and thinly sliced
1 carrot, cut into matchsticks
1.5ml/¼ tsp salt
60ml/4 tbsp vegetable stock
115g/4oz cooked peeled prawns, thawed if frozen
75g/3oz lean ham, cut into 1cm/½in cubes
15ml/1 tbsp light soy sauce

Serves 4

1 Soak the rice vermicelli in a bowl of boiling water for 4 minutes, or according to the instructions on the packet, then drain thoroughly and set aside until required.

2 Heat 5ml/1 tsp of the oil in a non-stick frying pan or wok. Add the egg and scramble until set. Remove with a slotted spoon and set aside. Clean the pan.

3 Heat the remaining oil in the clean pan. Stir-fry the garlic and chilli for a few seconds, then stir in the curry powder. Cook for 1 minute, stirring, then stir in the peppers, carrot sticks, salt and stock.

4 Bring to the boil. Add the prawns, ham, scrambled egg, rice vermicelli and soy sauce. Mix well. Cook, stirring, until all the liquid has been absorbed and the mixture is hot. Serve at once.